The MORTIMERS
of WIGMORE 1066–1485

The MORTIMERS
of WIGMORE 1066–1485

Dynasty of Destiny

edited *by* PAUL DRYBURGH
and PHILIP HUME

LOGASTON PRESS

First published in May 2023 by Logaston Press
The Holme, Church Road, Eardisley HR3 6NJ
www.logastonpress.co.uk
An imprint of Fircone Books Ltd.

ISBN 978-1-910839-65-2

Designed and typeset by Richard Wheeler in 11.5 on 15 Garamond.
Cover design by Richard Wheeler.

Printed and bound in Poland wwwlfbookservices.co.uk

Logaston Press is committed to a sustainable future for our business, our readers and our planet.
The book in your hands is made from FSC® (Forest Stewardship Council®) certified paper.

British Library Catalogue in Publishing Data.
A CIP catalogue record for this book is available from the British Library.

CONTENTS

LIST OF MAPS & PLANS

LIST OF FAMILY TREES

THE MORTIMER HISTORY SOCIETY

The Mortimer History Society promotes the study and dissemination of information about both the Mortimer family of Wigmore and the medieval Marcher lordships. The Society's conferences and events, journals, annual Essay Prize, newsletters and website are a mine of information: mortimerhistorysociety.org.uk

The society for everyone interested in the medieval Mortimers and the history of the Welsh Marches
www.mortimerhistorysociety.org.uk • Charity number: 1171392

The fifth in a series of publications for the MHS.
This book is published to mark the 700th anniversary of the escape
of Roger Mortimer from the Tower of London on 1 August 1323

Ludlow Castle, which became a main home of the Mortimers at the start of the fourteenth century. Roger Mortimer (d.1330) added new buildings to create a palatial residence (© Philip Hume)

ACKNOWLEDGEMENTS

First and foremost, we must give our thanks to the authors of the essays in this volume. Each one has enthusiastically supported the project, willingly giving their co-operation and time to research and write essays that help to illuminate the fascinating history of the medieval Mortimer family. We are grateful that, from the outset, the Mortimer History Society has championed and endorsed this book as well as providing financial support. We are extremely grateful to the individuals and organisations that have generously allowed us free use of their images that enhance and complement the text, including Jason Appleby, Paul R. Davis, John Fleming, Nick Goonan, Andy King, Charlotte May, Rob Orland, Julian Ravest, Laura Shepherd, Hugh Wood, Herefordshire Archives and Record Centre (HARC), Hereford Cathedral, the Foley Archives, the Office of Public Works at Dublin and Kilkenny Castles, St Mary's Collegiate Church in Warwick, Hatfield House Estates and Paul Johnson at The National Archives. We are also grateful to Rosalind Caird for helping to source some of the images.

The editors are especially grateful to Su and Richard Wheeler of Logaston Press: firstly, for supporting the project as the fifth book that they have produced in conjunction with the Mortimer History Society, and secondly for their enthusiasm and skill in designing and seeing through to publication the finished product.

The editors, the publisher and the Mortimer History Society are particularly grateful to the Trustees of the Marc Fitch Fund for the generous grant that has enabled this book to be published at a price that will hopefully make the book accessible to a wider readership.

MARC FITCH FUND

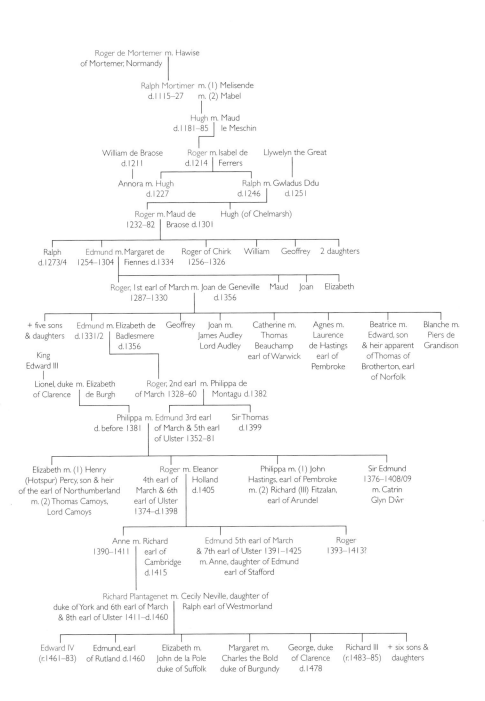

Roger de Mortemer m. Hawise
of Mortemer, Normandy

Ralph Mortimer m. (1) Melisende
d.1115–27   m. (2) Mabel

Hugh m. Maud
d.1181–85   le Meschin

William de Braose   Roger m. Isabel de   Llywelyn the Great
d.1211   d.1214   Ferrers

Annora m. Hugh   Ralph m. Gwladus Ddu
d.1227   d.1246   d.1251

Roger m. Maud de   Hugh (of Chelmarsh)
1232–82   Braose d.1301

Ralph   Edmund m. Margaret de   Roger of Chirk   William   Geoffrey   2 daughters
d.1273/4   1254–1304   Fiennes d.1334   1256–1326

Roger, 1st earl of March m. Joan de Geneville   Maud   Joan   Elizabeth
1287–1330   d.1356

+ five sons   Edmund m. Elizabeth de   Geoffrey   Joan m.   Catherine m.   Agnes m.   Beatrice m.   Blanche m.
& daughters   d.1331/2   Badlesmere   James Audley   Thomas   Laurence   Edward, son   Piers de
     d.1356   Lord Audley   Beauchamp   de Hastings   & heir apparent   Grandison
       earl of Warwick   earl of   of Thomas of
King   Pembroke   Brotherton, earl
Edward III   of Norfolk

Lionel, duke m. Elizabeth   Roger, 2nd earl m. Philippa de
of Clarence   de Burgh   of March 1328–60   Montagu d.1382

Philippa m. Edmund 3rd earl   Sir Thomas
d. before 1381   of March & 5th earl   d.1399
      of Ulster 1352–81

Elizabeth m. (1) Henry   Roger m. Eleanor   Philippa m. (1) John   Sir Edmund
(Hotspur) Percy, son & heir   4th earl of   Holland   Hastings, earl of Pembroke   1376–1408/09
of the earl of Northumberland   March & 6th   d.1405   m. (2) Richard (III) Fitzalan,   m. Catrin
m. (2) Thomas Camoys,   earl of Ulster   earl of Arundel   Glyn Dŵr
Lord Camoys   1374–d.1398

Anne m. Richard   Edmund 5th earl of March   Roger
1390–1411   earl of   & 7th earl of Ulster 1391–1425   1393–1413?
     Cambridge   m. Anne, daughter of Edmund
     d.1415   earl of Stafford

Richard Plantagenet m. Cecily Neville, daughter of
duke of York and 6th earl of March   Ralph earl of Westmorland
& 8th earl of Ulster 1411–d.1460

Edward IV   Edmund, earl   Elizabeth m.   Margaret m.   George, duke   Richard III   + six sons &
(r.1461–83)   of Rutland d.1460   John de la Pole   Charles the Bold   of Clarence   (r.1483–85)   daughters
          duke of Suffolk   duke of Burgundy   d.1478

Select Mortimer family tree

INTRODUCTION
Don't Mention the Mortimers

This is a book about a family. A single medieval noble family, and its impact and influence across the islands of Britain and Ireland, and beyond, over four centuries. From their arrival in the aftermath of the Norman Conquest, the Mortimers of Wigmore in north-western Herefordshire grew to become one of the most important and dominant aristocratic dynasties. The family's rise culminated with the accession to the throne in 1461 of Edward, earl of March, who gloried in sharing the family's blood, when he was crowned King Edward IV. The monuments to their power and influence continue to stand out in the landscape. And while some retain their magnificence, such as the castles of Trim and Ludlow, others are now clad in ivy and hawthorn – forlorn witnesses to the passage of time and the fading of the family from view. Indeed, beyond 'Mortimer Country' in the central borderlands of England and Wales,

Early fourteenth-century Mortimer coat of arms, St Laurence's Ludlow (© Shaun Ward)

the family's past glories are only now beginning to reach public consciousness. Even for professional historians, the family and its prominent individuals have largely proved incidental until recently: the article of faith 'Don't Mention the Mortimers', which Chris Given-Wilson (Chapter 9) argues almost came to define the reign of the usurper Henry IV, could almost be applied to the broad sweep of history-writing over the past two centuries.

As a Norman family which came to England in the aftermath of the Conquest in 1066, which then survived in the direct male line until 1425, and through a nephew to 1485, the Mortimers of Wigmore were one of the longest-lived of the medieval period. Indeed, one historian, A.C. Reeves, has remarked that 'for the Mortimers to have survived for over three centuries as Marcher lords was a political and biological feat' (*The Marcher Lords*, 41, Llandybie, 1983). The longevity of the family means that the study of the Mortimers provides many windows into the late medieval history of three countries. When you add in further factors such as their impact on national politics from the mid-thirteenth century onwards, through which individual members of the family shaped and influenced the fortunes of England, Wales and Ireland, the Mortimers deserve greater prominence than they have had thus far.

Fortunately, the twenty-first century has seen a sudden and welcome flourishing of research and publication, one catalyst for which has been the emergence of the Mortimer History Society, through which this anthology has been developed. In 2002, Charles Hopkinson and Martin Speight published *The Mortimers: Lords of the March* with Logaston Press. This brought together in one place a coherent narrative history of the family from the Conquest, combined with an analysis of the family's lands and properties – notably its castles and towns, as well as an introduction to the branches extending from the main line of the family tree. Their work provides a more focused study of Mortimer lordship in the Marches, for which Professor Sir Rees Davies' classic works *Lordship and Society in the Marches of Wales, 1282–1400* (Oxford, 1978) and his *Age of Conquest: Wales, 1063–1415* (Oxford, 1991), remain the standard authorities. A year later, in 2003, Ian Mortimer published the first academic biography of the most famous Mortimer, Roger, 1st earl of March (c.1287–1330) with his *The Greatest Traitor: the Life of Sir Roger Mortimer, Ruler of England, 1327–1330* (London: Jonathan Cape, 2003).

In this and Dr Mortimer's subsequent publications on the early fourteenth century – as well as a raft of academic and popular biographies such as the Yale English Monarchs series on *Edward II* (Seymour Phillips, 2010) and *Edward III* (W. Mark Ormrod, 2011), and Kathryn Warner's *Edward II: The Unconventional King* (Amberley, 2014) and *Isabella of France: The Rebel Queen* (Amberley, 2020) – we now have a rich and rounded portrait of the man whose career involved dedicated military service, rebellion, conspiracy, leadership of an invasion army, the engineering of an unprecedented forced abdication of an anointed English king, a potential sexual relationship with the queen consort, acting as the *eminence grise* at court over four years (enriching himself in the process), treason and execution. Roger also sits at the centre of a growing, if probably irresolvable controversy over the fate of King Edward II (1307–27). To some extent, therefore, the 1st earl now dominates research into the family, and certainly most readily captures the popular imagination; no more is he simply the brooding presence of Christopher Marlowe's *Edward II*.

The launch of the Mortimer History Society's journal in 2017 has brought other more diverse and vibrant scholarship to the fore, which contextualises the Mortimers within their chief spheres of influence, and illuminates their careers. We now have, for example, both new insights into the early history of the family in England and Wales, the place of women in the Marches, the career of Roger Mortimer, 2nd earl of March (1328–60) and the literary history and associations of the family. There is also doctoral research being undertaken at a variety of academic institutions within Britain and Ireland that promises both to bring new discoveries but also to widen the source-base on which studies of the Mortimer family can be (re-)written. This anthology attempts to ride this wave.

By the time of the compilation of Domesday Book, the Mortimers had lands that spanned 12 English counties, with their administrative centre at Wigmore in north Herefordshire. By the early thirteenth century, they were important regional barons though not in the first rank of the barony nationally. Whilst the biological and genetic strengths of the family, as extolled by Reeves, are outwith our scope, this collection presents 11 essays from established and up-and-coming scholars on various aspects of the political, military, social and legal history behind the family's rise to prominence across four centuries, as well as the economic assets which underpinned their wealth, power and influence. It charts their dramatic success in navigating the choppy political waters of medieval England until a Mortimer could assert and exercise a claim to the throne.

The first 200 years of Mortimer presence in England and Wales, from shortly after the Conquest of 1066 through to the conquest of Wales in 1282, are usually recounted in terms of the exploits of the male lords of Wigmore, 'who have long "hogged the limelight" of Marcher historiography'. Our first essay, though, provides a necessary corrective as it brings to the forefront the essential contributions made by women as mothers, wives, sisters and daughters across the five generations during which the Mortimers established their position and grew

Wigmore Castle
Engraving, 1806
(© Herefordshire
Archives and
Record Centre ref
K38-D-1211)

in power along the Welsh Marches. Against the backdrop of the Mortimers' arrival in England in the years after 1066, their acquisition of lands in England and conflict in Wales, their relationships with the Crown, through to their emergence as one of the leading baronial families in the country, Emma Cavell's essay demonstrates the fundamental importance of the female members of the Mortimer family, 'some of them arguably more dynamic and capable than their male counterparts'. Emma evidences

> how these women not only conveyed new lands and connections between
> their own and other elite families, but also managed and defended estates,
> households and castles, founded religious houses and tended to the souls
> of departed kin, and even involved themselves directly in high politics and
> intrigue.

It was during the middle period of the thirteenth century that the fortunes of the Mortimers changed dramatically, when Roger Mortimer (d.1282) propelled them towards the forefront of national affairs. The son of Ralph Mortimer and Gwladus Ddu (daughter of Llywelyn ab Iorwerth, prince of Gwynedd and ruler of Wales), Roger was first cousin to Llywelyn ap Gruffudd, who was recognised by the 1267 Treaty of Montgomery as the 'Prince of Wales'. Furthermore, Roger developed a close friendship with the Lord Edward, forging a strong bond which lasted throughout Edward I's reign until Roger's death in 1282, with the king deeply mourning the loss of his friend. Emma Cavell charts the importance of Roger's wife, Maud de Braose, throughout this period. In addition to bringing to the Mortimers an extensive inheritance of lands in England, the Marches and Ireland, Maud stands out as a 'frontier *barones*' in her own right. She was active as a litigant with her husband to secure and protect her inheritance, and defended her castles during the Montfort rebellion. She was involved, together with her husband, in the escape of the Lord Edward from his captivity, and the subsequent defeat of Simon de Montfort at the battle of Evesham after his death at the hands of Roger (followed by Maud's receipt of de Montfort's severed head). Maud had an active role in the downfall of Llywelyn ap Gruffudd, whilst also being responsible for managing castles and estates in the absence of her husband.

The Welsh Marcher context of the establishment and growth of the family's power, forms the canvas upon which David Stephenson paints a vivid but nuanced picture of conquest, conflict and co-operation. From the late eleventh century, the Welsh *cantref* of Maelienydd, which lay immediately west of Wigmore, within the region that became known as *Rhwng Gwy a Hafren* ('between Wye and Severn'), was the obvious target for Mortimer expansion into Wales. Although it was first annexed probably towards the end of the eleventh century, Mortimer control was never secure; and, indeed, it was in the hands of the native rulers for over half of the subsequent 200 years. A backdrop to much of this period was the bitter and personal feud that developed between, on the one hand, Hugh Mortimer (d.1181–5) and his son Roger (d.1214) and, on the other hand, the native rulers of Maelienydd – a deadly feud that saw the deaths of the native ruler and his brothers at the hands of Hugh and Roger Mortimer in the period between the mid-1140s and 1179. The violent nature of the early years has often coloured assumptions about the relationships between the Mortimers and the native Welsh lords, gentry and retainers in the swathe of lands across the Middle March – the location of the lordships that became the backbone of their wealth and influence. In an essay that is full of fresh insights, and which opens up a range of possibilities for further research, David Stephenson provides a much more careful and subtle analysis of 'the relations between the Mortimer lords and the Welsh populations of their lordships, who might on occasion threaten Mortimer control, and at other times might provide the sinews of Mortimer power'.

The picture that emerges is a complex one in which, at times, the Mortimers could be seen as harsh masters, whilst at other times being at the forefront of promoting local Welsh gentry to positions of influence and importance. David reminds us that

> those frequently ambiguous relationships were the product of a blend of mutual, sometimes grudging, acceptance and impatient self-interest that defies clear definition. We are reminded that in the March, especially, few things are as simple as they may at first appear to be.

Crucial to the defence, survival and territorial expansion of those barons whose lives in the earlier generations were forged in conflict in the Welsh Marches, castles form an essential element to the Mortimers' story. As Marcher lords they could exercise the right to build castles without requiring permission from the Crown. When later generations were ranked amongst the most wealthy and powerful in the kingdom, the Mortimers required castles that reflected their rank and status, and which provided palatial living accommodation both for a comfortable lifestyle and to impress visitors and onlookers. Consequently, across the centuries, the Mortimers owned or are associated with a great many castles. In his essay, John R. Kenyon examines the architecture of the main castles that are associated with the Mortimers, and which were built, rebuilt and developed by successive generations. Inevitably, John starts with Wigmore. Although first founded by William fitz Osbern (d.1071), it became the home and *caput* of the Mortimers from the mid-1070s, and the centre of a major lordship in the central Welsh Marches for over four centuries. It was successive Mortimers who first built structures in stone at Wigmore, gradually developing one of the largest and most imposing castles in the country. Another castle, Chirk, first built at the end of the thirteenth century by a Mortimer (a younger son, Roger Mortimer of Chirk), is still impressive today. As Emma Cavell also notes, strategic marriages to wealthy heiresses played an important part in the Mortimers' accumulation of lands and wealth, bringing many existing castles into their ownership. Of these, one of the most important was the acquisition of Ludlow when Roger Mortimer (d.1330) married Joan, the sole heir of the large de Geneville/ de Lacy inheritance. Already a splendid castle, at the height of his power Roger added magnificent buildings, creating one of the finest domestic ranges in any Marcher castle. John demonstrates, though, that Roger also spent equal sums at Wigmore, a short distance away, and challenges the idea of decline there. Although Wigmore, Chirk and Ludlow are the most impressive of the Mortimer castles, John reminds us of the large number of castles that the Mortimers owned, built and developed, of which often little remains today; and that their strategic sighting and innovative construction helped cement the family's hold on disputed territories and brought them into conflict both with Welsh lords and the English Crown.

It was at or near his castles of Wigmore and Ludlow that Roger Mortimer, the 1st earl of March, entertained the king, queen mother and Court in 1328/9. Here, fabulous tournaments were held to mark the marriage of some of his daughters into other powerful noble dynasties, not to mention his elevation in October 1328 to the unprecedented earldom of March. This, as Paul Dryburgh discusses, was a title that taken literally asserted authority over a swathe of independent lordships and jurisdictions, and perhaps also made similar plays to authority in the frontier areas of Mortimer power in Ireland. Roger's rise to national prominence was multifaceted, with both good fortune and an extraordinary logistical talent coming to the fore.

This is arguably best demonstrated by Roger's daring escape from captivity in the Tower of London on 1 August 1323, the feast of St Peter ad Vincula (St Peter in Chains) – an event whose 700th anniversary is marked by the publication of this anthology. The Tower had been his prison since the abject submission of Roger and his uncle of Chirk to Edward II during the civil war of 1321/2, which ended in the king's total victory. Perhaps only their long career of loyal service to the king and his Crown in Wales, Ireland and at Court saved them. However, in a striking new assessment of the chronicle accounts and government records relating to the escape, combined with her professional knowledge of the layout of the Tower, Laura Tompkins rallies new insights to enable us to understand how the break-out happened and who was involved. She demonstrates the careful planning which must have lain behind the escape and the

Terracotta tile with the Mortimer coat of arms, from St Peter's Chapel in Ludlow Castle (© Hugh Wood)

small circle of individuals involved on the inside and outside. She discusses the possibility that Queen Isabella played a role and whether anything can be said about the nature of the relationship between Isabella and Roger at this point.

The story of Roger Mortimer's subsequent flight to France, the spectre of conspiracy and paranoia this generated – particularly following Queen Isabella's own exile in the court of her brother, Charles IV, king of France – is well known. As is the political alliance between Roger and Isabella, which led to a return to England where, having engineered a bloodless coup, they forced Edward II to abdicate in favour of his teenage son. Following this Roger held the young king and the country in his thrall, during the minority of Edward III, until 1330 – and this without even achieving formal recognition of his power. In Edward III, however, Roger met his match. After nearly four years of domination, Roger had gained many enemies. With the young king chafing under the tutelage and control of Mortimer and his mother, some of Edward's associates gained access to Nottingham Castle, using its underground tunnels to evade the guard, to capture Roger. Quickly transported to the Tower of London, he was tried, found guilty by his peers and executed.

Nevertheless, in a republished edition of an important if little-known pamphlet of 1998, Barbara Wright explores Roger Mortimer's death – by hanging, rather than the more barbaric forms of execution suffered by others such as the younger Hugh Despenser, hanged, eviscerated and castrated at Hereford in November 1326. She does this in the context of the 'series of semi-constitutional executions spanning almost 50 years which had destroyed the confidence of the barons in the royal system of justice'. This was a process of political mutilation of his enemies that had begun during the reign of Edward I with the horrific execution of Dafydd ap Gruffudd in 1283. Through examining the treatment of traitors' corpses and the circumstances which affected their proper internment, combined with a detailed assessment of the records, Barbara resolves the confusions over the whereabouts of Roger Mortimer's corpse. The exasperation of the young king is clear from a clerk's annotation when declining a petition from Joan, his widow, to move the corpse to Wigmore: *'Demoerge le corps en peis encore'* ('Let the body remain in peace now').

Following the execution of Roger Mortimer in 1330, his family was not treated as harshly as it could have been when Edward III chose not to extinguish the earldom and to restore the family's primary estates. Within a relatively short period, Joan was permitted to regain control of her own lands. This allowed for the full rehabilitation of the Mortimers within a generation. An infant at his grandfather's execution in 1330 and his father's premature death in December 1331, Roger Mortimer (1328–60) entered an inheritance in dangerous circumstances. As he grew to manhood, the young Roger proved his mettle gloriously. His success, both in tournaments and as a military commander, brought him great esteem from the king, in the process becoming a protégé of the heir to the throne, Edward of Woodstock, the Black Prince. Having fought in the tumultuous English victory at Crécy in 1346, Roger became one of the founder-members in 1348 of Edward III's new prestigious, chivalric 'Order of the Garter'.

As Andy King discusses in the first of a series of chapters which examine different facets of the Mortimers during the fourteenth century, Roger's actions mirrored, perhaps exceeded, the exploits of his illustrious forebears. All the Mortimer earls of March frequently saw military service. Starting with his military service in Scotland and Ireland during the early career of Roger Mortimer, later 1st earl of March, Andy charts the experiences in warfare of the five earls, and other senior Mortimer men such as Sir Thomas (d.1399) and Sir Edmund (d.1409). Encompassing campaigns and battlefields across Ireland, Wales, Scotland, England and France, he argues that:

> The military careers of the Mortimers show how war could bring a noble family both social advancement and political disaster; and how military service could provide a route back from the political wilderness. Their careers thus provide a window into the interplay of war, military service and politics across late medieval Britain, affording a view of the symbiotic relationship between king and noble which underlay it.

A culmination of the route back from the wilderness came when, in 1354, Edward III himself pushed through Parliament an annulment of the verdict of treason on the 1st earl, thus restoring to the family the title 'Earl of March'. Roger, now 2nd earl of March, also received the lands his grandfather had acquired at the height of his power (except for Chirk).

The king and his heir evidently had a high personal regard for Roger Mortimer, and the rehabilitation of the family was cemented in 1358 when he was allowed to betroth his six-year-old son, Edmund, to Philippa, the only child of Lionel of Antwerp, duke of Clarence, the king's second surviving son. Although Roger died, aged only 31, whilst on campaign in France in 1360, the marriage between

The 2nd earl of March with his wife, Philippa Montagu, from the Salisbury Roll S-32-77
(The Heraldry Society BL Addnl Ms 45133)

Edmund and Philippa took place in 1368. When Lionel died shortly after, following his own second marriage in northern Italy, the couple became one of the wealthiest families in the country. From Philippa's mother, they inherited extensive estates across Ireland and England, including the earldom of Ulster, to add to Edmund's existing one of March. Further, the death of her father without any more children meant that Philippa and Edmund's children would have a potential claim to the throne. This landed settlement represented the zenith of the family's territorial endowment in the Middle Ages – the establishment, development and enhancement of which is the focus of Paul Dryburgh's chapter on the Mortimer estates and economy. His essay charts the steady accumulation of estates, which at the time of Domesday were scattered across 12 English counties (though centred on the former wasteland at Wigmore), and their concentration on several key centres on the March before the huge territorial gains in East Anglia, centred on Clare (Suffolk), in the late fourteenth century. It also documents the family's entry into Ireland, one of the greatest and repeated benefits of an astute marriage policy, and the recurring (and in some areas futile) struggles to defend, maintain and even expand a transnational lordship. There is also an analysis of the diverse nature of the economy of the estates, and of their fluctuating value which was dependent, as so much in the late Middle Ages, on climate, topography, epidemics and the commercialisation of markets.

As the lords of Wigmore for 350 years and earls of March for a century, the Mortimers could also rely on an extensive affinity of gentry, tenants and retainers whose families served the Mortimers for many generations. They have largely been neglected by previous researchers. More study and research of this topic could provide fascinating insights into the relationships between lordly families and their supporters, and the chapter by Patrick McDonagh gives a productive example of the potential of further research. He tells the story of a dramatic and fiery attack on the leading Anglo-Irish earls of Ormond and Desmond by the bishop of Cloyne from the pulpit of the chapel in Dublin Castle. This occurred in the presence of Edmund Mortimer, 3rd earl of March and lord lieutenant of Ireland, and his wife, Philippa of Clarence, and resulted in 'a plaint of slander and injury' against the bishop. A notarial instrument composed by Henry Hopton (clerk of the diocese of Hereford, and therefore an eyewitness to these events), lists 16 'reverent and discreet men' who had also been present, all connected to the 3rd earl, with some of them leading members of the Mortimer affinity. Patrick's detailed investigation of these 16 men, deploying a vast range of source material, much of which has not been employed before, demonstrates the potential to see 'the real world of relationships' that underpinned a lord, and the solid core of followers who surrounded him and were regularly in his company.

Like his father before him, Edmund, the 3rd earl, died at a young age. Indeed, in the 95 years after the execution of the 1st earl, none of his successors lived beyond the age of 33, on each occasion leaving a young child as their heir: Edmund (d.1331/2, aged 29/30); Roger (d.1360, aged 31); Edmund (d.1381, aged 29); Roger (d.1398, aged 24); and Edmund (d.1425, aged 33). The fortunes of the later medieval Mortimer family were almost wholly dictated by recurrent minority, as Chris Given-Wilson points out in his chapter. This was in marked contrast to the fortunes of the family during the *c.*250-year period from the mid-1070s to 1330, during which most of the Mortimer lords lived well into middle age and some into old age.

Throughout the 71 years following the restoration of the earldom in 1354 and the full rehabilitation of the family, argues Chris,

> there were around 33 years during which the earldom was held by an active
> adult earl and 38 years when it was held in wardship for a minor; and not just
> any minor, but a succession of boys with an emerging and plausible claim to
> be the next king of England.

He proceeds to demonstrate, 'as ambitious rivals circled for prey', the role of the whole family, including the other great families linked through marriage, in maintaining not just the inheritance itself of the successive Mortimer heirs, but also the Mortimer claim to the throne. Ultimately, he concludes:

> Collectively, the Mortimer clan and its allies in the years between 1380
> and 1425 had refused to allow the rights inherent in the name Mortimer
> simply to fade away, despite the attempts made by Henry iv and Henry v to
> airbrush them out of history.

This theme is taken up by Ian Mortimer in a chapter analysing who the enigmatic Sir John Mortimer might have been, and why he was 'judiciously murdered' by the Lancastrian regime in 1424. This analysis shows that Sir John was possibly a member of a minor family itself descended from a younger son of a cadet branch (Chirk) of the Mortimers of Wigmore. Yet, despite his obscurity, the full apparatus of the government was used to imprison him illegally, temporarily change the law to trap him into committing treason, and to ensure his violent execution. Ian concludes:

> Henry v might have come down to us via Shakespeare as "the golden boy of the fifteenth century" (to quote Anne Curry) but that is not how he appears from a Mortimer perspective. Sir John Mortimer was not imprisoned because he himself had a claim to the throne. He was imprisoned by Henry v, and judicially murdered by the Lancastrians, as an example to all those who believed the earl of March was the rightful king – including the earl of March himself.

Although the violent conflicts during the second half of the fifteenth century for the Throne of England, subsequently known as the Wars of the Roses, have popularly been seen as a struggle between the Houses of York and Lancaster, Chris Given-Wilson's chapter and the two which follow it demonstrate that the antecedents lay in the conflict between the houses of Mortimer and Lancaster. Indeed, as Joanna Laynesmith argues, with the white rose originating as a Mortimer symbol, their blood suffused the Wars of the Roses. It was certainly their Mortimer blood that gave Richard, duke of York and Edward iv a claim to precedence over the Lancastrian dynasty; and it was the Mortimer wealth, estates and titles (particularly in the Welsh Marcher lordships) that gave the York family the powerful position and support to take advantage of that lineage.

Thus, in the final chapter, Joanna Laynesmith explores the significance of Anne Mortimer's legacy for the House of York, both in providing legitimate and legendary dynastic claims to kingship, and in transmitting the right to the Mortimer family estates which provided a power-base to make good those claims. When Edmund Mortimer, 5th earl of March, died childless in 1425, his heir was the only son of his sister Anne Mortimer, who had married Richard of Conisburgh, later earl of Cambridge. Anne died in 1411, shortly after giving birth to her son. Richard was executed in 1415 for his part in the so-called 'Southampton Plot' which had aimed to place his brother-in-law, Edmund Mortimer, on the throne. Thus, aged four, their son was orphaned and, shortly after the execution of his father, his paternal uncle, Edward duke of York, was killed whilst fighting at Agincourt. Already heir to the duchy of York, when his Mortimer uncle died in 1425, the young Richard became heir to the vast empire of Mortimer lands and titles that spanned England, Wales and Ireland – and crucially the Mortimer claim to the throne. Joanna makes extensive use of the richly-illustrated manuscripts (many reproduced in her chapter) created to celebrate and communicate the House of York's royal heritage, derived from their Mortimer lineage. She contends that the Mortimer family's stories and iconography provided a significantly more impactful legacy for their royal descendants than is commonly appreciated. It was Anne Mortimer's descent from Lionel, duke of Clarence, and his daughter, Philippa, that enabled the House of York to claim precedence over the Lancastrian dynasty.

Although the line of Yorkist kings was abruptly halted at the Battle of Bosworth in 1485, the importance of the Mortimer lineage continued – not just their descent from Edward III, but also their purported descent from King Arthur and the princes of Wales, which came from the marriage between Ralph Mortimer (d.1246) and Gwladus Ddu, the daughter of Llywelyn ab Iorwerth, prince of Gwynedd. Through his marriage to Elizabeth of York, the eldest daughter of Edward IV, Henry VII drew on the legacy and lineage of the Mortimers, naming his eldest son, Arthur, and placing him at Ludlow, the Mortimer and Yorkist stronghold of the fourteenth and fifteenth centuries. Many of the Mortimer properties remained in royal hands long after, and both the Mortimer white lion and the black bull of Clarence are among the heraldic beasts still used by the modern royal family.

Intriguingly, the chapter (and this book) finishes with the insight that when Edward IV

> successfully established his sovereignty on the basis of descent through Anne and Philippa, he ensured that the English Crown would never be constrained as the French was by the exclusion of women.

It is with some irony, then, that Henry Tudor, pressed his claim to the

> red dragon prophecy ... that rested not only on his mother but also his future wife, Edward IV's daughter. It would be more than five centuries before a queen regnant finally succeeded in pushing this to its logical conclusion so that women could inherit the English throne on equal terms with their brothers.

LEFT: Mortimer horse trapping from the 1300s found near Wigmore. It shows the Mortimer coat of arms with three red enamel bars across the shield, the 'difference' indicating it belonged to a member of the Mortimer family but not the lord of Wigmore himself (© Hugh Wood). ABOVE: the trapping recoloured as it might have looked

The late John Grove, who had the foresight to establish the Mortimer History Society in 2009 to encourage the study of the Mortimers and the Welsh Marcher lordships, was fond of saying that, across the span of five centuries, the Mortimers and the Marcher lordships provide windows into so many aspects of late medieval history. This collection of essays opens some of those windows, but in doing so it also highlights the scope for further research. Given the centrality of the Mortimers to the relationship between Crown and nobles, and the governance of the country, it is fitting that the collection is published to mark the 700th anniversary of Roger Mortimer's escape from the Tower of London, on the feast of St Peter ad Vincula (St Peter in Chains) on 1 August 1323. Our hope is that our readers will find plenty to interest and inform them, and to encourage them to begin or continue their own research journeys into the history of this fascinating family, this dynasty of destiny.

PAUL DRYBURGH AND PHILIP HUME, 2023

Detail of a print of an 1815 drawing of Wigmore Castle, reproduced by kind permission of the Foley Archive (Herefordshire Archives and Record Centre, E12/IV/227/39)

Dr Emma Cavell

Mortimer women, dynastic power and the Welsh frontier *c.*1066–1282

THIS first chapter looks not at the barons of Wigmore, who have long 'hogged the limelight' of Marcher historiography, but at the women of the Mortimer family. In the two centuries between their establishment at Wigmore in the aftermath of the Norman Conquest of England and their contribution to the final conquest of Wales by Edward 1 in the 1280s, the Mortimers emerged as one of the leading families of the March of Wales. While so much of their success has been attributed to the actions of men, the part played in the rise of the dynasty by the women, some of them arguably more dynamic and capable than their male counterparts, is scarcely acknowledged, much less explored. Across the generations from the late eleventh century to the late thirteenth, these women not only conveyed new lands and connections between their own and other elite families, but also managed and defended estates, households and castles, founded religious houses and tended to the souls of departed kin, and even involved themselves directly in high politics and intrigue. In considering a selection of the women who married, or were born, into the Mortimer family of Wigmore during the central medieval period, this chapter will demonstrate the fundamental importance of female members of elite families like the Mortimers, and contribute to a more holistic impression of the Mortimer family and March of Wales in the inter-conquest years.

Our necessarily cursory examination of the women of the Mortimer family begins with Melisende, wife of the Domesday lord of Wigmore and conqueror of Maelienydd, Ralph Mortimer (d.1115–27). Little is known of Melisende, or indeed of her successor in marriage to Ralph Mortimer, a woman called Mabel. Yet the significance of Melisende's marriage, like that of Mabel after her, indubitably lay in what she brought to the Norman baron who, by 1086, was in possession of border territories that had once belonged to Eadric the Wild, to the fallen earl of Hereford, Roger de Breteuil, and to Queen Edith of Wessex. Perhaps the interests Melisende carried to her husband, whether in land or alliance, lay in the vicinity of St-Victor-en-Caux, the *caput* of her husband's lordship in Normandy, or closer to Mortemer-sur-Eaulne, some 30 miles north-east of Rouen, where Ralph's father Roger held a castle until 1054.[1] Perhaps the interests lay elsewhere in the duchy, or even beyond its limits. We simply do not know enough of Melisende's background to do much more than emphasise the fact that considerations of alliance and network, if not also of land acquisition, will have informed the marriage arrangement.

What we do know, on the other hand, is that somewhere around 1100 Ralph and Melisende's daughter Hawise married the Conqueror's own nephew, Stephen, count of Aumale (d.1127), thereby bolstering the bonds of kinship with the Norman ducal house that Mortimer himself was said to have enjoyed.[2] Hawise and her husband were already very distantly related. In addition, fragmentary, circumstantial evidence recently outlined by Paul Remfry hints at the existence of another daughter born to Ralph and Melisende, and of a marital union that carried interests in Mortimer land in Lincolnshire to John FitzRichard, father of brothers Eustace and Pain FitzJohn (two of the best known 'new men' of Henry I's reign) and thence to Eustace and his descendants.[3] Whatever the latter case, Melisende was dead by 30 March 1088 and her widower remarried, for this was the date on which 'Ralph son of Roger de Mortemer and Mabel his wife' were the first to place their crosses on a vassal's charter of donation to the abbey of Jumièges in northern Normandy.[4] Melisende was remembered a decade or so later in a charter issued to the Cluniac monks of St Martin de Champs, Paris, by Stephen, count of Aumale. This was done with the consent of the count's wife Hawise and of her father, since – so the charter tells us – the Mortimer inheritance had furnished the bequest.[5] Perhaps Countess Hawise entertained an expectation of inheritance in her father's lands at this point.

Although the information on the wives and daughters of the Domesday baron of Wigmore is frustratingly scanty, and we are compelled to write about them in a manner that makes them seem little more than commodities, it remains a fact that noblewomen of the Anglo-Norman milieu had a critically important role to play as transmitters of land and alliance between men. To consider this role, even before questions of female power and agency compel us to explore the women's active contributions to family and society, is to understand more fully a dynasty's priorities and aspirations. This ostensibly passive role as a conduit of land and alliance between men should not be confused with powerlessness. Women came to their marriages with their own priorities and concerns, pragmatic and ideological, personal and familial, and the interests that they brought with them to marriage typically shaped those concerns and influenced their actions. Although we have limited information on Melisende and Mabel, Hawise Mortimer serves to illustrate the point. In the 30 years between about 1088 and 1118, Ralph Mortimer and Stephen, count of Aumale, remained united in their (shifting) loyalties to the Conqueror's sons.[6] Hawise's turn-of-the-century marriage to Count Stephen was part and parcel of this alliance, and her own interests were evidently compatible with those of her husband and father. Orderic Vitalis tells us that when Count Stephen rebelled against Henry I in 1117–18 and gave shelter to the king's enemies, it was Hawise whom the king held responsible; and when Henry erected a castle to subdue the rebellious couple, at Rouen-sur-Bresle ('Old Rouen') near Aumale, he named it 'Whore-humbler' (*Mate-putain*) to spite Hawise![7]

It seems likely that Ralph Mortimer's son and successor Hugh, who perhaps followed an elder brother Roger, was a product of Ralph's second marriage – if chiefly because Hugh seems to have lived on until February 1185, having retired from active life a few years earlier.[8] Indeed, it is possible that Hugh and his brother were born only after the above grant to St Martin de Champs, if Hawise's association with a Mortimer 'inheritance' in that deed refers to something other than a *maritagium* (marriage portion in land). Hugh's own wife, Maud, was a daughter and ultimately co-heiress of William le Meschin, baron of Egremont in Cumbria and, through his wife, lord of Skipton-in-Craven in Yorkshire.[9] Although the land she inherited lay in the north of England, Maud le Meschin had recently been married to Philip de Belmeis (d.c.1145), the late lord of Tong in Shropshire, with whom she had been closely involved in the endowment of the Shropshire abbey of Buildwas and of a new community of Arrouasian canons who, by 1148, had settled at Lilleshall. Although the land given to Buildwas and the 'Lilleshall' canons derived from the Belmeis fief, Maud was a leading witness to her husband's acts and received, in turn, spiritual remuneration that included confraternity with the monks of Buildwas and the entire order to which the abbey then belonged, Savigny.[10] At the time of her marriage to Hugh Mortimer, Maud is likely to have held landed interests in Shropshire, in the form of dower in her first husband's land.

3

Maud le Meschin, wife of Hugh Mortimer (d.1181–85), was involved with her first husband in the endowment of Buildwas Abbey, Shropshire (© Philip Hume)

As the niece of the late Ranulph le Meschin, earl of Chester (d.1129), and first cousin of the younger earl of Chester, Ranulph de Gernon, Maud le Meschin also had impressive kinship connections in and around the Welsh frontier. She was, moreover, the first cousin of William, earl of Lincoln, Earl Ranulph's maternal half-brother. As one scholar has already demonstrated, Maud's second marriage was likely one of several political unions arranged by Hugh Mortimer and his nephew, William le Gros, now count of Aumale, as the two men aligned themselves with the earls in the service of King Stephen.[11] Nor, evidently, were Maud's lands and connections her only attribute as a marriage partner from Mortimer's perspective. She proved her mettle in the early days of their marriage when – if the Anglo-Norman Chronicle of Wigmore is to be believed – she managed to lay her hands on the impressive sum of 3,000 silver marks (£2,000), along with all of her husband's plate and his horses and hunting birds, to free him from captivity. He had been imprisoned in Ludlow Castle by his enemy Joce de Dinan sometime in late 1148 or 1149.[12]

Lest we too readily write off Maud's actions as a fabrication, extraordinary though the alleged ransom was, Hugh's daughter-in-law, Isabel de Ferrers, was likewise compelled to raise a sizeable ransom on behalf of her own husband, Roger Mortimer, in 1205. The younger Mortimer, who at the time of his father's retirement in 1181 had been in a royal prison in England for his part in the

1179 murder of Cadwallon ap Madog, was a prisoner of the king of France in Normandy in 1205.[13] During Roger's enforced absence his father's monastic foundation was burned to the ground, perhaps by the princes of Rhwng Gwy a Hafren; but, with a loan from King John and permission to collect scutage on the knight's fees which her husband held in chief, Isabel raised the 1,000 marks (c.£667) needed to see him back in control of his Marcher dominions.[14] Though still in captivity on 28 December 1205, Roger Mortimer was in England by June 1207.[15] The impressive sums involved in the ransoms raised by these two women is clear by comparison to the statutory relief (the amount paid by an heir for lawful possession of his inheritance) on an entire barony in this period: this stood at £100.

Maud le Meschin and Isabel de Ferrers were similar in other respects, too. Like her mother-in-law, Isabel had a natal family background in Normandy and lowland England. She was the daughter of Walkelin de Ferrers, the baron of Oakham in Rutland and a trusted companion of Richard I. Her father also held the castles of Ferrières-Saint-Hilaire and Chambray in Normandy. Like Maud le Meschin, Isabel also cultivated charitable interests outside the March itself but in an English county that bordered Wales. Where Maud's interests lay in Shropshire, Isabel's were in Gloucestershire. Here, most notably, Isabel and her second husband, Peter FitzHerbert, founded the hospital of St John the Baptist at Lechlade, a foundation to which she remained committed until the end of her long life. Lechlade was Isabel's own property, purchased from King John with other Ferrers lands which the king had seized as *terrae Normannorum* ('lands of the Normans') in 1204.[16] This manor seems to have been a greater priority for Isabel than the other family lands she acquired from the king in the middle years of her first marriage. It was far closer than Oakham in Rutland to Mortimer's frontier interests and, Sethina Watson argues, 'offered a geographical presence that mirrored the Mortimers' political expansion in these years'.[17] Its convenient location and its economic value at Isabel's death in 1252 were such that Isabel's grandson, Roger Mortimer (d.1282), was embroiled in a long-running political-legal dispute over the manor with Henry III.[18]

Nevertheless, there is little evidence of Isabel's involvement with Lechlade during the years of her first marriage. Married women's relative absence from the documentation aside, it may be that Isabel was involved to a greater extent with the territorial and charitable priorities of her husband and the frontier dynasty whose continuity she had helped to ensure. The Anglo-Norman Chronicle of

Wigmore tells of her intercession with her husband on behalf of the Wigmore canons after an illness during pregnancy that seems to have claimed the life of her infant. The male child was born *en route* at lodgings in Snitton (Shropshire) and, dying soon after, was interred at the church in nearby Cleobury. Isabel attributed the infant's demise and her own suffering to her husband's seizure of Snitton from the canons – precisely because Snitton was a convenient stop-over on the road between Wigmore and Cleobury – and tearfully beseeched him to return the property. Her words hit their mark. According to the Chronicle, Mortimer agreed to recognise the canons' right to hold Snitton and its parent manor, Caynham, *a remenaunt* ('forever').[19] Roger Mortimer died in 1214, and the same narrative tells us that, following Mortimer's death, Isabel founded a religious house at Lechlade for the health of her husband's soul and her own, and that she was ultimately buried there.[20]

Watson has demonstrated beautifully the 'creative agency' which Isabel brought to the development of Lechlade Hospital and the interconnection of the hospital's evolution in the 1230s and 40s with the fortunes of her Mortimer children.[21] With at least five surviving children to Roger Mortimer (but none to FitzHerbert), Isabel was the mother of two sons who became, in turn, baron of Wigmore: the childless Hugh, killed in a tournament in the November of 1227, and Ralph, baron and *paterfamilias* from late 1227 until his own death in 1246.[22] She was also mother of sons Roger and Philip, and of daughter Joan.[23] Isabel was probably already married to Peter FitzHerbert, her second husband, when she turned her attention properly to Lechlade, first using it to make provision for her younger sons, in the manner of her father before her, and then beginning work on the hospital there in 1228.[24]

Although the earliest work on the hospital was recorded chiefly in Fitzherbert's name, as one would expect of a married woman's activities in medieval England, there can be little doubt that, just as the Anglo-Norman Wigmore Chronicle and the Latin Founders' *Fundatorum Historia* tell us, this was Isabel's project.[25] Between 1224 and November 1227 death claimed four of Isabel's children – Roger, Joan, Philip and Hugh, lord of Wigmore. But it was the latter's demise that Watson suggests drove Isabel to begin developing Lechlade as a new hub for the barony, and the hospital as a centre of personal and filial commemoration.[26] In a deed dated somewhere between 1237 and 1246, provision was made for a lamp before the altar of the Virgin Mary in the newly-built chapel and a chaplain to say masses, in perpetuity, for her soul and that of her son Hugh.[27] Perhaps, then, the Anglo-Norman Chronicle of Wigmore named the wrong kinsman as the focus of her foundation's salvific function. In August 1246, Ralph Mortimer of Wigmore, Isabel's last remaining son, died, leaving the underage Roger Mortimer as his heir. The following year, the Lechlade brethren assumed the Augustinian rule, an initiative that appears to have belonged to Isabel's efforts to secure the future of Lechlade manor and its hospital as she approached the end of her own life. Dispensations for the organisation of the hospital and its property were followed by arrangements for the descent of Lechlade to her young grandson Roger, now the baron of Wigmore. When she died in 1252, Isabel was laid to rest in the hospital's chapel.[28]

It was during Isabel's lifetime, however, that the records of Mortimer marriage patterns indicate a 'frontier turn', if we can call it that, when the barons of Wigmore began marrying women of the Marcher dynasties proper. Far from representing a 'contraction of ambitions', as Brock Holden suggested, this was a shift in emphasis which greatly enhanced the Mortimers' standing in the March, and likely played a critical role in their emergence among the most powerful barons in England towards the end of the thirteenth century.[29] At the heart of the Mortimers' fortunes in the thirteenth century lay their multiple links to the mighty but troubled Braose dynasty. Isabel de Ferrers' son Hugh had married

Depiction of a high-status marriage ceremony in 'Decretals of Gregory IX', from the late thirteenth century (Hereford Cathedral Archives O.7.7 f.156r, © Dean and Chapter of Hereford Cathedral)

Annora de Braose, a daughter of William de Braose (d.1211) and his formidable wife Matilda de St Valéry (d.1210). Like her parents, Annora was pursued by King John: she was captured in Scotland with her mother and other family members and was confined to a royal prison from 1210 until 1214, the year her husband succeeded to his lands.[30] After Mortimer's death, Annora opted for the life of a religious recluse, confined within a cell attached to Iffley Church, outside Oxford, and sustained by regular gifts of consumables and clothing from Henry III and a substantial income of 100s a year from her *maritagium* in Tetbury, Gloucestershire.[31] She survived until at least 1241; and it is not beyond the realms of possibility that, as one scholar suggested, the extant French translation of *Ancrene Wisse* (an anonymous monastic rule for anchoresses) was produced for Annora's use.[32] Certainly, the March of Wales provided fertile ground for the anchoritic tradition. Annora was one of several Marcher women of the thirteenth century, including her own sister Loretta, who traded the turbulence of Marcher life for the peace of the anchorhold in widowhood.[33]

At some point shortly after Hugh Mortimer's death, his younger brother and successor to the barony of Wigmore, Ralph, married the widow of Annora's own brother, Reginald de Braose (d.1227/8). This widow was Gwladus Ddu, a daughter of Llywelyn ab Iorwerth of Gwynedd and either his lawful wife Joan, an illegitimate daughter of King John, or his long-term partner, Tangwystl Goch, who preceded Joan. As J.L. Laynesmith demonstrates in her chapter, it was through Gwladus that later generations of the Mortimer clan claimed descent from King Arthur and other legendary Britons of ancient lore; and it was Gwladus whose (alleged) relationship to King John could be used to reinforce the Mortimers' claim to the English throne in the fourteenth and fifteenth centuries.[34] But in the first half of the thirteenth century, the demise of Gwladus's stepson, William de Braose, sealed the fate of the main line of his dynasty. In 1230 William de Braose, who had not long succeeded his father Reginald as *paterfamilias*, was executed by Llywelyn of Gwynedd for a liaison with the prince's wife, Joan.[35] Besides his widow, Eva Marshal, the hanged baron left behind four young daughters: Isabel, who was soon married to Llywelyn's son and heir Dafydd, along with Maud, Eva and Eleanor. The Braoses' loss was the Mortimers' gain.

It was the second of these daughters, Maud, still just a child when her father died, who grew into one of the most remarkable of the women who married into the Mortimer family in the central medieval period. In November 1246, Maud de Braose became the wife of Roger Mortimer, the teenage son of Ralph

Mortimer and Gwladus Ddu and, ultimately, the best-known Roger Mortimer before the rise of his grandson and namesake, Roger Mortimer, 1st earl of March (d.1330).[36] Maud was the last of the sisters to marry and was already in her twenties at the time. In addition to being a member of the Braose clan, she brought her husband a series of kinship links to leading dynasties that included the Marshals and de Clares. She was also an heiress to a substantial fortune. Besides her own portion, including the lordship of Radnor, in her father's extensive ancestral lands in the Marches and Sussex, she also inherited that part of the Brewer lands in south-western England that her father had inherited from his own mother Gracia, daughter of the Angevin *curialis* William Brewer (and Reginald de Braose's first wife).[37] Moreover, by 1245 all five of the girls' Marshal uncles were dead, without a child between them, leaving the Braose sisters in line to inherit that fifth part of the vast Marshal fortune that fell to their mother.[38] The marriage in November 1246 offered Roger Mortimer, who was then still three months away from being granted possession of his own estates, promise of an impressive additional windfall. More importantly, it also offered Roger a dynamic and compatible life partner, whose function as a linchpin of the central Marcher 'reshuffle' in the mid-thirteenth century informed her identity and sense of purpose for the rest of her life.

The couple's first daughter, Isabel, seems to have been born toward the beginning of her parents' marriage and may have been their eldest child. Since she and her sister Margaret had several brothers, only a dynastic catastrophe, such as befell their mother's family, would make them heiresses. In the spring of 1260, when she was very much younger than her own mother had been at marriage, Isabel became the wife of John Fitzalan (d.1272).[39] Fitzalan was the heir apparent to the baronies of Clun and Oswestry in the March adjacent to Shropshire, and to the earldom of Arundel, although the earldom was destined to remain in the hands of his wealthy and influential grandmother, the dowager countess Isabel d'Aubigny, until after he himself had died. Marriage to Isabel offered her husband no great territorial gain, but it created a dynastic alliance and territorial alignment in the Shropshire and Herefordshire frontiers that was to prove critical some years later. John Fitzalan was only about 25 when he died in the spring of 1272, leaving Isabel with at least two young children, Maud and Richard, and perhaps another son, John.[40] The five-year-old Richard was soon placed, together with some of his patrimonial land, in the wardship of his maternal grandfather, Roger Mortimer.[41] Far more visible in the records during widowhood than as a married woman (as one would expect),

Isabel Mortimer married John Fitzalan, lord of Clun Castle. After her husband's early death in 1272, her father was given custody of Clun, where Isabel's mother, Maud, was often found quite literally 'holding the fort' (© Andy King)

Isabel was to spend 13 years actively involved in Marcher affairs alongside her parents, before marrying again in 1285 and largely disappearing from the records. Isabel died in 1292, but her mother lived on until 1301.[42]

Mother and daughter stand out for their active roles as frontier *barones* (a term chosen deliberately). Isabel made her mark in widowhood and Maud, rather more remarkably, as much during her marriage as in the years after Roger's death in 1282. During the de Montfort rebellion of the 1260s, and again in the period of the Anglo-Welsh wars in the '70s and '80s, Maud could be found quite literally 'holding the fort' at strategic posts on the frontier of Shropshire and Herefordshire while her husband was in the field. Although Maud's precise activities are shadowy, captured only in documentary fragments and the evidence of circumstance, there can be little doubt that she was an important contributor both to the royalist victory at Evesham in 1265, and to the destruction of Llywelyn ap Gruffudd at the end of 1282. She was probably drawn into the violence of her husband's feud with Simon de Montfort in early 1264, when an army led by de Montfort's eldest sons, Henry and Simon, descended into a frenzy of violence and destruction on Wigmore and Maud's own barony of Radnor.[43] Maud may well have been at one of these locations and subjected to abuse, as David Carpenter has suggested.[44] She certainly appears to have been at Wigmore in late May the following year, when, according to the metrical chronicle attributed to Robert of Gloucester, she received the Lord Edward as he fled from Montfortian captivity; and it was at Wigmore once more that she is said to have learned, in gruesome fashion, of the outcome of the battle of Evesham on 4 August.[45] Simon de Montfort had been butchered and dismembered. The earliest and most graphic accounts of his demise, contained in Robert of Gloucester's metrical chronical and in the *Cronica Maiorum et Vicecomitum* of Arnold fitz Thedmar, tell us that the earl's severed head, and perhaps also his testicles affixed on either side of his nose, were conveyed to Maud at Wigmore.[46] Since both accounts of Evesham and its aftermath contain eye-witness detail and intimate local knowledge, we ought not doubt the strength of Maud's ill-feeling toward de Montfort and the depth of her involvement in the affair.

While Maud was at Wigmore from May to August 1265, she was probably at or near to Clun around March 1274, when she received word that Llywelyn ap Gruffudd, prince of Wales, was planning to visit the area. In what was essentially an intelligence report, Hywel ap Meurig, a long-standing servant of the Mortimers and others in the central March, informed Maud that Llywelyn intended to visit the borderlands in the coming week. He advised her to have Clun ready and to pass the news on to her husband.[47] According to Hywel's dispatch, Llywelyn was planning to visit his new castle (Dolforwyn) in Cedewain and to find a suitable location for an additional fortress within the forest of Clun (which he had wrested from its Marcher lord several years earlier). It had also been reported to Hywel that a party of leading nobles of England were planning to meet the prince there, but their intentions were unknown. We may just have evidence that Maud followed Hywel's advice, because there survives today a badly damaged letter from Roger Mortimer to Robert Burnell, then archdeacon of York. It was written around the same time as Hywel ap Meurig's letter and informs Burnell of the news that Mortimer has received of Llywelyn's coming. The identity of Llywelyn's destination has been obliterated, but Mortimer's letter refers to Shrewsbury, Oswestry and other places in and near the Shropshire and Herefordshire borders. There is also a reference, partly lost, to the intended arrival of an English party.[48] Since both letters are now among the Crown correspondence housed at the National Archives, it is possible that Mortimer enclosed Hywel's letter to Maud with his own letter to Burnell, dispatching both in haste as tensions in the Middle March began to increase.

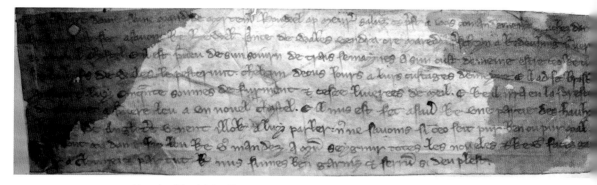

Hywel ap Meurig's intelligence report to Maud about the activities of Llywelyn ap Gruffudd in March 1274 (© TNA SCI/11, no. 47)

In fact, the Clun barony belonged not to the Mortimers but to the Fitzalans, but with the untimely death of Isabel's husband two years earlier, Roger Mortimer had been granted oversight of the barony. He had probably been keeping an eye on the region since 1267, the year in which the Treaty of Montgomery formalised Llywelyn's hold on the upland regions of western Clun, and the barony itself passed to Mortimer's young son-in-law, then aged just 22. Mortimer had also lost territory to Llywelyn, his cousin, in the years that preceded the treaty, and its failure to settle the contested position of Maelienydd simply heightened the hostility between them.[49] In contrast, Isabel and her parents appear to have enjoyed a cooperative relationship, and in the years immediately following the death of Isabel's husband, the increasing reach of her natal family's power along the frontier called for a working partnership with her parents.[50] Isabel's dower in the Shropshire border included the fortified manor of Shrawardine, a third of the wardship of Clun in peacetime, and a range of rights in Oswestry, including incomes from Oswestry borough (fairs, markets and the like), and knights' fees held by fellow Marcher powerbrokers like Fulk FitzWarin and John Lestrange.[51] In 1279 she requested, and was granted, keepership of the manor and castle of Oswestry and subsequently set up a garrison in the castle.[52] She now controlled much, if not all, of Oswestry barony and her interests lay cheek-by-jowl with those of her father, who had taken control of Clun and its fortifications.[53] In the run-up to the final war with Wales, father and daughter had assumed responsibility for much of the Anglo-Welsh border from the lower edge of Cheshire down to southern Herefordshire. Arrangements for Richard's wardship probably also necessitated communication and cooperation between the boy's mother and maternal grandparents.

Llywelyn ap Gruffudd and Roger Mortimer, first cousins and avowed enemies, died only weeks apart in late 1282. Around 26 October, Roger succumbed
to illness at the old Braose castle at Kingsland and was buried at Wigmore Abbey
with his ancestors.[54] On 11 December, Llywelyn was ensnared near Cilmeri, in
a trap that Maud had helped to set, and slaughtered by a group of leading men
from the Marches led by Maud and Roger's son and heir, Edmund, the new
baron of Wigmore. The newly-widowed Maud was again (or still) at Clun after
29 October when the escheators where ordered to take all of the lands held by
Roger Mortimer into the king's hands, as was standard practice on the death of
a tenant-in-chief pending the identification of the heir/s.[55] However, when Roger
Springhose, the sheriff of Shropshire, reached Clun he found that Maud had
garrisoned the castle against him.[56] His complaints about Maud's behaviour to
Robert Burnell, now the bishop of Bath and Wells and Lord Chancellor, seem to

have fallen on deaf ears. In December,
Springhose received an order from the
royal chancery not to interfere any further with the custodial arrangements
for Clun.[57] No doubt Edward 1, whose
gratitude for Mortimer's long service
and sorrow at his death were genuine,
held Maud in equally high regard.[58]

Even for the Mortimer clan, however,
frontier life was not all high drama; and
the greater range and number of records
that survive from the thirteenth century
also allows us to see some of the more
routine activities in which Maud and
Isabel were involved. These activities
were just as critical (if not more so) to
dynastic enterprise and personal quest
than the destruction of a rebel earl or
the last native prince of Wales. I have,
elsewhere, discussed in considerable
detail these women's active engagement
with the management of their estates
and, in particular, their exploitation of

The coat of arms of Maud de Braose/ Mortimer
depicted in glass in St Michael's Church, Kingsland.
In addition to all her other activities, Maud was
responsible for the building of the church towards
the end of the thirteenth century, a project that
was completed by her daughter-in-law Margaret
de Fiennes (© Philip Hume)

channels of redress offered by the royal justice system when things went wrong.[59] Though frequently hostile to royal interference in their activities, powerbrokers in the March were nevertheless willing to invoke the king's judicial powers when necessary. In the king's lawcourts Maud and Isabel could be found in pleas relating to land rights of one sort or another. For the English aristocracy land equalled wealth, prestige and power. The Mortimer women were no less likely than their husbands, sons and brothers to use the lawcourts in determined defence of their rights.

Maud turned to the royal lawcourts almost as soon as she was married, when she and her husband together began determinedly pursuing and defending Maud's extensive rights against the parallel and competing expectations of a range of adversaries.[60] A married woman had, in theory, no separate legal identity or capacity from her husband and all real action relating to Maud's possessions required Roger's participation. The couple's in-court adversaries included Maud's two younger sisters and their husbands, other leading families of the realm who had a stake in the Marshal inheritance, and eight dowagers, including Maud's mother, Eva (d.1246), her grandfather's widow Gwladus Ddu (d.1251) and four Marshal widows.[61] The eldest Braose sister, Isabel, played no part in the litigation. She had effectively been dispossessed of her inheritance by an English king determined to diminish the power of her husband Dafydd, the new prince of Gwynedd; and she had died childless at Godstow nunnery in 1247, a year after Dafydd himself.[62] Over the years and decades, Maud and Roger were involved in multiple interconnected lawsuits that outlasted many of the original suitors and led to multiple reallocations of the Braose and Marshal estates.[63] In addition, the couple claimed the right of 'esnecy' in the inheritance they shared with Maud's sisters. This was their legal prerogative, as the senior Braose heirs, to have first choice of the divided estates. With Isabel de Braose's death, Maud and Roger could now pursue the financial and practical benefits, and social capital, attached to having – for example – the main castle of the old Marshal barony of Offaly (modern-day co. Laois in Ireland) when that barony was apportioned to the Braose sisters.[64]

Maud's maternal inheritance looms large in the couple's joint litigation. Every birth and death in the extensive Marshal kinship network further complicated the patterns of expectation and disagreement and drew the couple, with Maud's sisters and their husbands, into a web of action over Marshal property that rumbled on for many years. Among other things, Maud and Roger demanded certain properties and incomes as their right, pursued errant suitors to their own seigneurial courts, joined forces with their fellow heirs in plaint and defence and responded to accusations of misconduct and requests for warranty (a guarantee of the plaintiff's seisin). The lordship of Haverford in the earldom of Pembroke was one bone of contention that not only brought the Marshal co-heirs, especially the Bohun and Valence families, to court repeatedly, but even resulted in direct, violent intervention in the lands themselves. On one occasion, Roger Mortimer was accused of thuggish and destructive behaviour in the Valences' liberty in Pembroke.[65]

Yet, for each lawsuit that placed Maud and Roger in opposition to Maud's sisters and other members of her extended kingship network, there were several more that brought family members together. The presence of dower in shared territories could sometimes be a force for unity or common purpose among co-heirs in the courts. The de Braose sisters and their husbands had to navigate their way around the dower of no fewer than four Marshal widows, in court and out. Perhaps the most difficult of these widows to counter was Margaret de Quency, countess of Lincoln in her own right and relict of both John de Lacy (d.1240), hereditary constable of Chester, and Walter Marshal (d.1245). Margaret enjoyed greater social standing and political influence than most of her adversaries and, supported by the Crown, enjoyed some of the best of the Marshal territories as her dower. When, in 1248, she was awarded the entire county of Kildare and more in Ireland, Margaret encroached onto interests that had already been assigned to Maud and her Ferrers cousins, the seven daughters of Sybil Marshal and William de Ferrers.[66] With Margaret's dower seemingly protected from diminution, her adversaries were simply compensated directly from the shares of the other Marshal heirs.[67]

Maud Mortimer's involvement in litigation relating to aspects of her own inheritance continued into her widowhood in late 1282, as family wrangling showed little signs of abating.[68] Maud now also had her own dower to think of. Unless she married again and was once more under a husband's tutelage, a widow of full age did not need to involve a male guardian in her litigation. Maud did not remarry after Roger's death, and the burden of litigation in which she was involved after 1282 she alone carried. By that time, her daughter Isabel had been an independent litigant for a decade already, engaged in a dower-quest that may have been rendered more pressing by the fact that she had no great inheritance of her own. Dower was essential to a widow's maintenance and a widow's right to dower unassailable, no matter what her own personal wealth – as Margaret de Quency's case clearly attests. For an English aristocratic widow in the 1270s, dower represented a third of her late husband's estates, most frequently assigned by administrative process after the husband's death. The seizure of the westernmost lands of Clun by Llywelyn ap Gruffudd in the 1260s, and the formalisation of his territorial gains in the Treaty of Montgomery (1267), removed that district from Isabel's reach. Alternatives had to be found to make up the shortfall in her dower. One measure was a 'stop-gap' grant from her father out of those Fitzalan baronial lands which he held in custody.[69] Although Roger Mortimer drove Llywelyn out of western Clun in 1277, no attempt was made to dower Isabel in the region until two years after both Mortimer and the Welsh prince had died, and Isabel initiated no pleas for that land.[70] Elsewhere, however, she sued tenants, kin and neighbours for what she felt were her dower rights.[71]

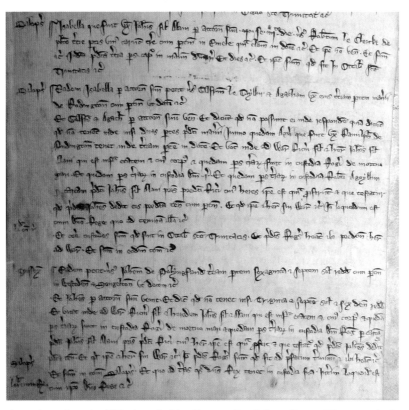

A membrane from the 1273 plea roll of the Common Bench (later Court of Common pleas), shows Isabel Mortimer (d.1292), daughter of Roger and Maud, suing for dower in the FitzAlan lands in Shropshire and Sussex. (© TNA, CP 40/2A, m. 5d.)

A striking feature of dower litigation among landholders in the thirteenth century was the frequency with which widows sued family members. Isabel's earliest dower litigation brought her to court not just against the tenants of knights' fees that she felt belonged to her portion, but also against her mother-in-law and fellow dowager, Maud de Verdun, the widow of John Fitzalan (d.1267). All too often a noble family's estates would need to accommodate the life-interests of widows from different generations of the family. In the lands traditionally earmarked by the Fitzalans for widows' maintenance – stable, secure and away from the main holdings – Isabel's expectations clashed with those of Maud de Verdun and Maud's second husband, Richard de Mandeville. Isabel attempted (not always successfully) to secure additional lands, rents and services from the dower portion of Maud de Verdun.[72] Furthermore, when her father died in late 1282, Isabel was also sued by her mother for dower in the manor of Dodington in Shropshire, which had been part of Isabel's *maritagium* back in 1260.[73] We should not automatically assume that adversarial pleading in court was associated with personal animosity between the parties, since litigation presumably also functioned as a means of amicable settlement and the registration of agreement; but it is difficult not to wonder what the emotional effects of parent-child or sibling litigation were. The intra-familial litigation of the Mortimers at this stage was certainly knotty. While Isabel sued her brother Edmund, the new lord of Wigmore, to warrant her property rights against her mother's dower demands, Maud herself was suing Edmund, and his younger brother Roger, for more dower.[74] Negotiating with the new baron of Wigmore was particularly awkward, since he appears to have been reluctant to relinquish any property either to his mother as dower, or to his siblings to warrant their claims.

In-court litigation was not the only path to justice and remedy taken by Maud and Isabel. From the reign of Edward I (1272–1307) there survive a number of written appeals by women landholders of the Welsh frontier, to the king or his chief advisors, for redress that could not easily be provided by the royal law courts. Both Maud and Isabel made written appeals for grace and favour that were independent of any known lawsuits. A faded piece of correspondence addressed to Edward by the newly-widowed Maud in late 1282 asks for the return of her inheritance, which had been seized into the king's hands on her husband's death. Her husband has been 'called to God' (*a Deu comande*), she says, as Edward has heard from others, and she is troubled by being kept out of her inheritance for so long.[75] A second letter to the king also survives, written

The letter, now faded, from Maud to Edward I in late 1282 asking for the return of her inheritance which has been taken into the king's hand after RM's death (© TNA SC 1/19, no. 130)

some 14 years later, in which Maud requests the return of lands she had given to her younger son William, who is now dead. In a far briefer and less emotive fashion than before, she states that the king's escheators have seized the lands she granted to William for himself and the heirs of his body, and that William has died without such heirs.[76] Both appeals appear to have achieved their desired effect. In the latter case we have Edward's own response, dated 14 November 1296, confirming Maud's claims and commanding the relevant officer not to interfere any further with Maud's properties.[77] In the earlier case, Maud was in possession of her inherited lands by early 1283.[78]

Nevertheless, it is arguably two surviving petitions of 1279–80 relating to Isabel's interests that offer most insight into a Mortimer woman's appeal to the discretionary powers of the king and her sense of place within thirteenth-century frontier society. Written in the third person throughout and addressed solely to the king, though perhaps for consideration in parliament, these two petitions furnish straightforward requests. The first is her request, mentioned above, that she be appointed to the keepership of the lands and castle of Oswestry during the minority of her son. This she was duly granted on 28 April 1279.[79] The second petition, written a short time later, is a request for exemption from paying scutage, doubtless that scutage, or 'shield money', levied by Edward in 1279 in connection with the Welsh campaign of 1276–7. Isabel's justification for her request is telling: she has, says her petition, 'defended her March as well as her other neighbours' (*ele systint sa [m]archa ausi autant cum ses autres voisins*).[80] Perhaps she referred to male lords like her father. She further pledges that, if granted this waiver, she will redirect the same money to the repair of Oswestry Castle, which is run-down (*decheu*).[81] Unfortunately, the king's response to Isabel's request does not appear to survive.

Here we must leave the Mortimer women. There is much more to be said about the female members of the Mortimer family of Wigmore in the period between the Norman Conquest of England and Edward I's conquest of Wales. Women from the cadet branches of this frontier family, such as Agatha Mortimer (née Ferrers) of Chelmarsh and Lucy le Waffre of Chirk, also have stories to tell. Yet the evidence outlined briefly above, though less than is available for the men, serves as a powerful indicator of the place of women at the heart of one of the best-known baronial families of the Anglo-Welsh frontier. From spearheading a revolt against Henry I at the beginning of the twelfth century, to collaborating in the war efforts against Simon de Montfort and Llywelyn ap Gruffudd in the second half of the thirteenth, these women were not compelled by their gender, and the violence of medieval political upheavals, to remain in the shadows. Some aristocratic women did, of course, elect to withdraw from society (as did some noble men). Annora de Braose chose the life of an anchoress after the death of Hugh Mortimer in 1227; but this was a personal choice and probably born as much of a spiritual yearning as a desire to escape the demands of frontier life. In contrast, Maud le Meschin and Isabel de Ferrers, at once both deeply pious and uncompromisingly worldly, sought salvation and dynastic commemoration through religious patronage and benefaction. Isabel even established a hospital and new baronial administrative centre on patrimonial lands she had purchased at great cost from King John in the opening years of the thirteenth century. With more evidence produced in, and surviving from, the thirteenth century, it becomes possible to observe the Mortimer women's administrative and legal activities in greater detail, as they ran the great households, managed estates and, as I have shown above, litigated in the king's lawcourts. Maud de Braose and Isabel Mortimer, mother and daughter, were no more disempowered by theoretical legal disability than by the exigencies of aristocratic life on a militarised frontier. Thus, it is only when we allow for these women's contributions to family enterprise can we get the full measure of an impressive border family which, in the fourteenth century, stood on the national stage. Only when we develop a more holistic impression of the Mortimer family (and of neighbouring dynasties), an impression which captures the activities of the women, can we really understand the March of Wales.

2

Dr David Stephenson

The Mortimers and their Welsh tenantry: some observations

F OR approximately 200 years, from the later eleventh century until the point at which Edward I achieved something approaching a Welsh supremacy in the 1290s, the Mortimer family had to fight and manoeuvre to establish their mastery in much of the Middle March and subsequently across huge swathes of Wales. In many respects the core territory of the Mortimer dynasty was the Marcher territory of Maelienydd. This was the most substantial of the *cantrefi* of the region which became known as Rhwng Gwy a Hafren ('between Wye and Severn'), sometimes designated as the 'Middle March'. It is on developments in this *cantref* that the present study will focus, partly because of the limited space available, but also because of its manifest importance in the eyes of the Mortimers, and because the evidence is more consistent and more enlightening for Maelienydd than for most other Mortimer territories. It will of course be necessary to examine those other territories when appropriate.[1]

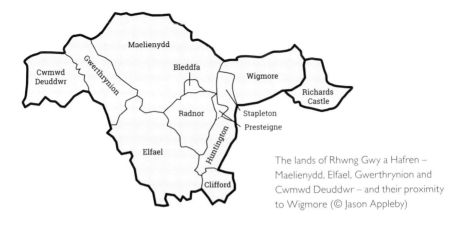

The lands of Rhwng Gwy a Hafren – Maelienydd, Elfael, Gwerthrynion and Cwmwd Deuddwr – and their proximity to Wigmore (© Jason Appleby)

The lands within which the Mortimers exercised lordship in the March of Wales have, unsurprisingly, been the subject of much previous investigation. This has included the remarkable doctoral thesis produced by Penry Evans in 1934, elements of Rees Davies's magisterial study of the March published in 1978, and a flurry of studies ranging from very competent broad surveys to truly ground-breaking work in recent decades.[2] But what is perhaps surprising is that little attention has been given to the relations between the Mortimer lords and the Welsh populations of their lordships, who might on occasion threaten Mortimer control, and at other times might provide the sinews of Mortimer power.

During their long struggle to establish their lordship in the period from the late eleventh to the thirteenth century the Mortimers enjoyed some striking successes which were for long periods balanced by dramatic setbacks. Some periods of that story are obscure, but it is at least clear that the Mortimer family exercised meaningful control of the Middle March for less than half of the period from the 1080s to the 1270s. A narrative embraces initial occupation, marked by castle-building, then expulsion in a period of Welsh revival in the 1130s, re-establishment in the 1140s followed by renewed expulsion in the 1150s. Control is only restored in 1195 – for some 20 years – and then follows renewed expulsion at the hands of Llywelyn ab Iorwerth and his allies and dependents from the indigenous dynasty. Mortimer ascendancy was restored in 1241, but was undermined by developments in the early 1260s only to be revived in the middle of that decade. The family's position was consolidated in the war between Edward I and Llywelyn ap Gruffudd in 1277, when Mortimer forces were an important element in the restoration of the Marcher dominance in the Middle March which was to be an enduring feature of the political landscape of the fourteenth century. In the case of the Mortimers, however, that dominance, particularly in the mid- and later-fourteenth century, was limited by recurrent minorities which saw the Mortimer lands pass into the hands of custodians,[3] and by dower provisions for lords' widows.[4]

This pattern of sporadic Mortimer lordship punctuated by fighting and periods of control exercised by the indigenous dynasty, as well as by intrusive Welsh rulers such as the imperialistic Llywelyn ab Iorwerth of Gwynedd, was a crucial element in the developing nature of the relationship between the Mortimer lords and the Welsh communities of the Middle March. It almost certainly had the effect of limiting the capacity of the Mortimer lords to exploit the resources of the land. Though it involved, unsurprisingly, recurrent violence it also necessitated accommodations with the Welsh population. The more prominent elements in that population were clearly vociferous in their determination to maintain their rights and privileges, as when it was reported that the *optimates*, the more prominent and locally powerful members of the Welsh community, had declared that they would not suffer the domination of any prince over them.[5] That declaration was undoubtedly aimed at Llywelyn ab Iorwerth, but was symptomatic of a determination to resist any external lordship. And there are interesting hints that at times the Mortimer lords were obliged to make concessions within the lands over which they were striving to establish lordship to members of the indigenous dynasty. We should note in this connection the suggestion that Roger Mortimer (d.1214) may have agreed to install a member of the indigenous dynasty, Madog ap Maelgwn ap Cadwallon in part at least of the lands which Madog saw as his patrimony. The evidence is far from conclusive, but it is an attractive interpretation.[6] Most importantly, the scanty evidence does suggest that the Mortimer lords were amongst the first Marcher magnates not just to attempt to conciliate, but to draw into their entourages, some of the leading figures in the Welsh communities which they were striving to control. An early sign of this process is provided by the charter issued to Cwm Hir abbey in 1199 by Roger Mortimer (d.1214). While the charter includes a pointed reference to Mortimer's conquest of Maelienydd (*c.*1195) it is perhaps just as significant that the witness-list includes the names of several Welshmen. By the time of the issue of documents in the early 1240s, which marked the effective removal from real power of members of the old Welsh dynasties of Maelienydd/ Gwerthrynion, it is clear that the Mortimer entourage included significant Welsh figures, some of whom, the descendants

The charter issued by Roger Mortimer (d.1214) to Abbey Cwm Hir in 1199, which includes the names of several Welshmen in the witness-list (Archives of University College, London)

of Meurig ap Philip, were destined to become figures of major importance in the administration of Mortimer lordships, including Maelienydd.[7]

It is clear therefore that in several ways the Mortimer lords of Maelienydd and associated territories found it advisable to make accommodations with some elements amongst their tenantry in order to maintain their position. Such manoeuvres had institutional consequences which reached far down through Welsh society. Not the least was the toleration by the lords of the effective autonomy of the Welsh community. One sign of this was the very limited territorial control exercised by the lords, as exemplified by the fact that the lord's rental income from Maelienydd in 1356–7 amounted to only £15 out of a total gross yield of £215. It was of course inevitable that the lords would attempt to increase revenues by other means, which would impact on their Welsh tenantry, and it was to be expected that this would produce tensions and resistance. There are certainly some indications of such strains developing in the course of the thirteenth century.

For the period of spasmodic Mortimer control in the Middle March in the century and a half after c.1277, which saw a more settled ascendancy punctuated by short periods of dynastic crisis such as the dramatic upheavals which beset the family in the years from c.1322 to the fall and execution of Roger, first earl of March in 1330, it is clear that the Mortimers' Marcher possessions played a central role in their rise to importance and power within the realm. And it was not simply a matter of the extent of their Marcher territories, but also one of their relationship with the tenantry, particularly the Welsh tenantry, of those lands.

Their proliferating Welsh territories provided the Mortimers with many of the sinews and trappings of power: such was the case when Roger Mortimer, fourth earl of March, came of age in 1393 and celebrated that fact with a forty-day progress around his Welsh territories. Roger was continuing a family tradition of attempting to maintain, whenever possible, close personal connections with his lordships in the March.[8] He was also announcing not just his coming of age but his acquisition of a political and military strength which put him amongst the front rank of Richard II's aristocracy.[9] And sometimes such a declaration could be even more pointed and forceful, as when in mid-1321, the rebellious Roger Mortimer of Wigmore led his followers, including many Welsh tenantry, through London clothed in his livery.[10] Similarly when Roger, fourth earl of March, arrived in Shrewsbury to attend a parliament in January 1398 he was allegedly greeted by 20,000 of his followers and tenants.[11]

Though the numbers involved were almost certainly exaggerated, we can glimpse the impact of the support which the Mortimer lord could muster from an inquisition of 1322 which heard that:

> the chase of Wyre is in a poor state of vert and a reasonable state of venison, but not as it used to be, because 10,000 Welshmen of Brycheiniog, Maelienydd, Gwerthrynion, Ceri and Cedewain [all but the first being Mortimer territories], fifteen days before the surrender of Roger Mortimer of Wigmore stayed in the said chase for nine days and took forty bucks ... The park of Cleobury is in a good state of vert and a poor state of venison because the said Welshmen took two hundred bucks and does at least ...[12]

But as the Mortimer hold on extensive territories in the Middle March of Wales strengthened in the middle decades of the thirteenth century, another facet of their relationship with their Welsh tenantry came increasingly to the fore. This was the issue of the nature of Mortimer governance, and in particular that of lordly exaction and community resistance. Chronicle evidence relating to 1262 suggests that Roger Mortimer (d.1282) was facing serious problems with the Welsh inhabitants of some of his Welsh territories. The accounts of events recorded in both the Peniarth 20 and Red Book of Hergest versions of the Welsh chronicle *Brut y Tywysogion* are in close agreement:

> That year, about the feast of Andrew the Apostle [30 November] certain people by their own counsel came from Maelienydd to the new castle which then belonged to Roger de Mortimer. And they took the castle and seized Hywel ap Meurig, who was constable of the castle, and his wife and his sons and his daughters, after killing the gate-keepers. And they made that known to the Lord Llywelyn's seneschal and constable. And those came in haste and burned it to the ground. And when Roger heard that, he came with many leading men as his supporters in arms. And he stayed within the castle walls for a few days. And the Lord Llywelyn's officers made that known to him. And he gathered a host and came to Maelienydd, and he received the homage of the men of the land, and took two other castles ...

The page of the *Brut y Tywysogyon* in the Red Book of Hergest that recounts the capture of Cefnllys in 1262 (the account starts just below the repair in the left-hand column). Oxford, Jesus College MS. 111, f.87v
https://digital.bodleian.ox.ac.uk/objects/9bf187bf-f862-4453-bc4f-851f6d3948af/

From these chronicle notices we can establish that the capture of Cefnllys Castle was not the result of an initiative taken by Prince Llywelyn or by his local officials – the men described in the *Brut* as his seneschal and constable. It is quite clear from the testimony of the Welsh chronicle that the seizure of Cefnllys was carried out by members of the community of Maelienydd. The key text here is that of the Red Book of Hergest version of the *Brut*.[13] This makes it clear that the capture was effected 'by the counsel of the men of Maelienydd'. We are dealing therefore not with an attack planned by the prince or his commanders, but by elements of the Mortimer tenantry. At the same time, it is clear that what we may see as a Mortimer policy of attracting senior figures in parts of the March into the service of the dynasty had succeeded in the case of Hywel ap Meurig and his family, as in a number of other cases.

Additional information about the events of late 1262 is provided by another chronicle source – the so-called B-text of *Annales Cambriae*. It has been argued that the annals for the late 1250s and the early 1260s represent contemporary or near-contemporary chronicling in the nearby abbey of Cwm Hir, as opposed to the two main versions of *Brut y Tywysogion*, which reflect chronicle entries being made at Strata Florida.[14] It therefore constitutes a significant additional source of evidence for the events now being analysed. The *Annales Cambriae* B-text section in question runs as follows:

> In that same year on the vigil of St Andrew the Apostle the castle
> of Cefnllys was captured and destroyed by the efforts of the men of
> Maelienydd. On the same day the castle of Bleddfa was taken and
> destroyed ...[15]

It would seem that local men were aiming to capture castles simultaneously in several parts of the Mortimer lands of the Middle March. What is perhaps most striking about the B-text entry for this episode is the emphasis it places on the role of the men of Maelienydd. Even more than the entry in the *Brut*, the B-text makes it clear that the taking of Cefnllys was the product of a local insurgency rather than part of Prince Llywelyn's campaign of conquest. It is possible that the members of the community who attacked Cefnllys were asserting their autonomy in the face of the development of a new bastion of Mortimer power in Maelienydd and that Roger Mortimer had begun to threaten the delicate balance of power between lord and community.

The natural ridge at Cefnllys. The site of Roger Mortimer's castle, captured in 1262, is at the north (near) end; he later built a castle at the southern end (© CPAT image 4236-2025, photograph by Julian Ravest)

But it remains possible that the Welsh of the Mortimer marchland may have been not so much in revolt against Mortimer lordship *per se* in 1262 as stirred by fear of the instability that might follow Roger Mortimer's absorption in the increasingly turbulent politics of Henry III's realm, which saw Mortimer emerging as a principal target of the hostility of the baronial faction. There may be a link here with the report of Roger Springhose to Edward I in late 1282. Springhose, an experienced administrator with strong connections in the March, had been sent to report on the Mortimer lordships in the March following the death of Roger Mortimer in late October 1282. In the first of two reports by Springhose to the king, probably written in early November of 1282, he stated that the lands and castles of the late Roger had been found in good order, that he and his fellow commissioner (clearly Grimbald Pauncefoot) had comforted the Welshry and left them, as far as they could discover, well disposed towards the king. The situation seems to have changed by the time a second report was submitted by Springhose. This has been dated, surely correctly, to the period immediately before 24 November of 1282.[16] On that occasion, Roger reported that he had surveyed and furnished the castles which had belonged to Roger Mortimer, and had negotiated the inhabitants into the king's peace as far as he had been able. His further comment seems to be of great importance: he had found the inhabitants of Mortimer's lands 'very fickle and haughty, as though they were on the point of leaving the king's peace, because they have no definite lord.' Springhose noted that he did not believe that the inhabitants of the Mortimer lordships would long continue to keep the peace unless their lord came to them. He concluded his analysis by emphasising that it would be a good thing for the security of the land if the matter of the heir were hastened.[17] Springhose was referring to an apparent delay in confirming Edmund Mortimer as the late Roger's heir, and transferring Roger's lands to him. This was done on 24 November when Springhose was ordered to give Edmund seisin of his late father's lands. The key point here is that the tenantry were not regarded by Springhose as being discontented with Mortimer lordship, but rather with the absence of such lordship.

It is, however, to the 1290s that we must look for indications of apparently serious tensions between a Mortimer lord – now represented by Roger Mortimer's son, Edmund – and the men of Maelienydd. Those indications seem to be made evident in two charters granted by Edmund in June 1297. These charters are of prime importance for an analysis of the relations between lord and community in Maelienydd and must therefore be considered in detail. The first begins by stating that Edmund's grant had been made in response to complaints by the men of Maelienydd alleging oppressions committed by officers of the lord, both in Edmund's time and in that of his father. The charter thus emphasises the role of the community in challenging the ways in which lordship had been exercised, and suggests that some at least of the complaints were by no means new. It sets out a procedure for dealing with grievances relating to lands, tenements, mills, woods or chattels which have been unjustly taken from a complainant, or to other injuries or trespasses suffered at the hands of Edmund, his father or his bailiffs. The plaint is to be brought into the court of Cymaron, to be dealt with by judgement of twelve jurors, according to the laws and customs previously used there. Edmund thus appears to be picking up long-standing grievances which are to be remedied in accordance with time-honoured customs. A proviso is introduced that no-one should bring any plaint regarding the demesnes of the castles of Cefnllys or Knucklas, and the lands of Pilleth. In what looks like a partial repetition (perhaps an indication of hasty drafting) it is stated that cases touching fees 'or other matters' should be determined in the court of Cymaron by verdict of twelve jurors. It is then provided that the goods and chattels of the freemen of Maelienydd should not be taken for the lord's use, unless in cases of necessity. If those goods should be saleable they should be taken at a just price, to be paid within three weeks. It was also provided that if anyone had been taken and imprisoned, but was according to the laws of Maelienydd 'repleviable or manucapable' (i.e. fit to be released upon finding suitable pledges) he was to be released upon finding such pledges. For every crime whatever, the common law should be granted without money ransom.

A further section of the charter relates to mercantile matters and notes that all pleas touching the lord's tolls (*tolnetum patriae*) in that land should be held in the 'hundred' (i.e. court) of Cymaron, as was usual in the time of Edmund's father, though those relating to the markets of Cefnllys and Knucklas should be held in those places. These mercantile provisions were important firstly in that they do, in contrast to others, suggest that problems had intensified in the time of Edmund Mortimer, while they imply that the courts of the urban foundations attached to the castles of Cefnllys and Knucklas were a special source of lordly

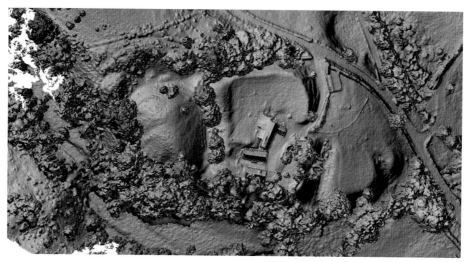

The site of Cymaron Castle, probably first built by the Mortimers in the 1090s, but subsequently retaken by the native Welsh rulers on three occasions, on the last occasion being destroyed in 1215 and not rebuilt. However, it remained an important centre of administration with the Mortimers building a courthouse there. Photogrammetric view made from 43 individual drone photographs processed to construct a 3-D digital model and recoloured red for the highest points (some tree tops) down to green. (© CPAT image 1112-002, photograph by Julian Ravest)

revenue. The dispositive clauses of the charter conclude with a provision that anyone holding wood or pasture in the land of the abbot and convent of Cwm Hir by the monks' grant should enjoy those rights peacefully.

A second charter, with the same date, place of issue and witnesses as the first, granted the men of Maelienydd the right to hunt and take deer in that land, with the exception of the demesne lands of Knucklas and the demesne of the wood of Swydd, as well as in the lands and demesnes of the abbot and convent of Cwm Hir, though three granges of Cwm Hir were withdrawn from this prohibition. It provided that if anyone should hunt beyond the permitted bounds and should kill any kind of game and should be convicted by being taken in the act or by the inquisition of twelve lawful men, the following penalties should apply: 20s for a stag, 10s for a hind, 5s for a young hind, 5s for a roe-deer, 10s for a boar and 5s for a sow. If the hounds should go beyond the permitted bounds and take deer, the beasts should remain the property of the lord and the hounds should be given back to their owners. In addition, it was provided that the whole of the River Ithon from the bridge of Llanddewi to the ford called Rhyd yr hen bont should be free for hunting.

The reason why two apparently separate grants were made at the same place and time and with the same participants is not explained in the charters, but a probable reason may be suggested which may be of importance. It seems likely that the first charter was drawn up in advance of its issue, and represents an initiative by Edmund Mortimer or his officials. The second charter may represent a response to demands or requests put forward by the men of Maelienydd at a later stage, perhaps at a meeting to hand over the first charter. If correct, this scenario may be of importance in establishing the nature and context of the grants.

The importance of the grants is underscored by the distinguished group to witness the issue of the charters. The list is headed by Richard, earl of Arundel, another great Marcher magnate, lord of Clun and of Oswestry, who had been raised to the earldom of Arundel in 1289. Arundel was a veteran of Welsh wars of the late 1280s and the 1290s, had fought in Gascony and was close to Edward I. Also present were the abbots of Wigmore and of Cwm Hir, two knights, Philip ap Hywel, Mortimer's steward, and John de Lingeyn, a significant Mortimer tenant.

The grants of 1297 together constitute a major, wide-ranging statement of liberties to be enjoyed by the men of Maelienydd. It appears to demonstrate the power of the community against that of the lord. But there are factors which throw this verdict into some doubt. The last clause of the second charter before the witness-list which completes it is most instructive, for it records that the men of Maelienydd have paid £500 for the grant. Edmund Mortimer had indeed made concessions to the community, but had underlined the strength of his lordship by exacting a significant payment in exchange.[18] A further clause noted that the men of Maelienydd would hold the liberties granted in the charter as long as they kept themselves in the king's peace. The introduction of the king into the text is particularly important: Mortimer was amongst the great lords of the March, but the political environment was dominated by the king.

This last point raises the question of Edward I's role in the granting of the charter to the men of Maelienydd. By a fortunate chance this can be established by reference to a document recorded on the Close Roll for 1297. A royal mandate of 16 May addressed to Edmund Mortimer ran as follows:

> The king has received divers complaints from the community of Welshmen of Maelienydd, Edmund's men and tenants, setting out that he grievously disquiets and molests them by imprisonment of their bodies and the taking and carrying away of their goods and chattels and by various ransoms, wilfully and without reasonable cause, contrary to justice and contrary to the law and custom of those parts, so that they are now so impoverished that they have little or nothing to live upon, as they assert ; and the king, pitying their estate, has given them a day before him in parliament at London in the octaves of Holy Trinity to show their complaints there before him and his council: he therefore orders Edmund to be present in person on that day to answer to the said Welshmen for the aforesaid grievances and other things that they will object against him, and to do and receive what the court shall consider in the premises. He is ordered not to aggrieve or molest them in any way in the meantime in their persons or goods by reason of the complaints aforesaid or for any other reasons.[19]

The first point to note here is that the content of this mandate shows some obvious relationships to that of the first charter itself, which appears to have been a direct response to the royal order. The second important point is that the hearing of the claims against Edmund Mortimer was to take place on the octave of Holy Trinity (16 June), whereas the charters were granted on the morrow of that feast, almost a week earlier (10 June), thus presumably obviating the need for the proposed hearing. It seems that Mortimer had bowed before the king's

Statue of Edward I, Burgh by Sands (© Rose & Trev Clough, Geograph)

threat of legal proceedings and had issued the first charter as a way of escaping from them.[20] The charters were then conveyed from Wigmore to Westminster where they were subjected to inspeximus and confirmation on 1 July.

It is very instructive to compare at this point the issue of a charter to the Welsh tenantry of Humphrey de Bohun, earl of Hereford, in the lordship of Brecon in the same year.[21] The charter was granted as a means of countering an attempt by Edward 1's agent Morgan ap Maredudd, acting on the king's secret orders, to provoke disturbances which would almost certainly have allowed the king to take the lordship into his hand – as he had done in Glamorgan in 1295. The grant of the charter left the Welsh community of Brecon lordship 'at one with their lord'.[22] There is a distinct similarity between events in Brecon and those in Maelienydd: in both cases the fact or threat of royal intervention was met by the prompt issue to the Welsh community of a charter which was intended to reconcile the tenantry to their lord. The figure who was common to both the issue of the Maelienydd charter and that to the men of Brecon was Philip ap Hywel, who was the steward to both de Bohun and Mortimer. Philip was the highly influential son of Hywel ap Meurig, who had occupied a similar position in the previous generation. It is difficult to resist the suggestion that Philip ap Hywel may have been behind the tactic of issuing a charter in both cases. This in turn raises in striking fashion the important question of the identity of those actually responsible for relations with the tenantry. It is true that the Marcher lords might on occasion make crucial policy decisions on their own initiative, without reference to, or in spite of the advice of, their councils or leading officials.[23] But we must be alert to the possibility that those senior figures in a lordship, like Philip ap Hywel, with close relations with the Welsh community, might on occasion prove to have been the mainsprings of lordly policy.[24]

It is clear that Edward I was adept at using the grievances of Welsh communities in the March to put pressure on the Marcher lords or to exact financial penalties from them in a period when the king was in great need of money. This in turn raises the question of how far the grievances may have been stirred up or exaggerated by the king and his officers. We should perhaps note that there is no evidence of participation by the men of Maelienydd in the risings of 1294–5. It is true that absence of evidence does not constitute evidence of absence, but in this case we can go a little further. The Mortimer chronicle covering the years 1066–1306 (John Rylands Library MS 215) edited by Penry Evans contains a particularly interesting entry under 1294, recounting how 'the Welsh unanimously withdrew from the king's peace, so that no Welsh-speaking land remained which had not risen against the king, with the exception of Maelienydd and *tebeset*'.[25] So Maelienydd had apparently not been affected by the risings of 1294–5, which had convulsed so many parts of Wales.[26] This is perhaps surprising if we attempt to paint a picture of widespread discontent in that *cantref.*

The background to the issue of the 1297 charters is therefore a complex one. But their importance may be underscored by their confirmation in the period before Bannockburn in 1314, when Edmund's son, Roger (d.1330), may have been anticipating problems resulting from the absence of the king from the realm with a significant body of troops; an alternative possibility is that Mortimer was preparing to join King Edward's force and was perhaps guarding – in either case – against possible turbulence in Maelienydd.[27] It seems possible that Roger Mortimer of Wigmore took that step in an attempt to placate the Welsh population of Maelienydd during his projected absence on campaign. But charters of liberties, however buttressed by confirmations, could not of themselves guarantee stability and peace – a fact acknowledged by Penry Evans in his investigation of the Mortimer lordships.[28]

It is fairly easy to find examples of oppressions committed by Mortimer lords. Such is the case of Cadwgan Goch, originally of Arllechwedd in Gwynedd. It is probable that he had served Llywelyn ap Gruffudd in Cedewain after that prince's seizure of that territory in the early 1260s. In a probable reference to the war of 1282–3 he wrote to Edward I to remind the king that he had been admitted to the king's peace 'in the present war' and had been restored to his lands in Cedewain by royal letters. In spite of this, Cadwgan reported, Edmund Mortimer, without observing any rule of right, was keeping him in irons in his castle of Wigmore. He therefore prayed for justice, liberation, and the restoration of his lands.[29] In a rather different case, we may suspect a significant degree of coercion on Edmund's part when we learn of his apparent dispossession of the last of the native lords of Ceri, when Gruffudd Goch ab Owain 'Cendamy' relinquished to Edmund all of his rights of lordship in that land.[30] But it must be remembered that these relate to individual cases, and that we do not usually know the detailed background to them. It is unsafe to form rapid judgements and to generalise. On the other hand, it has to be observed that the attempt by B.P. Evans to support his comment that 'the picture is not wholly unrelieved, however, by acts of consideration on the part of the [Mortimer] lord towards his Welsh tenants' is supported by very few instances of such generosity.[31]

Chirk Castle, built by Roger Mortimer of Chirk (d.1326).
The tenants of Chirk complained about his harsh rule (© Philip Hume)

The Mortimers can easily be depicted as an exceptionally hard-nosed, even vicious dynasty, as evidenced by the brutal way in which the first and second earls of March participated in the effective destruction of even their own kinsmen, the Mortimers of Chirk.[32] This aspect of Mortimer lordship is well evidenced by the lamentations of the tenantry of Chirk in 1330–31:

> There was no forest or warren in the land of Chirk until it was given to Roger Mortimer the uncle, or for twelve years after he had seisin, but he made forest and warren in waste lands and woods so that the men and tenants of the land could not have common of pasture for their animals, or hunt in the said woods, or take other profits, as they were wont to do. Forest tax and hound tax were not exacted before the time of the said Roger beyond 5s 7d which of right ought to be paid in the name of hound tax, but now the tenants pay £6 14s 5d. The said Roger used to take from his free tenants heriots and leyrwites.

> All the free tenants used to have their own mills on their own soil, without paying any rent to the lord; but the said Roger after about twelve years by distraints made them pay him a certain rent yearly, viz. £7 and unjustly took pannage and toll. After his death, Roger Mortimer, earl of March, continued these things all his time.[33]

Perhaps inevitably, there were clearly many instances of upheaval on his estates in the aftermath of the fall of Roger Mortimer, earl of March, in 1330. But we should note that much of the activity was not confined to the Welsh community, as witnessed by the removal of wooden palings from the palisade of the park at Dolforwyn by a crowd of Welshmen from Cedewain, aided by a party of English from Montgomery who arrived with carts to transport the looted timber. Evans emphasised what he called 'outraged national feeling' as the motive behind the attacks on Mortimer property after the fall of the earl of March in 1330, but immediately cast doubt on this as a complete explanation by referring to the actions of one Gruffudd Llwyd 'with certain unknown Englishmen' in breaking into Chirk Castle and seizing the Receiver's possessions.

Finally, we must examine perhaps the most notorious episode in the long story of the relationship between the Mortimers and their Welsh tenantry. In 1402, the rapidly emerging leader of demands for an autonomous Welsh polity, Owain

Glyn Dŵr, led a significant foray into the Welsh March and the lands which had long been associated with Mortimer rule. Forces of the Herefordshire gentry led by Sir Edmund Mortimer, uncle of Edmund, the young heir to the Mortimer lands, moved to confront Glyn Dŵr's men at Bryn Glas in Maelienydd. The Herefordshire men were augmented by a strong force of archers drawn from Maelienydd. In the course of the battle the Maelienydd men changed sides and fired into the English ranks, a move which proved decisive in the outcome of the battle. In weighing up the factors which led the Maelienydd men to turn their weapons on Sir Edmund Mortimer's force, we should note that the death of the earl of March in 1398, and the inception of yet another Mortimer minority had deprived the tenantry of that personal 'good lordship' which was so important in maintaining goodwill and stability. But it may be relevant to recall that the alternative name for Bryn Glas is that of Pilleth. We have encountered that name in the text of the first of the 1297 charters, when Pilleth was one of three territories from which the rights confirmed to the men of Maelienydd were excluded. It is

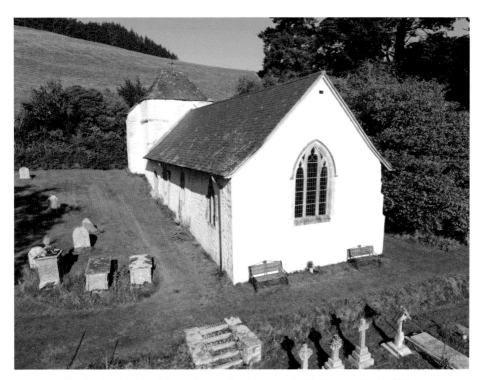

The site of the battle of Bryn Glas rises from the church of St Mary our Lady of Pilleth
(© Laura Shepherds, Lens Photography www.laurashepherdslensphotography.com)

tempting to speculate on how far being ordered to confront Glyn Dŵr's force at Pilleth was a step too far for the Maelienydd men, in that they were not defending their own community from the northern incursion, but a territory which had long association with Mortimer control and exclusion of Welsh rights.[34]

The foregoing brief examination of aspects of the relationship of Mortimer lords and their Welsh tenantry serves to emphasise the problems of interpreting what often turns out on close scrutiny to be the ambiguous evidence involved. The detailed analysis of the charters to the men of Maelienydd of mid-1297 carried out above reveals something of the complexities surrounding what are on the surface relatively straightforward documents. Complexity also surrounds many other superficially simple situations, such as those of Roger Springhose's reports to Edward I in 1282.[35] Accounts of tensions between Welsh communities of tenantry and their Mortimer lords must be set out with due regard for such factors as English individual or community participation and support in their actions, the strong possibility that what may superficially look like a rejection of Mortimer lordship in fact represents a reaction to the lack of such lordship, and the fact of royal connivance at, and encouragement of, the expression of grievances against Mortimer lords by their Welsh tenantry. It is easy to picture 'the mercilessly grasping lordship of the Mortimers',[36] and in some cases such a description is amply justified by the record sources. But we should note that there is clear imbalance in the sources – in documentation like petitions and inquisitions we are far more likely to hear complaints against magnates like the Mortimers than to encounter commendations for kindness or generosity.

The complaints of Welsh communities against Mortimer lords and lordship can be set against the remarkable praise-poem addressed to Roger Mortimer, 4th earl of March, by Iolo Goch, himself a Mortimer tenant in the lordship of Denbigh.[37] A poem composed in Welsh was of course aimed at a Welsh and Welsh-speaking audience. It reveals something of the esteem in which Roger was held at least amongst the favoured members of the Welsh community of his lands. As well as his eminence in Ireland, where he was appointed to numerous high offices, culminating in that of lord lieutenant of all Ireland in 1397, Roger's dominant position in both Welsh and English political society is emphasised, as the descendant of the royal house of Gwynedd and one who had a claim to be heir to the throne of England. The poem emphasises his martial qualities, in lines such as *'Rhyswr, cwncwerwr can caer'* (a hero, conqueror of a hundred fortresses).

Such a depiction of Roger, as well as an emphasis on his wide dominion in Wales, England and Ireland, promises the capacity and the will to defend the interests and to further the careers of his followers. A reference to *glod Elystan*, (having the renown of Elystan) is a reference to the celebrated but elusive Elystan Glodrydd, eleventh-century ruler of Rhwng Gwy a Hafren. This brought Roger close to the many distinguished families of the Middle March who traced their descent from that king.

Most interestingly and tantalisingly, one phrase (l.14) of Iolo's poem has a special significance. In it Roger is characterised as *burffrwyth iôr Aberffraw* (the pure fruit of the lord of Aberffraw). The reference to Aberffraw links him to the place of that name, which was the chief court of Gwynedd, and by extension of Wales, of the great princes (Llywelyn ab Iorwerth and Llywelyn ap Gruffudd) of the thirteenth century. Indeed, the former used the designation *princeps Aberffraw* (prince of Aberffraw) in his title.[38] What is particularly striking, however, is that the phrase is identical to one employed in another poem by Iolo Goch, this time to Owain Glyn Dŵr.[39] That Iolo aligned the two men in that way is an extraordinary testimony to the way in which he sought to present Roger Mortimer.

The poem of Iolo Goch to the fourth earl of March thus serves as a reminder, if one were needed, that 'good lordship' as well as lordly oppression, might be a feature of the relationships between the Mortimer lords and at least some of their Welsh tenantry.[40] Those frequently ambiguous relationships were the product of a blend of mutual, sometimes grudging, acceptance and impatient self-interest that defies clear definition. We are reminded that in the March, especially, few things are as simple as they may at first appear to be.

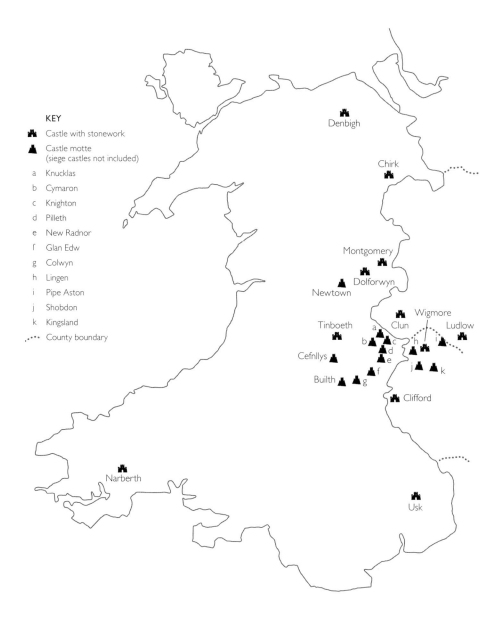

KEY

⚔ Castle with stonework

▲ Castle motte
  (siege castles not included)

a Knucklas
b Cymaron
c Knighton
d Pilleth
e New Radnor
f Glan Edw
g Colwyn
h Lingen
i Pipe Aston
j Shobdon
k Kingsland

·⸱·· County boundary

Denbigh

Chirk

Montgomery

Dolforwyn

Newtown

Wigmore

Tinboeth   Clun   Ludlow

          a
        b   c
          d
Cefnllys   e
          f

Builth   g

Clifford

Narberth

Usk

The key Mortimer Castles in and near to the Welsh Marches

40

3

Dr John R. Kenyon

The castles of the Mortimers: an overview

THIS contribution examines the architecture of the main castles that are associated with the Mortimers, as opposed to sites that varied in ownership during different periods of Welsh and English ascendancy. For example, the builder of the motte and baileys of Rhyd yr Onen in the later twelfth century in what was Arwystli, to the north-east of Llangurig (Montgomeryshire), could have been any one of a number of people, including Roger Mortimer (d.1214).[1] There are several lesser sites, mainly surviving as earthworks, that can be seen in lands over which the Mortimers held sway at one time or another, and the Mortimer History Society's website lists a range of castles with some form of Mortimer connection. (See also *On the Trail of the Mortimers in the Welsh Marches*.)[2]

The greatest castles in terms of their architecture are, of course, Wigmore, at the heart of the Mortimer lands, Ludlow and Chirk. However, there is a group of fascinating sites deep into Wales, in the *cantref* or lordship of Maelienydd in what is now Radnorshire. This was a territory that the Mortimers fought over with the Welsh for around two centuries, much of that time being a period when the Welsh held sway, capturing and sometimes holding the castles of the Mortimers.

It is not always possible to assign phases of works to some of the castles, such as Montgomery and Dolforwyn, when there were times that these castles were in the hands of the Mortimers, mainly in the fourteenth century, and even the plans in the guidebook to these two sites simply date new works to the later thirteenth century through to the late fourteenth century.[3]

For a general study of the Marcher lordships, including castles and other buildings, then the Logaston Press book on the central and northern lordships is recommended, the first of a three-volume study.[4]

41

1731 Engraving of Wigmore Castle by Samuel and Nathaniel Buck
(© Herefordshire Archives and Record Centre, L67-1)

WIGMORE, HEREFORDSHIRE

The castle of Wigmore is important for two reasons: first, although founded by William fitz Osbern (d.1071), it became the home of the Mortimers from the late eleventh century and centre of a major lordship in the central Welsh Marches for some four centuries; second, as a recent example of an imaginative method to conserve and display a major monument without proceeding along the lines of 'ministry' work of the 1970s and earlier and other sites in state care, a method not without its critics.[5]

As part of the conservation of the castle, two small-scale excavations were undertaken in 1996 and 1998, work that nevertheless emphasised the richness of the deposits within the walls.[6] Although there is much to commend regarding English Heritage's work, 'in many ways, Wigmore Castle still remains some-thing of an enigma'.[7]

The castle is approached from the village through the rectangular outer bailey, with no physical evidence today of masonry defences, although these have been suggested by resistivity surveys. Between the village and this outer bailey there are earthworks which may be the remains of a siege castle when Wigmore was besieged by forces of the Crown.[8] The conjectural reconstruction by Dominic Andrews[9] shows the whole of the main part of the castle, that is, the inner and the upper baileys, enclosed by a curtain wall. The most imposing buildings are the half-buried main gatehouse and the two rectangular towers to the west of it. The gatehouse dates to the thirteenth and fourteenth centuries, the south-west towers with their ogee windows and seats, as well as fireplaces, forming part of the fourteenth-century refurbishment of the castle. Of these two towers, that to the west of the gatehouse is the best surviving piece of architecture in the castle. Originally of at least two storeys with a basement, fireplaces and windows with seats in the embrasures, these features indicate a structure of domestic significance.

The D-shaped south-east tower is earlier, and on slightly higher ground within the bailey is a platform that may have held the great hall, and behind it, on the curtain wall, is the outer face of a fourteenth-century polygonal tower. So, clearly major improvements were made to the castle by Roger Mortimer, earl of March (d.1330), at the same time as new accommodation was being built at Ludlow.

Future work on the castle needs to concentrate on the so-called motte and shell-keep, at the highest point of the castle. The plan on the English Heritage website simply calls this area 'Lord's apartments', and its very position marks this area as the site of the most private accommodation of the Mortimers. The view of the castle by Samuel and Nathaniel Buck, published in 1733, gives some idea of what was standing at that time in this part of the castle.

The term 'shell-keep' for the curtain wall is a misnomer – it is simply an upper enclosure with curtain wall and seemingly a polygonal tower of some importance at the highest point, although little remains. The recent work on shell-keeps by Dr Bob Higham, with Neil Guy, rightly omits Wigmore from its gazetteer, but it is a term that has been used often regarding Wigmore, possibly from the time of the survey by the RCHME.[10]

The ultimate failure of the rebellion against King Edward II led by Thomas, earl of Lancaster, in 1321–2, which brought about the earl's execution, led to Roger Mortimer, the future earl of March, and his uncle, Roger Mortimer of Chirk, being imprisoned in the Tower of London. In 1322 an inventory was made of the contents of the castle of Wigmore, of which more below.[11]

Although the castle continued to be used from the Tudor period onwards, not least by the Council of the Marches in Wales, and some repairs were undertaken, more often comments related to the poor condition of the castle and its possible slighting in the wars of the 1640s.[12]

Ludlow Castle: the north range at the top of the photo in the inner bailey is one of the finest surviving examples of a medieval domestic range (© Laura Shepherds Lens Photography. www.laurashepherdslensphotography.com)

LUDLOW, SHROPSHIRE

Of all the Mortimer castles, Ludlow, founded by the de Lacy family, is the most imposing,[13] although it was only directly in the hands of that family for a relatively short period. It was a Mortimer home from the early fourteenth century through to the time when it passed through the female line into the house of York in 1425, when a minor, Richard Plantagenet, duke of York, inherited the Mortimer estates through his mother, Anne, sister of the fifth and last earl of March, Edmund. It would seem that Ludlow became the favoured seat of the Mortimers, rather than the patrimonial centre at Wigmore.

Unlike Wigmore, Ludlow Castle continued to flourish in the sixteenth and seventeenth centuries, although stripped of much of its contents in 1650. Leased to the Powis estate in the eighteenth century, its eventual acquisition by the earl of Powis in 1811 could be said to have saved the castle from further deterioration, although it was not until the 1970s onwards that the fabric was stabilised.[14]

The collection of essays on the castle cited in note 13 provides a full description of the castle in several chapters, but here we are concerned with the Mortimer period, notably the work of Roger Mortimer, the first earl of March. The castle contains many a fine building, such as the great tower and the Norman chapel with is circular nave, but it is the domestic complex on the north side of the inner bailey that concerns us here primarily.

This range can be divided into two phases. The western half, which consists of the solar and the great hall, probably dates to the late thirteenth century, its Y-tracery windows being a feature of this work. The range is the work of the Geneville (Joinville) family, either Geoffrey or his son, Peter, Geoffrey having married a de Lacy heiress, Maud, by the summer of 1252. We are concerned with the eastern half, with its fourteenth-century ogee windows in the great chamber, and this is the work of Roger Mortimer, although the rooms adjacent to the Norman Pendover Tower at the north-east corner were modified in the fifteenth and sixteenth centuries.[15]

Roger, the future first earl of March, was betrothed to the Geneville heiress, Joan, in 1301, and is unlikely at his young age to have instigated the Mortimer work at that time, and especially as he was to spend the opening decades of the fourteenth century on the family estates in Ireland. So, we are looking at a date from around 1320 for his transformation of the north-east corner of Ludlow's inner bailey.

The great chamber consists of two very fine rooms over a ground floor or basement, all the floors heated, the corbelled-out fireplace on the first floor being the most handsome, with its two sconces consisting of carved heads, perhaps representing King Edward II and his queen, Isabella. A large Tudor window replaced the Mortimer one in the sixteenth century when this range was occupied by the presidents of the Council of

Ludlow Castle – internal view of the Great Chamber, first built by Roger Mortimer (d.1330). When the first floor was refurbished for the Council of the Marches in Wales in the sixteenth century, a large Tudor window replaced the original (© Rosalind Caird)

the Marches in Wales. The fireplace and north window of the uppermost chamber also indicate a room of importance.

The Mortimer range of the great chamber and the accommodation to the east of it was served by a massive four-storey garderobe tower that projects from the Norman curtain wall, its five chutes serving a number of latrines. The lowest two storeys had two small rooms or closets per floor, with a single closet or bedchamber on the two upper floors, rooms with commanding views to the north.

Ludlow Castle: external view of the massive four-storey garderobe tower built by Roger Mortimer (© Philip Hume)

Although there is a stair turret off the north-east corner of the great hall, there must have been access to the great chamber block from within the inner bailey, and Thompson has postulated that there is evidence for an external stair turret just to the west of the existing Tudor equivalent.[16]

The one Roger Mortimer building to which a date can be assigned with some accuracy is St Peter's Chapel in the outer bailey. It was built as a chantry chapel for two priests to give thanks for Mortimer's escape from the Tower of London in August 1323.[17] Although altered in the sixteenth century to serve as the courthouse for the Council of the Marches in Wales, during the presidency of Sir Henry Sidney, the chapel's remains include one blocked Y-tracery window and evidence for another, a design that we have seen in the late thirteenth-century solar and great hall of the Geneville period. However, we should not be surprised to find these two types of windows in Mortimer work – Y-tracery and ogee – for the fine church at Kingsland in Herefordshire has both, the church considered to be a Mortimer endowment of around 1320–40.[18]

46

CHIRK, DENBIGHSHIRE

The baronial castles erected following the conquest of Wales and established in the north-east of that country, in the counties of Denbighshire and Flintshire, have recently received long-overdue assessment.[19] Henry de Lacy, earl of Lincoln, built the castle at Denbigh which is, of course, well known and is the best surviving of this group of monuments. Hawarden, in private hands, has a remarkable round keep on a motte which bears comparison with Edward I's great tower at Flint Castle. Ruthin Castle, absorbed into the grounds of an hotel, has become better known through the recent work of the Ruthin Castle Conservation Trust and substantial repairs funded by Cadw. The castle at Holt, built by John de Warenne, earl of Surrey, has all but disappeared, but sixteenth- and seventeenth-century plans and an inventory of 1484 have enabled a detailed study with a digital reconstruction to be undertaken.[20] This leaves us with Chirk, in the care of the National Trust.

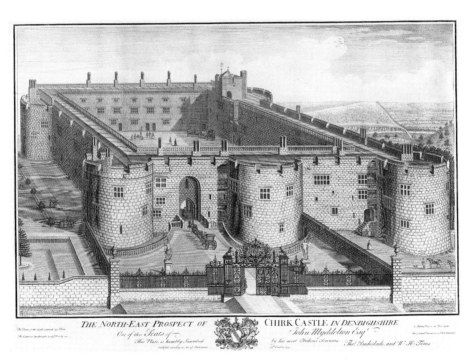

An eighteenth-century engraving of the north-east prospect of Chirk Castle in Denbighshire, first built by Roger Mortimer of Chirk. 1735 Engraving by W.H. Toms, after Thomas Badeslade, artist
(© Nantional Library of Wales)

Roger Mortimer (of Chirk, d.1326), third son of the Roger (d.1282) who played a major role in Edward I's initial conquest of Wales, was granted the new lordship of Chirkland in 1282, but the precise date for the castle's construction is not known. It may even be from the time of Roger's appointment as justiciar of Wales in 1308. The quadrangular plan of the castle, with massive mural towers, has led to comparison with the king's castle of Beaumaris on Anglesey, the core of this unfinished castle dating to 1295, although Chirk lacks a great twin-towered gatehouse, two of which were planned and partly built at Beaumaris. Nevertheless, the Chirk gatehouse is impressive, with loops covering the vaulted entrance passage. The cost of building such a castle as Chirk *ab initio* must have been enormous when one thinks that some £6,000 in the money of the day was the cost of work at Beaumaris over the first six months, and this may be the main reason behind Chirk's presumed unfinished state.

So, the castle was never completed, assuming that the idea was to have a quadrangular castle with great mural towers at each corner and in the centre of the curtain walls. These mural towers must be amongst the most thickly-walled corner towers in England and Wales. Certainly, what had been left unfinished was habitable, for in 1329 major repairs were needed for the tiled roofs.[21] The entrance, over which may have been a carving of the Mortimer coat of arms, lies in the north-east corner of the north curtain. To the west are the medieval middle and Distil towers, the curtain running south of the latter also medieval, leading to the Adam's Tower. This last tower is the finest part of the Mortimer castle, with its large rooms, spacious window embrasures, and the stairs leading up to the first floor being covered by murder holes; examples are also to be seen over doorways.

The equivalent towers on the east side are dated on National Trust plans as late seventeenth century, but probably represent a thinning of the original Mortimer build. The south range has been dated to around 1400, certainly fifteenth century, and contains a chapel in the south-east corner. However, during two workshops held at the castle in July and August 2018 some attendees came to the tentative conclusion that whilst the eastern end of the south range started life as a partly-free-standing chapel, the secular nature of some of the current features seen in the chapel suggested that this may have been partly used as the great hall of the castle at a later date, perhaps when the rooms along the range were extended westwards in the late fourteenth century. A chapel may have continued to function in an internally shortened/ divided section of the space towards the east window.

John Goodall has drawn our attention to the early fourteenth-century inner wards of the castles at Skipton in Yorkshire and Alnwick in Northumberland – respectively the work of Robert Clifford and Henry Percy – comparing the compact nature of their inner wards with those built or planned at Chirk, with powerful mural towers which are relatively closely spaced.[22] Wide window embrasures can also be seen at Skipton, as well as at both Flint and Hawarden (2018 workshops).

NARBERTH, PEMBROKESHIRE

A castle at Narberth[23] in south-west Wales first appears in the records in the year 1116 when it was burnt by the Welsh, but the Mortimer connection dates from 1247. In this year the estates of the great Marshal family were subdivided following the death of the last male earl of Pembroke, Walter, in 1245. Roger Mortimer (d.1282) had married Maud de Braose, the daughter of Eva Marshal, and he received Narberth and other lands in south-west Wales.

The south range of Narberth Castle viewed from the north, from within the castle (© Philip Hume)

It is not known what state Narberth was in when acquired by Roger, but it certainly was not strong enough to sustain Welsh attacks in 1257 by Llywelyn ap Gruffudd of Gwynedd. The ruins of the castle that stand today must date to a rebuilding of the castle by Roger after 1257 and it remained in the family's hands, by and large, until the end of the Mortimer male line and the passing of the Mortimer estates to Richard, duke of York, by 1432.

The castle stands on a spur overlooking the town to the north. The castle consists of four round towers enclosing a rectangular ward, the largest of which, the very ruinous north-east, might be seen as the donjon or great tower, so called in the 1539 survey. It consisted of four storeys and had fireplaces and latrines. The best surviving tower lies at the south-west corner, has windows but no fireplaces, while virtually nothing remains of the north-west tower. The southern towers consisted of three storeys. In the centre of the long east and west sides of the castle there are the remains of a small tower or turret.

To the north there may have been an outer ward, but there is no evidence surviving of the main entrance to the castle, though the 1539 survey of Narberth mentions a passage between two chambers. The gap between the two northern towers is too small for there to have been a twin-towered gatehouse, so perhaps the entrance was akin to the main entrance to Conwy Castle of the 1280s.

The masonry does indeed suggest a later thirteenth-century date for the rebuilding of the castle by Roger Mortimer, although the fragmentary remains of the domestic buildings suggest a date for these of around 1300, when Narberth was in the hands of Roger Mortimer of Chirk. A vaulted building on the south-east side appears to have supported a first-floor solar. Running across the south end of the castle lay the hall, part of the inner wall surviving. The hall was on the first floor, the 1539 survey stating that a kitchen lay below it. A list of the castle's goods in 1330 mentions timber for a mangonel (stone-throwing artillery), presumably either wood for one to be made or indicating that the mangonel was dismantled for storage purposes.

In his paper, Neil Ludlow stresses that the masonry of the great hall is different to that in the main towers, and the few surviving diagnostic features also indicate a later date, perhaps a rebuild after Narberth was burnt in 1299.

CEFNLLYS, CWM ARAN, KNUCKLAS AND TINBOETH, RADNORSHIRE

There are numerous sites of interest in the Welsh *cantref* or lordship of Maelienydd, both archaeologically and historically,[24] and the four under consideration here have a particular Mortimer connection. One only has to stand on top of Cefnllys or Knucklas for example to realise the importance of these castles in overlooking routes between Welsh- and Anglo-Norman-held territories.

Of all the sites in Maelienydd, Cefnllys is arguably the most interesting, as the site consists of two Mortimer castles at either end of a naturally strong hill, a ridge known as Castle Bank. The site has been the subject of investigation by the Royal Commission on the Ancient and Historical Monuments of Wales.[25] It is thought that the northern castle was built by Ralph Mortimer (d.1246) in 1242, when a castle was built in Maelienydd, a structure that was destroyed by Llywelyn ap Gruffudd in 1262. It appears that Ralph's son, Roger (d.1282) began to repair the damage soon after the Welsh destruction but abandoned the attempt in order to build a new castle in 1267, and this second castle occupies the southern end of the hill. It was still under construction in the 1270s, for in a letter dated 1273 or 1274, Llywelyn ap Gruffudd complained to King Edward that Mortimer was doing more than repair a castle but was digging a wide and deep ditch, with stone and timber brought in to build a castle.[26]

Repairs were undertaken in 1356–7 on the keep and a barn was thatched, and although the castle was in the hands of the Crown at different times, as well as Mortimer descendants, it was still occupied in the later Middle Ages and garrisoned during the Owain Glyn Dŵr uprising of the first decade of the fifteenth century. In a poem written by Lewys Glyn Cothi in the fifteenth century, when Cefnllys formed part of the inheritance of Richard, duke of York (d.1460), the poet describes the hall of the constable of the castle, Ieuan ap Phylip, possibly located on the ridge between the two castles.[27]

The first Mortimer castle had a main tower within a curtain wall with two wards or baileys, but the appearance today is grass-covered rubble and later quarrying makes distinguishing medieval features difficult to interpret. The later castle had a massive ditch cutting it off from the rest of the hill, a ditch that is still apparent to this day. This new castle also had a keep or main tower, and it may have been polygonal, for it is described by Lewys Glyn Cothi as an 'eight-sided fort'.[28] The aerial views clearly show that the keep was set within a square or rectangular curtain-walled enclosure, with traces of corner towers facing the approach from the ridge.

The second castle considered in this section, Cwm Aran or Cymaron, consists of a substantial rectangular motte with bailey and dates to the twelfth century. It may have been established by Ralph Mortimer (d.1115/27) and rebuilt after falling to the Welsh by Hugh Mortimer (d.1181/85), Ralph's son, in 1144.[29] It was then repaired in 1179 at a cost of £10 to the Crown. Falling into Welsh hands in 1182, it reverted to a Mortimer castle in 1195, when Roger (d.1214) refortified it with a grant of £20 from the Crown.[30] After its destruction by Llywelyn ab Iorwerth's supporters in 1215, it appears that no further use was made of the site. A Scheduled Monument, the scheduled area was extended in the early 1990s to

Knucklas Castle
dominates the
Teme Valley
(© CPAT image
4236-3419,
photograph by
Julian Ravest)

take account of the earthworks that may have been a siege castle in one of the many attacks on the castle.[31] There is no visible evidence for masonry.

Knucklas Castle, set within the confines of a possible Iron Age hillfort, is first mentioned in 1246, on the death of Ralph Mortimer, although it may date to the opening years of the thirteenth century. Taken by the Welsh in 1262, it may never have been permanently occupied thereafter. There is evidence of a square structure, perhaps a keep or small inner ward, with small corner towers, although the south-west tower may have been larger than the others.

Tinboeth, or Dinboeth, is the fourth castle in Maelienydd mentioned in this section. It was built by Roger Mortimer (d.1282), so dates to the late thirteenth century. It is a massive ringwork castle, possibly, like Knucklas, set within a hillfort. A deep rock-cut ditch delineates the enclosure, and the turf covers a wealth of evidence for masonry defences and buildings. The remains of a twin-towered gatehouse stand above ground and bases of a faceted curtain wall and at least three small angle towers or turrets can be traced. There is also a massive flat-topped outwork or barbican facing the approach to the east, similar to that in front of the inner ward at New Radnor and the bailey of Wigmore. The castle does not appear to have remained occupied for long, and even though included in the possessions of Roger Mortimer (d.1330) taken by the king in 1322, there is no reason to assume that it was a functioning fortress.

Formidable Tinboeth Castle built by Roger Mortimer (d.1282) (© CPAT image 962-001, photograph by Julian Ravest)

NEW RADNOR, RADNORSHIRE

The wife of Roger Mortimer (d.1282) was Maud de Braose, and it was through her that Roger came to own this castle upon their marriage in 1247. The great earthworks of the castle overlook the medieval town with its grid of streets. The town was enclosed within defences for which murage grants were made in the second half of the thirteenth century.[32]

The castle occupied a natural hillock, double ditches dividing two enclosures from one another, the outer very large and the inner defended by two lines of massive ditches, including a very broad outer bank similar to those at Tinboeth and Wigmore. Although there are traces of masonry, the castle has never been

Radnor Castle dominated both the town and plain (© CPAT image 4236-3409, photograph by Julian Ravest)

53

explored systematically. It is presumed that the form of the castle is owed to the time that it was in the hands of the de Braose family, but there may have been Mortimer rebuilding. Earl Richard of Cornwall commenced rebuilding in March 1233, but by 1235 the castle was in the hands of Ralph Mortimer. In 1264 the castle and town were burnt by the sons of Simon de Montfort who were in alliance with Llywelyn ap Gruffudd. The castle played a major role on behalf of the Crown during the Owain Glyn Dŵr uprising, being well-garrisoned, especially in the period from the summer of 1402 to January 1405 at a cost of nearly £900.[33]

OTHER CASTLES IN WALES WITH MORTIMER CONNECTIONS

One of the most impressive of the native Welsh castles is Dolforwyn,[34] the last castle to be built by an independent prince of Wales, Llywelyn ap Gruffudd (d.1282), constructed in the early 1270s. Overlooking the Severn Valley, the position of Llywelyn's castle was problematic as far as the English Crown was concerned, being close to the royal castle and town of Montgomery. Following King Edward I's first Welsh war of 1277, in which Dolforwyn was besieged and taken by Roger Mortimer in April of that year, with at least one siege engine coming from Wigmore, Roger was given the lordship of Cedewain, including the castle. The castle, which had been damaged during the siege, remained in Mortimer family hands, apart from some short-lived forfeitures, until the male line died out and Mortimer possessions came to the house of York.

Little of the castle survived above ground before excavations that ran from 1981 to 2000, led by Lawrence Butler, but what they revealed was Llywelyn's substantial castle, with a rectangular keep at one end of the castle and a great round tower at the other, as well as an apsidal or D-shaped tower on the western side.[35] The excavations also revealed repairs to the keep and a reordering of the internal buildings by the Mortimers, including a hall, storeroom, bakehouse and brewery. When the castle was forfeited in 1322, the survey that ensued listed a range of buildings, including the main towers, the round one of which housed the armoury, a chapel, hall, pantry and buttery, as well as garners for the storage of grain.[36]

Montgomery Castle, although a royal castle, came into the hands of Roger Mortimer (d.1330) courtesy of the king, and became a Mortimer castle in perpetuity other than when it was forfeited. A major refurbishment of the castle was made in the 1280s by the Crown. The castle was in a poor state in 1310, with the well tower on the point of collapse, and repairs were made in 1331, after forfeiture from the Mortimers, with £20 spent on the castle's bridge and other buildings. It is impossible to assign any of the surviving buildings in the inner and outer wards to any one person, although it was the king who funded those works that we know about.[37]

Denbigh Castle[38] came into the hands of Roger Mortimer, 1st earl of March, after the deaths of Hugh Despenser (1326) and Edward II (1327). Following the earl's own death in 1330, the castle was forfeited and not regained by the family until 1355, and then largely held until the death of Edmund, the last of the male line, in 1425. As far as the fabric of the castle is concerned, little appears to have been done when in Mortimer hands other than upkeep and repair. Surviving accounts mention work at various times when in the hands of the Crown, such as on the Red Tower in 1374.[39]

Usk Castle in Monmouthshire[40] has a connection with the Mortimer family as earls of March in the period 1368–1425, from the time that Edmund married Philippa, the daughter of Lionel and Elizabeth de Burgh, and their son, Roger, the 4th earl, was born there. It is possible that part of the outer gatehouse and the adjacent south tower (later a dovecote) may represent a Mortimer phase, but further study is needed here. It is known that in 1411–2 a new chamber was built at a cost of over £20.[41] However, Priestley and Turner have suggested that the outer ward of the castle dates to the early 1320s, the work of Elizabeth de Burgh and her husband, Roger Dammory.[42]

Two castles in Breconshire were in Mortimer hands at times in the fourteenth century, Blaenllynfi and Bwlch y ddinas, but it is unlikely that any works were undertaken on them, the value of these castles and their lands to the Mortimers being rents due.[43]

IRELAND

Although the Mortimers held lands in Ireland from the middle of the thirteenth century, there is little that we can say about their influence on the castles of that land. Roger Mortimer (d.1282) was the first to hold lands there, but the first member of the family actually to set foot in Ireland was his grandson, Roger, the future earl of March.[44] However, mention needs to be made of Trim in County Meath, Ireland, for Roger Mortimer, later first earl of March (d.1330), inherited the Irish lands of the Geneville family through his wife, Joan, as well as Ludlow.

Roger Mortimer (d.1330) inherited Trim Castle through his marriage to Joan de Geneville (© Hugh Wood)

Trim is one of the greatest medieval castles in northern Europe, let alone Ireland, but there is little firm evidence for Mortimer works at the castle. Although repairs and new building were undertaken in the fourteenth and early fifteenth centuries, one cannot assign them specifically to the Mortimers; documented repairs tend to relate to when the castle was held by the English Crown.

However, building phases dating to the later fourteenth and fifteenth centuries revealed by the excavations include the short-lived 'small hall' on the north side of the castle, adjacent to the earlier great hall. On the north side of the great tower a forework was added, protecting the tower from that side, with bridge access.

Bearing in mind the windows to be seen in fourteenth-century Mortimer additions to Wigmore and Ludlow, an ogee-headed window was added to a chamber on the third floor of Trim's great tower.[45]

CONCLUDING REMARKS

How much more can we learn about the form of the Mortimer castles? Without archaeological excavation at Wigmore and the castles in Maelienydd, which is unlikely to happen, then perhaps not much more. However, there is one major stronghold that needs an in-depth study, more than just the two workshop days in 2018, and that is Chirk. Apart from the domestic range at Ludlow built by Roger Mortimer, arguably the best surviving example of a Mortimer castle is that built by Roger's uncle, Roger of Chirk. An academic study of the castle and contemporary castles would be a major contribution to the study of castles of that period. As well as such links, the study should be combined with the influences gained from the Crown's 'office of works' through the thirteenth century and beyond. These influences may stem from medieval plans of kings' works, plans that are no longer in existence, but as Richard K. Morris has stressed, medieval masons, an itinerant profession, are just as likely to gain knowledge from actually seeing castles 'in the flesh', as it were.[46]

There is, however, one aspect that enables us to add some colour to the Mortimer castles, literally in some cases. This is through the finds made during the archaeological excavations at Wigmore, Dolforwyn and Montgomery, as well as through the surveys and inventories made when Mortimer castles were removed from the family's ownership.

The small-scale excavations at Wigmore consisted of a trench in 1996 running from the curtain wall into the interior, the trench being situated between the south and south-west towers, and a trench in 1998 backing on to the east tower.[47] The pottery assemblages were nothing remarkable, consisting of basic wares needed in the running of a medieval household. Other finds included glazed floor tiles, arrowheads, fragments of possible plate armour, horse equipment, dress accessories, and a variety of household objects such as keys. Other chapters in the Rátkai report cover the faunal and plant remains. What the finds from the two excavations have shown is that there must be a wealth of evidence relating to the building and life of the castle of Wigmore waiting to be explored at some future date.

Lawrence Butler's excavations at Dolforwyn[48] revealed some coins, dice and thimbles. Several catapult balls were found, either used against the castle during Roger Mortimer's siege of 1277 or stored on site for artillery mounted in the castle. An ivory book cover and a piece of painted window glass were amongst the finer finds. Another example of a fragment of fourteenth-century painted window glass was uncovered during the excavations of Montgomery Castle, depicting the head of a woman of rank.[49]

Decorated floor tiles were also amongst the finds at Montgomery, and an appendix to the report on the finds examined the remains of musical instruments, there being four later thirteenth- or fourteenth-century bone tuning pegs for harp or lyre.[50] Amongst the metalwork there was the usual range of clothing accessories, as well as arrowheads, spear and axe heads, and horse furniture.[51]

As a result of Roger Mortimer's fall from grace in 1322, an inventory was made of the contents of Wigmore Castle.[52] Amongst the items in the survey are weapons of war such as springalds, crossbows, arms and armour, as well as household objects and board games. The outer bailey enclosed cattle, as well as corn and hay, and Wigmore Abbey also housed armour, as well as furniture, garments and hangings said to belong to Roger's wife, Joan. In the same year, Mortimer's possessions at Dolforwyn were listed.[53] Arms and armour were stored in the round tower at the north end of the castle, including over 400 quarrels for crossbows. In the chapel were vestments and vessels for the Mass, the hall had several tables, Joan Mortimer's chamber housed a tub in which to bathe, and the various service rooms such as kitchen, brewery and larder all contained items that would ensure the smooth running of the household when the Mortimers were in residence.

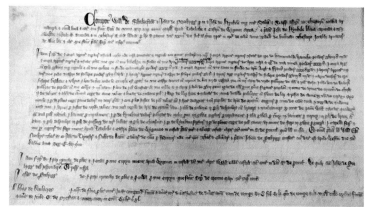

Enrolled copy of the account submitted by William of Shalford and John of Piercebridge itemising the possessions of Roger Mortimer at Ludlow and Wigmore after his death (TNA E 372_179, rot. 22d_m.2)

In November 1331, the plate, goods and chattels belonging to the late earl of March in the castles of Ludlow and Wigmore were itemised by William of Shalford and John of Piercebridge.[54] Mortimer's possessions ended up in London, being delivered into the royal treasury. There were several gilded silver cups and ewers listed at the beginning before the inventory moves on to a range of textiles, including a silk bed whose coverlet is worked with a castle of love (*castro amoris*) and a hanging of eighteen pieces with butterflies and the coat of arms of Mortimer of Chirk. Amongst the armour was a red velvet coat for jousts with the Mortimer coat of arms, various helmets and bascinets. In which castle these items were housed is not specified. The inventory, of course, is only concerned with the valuables in the castles, not the everyday objects.[55]

4

Dr Laura Tompkins

The escape of Roger Mortimer from the Tower of London, 1323

Roger Mortimer's escape from the Tower of London on the night of 1 August 1323 was a pivotal event in the reign of Edward II that would ultimately result in the king's forced abdication and death. After a dramatic flight across the sea – complete with poison, intrigue and rope ladders – once Mortimer reached France he became the focal point of the baronial opposition to the king and his hated favourite, Hugh Despenser the younger. It was here in late 1325 that it became widely rumoured that Mortimer had entered into a sexual relationship with the queen, Isabella of France, cementing his notoriety in history as 'the queen's lover' or 'paramour'. In September 1326, having been forced out of France in possible disgrace, the couple launched an invasion which soon gained popular support. Within months Edward II had been replaced on the throne by his son, Edward III, with Mortimer and Isabella acting as *de facto* regents. Despite its importance, however, because the story of Mortimer's escape itself is so entertaining, over the years it has become embellished and distorted to the point where it can be difficult to ascertain what is known – and what is not – about the details of what actually happened. Moreover, whilst the escape is discussed in numerous historical contexts, it has not been the subject of discrete study in its own right. This chapter will attempt to address these issues by bringing together and breaking down the individual pieces of evidence for the escape, identifying potential collaborators – including the queen – and offering some thoughts on exactly where Mortimer might have been held within the Tower of London.

BACKGROUND, REBELLION, AND IMPRISONMENT

Roger Mortimer (d.1330) was a powerful and prominent nobleman from a young age.[1] Born at Wigmore Castle in 1287, upon the death of his father Edmund in 1304 he became a ward of the Crown at the age of 17. Edward I granted Roger's

59

wardship to Piers Gaveston, the favourite of the then Prince Edward, but in 1306 Mortimer was knighted and given livery of inheritance despite still being a year from coming of age. For this, he apparently gave Gaveston 2,500 marks in compensation. In 1308 Roger performed a ceremonial role at the coronation of Edward II. The Mortimer estate had grown significantly under Edward I, with manors stretching across Herefordshire, Shropshire, Gloucestershire and Worcestershire, together with several important marcher lordships in central Wales, and property in Ireland. In 1301, Roger had married the wealthy heiress Joan de Geneville, whose numerous and strategically important lands, including Ludlow Castle, greatly enhanced Mortimer's regional territorial power in the west of England and the Welsh Marches. Perhaps most significant of all, however, was her substantial property in Ireland in the liberty of Trim, centred on its formidable castle, which made Mortimer one of the foremost English lords in Ireland. As a result, Mortimer spent much of his time between 1308 and 1320 in the country. In 1317, he was appointed as lieutenant of Ireland by Edward II with the task of defeating Edward Bruce, brother of Robert I of Scotland, and restoring order amongst both the native Irish and English settler lords. Mortimer did an exceptional job on most fronts, and in 1319 was reappointed by Edward II as justiciar, during which term he made great strides in improving the Irish administration and the general political stability of the region.

For many years, therefore, Mortimer had played only a modest role in domestic politics. Upon his return to England in 1318, after his first term of office as chief governor, he began to take up a more prominent position as a generally-respected, perceptibly neutral force in the acrimonious conflict between Edward II and Thomas of Lancaster. Most notably, in July 1318 he was part of the delegation that negotiated a truce between the king and his cousin, and in August he was appointed to the new council of sixteen men created as part of the resulting Treaty of Leake, together with a commission to reform the royal household. It was when Mortimer returned from Ireland for a second time in 1320, however, that he emerged as an opponent of the king as he came into conflict with Edward II's favourite, Hugh Despenser the younger, over the latter's territorial ambitions in the Welsh Marches. By early 1321 Mortimer and several other marcher lords were in open rebellion against the king's decision to grant Despenser the vast and profitable lordship of Gower. In May that year Mortimer led a number of attacks on Despenser lands in south Wales, capturing both Cardiff Castle and Swansea. Having formed an alliance with Lancaster at a meeting at Sherburn in Elmet (Yorkshire) in late June, in August Mortimer and other of the king's opponents marched on London and forced Edward to send both Despensers into exile. Mortimer, meanwhile, received a pardon for his previous devastation of the Despenser lands.

The tentative peace between the king and his magnates did not last long and hostilities soon resumed, but Mortimer now found himself on the back foot. After fierce fighting around Gloucester and Worcester in December, Mortimer was eventually outmanoeuvred by Edward II and forced to surrender at Shrewsbury on 23 January 1322. Despite apparent promises of mercy, both Mortimer and his uncle, Roger Mortimer of Chirk, were sent to the Tower of London. Following the defeat of the earl of Lancaster at Boroughbridge in March 1322, on 14 July Edward appointed judges to try Mortimer and his uncle for treason. They were found guilty of raising war against the king and other acts of felonious violence and in early August were condemned to be drawn and hanged, although interestingly by 22 July Edward II had already decided to commute this sentence to life imprisonment, prior to the verdict being publicly passed.[2] At this stage it seemed that Mortimer was in for a long acquaintance with the Tower, but just a year later he would make his miraculous bid for freedom.

Copy of proceedings and judgement pronounced on Roger Mortimer, the uncle, and Roger Mortimer, the nephew [1322] (TNA, E 163/24/12)

THE ESCAPE

Roger Mortimer's escape from the Tower of London is a remarkable tale that could come straight out of any action-adventure historical drama – indeed, it may have set the template for the fictionalised portrayal of many a daring prison break. To summarise the core narrative, on 1 August 1323, the feast of St Peter ad Vincula (St Peter in Chains), Roger Mortimer escaped from the Tower by drugging his guards and the Constable of the Tower, Sir Stephen Segrave, with a noxious drink that put them all into a deep sleep. He then broke through the wall of his cell, fled into the kitchen, out through the roof, and using a rope ladder scaled two of the castle's walls in order to reach the river, where men were waiting for him with a boat. He then crossed the Thames and travelled by horse to Portsmouth before taking a boat to France. A number of accounts also record that Mortimer received aid and assistance from collaborators at various stages of the escape process. The principal body of source material for this narrative is a number of chronicle accounts, many of which were written close to the time of the escape. Although some of the accounts were prone to creative licence, what is perhaps most surprising is that, in general, the version of events presented by the chroniclers is supported by the government records and therefore appears to have been broadly accurate, despite its fantastical nature. This section will focus first on the contemporary chronicle accounts, providing a full breakdown of exactly what is said in each of these texts, before turning to the government records and the official response from Edward II to Mortimer's escape.

Chronicle accounts
The most detailed of the chronicle accounts is that written by Henry de Blaneford, a monk of St Albans Abbey, whose text is a continuation of the *Annales* of John de Trokelowe and which survives for just one year between 1323 and 1324.[3] In full, his narrative of events reads:[4]

> In the year 1324 [1323], on the feast of St Peter called 'Ad Vincula', a noble man, lord Roger of Mortimer, lord of Wigmore, who was detained and secluded less honourably than was proper, in a very high up and confined place in the Tower of London with Lord Roger, his uncle, and with other nobles of the king, who (returning to the conflict between the king and the barons I recalled above) had submitted themselves to the king's mercy, out of the sight and hearing of the world, drew upon the depths of his intelligence to plot his secret escape. Thus, in the silent darkness of night on the said feast day, with the castle guards and many others having been put into a deep sleep by means of a certain noxious drink, he suddenly made his escape, not through the door of his chamber – which had been barred with many locks and bolts – but from another place, through a breach in the wall, into the kitchen which adjoined the king's palace and, coming out through

its roof, he came to the first of the castle walls. Then, using ropes ingeniously arranged into a ladder, which a friend had brought to him previously in secret, and with no little fear, he reached the second wall. And just as the Blessed Peter bound in Nero's chains, guided by an angel he passed over both the first and the second walls, and with the greatest difficulty he came at last to the water of the Thames where he found a certain fragile boat with his assistant and two others of his counsel. He got in and, by God's will, they quickly crossed the said water.

Blaneford then records that Mortimer and his companions travelled quickly to a harbour, avoiding the main public roads, where a boat had been waiting for them for some time. They embarked, and with the help of a propitious wind sent by God, soon arrived in France. Blaneford makes a couple of notable errors, the first of which being the year of the escape which he places in 1324 instead of 1323, and the second referring to St Peter being held by Nero, when the saint was in fact incarcerated by Herod (Acts 12: 3–19).[5] Blaneford's allusion to the biblical narrative is emphasised by the fact that he describes the Tower's two walls as *custodia* rather than the more literal *murus*, echoing the fact that St Peter escaped past two human guards (*custos*).

Another seemingly contemporary account is that of the enormously popular and well-circulated long continuation of the *Brut*. The author – or more likely authors – of this text is unknown but based on internal evidence it has been suggested that it was a secular work of London origin, possibly written by clerks based in Chancery. Despite this potential beginning within royal administration the text is firmly Lancastrian in its sympathies.[6] The *Brut*'s account of Mortimer's escape broadly agrees with that of Blaneford but differs in the detail:[7]

Sir Roger Mortimer of Wigmore broke out of the Tower of London in this manner: the aforesaid Sir Roger heard that he should be drawn and hanged at London in the morning after St Lawrence day [10 August], and on the day before he held a fair feast in the Tower of London and there was Sir Stephen Segrave, Constable of [the Tower of] London, and many great men with him; and when they should eat, the aforesaid Stephen sent for all the officers of the Tower; and they came and supped with him; and when they should take their leave of him, a squire who was in complete confidence with the aforesaid Roger, on his instruction, gave them all a drink such that all of them slept at least two days and two nights; and in the meantime he escaped away by water, that is to sea, by the Thames, and over the sea to France where he remained; wherefore the king was sore annoyed, and so put the same Stephen out of his constabulary.

The focus of the *Brut*, therefore, is predominantly on the role of the Constable of the Tower, Sir Stephen Segrave, and the poisoning of both him and the other officials.[8] This is a distinct contrast to Blaneford, who does not mention Segrave at all. The *Brut* also gives Mortimer greater agency in actually arranging the feast and inviting the officials in order to poison them, as well as introducing the character of a squire accomplice.

The *Anonimalle Chronicle* is the fullest version of the short continuation of the *Brut* for the years 1307 to 1333 and, like its longer counterpart, was possibly originally written by a government clerk who was based in London in the 1320s and then moved north to York in the 1330s.[9] A completely distinct text from the long *Brut* continuation for this period, the anonymous author, probably writing in the early 1330s, offers the fullest summary of the different contemporary accounts of Mortimer's escape which emerged in the immediate aftermath of events, and the variations in their narratives:[10]

> Next it so happened in the same year that Sir Roger Mortimer, lord of Wigmore, escaped from the Tower of London at night on the feast of St Peter ad Vincula [1 August]. There were various accounts of how he escaped, for some people said that he escaped by means of a cunningly concocted drink which was given the same evening to the guards of the Tower and to others, thanks to which they were soundly put to sleep; some said that he escaped by an ingeniously made rope-ladder which was shown the next day to several people at the Tower; still others said he walked through the doors of the said Tower. And when he escaped he fled to Portchester and there he speedily put to sea and went abroad into the lordship of the count of Hainault.

The short continuation of the *Brut* was the main source of information for the French *Chroniques de London*, which bears a strong resemblance to this descrip-tion, stating that on the night of the feast of St Peter ad Vincula, Mortimer gave a secretly made drink (*boivere sotilement*) to the lord constable and the guards of the Tower, together with others therein, before escaping using skilfully made rope ladders and then travelling to Portchester and over the sea to Hainault.[11]

The more unusual idea presented in the *Anonimalle Chronicle* that Mortimer simply 'walked through the doors' of the Tower, together with details of his escape to the south coast before travelling to Hainault, rather than France, appears to have been taken directly from the *Flores Historiarum*. The author of the *Flores* was the Westminster monk Robert of Reading, who, writing between 1327 and 1330, seems to have produced his work with the sole purpose of justifying Edward II's removal from the throne by Isabella and Mortimer in 1326–7. The style of the text could not be more different from the factual and analytical *Anonimalle Chronicle*, with Reading approaching his material in a literary fashion and writing – appropriately – in florid prose, which drew heavily on biblical quotations.[12] This is exemplified in his account of Mortimer's escape from the Tower, in which he draws directly on the liberation of St Peter from Herod's prison to describe his flight in terms of divine intervention:[13]

> ... behold *on the night* of St Peter ad Vincula, the Holy Ghost stood near and his grace was present in the prison cell, and touching Roger's heart *raised him up, saying 'arise quickly and follow me'*. And having stepped out, *he followed him*, because it is true that it was done by Christ; *thus he thought he saw a vision*. And passing the first and then the second guard he reached beyond the river Thames, and immediately mounting a horse which he found ready for him there, he quickly took the road towards the southern sea.

The *Flores* then records that he took a ship and was transported by favourable winds to the count of Hainault, William I, who would later support Isabella and Mortimer's invasion of England. The description by the author of the *Anonimalle Chronicle* of Mortimer walking through the doors of the Tower would therefore seem to refer to this account in the *Flores*, because although it is not explicitly stated by Reading, in the biblical account of St Peter's escape the prison doors opened of their own accord.

Like the *Flores*, the *Annales Paulini*, written under the auspices of St Paul's Cathedral in London, also makes little comment on the exact nature of Mortimer's escape route from the Tower, but it does provide much more detailed information of his subsequent flight across the country:[14]

And in that same year, on the night following the feast of St Peter ad Vincula, lord Roger Mortimer escaped from the Tower of London and crossed beyond the Thames until he reached the mill of John de Gisors. Nearby in the houses of an abbey there were seven horses ready, on which the lord Roger with seven persons travelled towards the sea, and in that place he found a boat organised by prior arrangement ...

Based in the capital, the anonymous author of the *Annales Paulini* was well informed of events both in London and further afield, and with none of the obvious bias or literary flare of the *Flores* this would appear to be the most accurate and detailed account of this phase of the escape.[15] It is from here that the author of the *Anonimalle Chronicle* probably took Mortimer's place of departure as being Portsmouth or nearby Portchester. In regard to the other major accounts of this period, the second chronicle written at St Paul's at this time, by the clerk Adam of Murimuth, only has one short sentence on the escape without any new details. Unfortunately, the section of the highly informative and near-contemporary *Vita Edwardi Secundi* that would have covered Mortimer's escape is missing from the single surviving manuscript, resulting in the loss of an important account of events.[16] Nevertheless, the wealth of chronicle material written at this time has resulted in a remarkably full and vivid picture of Roger Mortimer's audacious escape from the Tower in 1323.

A nineteenth-century depiction of Roger Mortimer in stained glass in the west window of St Laurence's Church, Ludlow (© Philip Hume)

Government records

Although they do not go into the same level of detail as the chronicle sources, what is perhaps one of the most surprising things about Mortimer's escape is that the wider narrative is broadly supported by Edward II's response to events as documented in the government records. At the time of Mortimer's escape, Edward II was at Kirkham in Yorkshire, where news reached him on 6 August. In an immediate response, the king wrote to the treasurer Walter Stapledon, bishop of Exeter, that:[17]

> the king understands for certain that Roger Mortimer of Wigmore, the
> king's enemy and rebel, who was imprisoned in the Tower of London, has
> broken the prison and escaped from the Tower by night, and that during the
> perpetration of this sedition Stephen Segrave, late constable of the Tower,
> and many others were poisoned by artifice [*subdole*], and that Stephen in
> consequence is so seriously ill that he is now insufficient for the safe custody
> of the Tower.

The king handed custody of the Tower over to Stapledon and ordered him to go there with his household and keep it safely, either directly himself or by another in whom he had complete trust. This document, therefore, confirms that poison was a key part of the plot, and that Segrave was one of those poisoned, as reported by the *Brut*. Indeed, it demonstrates that the *Brut*'s focus on Segrave was an entirely accurate reflection of Edward II's own reaction to the crisis.

The government records also provide a name for one of Mortimer's collaborators: Gerald de Alspaye, a sub-constable of the Tower of London. Alspaye's involvement is recorded in the chronicle of the Augustinian canon Henry Knighton, who, writing from Leicester, the Lancastrian centre, states that Mortimer escaped from the Tower 'by means of the help of a certain Gerald de Alspaye, who had custody of him under Sir Stephen de Segrave'.[18] Knighton was writing in the late fourteenth century and Alspaye's name does not appear in any of the earlier, contemporary chronicle accounts outlined above. His involvement is confirmed, however, by a pardon issued in March 1330 to a 'Gerard de Allespathe', for aiding the escape of Roger Mortimer from the Tower and accompanying him abroad.[19] Following the successful invasion of England in 1326 and subsequent deposition of Edward II, in February 1328 Mortimer had also previously granted Alspaye lands in Gloucestershire worth £40 a year for life, presumably as a reward for his assistance.[20] The fact that Alspaye also accompanied Mortimer abroad indicates that he either escaped from the Tower with Mortimer or, perhaps more likely, assisted him in the preparation by helping to make the hole in his cell, obtaining the rope and the poison, and facilitating general communication between Mortimer and his supporters, before meeting him on the outside, either with the boat on the Thames or with the horses across the river. This narrative is very similar to that of Mortimer's unnamed friend in Blaneford's account, and it seems highly likely, therefore, that this man was in fact Alspaye. Likewise, although he doesn't appear in any of the chronicle accounts, it is possible that Richard de Monmouth was imprisoned with and escaped alongside Mortimer, as in February 1327 he and Mortimer both received a pardon in the same writ 'for breaking prison at the Tower of London'.[21]

TIMING AND CAUSE

According to three of the chronicles – the *Brut*, the *Flores Historiarum* and the *Anonimalle Chronicle* – the reason behind Mortimer's decision to escape in the summer of 1323 was that Edward II was planning to execute him. As already quoted above, the *Brut* records that 'the aforesaid Sir Roger heard that he should be drawn and hanged at London in the morning after St Lawrence Day [10 August]'.[22] Similarly, the *Flores Historiarum* states that after the execution of the earl of Carlisle, Andrew Harclay, in March 1323, Edward 'sent his detestable, cruel ministers to the Tower of London' with the intention of bringing forth the younger Mortimer before the people and condemning him to a violent death (*acerba morte*).[23] It would be easy to dismiss these claims: both the *Brut* and the *Flores* claim that the escape took place on the night before Mortimer was due to be executed as a direct allusion to St Peter's escape from Herod.[24] Consistent with his wider biblical narrative, Robert of Reading in particular goes to the extra effort in the *Flores* of stating that Mortimer was 'bound by fetters', just as the saint was held in chains.[25] The same accusation cannot be made of the *Anonimalle Chronicle*, however. In this account, the author relates that letters had come from Edward II 'that the said Sir Roger was to be drawn and hanged within four days [of his escape] if he had remained in the Tower'.[26] When combined with the broader factual nature and tone of the *Anonimalle Chronicle*, this suggestion seems much more plausible.

The idea that Edward II was planning to execute Roger Mortimer at this time has certainly been viewed by historians as entirely feasible within the wider political context of this period. Paul Dryburgh, for example, has argued that Edward II made the decision to execute Mortimer in July 1323 due to a number of different factors. These included the strengthening of the king's own position following a truce made with the Scots at the end of May, and ongoing outbreaks of popular dissent and attacks on Despenser lands in Wales, the latter of which were primarily in support of Mortimer.[27] Most significant of all, however, was an alleged plot that emerged earlier in the year, which according to Blaneford saw all the imprisoned Contrariants attempt to rise up and seize the castles in which they were incarcerated, on the same night.[28] Edward II clearly believed this to be true, as on 7 April a commission was ordered to make enquiry in regard to 'the persons who planned the seizure of the castle of Wallingford, the Tower of London, the castle of Windsor and other of the king's castles'.[29] In November 1323, a recital of Mortimer's crimes also makes reference to the 'conspiracy to seize the said Tower and the castle of Windsor and Wallingford'.[30] Seymour Phillips has stated that although there is no documentary evidence to support the chroniclers' claims that Edward II was planning to put Mortimer to death, 'it is entirely possible', and that even if there were no fixed plans the likelihood of the king taking this action would have only increased with the growing number of conspiracies, giving Mortimer 'every incentive to escape at the earliest opportunity'.[31]

It certainly seems that regardless of if and when Mortimer found out about Edward II's plans, he had been plotting to make his escape on this specific day for some time. This point is interesting in itself, as much like the claims that Edward was planning to execute Mortimer, it would be easy to assume that the majority of the chroniclers placed the escape on the night of the feast of St Peter ad Vincula in order to emphasise the biblical comparison to the saint's own incarceration and liberation. The fact that the king had found out about Mortimer's flight by 6 August, however, means that there is no reason to doubt the authenticity of this date and it certainly rules out the escape happening on 10 August as stated in the *Brut*.[32] Moreover, there was a very practical, non-biblical reason for Mortimer choosing the night of 1 August, namely that St Peter ad Vincula was (and still is) the patron saint of the parish church of the Tower of London. It seems highly likely, therefore, that Mortimer purposefully plotted his escape to coincide with the saint's feast day, when the inevitable excesses and inebriations of the members of the Tower community – possibly actively encouraged by Mortimer as suggested by the *Brut* – would have provided him

St Peter's Chapel, Ludlow Castle, built by Roger Mortimer in gratitude to St Peter ad Vincula
for his escape from the Tower on his feast day (© Philip Hume)

with the perfect opportunity to execute his plan. Consequently, although the
fact that Mortimer escaped on the feast day of St Peter ad Vincula is entertain-
ingly appropriate, and something which the chroniclers, keen to prove a moral
message, were naturally quick to pick up on, it was an entirely practical choice.
Mortimer is said to have later built a chapel dedicated to St Peter ad Vincula at
Ludlow Castle in gratitude to the saint for his escape.[33]

INSIDE COLLUSION AND COLLABORATORS

One aspect of the escape which is clear is that to a lesser or greater extent Mortimer
received the help of collaborators both on the inside and outside of the Tower.[34]
Putting aside the *Flores's* angel, these include the unnamed friend who provided
Mortimer with the rope ladder – who was probably his known collaborator, the
sub-constable of the Tower, Gerald de Alspaye – and the two other accomplices
who were also waiting for him by the river with a boat as recorded by Blaneford;
the squire who helped him with the poisoning of the guards in the *Brut*; and
the mill owner John de Gisors, together with seven accomplices who rode with
Mortimer to the south coast, identified in the *Annales Paulini*. The *Annales* also
provides details of an inquiry that was held on 10 August in Portsmouth, which

reveals the most precise details of the final phase of Mortimer's flight abroad and the number of individuals involved.[35] The investigation found that on the feast of St Peter ad Vincula, Thomas Lessorte, a boatman of the Isle of Wight, led his boat to 'Barelorde', Portsmouth, where he had been told he would find a group of men who he was to guide onto the island. He had been told to do this by Alice de Borhampton, who herself had been instructed by Ralph de Bocton, a London merchant. Lessorte then led the men across the sea towards 'Notelshere' where they saw a ship that Bocton had previously procured from Normandy, which the men then embarked. The inquiry concluded that these men were indeed Mortimer and his seven accomplices and that Bocton had also been responsible for arranging the horses, which had been left with Alice de Borhampton following the men's departure to France. Bocton's involvement would seem to be confirmed by an order to the sheriffs in October to seize and imprison both him and Sir John de Patesmere for their adherence to Mortimer.[36]

The support of prominent Londoners unquestionably played an instrumental part in Mortimer's escape.[37] In addition to Bocton, John de Gisors was an ex-mayor and alderman, who went on to play a leading role representing London in the parliament which agreed to the forced abdication of Edward II in 1327.[38] Hamo de Chigwell, Hamo Godchepe, Edmund Lambyn and Roger Palmer all also came under immediate suspicion, receiving a remission 'of the rancour which the king had conceived against them' in early September, on condition of their future good behaviour.[39] The *Anonimalle Chronicle* – which is particularly well informed on events in the capital – and, following it, the *Chroniques de London*, both report that in November 1323 a clerk named Thomas Newbiggin, who had purchased the king's commission, charged citizens of London and other towns 'of having spoken with the said Sir Roger about maintaining and supporting him to go abroad, and of having aided and abetted his escape from the Tower of London'.[40] Although the citizens were once again cleared of all charges, it is obvious that the capital's sympathies lay with Mortimer and the baronial opposition more widely. This was a result of an assault on London's liberties (during which Gisors was deprived of his office of Alderman) and aggressive demands for indentured military service by Edward II in 1321–2.[41] At the end of June 1323, just before Mortimer's escape, the bishop of London had been ordered to prevent people from visiting St Paul's to venerate a tablet depicting Thomas of Lancaster, which the bishop had been profiting from, demonstrating that there was a large pro-baronial audience in the city for Lancaster's emerging cult.[42]

Edward II had evidently been paranoid about the security of the Tower of London in the build-up to the escape. Segrave himself had only been appointed as Constable in February 1323 in response to the growing number of plots to release the Contrariants, with the specific condition that he was to keep his prisoners safely imprisoned under threat of a penalty of 10,000 marks.[43] The tone of the letter the king sent to Walter Stapledon on 6 August makes it clear that he was genuinely worried that Mortimer's escape was the result of widespread betrayal within the Tower, and that the fortress had already fallen into the hands of the rebels. In particular, it is noticeable that Edward ordered Stapledon to enter the Tower on the pretext of visiting the treasury or for some other excuse, indicating that he was worried about his ability otherwise to gain access and take control.[44] At first, Segrave seems to have been suspected as being part of the plot, and once he had recovered from his poisoning, Edward II had his former constable imprisoned for his negligence. It soon became apparent that Segrave was not one of the conspirators, but he admitted that he could have kept Mortimer 'in deeper and closer imprisonment' than he did.[45] On 1 June 1324 Segrave was pardoned upon the acknowledgment that Stephen and his father John owed the king 10,000 marks.[46] It is possible that the man who was ultimately pulling the strings behind the escape was the bishop of Hereford, Adam Orleton, who was arraigned in parliament for his alleged involvement in February 1324 and, despite his denials, stripped of his temporalities the following month.[47]

1320 Seal of Adam Orleton, Bishop of Hereford, who was accused of involvement in Roger's escape from the Tower (Hereford Cathedral Archives HCA1320, © Dean and Chapter of Hereford Cathedral)

MORTIMER AND ISABELLA

No discussion about Roger Mortimer's conspirators would be complete without mentioning the most famous potential collaborator of all: the queen, Isabella of France. It is of course well known that Mortimer and Isabella entered into a relationship, strongly rumoured to be sexual, after the queen joined him in France in

1325. There is a long tradition in both academic and popular histories, however, that the couple's affair began during the time of Mortimer's incarceration in the Tower and that Isabella played an instrumental role in securing Mortimer's initial pardon and his subsequent escape.[48] In the latest version of the official history of the Tower published by Historic Royal Palaces, Tracy Borman states that it was said that Isabella spent many lonely hours at the Tower whilst her husband pursued his male favourites, passing her time reading romances which 'may have inspired her to strike up an affair with Mortimer'.[49] There is evidence to support this idea. First, it is known that Isabella did spend time in residence at the Tower during Mortimer's incarceration, while Edward remained in the north of England with his favourite Hugh Despenser. Second, Louis de Beaumont, bishop of Durham, may have played a role in persuading the king to commute Mortimer's original sentence from death to life imprisonment, and as Beaumont's patron this might suggest the queen's intervention.[50] Finally, on 17 February 1323, Isabella wrote to the lieutenant of the treasurer, William Norwich, requesting that Mortimer's wife Joan should receive the funds allocated for her sustenance while she remained under house arrest.[51] Based on this final document, Ian Mortimer has stated that Isabella and Mortimer were 'more likely than not' in collusion (if not a full intimate relationship) at this stage, and that the queen was the one who informed Mortimer of Edward II's plans to order his execution prior to his escape.[52]

Several historians have disagreed with this conclusion, however. As part of a thorough assessment of the evidence for Isabella's actions during this period, F.D. Blackley makes the point that the queen cannot be specifically associated with Mortimer until December 1325 and that it would have been a very strange decision to send Isabella to France to treat with the French king had her loyalty been in question.[53] Natalie Fryde agrees with this assessment, albeit with the suggestion that Isabella already had an ulterior motive to travel abroad by this time. Phillips states that there is nothing to support Ian Mortimer's argument that Isabella aided Roger in his escape, and concludes that, on balance, a connection between the pair in 1323 cannot be ruled out but it seems unlikely.[54] Most recently, Kathryn Warner poured cold water on the notion of any romantic trysts in the night at the Tower during this period and states that any idea that they spent time together is based solely on the knowledge of their later relationship.[55] Both Warner and Phillips have made the point that the queen's companion Eleanor de Clare, who was with her in the Tower in February 1323, wrote an almost identical letter regarding the maintenance of Mortimer's wife Joan on the same

Fig. 1 Reconstructed view of the Tower of London from the south-west in about 1320
(© Historic Royal Palaces. Drawing: Ivan Lapper)

Fig. 2
Reconstructed
view of the
Tower of
London with
the Great
Hall, 1300
(© Historic
Royal Palaces.
Drawing: Ivan
Lapper)

date as Isabella, negating the strength of the use of this document as evidence for collusion between the queen and Mortimer.[56] It is certainly true that there is no direct evidence to suggest that Isabella was conspiring or conducting an affair with Mortimer in the Tower at this time, and as has been seen there is nothing in the English chronicle sources to suggest that she played any part in his escape. Nevertheless, the idea that they had some form of contact cannot be ruled out, as it is probable that Mortimer was held closer to the queen's apartments and with weaker security than perhaps might be assumed.

THE ESCAPE ROUTE

One of the points which Warner makes to support her argument that Mortimer and Isabella would not have come into contact is that 'the prison cells were, of course, far away from the royal apartments where she lived'.[57] However, one of the most interesting aspects of the history of imprisonment at the Tower of London is that prisoners were kept in a large variety of locations at any given time; no part of the Tower was specifically built as a prison and there were no defined 'prison cells'.[58] Thus, in many cases it is not known exactly where a prisoner was held, with contemporary sources simply referring to the Tower more broadly, with no further distinction provided. This includes the incarceration of Roger Mortimer in 1322–3. We are left, therefore, to make reasoned speculation regarding the location of Mortimer's imprisonment and the route of his escape based on two principal sources: the description of his escape by the chronicler Henry de Blaneford and the topography of the Tower in the 1320s, which has been reconstructed by architectural historians based on building accounts and other contemporary records.

Turning first to the Tower's layout, by the time of Mortimer's escape in 1323 the Tower had already been expanded to achieve its broad outline structure that is still recognisable today (Figs 1 & 3).[59] Both Henry III (1216–72) and Edward I (1272–1307) made significant military improvements, creating the first and second complete rings of concentric towers – the two walls which are referred to in the narrative of Mortimer's escape. As part of this work, Edward I ordered the construction of St Thomas's Tower, more commonly known as Traitor's Gate, although it is important to note that at this stage the Tower Wharf had not been extended along the length of the building, meaning that the south wall and towers of the castle sat directly on the river.[60] Another significant development under Edward II's two predecessors was the creation of the – sadly now largely lost – medieval palace, with Henry III in particular spending vast sums of money on the transformation of the fortress into a modern, thirteenth-century royal residence (Fig. 2). The palace buildings were located in a newly-created gated inner bailey directly to the south of the White Tower known as the Inmost Ward. They included ranges of royal apartments for the king and queen in the Wakefield and Lanthorn Towers with their accompanying chamber blocks, which were situated at either end of the magnificent great hall built against the south wall looking out onto the Thames.[61] Perhaps most importantly for understanding Mortimer's route out of the Tower, Henry's building works also included the construction of a 'great kitchen', which architectural historians have concluded probably lay in the area immediately to the west of the great hall.[62] This was almost certainly the 'kitchen which adjoined the king's palace' in Blaneford's account of Mortimer's escape.

The only significant addition to the medieval palace under Edward I was the creation of a new suite of royal apartments in St Thomas's Tower, which are believed to have been created for the king's own use. These rooms were connected to the Wakefield Tower via a bridge over Water Lane, in roughly the same location as the current nineteenth-century enclosed walkway. Apart from this the structures of the main palace complex within the Inmost Ward remained largely the same, with evidence indicating that Edward I ensured that they were kept in good repair.[63] The same was not true of Edward II, who after an initial flurry of activity to improve fortifications at the very start of his reign appears to have taken relatively little interest in the maintenance of the Tower until the period after Mortimer's escape.[64] In 1321, the Constable John de Cromwell was dismissed after allowing the buildings to fall into such a dilapidated state that when Queen Isabella arrived to give birth to her daughter Joan, rain apparently came through the roof of her apartments onto the bed.[65] The condition of the Tower almost certainly aided Mortimer's escape. Although repairs were made to the 'great kitchen' in 1315, when new works began in 1324 it was recorded that the kitchen roof needed to have all its timbers replaced and be completely re-tiled, as did the adjoining pantry and buttery.[66] The king's great chamber block next to the Wakefield Tower was also in a terrible state and in need of considerable work.[67] As a result of this, it appears that the king's apartments were expanded to the Lanthorn Tower, while the queen's chambers were now in a new range situated somewhere between the Lanthorn and Wardrobe Towers against the eastern wall of the inmost ward.[68] There is no evidence, however, that the kitchen and other service buildings had moved from where they were built at the west end of the great hall under Henry III.

The layout and function of the buildings of the medieval palace under Edward II present a number of options for the location of Mortimer's incarceration, and his subsequent escape route. Henry de Blaneford describes Mortimer as being held in a 'very high up and confined location' (*in eminentiori et arctiori loco*).[69] This has been interpreted to mean that Mortimer was held in the indomitable fortress of the White Tower, where several high-profile prisoners are known to have been held, including Ranulf Flambard, bishop of Durham (1100), Gruffudd ap Llywelyn, who fell to his death trying to escape in 1244, and John II, king of France (1360).[70] This is possible, but even taking the vagueness of medieval chroniclers into account, it seems strange that this iconic location was not referred to in any of the contemporary sources. Moreover, an escape from the White Tower arguably does not ring true with the rest of Blaneford's account, namely that he escaped 'through a breach in the wall, into the kitchen which adjoined the king's palace, coming out through its roof he came to the first of the castle walls'. It was only *then* that Mortimer apparently used his ingeniously crafted rope ladder to traverse both this and the second, outer wall, in order to reach the Thames.[71] In combination with Segrave's admission that he could have held Mortimer more securely, it seems more likely, therefore, that rather than the White Tower, Mortimer was imprisoned somewhere within the complex of the medieval palace in the Inmost Ward. Of these apartments, one of the strongest possibilities is that he was held in the Lanthorn Tower or its adjacent chamber block, where Mortimer was probably held when he was imprisoned in the Tower for a second time in 1330.[72] Interestingly, although, as noted above, the queen's apartments appear to have moved out of the Lanthorn to a separate range by this stage, this would have still placed Mortimer's cell in reasonably close proximity to Isabella's rooms. From the Lanthorn, Mortimer could have feasibly fled across the open ground of the Inmost Ward, and into the kitchen at the western end of the great hall.

There is also another intriguing option, however, that Mortimer was held in the Wakefield Tower or its neighbouring chamber block. This suggestion is based in part on Blaneford's description of Mortimer escaping through a breach in his cell *into* the kitchens. This could of course mean, as in the other scenarios, that he first managed to get out of his cell, before making his way to the kitchens. If taken in its most literal form, however, this could be interpreted as the room

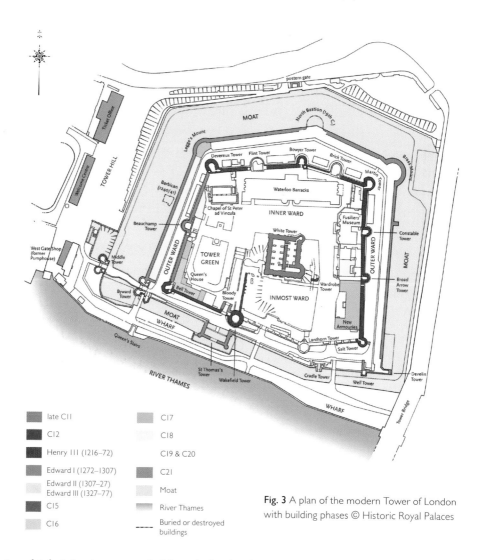

late C11	C17
C12	C18
Henry III (1216–72)	C19 & C20
Edward I (1272–1307)	C21
Edward II (1307–27) Edward III (1327–77)	Moat
C15	River Thames
C16	Buried or destroyed buildings

Fig. 3 A plan of the modern Tower of London with building phases © Historic Royal Palaces

in which Mortimer was held and the kitchens lying directly adjacent to each other and that the hole in the wall gave Mortimer direct access to the kitchen. This is entirely possible, as although both Simon Thurley and Jeremy Ashbee have suggested that the kitchens were separated from the Wakefield Tower by a space of open ground, the exact details of the layout of these buildings is far from certain and therefore the kitchens, or at least a connecting chamber, may have directly abutted the royal apartments.[73] Ashbee notes there is a recess on the external north-east corner of the Wakefield Tower, which may indicate another structure in this area.[74] If this was the case then Mortimer could have escaped from incarceration either in the Wakefield Tower or perhaps more likely in the neighbouring chamber block pretty much directly into the kitchens. On a more practical level, the dilapidated state of the chamber block and Edward II's subsequent expansion of his own apartments into the Lanthorn Tower meant that it was almost certainly not being used as royal accommodation by the early 1320s. This increases the likelihood of it being a location for Mortimer's imprisonment, not to mention his ability to escape through its apparently crumbling walls.[75]

Whichever way he got there, once in the kitchen Mortimer appears to have been able to get out through the – again poorly-maintained – roof with relative ease. (A new tradition has taken hold in more recent versions of the story that he climbed up through a chimney, but this appears to be a nineteenth-century invention.)[76] From here, it can be reasonably estimated that Mortimer took a route which saw him first climb down the inner curtain wall into Water Lane and then quickly traverse the outer wall at somewhere to the east of St Thomas's Tower, before dropping down to the Thames. The strongest evidence to support this is the fact that when Edward II began his building works in 1324–5, one of the most significant pieces of work to be undertaken was the rebuilding of 412 feet of the outer curtain wall between St Thomas's Tower and St Katherine's Hospital to the east, so that it was 'broader and higher'.[77] Described in the *History of the King's Works* as 'the only important contribution to the development of the Tower made by Edward II', this work indicates that this section of wall almost certainly formed the final part of Mortimer's escape route.[78]

Any speculation on the location of Mortimer's place of imprisonment and escape needs to be treated with a high degree of caution. Whilst the chronicle sources are numerous, ultimately we are predominantly reliant on Henry Blaneford's account, which itself is influenced by the biblical account of St Peter's escape from imprisonment by Herod. Nevertheless, by combining this text with buildings accounts and the subsequent reconstruction of the architecture of the Tower's medieval palace by architectural historians, it is possible to offer a number of reasonable scenarios to locate this most daring of escapes.

Conclusion

Following Mortimer's flight, Edward II frantically sought to establish where his enemy was hiding and who had aided him in his escape. Eventually, after numerous commissions and orders, by 1 October 1323 it was established that Mortimer was in France residing with his cousins and a number of other rebels who had joined him there. There is no evidence that Mortimer first went to Hainault as some of the chroniclers claimed. In March 1325, Edward II sent Queen Isabella to France to broker peace with her brother the French king. The resulting treaty could have brought about the collapse of Mortimer's plots and machinations against the king. Instead, Isabella and Mortimer entered into their now infamous relationship, forming a powerful personal, political and military alliance. In September 1326 they launched a successful invasion, which ultimately resulted in the forced abdication of Edward II and the succession of his son Edward III in January 1327. Once again, London played an instrumental role in events. On 9 October, Isabella wrote an open letter to the citizens asking for their support against Hugh Despenser the younger, which resulted in the city coming out in full support of the queen and Mortimer. In the riots that followed, the Tower was raided and all the remaining prisoners released, including Mortimer's two sons. John de Gisors was rewarded for his previous loyalty to the cause by being appointed as the new joint keeper of the Tower alongside Richard de Bethune by a writ issued by Queen Isabella on 6 November 1326.[79] This was not the end of Mortimer's relationship with the Tower, however. After three years of ruling alongside Isabella and personal aggrandizement, Mortimer had gained many enemies and on the night of 19 October 1330 he was arrested at Nottingham Castle in a move that would mark the beginning of Edward III's personal rule. Once more Mortimer was sent to the Tower, and this time he would not escape.

5

Barbara Wright

The execution and burial of Roger Mortimer, 1st earl of March (1287–1330)

W HEN Roger Mortimer of Wigmore, earl of March, was hanged for treason in November 1330, it marked the end of a series of semi-constitutional executions spanning almost 50 years which had destroyed the confidence of the barons in the royal system of justice. The comparative benevolence which pervaded Mortimer's exit from this world was in marked contrast to the brutalities inflicted on their enemies by Edward I, Edward II and, indeed, by Mortimer himself. Though one might have expected some injudicious actions in the face of Edward II's weak reign or the turmoil of Mortimer and Isabella's usurpation, it was Edward I, the 'English Justinian',[1] who initiated personal vengeance and the political mutilation of his enemies.[2] This paper looks at the treatment of traitors' corpses in the three reigns, and at the circumstances which affected their proper interment.[3]

The execution of Roger Mortimer, though a fitting reward for his most recent actions, has long been seen as an injustice upon a man whose king had failed him on many occasions.[4] Mortimer's rebellion against Edward II established itself after he became involved in an intimate relationship with the Queen, Isabella, begun when they shared a form of exile in France in 1325 and 1326. This alliance had provided the backing Mortimer needed to restore himself as one of the premier barons in England after Isabella's invasion of 1326 and the deposition of her husband, Edward II. Though Mortimer was not included on Edward III's regency council,[5] he was the one to whom Isabella turned for advice and support. He was rewarded with gifts of land and money, and, in 1328, with the newly-created title earl of March.[6]

The favours given to him mirrored the excesses for which Edward II had been deposed, and the power achieved by Mortimer and Queen Isabella during the minority seems to have blinded them to the reiterative nature of their actions.

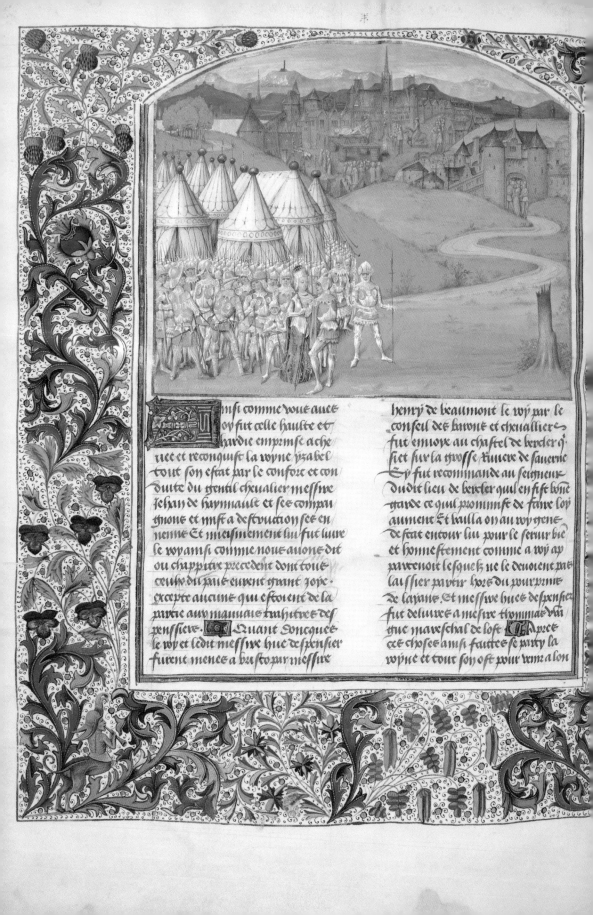

ansi comme vous aues
oy fut celle haulte et
hardie emprinse ache
uee et reconquist la royne ysabel
tout son estat par le confort et con
duite du gentil cheualier messire
Jehan de haynnault et ses compai
gnions et mist a destruction ses en
nemis Et meismement lui fut liure
le roy ainsi comme nous auons dit
ou chappitre precedent dont tous
ceulx du pais eurent grant Joye
excepte aucuns qui estoient de la
partie aux mauuais trahistres des
penssiers [O] Quant doncques
le roy et ledit messire hue despensier
furent menes a bristo par messire

henry de beaumont le roy par le
conseil des barons et cheualiers
fut enuoye au chastel de berclei si
siet sur la grosse riuiere de sauerne
Si fut recommande au seigneur
dudit lieu de berclei quil en fist bonne
garde ce quil promist de faire loy
aulment Et bailla on au roy gene
de estat entour lui pour le seruir bie
et honnestement comme a roy ap
partenoit lesquelz ne le deuoient pas
laissier partir hors du pourprins
de laians Et messire hues despensier
fut deliure a messire thommas vai
hue mareschal de lost [O] Apres
ces choses ainsi faictes se party la
royne et tout son ost pour venir a son

The envy of the barons was, once more, aroused. Mortimer's position at court had no strong foundation. His only status there came through the queen's favour. The most influential post was that of head of the regency council, held by Henry, earl of Leicester, whose power was severely curtailed when Mortimer spuriously accused him of riding in arms against the king in 1329.[7] Leicester found himself banished from the court and forced to pay a hefty penalty of £30,000, as a result of which he became totally inimical to Mortimer.[8]

As a marcher baron, Mortimer had been accustomed to ruling as a king in his own lands, in which the king of England had no authority. How easy it must have been for him to assume a similar mantle in England where his chief competition was a mere boy! It seems that he may have underestimated his opponent, however. Edward III was growing up: impending fatherhood and increasing maturity made him aware that little could stand in Mortimer's way, and Mortimer's own actions gave further clear demonstration.[9] In 1329 Edmund (of Woodstock), earl of Kent, the king's young uncle, in a carefully contrived plot, was led to believe that his brother, Edward II, still lived. Mortimer subsequently accused Kent of treasonable acts in attempting to restore Edward II to the throne and had him executed.[10] The young king began looking for a way to take back his usurped power, spurred on by the birth of his first son in June 1330.

In turn, Mortimer became aware that the tide was turning against him. He became even more suspicious of those surrounding him. He must have known that the chief among his enemies was Edward III, and that the only safe way to contain him was by elimination. With the king removed, there was the possibility of an extended regency for the baby prince. Or did Mortimer have greater ambitions, based on his relationship with Queen Isabella?[11] Until he could make his next move, he made sure his back was well guarded. When, on 19 October 1330, the court came to Nottingham for a council meeting, Mortimer and Isabella, with their supporters, took control of the castle there, excluding even the king himself from the security of its walls, and locked the gates against intruders. During the night William Montagu, and other loyal friends of Edward III, entered the castle through one of the many tunnels that penetrate the rock on which it stands. After a brief scuffle with Mortimer and his bodyguard, during which three men were killed,[12] Mortimer was taken prisoner and quickly dispatched to the Tower.

OPPOSITE: Roger Mortimer greeting Queen Isabella outside Hereford
(© British Library Board, Royal MS 15 E IV f.316v)

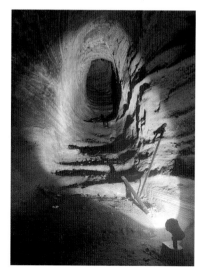 

The caves and tunnels beneath Nottingham Castle through which access was gained to capture Roger Mortimer in 1330 (photographs © Charlotte May)

By a decision based on *common notoriety*,[13] Mortimer was convicted of all the crimes imputed to him, without being allowed to speak in his own defence. Whatever pretensions he might have had to the kingdom were not brought out during his trial. The main charges, of the 14 cited against him, were the murder of Edward II, the arrogation of royal power, his actions against Henry, earl of Leicester and Edmund, earl of Kent, and his acquisition of money and property through undue influence on the young king. For this, the official judgement was that he should be drawn to the gallows and hanged as a traitor and enemy of the king and kingdom.[14]

Drawing to the gallows (*tractus*) was originally a method of humiliating the prisoner by tying him behind a horse and dragging him along the ground to the site of the execution. Over long distances, the rigours could prove too much for some men, and the hangman was thus deprived of his victim, so the punishment was modified by the introduction of a hide or hurdle beneath the prisoner's body.[15] Even so, Mortimer was subjected to a painful journey through the filth and ordure of the medieval streets, exposed to the mood of the crowd who gathered for the spectacle. The hanging which followed was, in the Middle Ages, a protracted and shameful death. Not for its victims the *long drop* and the swiftly broken neck of modern executions; they suffered a public loss of control over their bodily functions as the rope slowly strangled them, frequently taking as much as twenty minutes to achieve its – and their – end.[16] It was considered a proper punishment for those who had failed to keep faith with their king.

Though he was condemned as an 'enemy and traitor of the king' the crime of treason was not yet formalised at this early date. Before 1282 fighting against the king was classed as a felony, and punished as such. Other barons before Roger Mortimer had ridden against the king 'with banners unfurled' (equivalent to a declaration of war) and suffered nothing worse than the confiscation of their lands, to be returned later when a suitable financial penalty had been paid to the king.[17] Some, admittedly, had been hanged or beheaded, notably Thomas earl of Lancaster, Edward's cousin and rival, in 1322, and some had suffered even worse fates.[18] Treason had, however, no set penalty and was not a mandatory capital offence until the 1352 Statute of Treason.[19]

In England only the king had power to execute felons after a trial; if private persons wished to have this right they required a special grant from the king.[20] In the normal course of events an execution would be supervised by the sheriff, who received payment from the Crown for his duties.[21] In Roger Mortimer's case, however, an order was made by parliament that the Earl Marshal should ensure the execution of the judgement, though payment was still made to the sheriffs of London for the expenses of the hanging.[22]

Roger Mortimer, the first earl of March, was hanged on Thursday, the vigil of St Andrews day, 29 November 1330, the same day that judgement was pronounced.[23] In the early evening, he was drawn at the tail of two horses, possibly with only an ox-hide to protect his body from the filth of the London streets, to his execution at Tyburn Elms.[24] From the scaffold he confessed that he had procured the death of the earl of Kent but, curiously, he did not admit to the murder of Edward II.[25]

LEFT: Plaque marking the site of Tyburn (© John Fleming). RIGHT: Tomb and effigy of Edward II in Gloucester Cathedral. On the scaffold, Roger Mortimer did not admit to the murder of Edward II (© Philip Hume)

Execution seems to have spelled the end of the matter as far as official sources are concerned. Even the chroniclers lose interest in dead traitors. A survey of 25 chronicles written in the fourteenth century finds all of them, except for the Wigmore Chronicle, mention the manner of Roger Mortimer's death: only eight cover the disposal of his body.[26] This failure to follow through *to the grave* is common in the recorded history of felons convicted of treason, and only with the most notorious is there any chance of discovering anything at all about the disposal of the body. The best-known *traitor* of Edward 1's reign was Llywelyn ap Gruffudd (d.1282), prince of Wales, who, having renounced his homage to Edward, was killed in an ambush at Cilmeri (Powys). His body was treated almost as if he *had* been judicially executed, with the severed head being sent to the king and later spiked on a pole on London Bridge where it remained for at least the next 15 years.[27] The torso was reputedly buried at Abbey Cwm Hir.

Dafydd (d.1283), who, after his brother Llywelyn's death, attempted to assume his princedom, suffered a more violent fate at the hands of vengeful Edward. Dafydd had once sworn fealty to the English king and his rebellion was taken as a personal insult. After being betrayed by his own people, Dafydd's fate was discussed at a convocation between the king and his barons, where he was deemed to be a rebel and enemy of the king.[28] A prepared judgement was announced at the formal trial; he was to be drawn to the gallows for his treason and hanged for homicide. Then the body would be disembowelled, and the entrails burnt. This was the punishment deemed appropriate for one who had committed sacrilege by pillaging churches in his fight against Edward. The corpse would finally be beheaded and quartered for plotting the king's death.[29]

Rhys ap Maredudd, a prince of South Wales, had taken Edward 1's side against Llywelyn and Dafydd, but after the conquest of Wales most of his power and lands were taken from him. In 1287 he raised an army and captured a number of castles, but the massive strength of the English army soon reversed the situation and Rhys fled, possibly to Ireland.[30] He returned a few years later with a new army, but was betrayed to Edward in 1292, when he was tried at York under common law, and sentenced to be drawn and hanged.[31]

The Scots rebel, William Wallace, taken to London in 1305, was already 'known to the king to be a rebel and traitor', so his trial was brief. He was not permitted to speak in his own defence and was executed in a manner similar to Dafydd of Wales. To judge from Edward's inclement treatment of other Scots rebels and members of the Bruce family who fell into his hands, the same harsh end could have been expected by the man who defied England and was crowned King of Scots in 1306. Fortunately for Robert Bruce, his antagonist died in the summer following and was succeeded by his less able son, Edward II.[32]

Edward II had great difficulty controlling his barons, with the result that it was initially almost impossible for anyone to be convicted of treason. However, in 1318 Gilbert de Middleton was convicted by the king's record, and suffered the traitor's death of being drawn to the gallows, hanged, beheaded and quartered for fighting against the king with banners unfurled.[33] In addition, for crimes against the Church, his internal organs were to be burnt.

By 1322 Edward II had a full-blown, armed revolt on his hands, sparked by an incident at Leeds Castle (Kent).[34] Bartholomew Badlesmere, held to be the instigator of the troubles, was drawn, hanged and beheaded.[35] Roger Mortimer, whose eldest son, Edmund, was married to Badlesmere's daughter, Elizabeth, was condemned to death along with his uncle, Roger Mortimer of Chirk. This sentence was commuted to life imprisonment, probably because the two Mortimers had surrendered to the king on a promise of life and limb in January.[36] Many more rebels were killed in the decisive battle at Boroughbridge (Yorkshire) on 16 March 1322, and the chief ringleader, Thomas earl of Lancaster, already reputed a traitor before the battle, was sentenced to death on 22 March after a mere pronouncement of his crimes.[37] His drawing to the gallows and hanging were rescinded because he was of the blood-royal, and he was beheaded after a humiliating ride through the town. Andrew Harclay, the captor of Thomas of Lancaster, was accused, only a year later, of having dealings with the Scots, and was drawn, hanged, beheaded and quartered at Carlisle without any prior reputing as a traitor.[38]

The death or exile of so many barons and knights after Boroughbridge provided a short interlude of peace in which Edward II was able to govern his kingdom without undue interference.[39] The return of his queen at the head of an invading army in 1326 unleashed another bloodbath on the country. Initial mob rule meant that some of the enemies of the new regime were disposed of without the need for a trial, but Hugh Despenser, earl of Winchester, who surrendered to Queen Isabella and Mortimer at Bristol on 27 October, did receive a semblance of one. He was drawn to his execution wearing his coat of arms, to focus attention on the shame he had brought to his family, and subsequently hanged and beheaded.[40] Edmund, earl of Arundel, was possibly tried in secret at Hereford, and beheaded there in November.[41]

The death of Hugh Despenser, Hereford, 1326 (© Bibliotheque Nationale de France, Frossart's Chronicles (Book 1), Fr 2643, f.011r.)

Hugh Despenser the Younger, Edward II's close confidant and advisor, was captured with his king and brought before the queen and Roger Mortimer at Hereford. From there he was paraded through the town wearing a crown of nettles before suffering a traitor's death with the embellishment of castration and having his entrails ripped from his still living body and burnt.[42] His head was taken to London by the victorious faction and carried in procession along Cheapside before being spiked on London Bridge. It was three and a half years before another execution for treason took place. Edmund, earl of Kent, entrapped by Mortimer's agents, was tried and executed at Winchester. His beheading was botched, and this added to the general horror felt at his death.[43] Mortimer's own trial and execution followed not long after and was the concluding act of the series.

More than 20 political opponents had been executed by Edward I, most of them Scots rebels.[44] His desire to make their deaths an example to others who dared to defy him led to the corpses being turned into symbols of his puissance. Though only Wallace was brought to London for trial, the heads of most traitors were exhibited on London Bridge until they disintegrated. Edward II seems to have been more interested in making his point in the locality where his enemy had been known. Badlesmere, a tenant in chief in Kent, was executed at Canterbury, Thomas of Lancaster outside his own castle of Pontefract, and Harclay in the seat of his earldom at Carlisle.[45] The initial executions of the Isabella-Mortimer regime were mostly expressions of revenge. No attempt was made to show justice being done, nor did they exhibit the corpses for political ends. The secrecy attached to the execution of Edmund, earl of Arundel was typical of that administration, and was repeated in the furtive murder of the deposed Edward II and, later, in the deception and contrived execution of the earl of Kent.

Edward III brought a calmer and more clear-sighted approach to the treatment of traitors, though the trials of both Roger Mortimer and his close ally, Simon Bereford, adhered to the dubious format of those earlier ones. Edward was not above using conviction by the king's record, or by common notoriety, when it suited him.[46] He did, however, see the need for the more formal legislation against treason, and its punishment, instituted in 1352.

When we look at the treatment of traitors' corpses, we see that some were dismembered and the parts scattered. Others were beheaded, with the head kept separate from the torso. A third category of men were beheaded but the corpse was seemingly buried entire. The remainder were hanged but not mutilated. Neither their alleged crimes, nor which king they betrayed, seem to have much bearing on the punishment. Personal status was a minor influence, causing a mitigation of the sentence in the case of those with royal blood.

In the Middle Ages it was important to one's progress in the after-life to be buried in an appropriate place. For high status persons this was likely to be in a church endowed by the family and used by them for burials.[47] This strengthened the power of any prayers said for the souls of the departed. The succour of souls was a continuing consideration in the medieval concept of the life-death cycle. It was believed that the body in which the soul had resided should be preserved as entire as may be in readiness for the resurrection. This being the case, it was seen to be a good thing to arrange for the proper burial of executed felons. A hanged man, if he had confessed and received the *viaticum*, was permitted a church burial.[48]

The fate of the particular corpses in this study beyond their punishment was much more diverse. The heirs of both Welsh princes were held captive in England for the rest of their lives.[49] Coupled with the disintegration of independent Wales and the wrath of Edward I, this meant that no one was in a position to ensure the proper and entire burial of Llywelyn and Dafydd. The heirs of Rhys ap Maredudd were likewise prisoners. Their father's body was left on the gibbet at Knavesmire (York) for three days before, presumably, being given charitable burial in the city.[50] William Wallace had no known heirs and came from only a minor gentry family. No Scot during the war for independence could hope to appeal to Edward I. Wallace's head and quarters must have remained at their posts until they shrivelled and wasted away.[51]

In Edward II's reign, both Gilbert de Middleton and Andrew Harclay, who had each been dismembered for their treason, died without issue. Middleton was excommunicate and therefore not entitled to church burial. Harclay's sister was able to use the antagonism of the Isabella-Mortimer regime towards acts of Edward II to reclaim his head and quarters for burial in 1328.[52] Bartholomew Badlesmere was neither dismembered nor beheaded. The king's cousin, Thomas of Lancaster, was interred with his severed head at Pontefract Priory. During Edward III's regency, the earl of Kent was similarly treated because of his royal connections. Following a petition to the pope by his widow and his heir in 1331, his body was transferred from the Grey Friars at Winchester and reburied at Westminster Abbey.[53] After hanging at Bristol, Hugh Despenser the Elder was beheaded and the head sent to Winchester, the city of which he was earl. His body was left hanging on the gallows for four days, after which it was cut into pieces and left for the dogs to eat.[54] The change wrought by Edward III's accession brought redress to those who had been brutalised by Mortimer and Isabella's reign of terror. In December 1330 permission was obtained to gather together the head and quarters of Hugh Despenser the Younger for burial.[55] The royal connections of his widow, Eleanor, a granddaughter of Edward I, probably eased the way in this case. No such concessions were necessary for Roger Mortimer. His head remained on his shoulders: his corpse was not mutilated. So what happened to his body?

Before removal of the corpse of an executed person from the gallows, the consent of whoever was in charge of the execution was required.[56] Mortimer's wife Joan and younger children were miles away at Ludlow on the Welsh border when he died. His eldest son Edmund was arrested at Nottingham with him, as was his younger son Geoffrey, a faithful companion during his exile and throughout the regency period. Both were still incarcerated in the Tower.[57] His immediate family, therefore, were unable to claim the body. It was customary for the Knights Hospitaller to collect unclaimed bodies of executed felons for

Ludlow Castle was part of the inheritance that Joan de Geneville brought to the Mortimer family
(© Laura Shepherds Lens Photography www.laurashepherdslensphotography.com)

burial in their churchyards,[58] but the friars seem to have usurped this custom as they did others. Burial was expected to be made in the graveyard nearest to their place of execution.[59]

The chroniclers of Roger Mortimer's burial apparently substantiate this view, saying that the corpse was taken by the Franciscans. The Bridlington and Lanercost chroniclers merely state that he was interred by the Friars Minor.[60] Murimuth adds that he was buried in London,[61] while the *Anonimalle Chronicle* gives the added detail that his body was handed over, by the king's grace, on Saturday evening and buried there on the Sunday following.[62] Walsingham seems to concur with this, saying: '... *Fratribus Minoribus corpus ejus conceditur et honorifice sepelitur*'.[63] The *Llandaff Chronicle* has the body buried by the Franciscans at Shrewsbury.[64] This would appear to be confirmed by the chronicle of the Mortimer family's own foundation at Wigmore:

Post hec ad Fratres minores Salopie in honore tumulatum in vigilia sancti Andree Apostoli Anno domini.Mº.CCCᵐᵒ.xxxjº.[65]

Can we believe that the friars would be allowed to transport the corpse halfway across the country? Why would they choose to bury it in Shrewsbury? Though the Mortimers had vast holdings in Shropshire, their interests were to the south of that county, and they had no direct connection with the Shrewsbury Greyfriars. Murimuth, usually a reliable source, tells us that Mortimer's body was transferred, much later, from London to Wigmore.[66] Surely, if that were the case, the Wigmore chronicler would have known about it and mentioned it? There is no other evidence available to substantiate Murimuth's claim; no burials list for Wigmore Abbey, no recording of any monument there.[67]

We have to look beyond the chronicles, however, to solve the conundrum. It is entirely conceivable that the London Franciscans took the corpse into their church for charitable interment. Though there is no burial recorded in the *Chronicle of the Grey Friars of London*, nor monument found in the church, nor grant towards the fabric, this proves nothing either way.[68]

The records of the Shrewsbury Greyfriars are extremely sparse.[69] There is not even any consensus on the founder of the friary. Dugdale, following Owen and Blakeway, opts for Hawise Gadarn de la Pole and her grandfather, Gruffudd ap Gwynwynwyn of Powys, while the *Victoria County History* provides more solid evidence for it being an English royal foundation.[70] There is in this, therefore, no help for our enquiry.

The *Dictionary of National Biography* suggests that Roger Mortimer was buried initially at Coventry, and transferred 'in November 1331' to Wigmore Abbey.[71] The author accepts Wright's assertion, made in 1826, that all five earls of March were buried in the abbey,[72] presumably in light of the accompanying reference.[73] This latter document, from the king to the Minorite friars at Coventry, dated 7 November 1331, orders them to deliver the body of Roger Mortimer to Joan, his widow, and Edmund, his son.[74] Edward III closely followed it with a mandate to his sheriffs and others to allow the body to be taken by the Mortimer family for burial at Wigmore.[75] If these orders from the king had been carried out, then the story would end here.

Roger's wife Joan was a considerable heiress in her own right, by her descent from the Anglo-Irish de Lacy and de Geneville families. The execution of her husband in 1330 for treason had also resulted in the confiscation of all his lands, both of his own inheritance and hers, and thus cut off all sources of income for the Mortimer family. Though the king had made prompt provision for payment of the expenses of Joan and her household, it was an urgent necessity for her to seek the return of her own lands at least.[76] Throughout the winter months of 1330 the sheriffs were making surveys and holding inquisitions to discover what lands Roger Mortimer held, and which of them were Joan's inheritance.[77] On 27 December the sheriff of Herefordshire restored her manors of Mansell Lacy and Wolferlow, and her lands in Ewyas and Walterstone were returned on 11 January 1331.[78] Orders were issued the next day for her property in Ludlow and Stanton Lacy (Salop) to be handed back, and also her inheritance in Ireland.[79] Her homage and fealty for these lands was respited until 29 September 1331.

One might imagine her then coming in in the autumn to Westminster, where the king and his magnates were assem-

Looking through to the ruins of the south transept of Wigmore Abbey. Founded on this site by Hugh Mortimer in 1179, some 19th century accounts said that all subsequent Mortimer lords, including the five earls, were buried there. In fact, the fifth earl was not, nor the first earl, Roger Mortimer.

bling for a parliament, in the company of Edmund, Roger Mortimer's eldest son and heir.[80] Together they must have lobbied such friends as they had among the peers, for during the parliament the magnates begged Edward III to show favour to Edmund concerning certain lands which had belonged to his father.[81] When the king asked for their counsel as to what he might honourably do for the man whose father had murdered his own father, they were unable to offer any advice. Nevertheless, the king was generous, and the castle and manor of Wigmore were restored to Edmund on 12 October 1331.[82] Shortly afterwards, the goods and chattels pertaining to Wigmore were also granted to Edmund.[83] It was in this atmosphere of renewed favour that the order was made to the friars at Coventry for the return of Roger Mortimer's body.

On 20 November Edmund Mortimer was sent his first writ of summons as a baron, to attend a parliament due to be held at Westminster on 20 January following.[84] Delivery of the goods and chattels relating to Wigmore was made to him at Westminster on 12 December.[85] Then tragedy struck. Within a few days Edmund was dead. The *Wigmore Chronicle* has him dying at Stanton Lacy on 16

December 1331,[86] a physically difficult – though not impossible – feat if he was at Westminster only four days earlier. He was certainly dead before 5 January 1332, when lands at Arley (Herefs. & Worcs) were recorded as being in the king's hand by reason of the minority of his heir.[87]

This was a disaster for the family. Edmund's son, Roger, was only three years old. As the heir of a tenant-in-chief, he and his inheritance came directly into the king's custody. With the family lands once more in royal hands, both Joan and Edmund's widow, Elizabeth, were again without any means of support.

It was probably in the March 1332 parliament at Westminster where Joan petitioned the king for the return of her liberty of Trim in Ireland.[88] She was asked to bring the supporting documents into Chancery for examination. At the next parliament, in the following September, she again presented a petition, this time with four separate clauses, and repeated her request for the return of Trim, on which the king had delayed his decision in the previous parliament.[89] The necessary documents must then have been available for the king's consideration for, within five days of the parliament commencing, he issued orders to Anthony de Lucy, as Justiciar of Ireland, to give back Trim.[90] On 18 September 1332 Joan surrendered the 1327 grant to Chancery, as she had been commanded, clearly in the belief that restitution had been achieved.[91] It appears not to have been, for, on 3 October, Edward III commanded the return of Trim by John Darcy, Justiciar of Ireland; Anthony de Lucy having been removed from office before he had executed the previous order.[92] This time the transfer seems to have proceeded smoothly, and on 28 December Joan appointed attorneys to act for her in Ireland.[93]

The fourth clause of her petition of September 1332 had asked for custody of the lands and heir of Edmund Mortimer, as the lands were subject to destruction and damage while in the king's custody, and were lying uncultivated.[94] In this case, too, a second petition had to be entered before Joan elicited any action on the matter, though the delay here may have been caused by the need to assign dower to Edmund's widow first of all.[95] As a result of her petition, Joan received wardship of the remaining two-thirds of Edmund's lands,[96] but custody of Roger, the heir, remained with the king. Joan's petition also has relevance to the fate of her husband's body, for its second clause informs the king that his letters and writs to the Friars Minor of Coventry, ordering them to deliver the body of Roger Mortimer to Joan, have not been obeyed. She asks Edward III and his council to decree a remedy for such disobedience, and that the body may be delivered to her as previously granted. The response endorsed on the petition seems to betray the king's weariness with the whole subject, almost two years after the execution: *'Demoerge le corps en peis encore'* (Let the body remain in peace now).[97] Perhaps Edward III felt that no further concessions were necessary to a felon. Roger Mortimer's body had been maintained decently intact and was, presumably, buried in a fitting manner at Coventry.

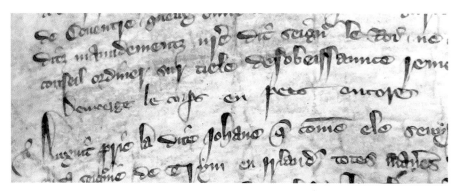

Clause 2 of Joan Mortimer's petition asking for the return of her husband's body in accordance with the King's former order. Edward III has written on it: *'Demoerge le corps en peis encore'* (let the body remain in peace now). Dated *c.* September 1332 (TNA, SC 8/61/3027)

Edward III had not been massively vindictive in his pursuit of his father's murderers. Mortimer and Simon Bereford he had had executed. Queen Isabella, his mother, was deprived of her power and much of her illicitly acquired lands, and allowed to live quietly away from court until her death almost 30 years later. Mortimer's younger son, Geoffrey, heavily involved alongside his father, was allowed to leave the country and went to live in Poitou, on lands he had inherited from his maternal grandmother.[98] Thomas de Berkeley convinced his accusers that he had been lying sick at his manor of Bradley when Edward II died in Berkeley Castle, and was eventually pardoned for any complicity.[99] The named murderers, John Maltravers, Thomas Gournay and William de Okeley,[100] all fled abroad. Okeley, a tenant of the Mortimers, was never heard of again. Gournay, finally captured in Italy, died very conveniently on the journey back to England. Maltravers found good employment as a knight in Flanders. When, in 1337, he made an approach to Edward III, he was visited by William Montagu, and served thereafter as an unofficial agent of the English government for a number of years.[101] In 1345 he offered to return and stand trial for Edward II's murder in order to clear his name. Edward III refused him a trial, but Maltravers was allowed back into England and, until his death in 1364, received increasing favour at the hands of the king.[102] Within a few years, therefore, of Mortimer's execution, the whole matter of Edward II's murder was concluded or suppressed, and the order to let Mortimer's body remain at Coventry seems to have been part of this desire to draw a line under the affair.

What further reason could there be to have Mortimer's body exhumed and removed to Wigmore? The main motivation would most likely be family pride and continuity.[103] To have all the members of the Mortimer family interred within the family foundation at Wigmore would be no more than what was fitting and proper, if it could be achieved. Joan, having had an answer to her petition of September 1332, was not in a good position to press the point. To have taken the matter further would probably have involved her in an expensive petition to the Papal Curia in Avignon. Roger, the Mortimer heir, was brought up at Edward III's court with the king's own children, far away from his ancestral home in the Welsh march. When he became a man, he fought at the king's side in the French campaigns, married the daughter of Edward III's most faithful companion, and continued to spend much of his time with the court. What knowledge could he have of his marcher ancestors? Both his son and his grandson inherited the restored earldom of March as minors; both grew up as wards of the king. The abbey church at Wigmore was completely rebuilt by Roger's son in 1379 – as a proud statement of his alliance with Philippa, Edward III's granddaughter – and the *Wigmore Chronicle* was written some time after that.[104] No wonder, then, that its chronicler was ignorant of the true location of the first earl's burial. There is no chronicle now extant from which he could have copied the correct information, and family memory had been uprooted and withered. No study appears to have been done on the sources used by the Wigmore chronicler,[105] and, as Giffin informs us, only 17 leaves of a total 70 are made generally available through Dugdale's transcription.[106]

As Roger Mortimer's body seems unlikely to have been moved, one is left with two questions. Firstly, why were the friars at Coventry unwilling to part with the corpse, and secondly, why was it in Coventry at all?[107] The first question may be partly resolved by looking at the financial aspects of the problem. Burial was the key to various forms of endowment. Binski tells us that from the thirteenth century 'an important and competitive economy grew up around bodies, extending that which had previously grown up around the relics of saints'.[108] *Capture* of the body of an important person might, therefore, enrich the community of the church wherein they were buried. Thefts of corpses were quite as much in evidence as commercial exchanges of holy relics.[109] Equally advantageous, financially, was the prospect of the cadaver turning out to be a saint, thereby bringing pilgrims to the church with a steady stream of gifts and oblations.[110] Since the friars first came to England in the early thirteenth century, they had encroached on the rights of the Church to bury the dead – a coveted source of income.[111] A papal bull of 1281 had removed the friars from the control of the bishops and this led to violent and aggressive protestations of rights by both friars and churchmen.[112]

The Bull *Super Cathedram* (1300) limited the activities of the friars, except where they had special licence, and diverted part of any burial fee they received to the parish priest.[113] Even after that, there was still a substantial income to be had from burials. The friars became an extremely popular force in the religious life of the day, with substantial support from many members of the nobility and the royal family.[114] In particular, the Franciscans were chief beneficiaries of royal patronage. Rebuilding of their London church, begun in 1306, was financed by Margaret of France, Edward I's second wife, with continuing support by Queens Isabella and Philippa.[115]

Showing the proximity of the Gatehouse of Cheylesmore Manor, owned by Queen Isabella, to the Greyfriars church (Christ Church Spire), Coventry (© Rob Orland, 2006)

The Franciscan friars had been established in Coventry since before 1250, when their dwelling-house by the park of Cheylesmore (which abutted the city) is mentioned in a deed of Roger and Cecily de Montalt.[116] In 1327 Robert de Montalt, their grandson, settled various lands and castles, including the manor of Cheylesmore, upon himself and his wife with remainder to Queen Isabella.[117] In 1330 she inherited the manor, and it remained in her hands beyond her fall from grace until her death in 1358.[118] She took an active interest in her rights acquired in Cheylesmore and the part of Coventry over which she had control. Though she was excluded from the politics of the court after 1330,[119] she was not the secluded nun that many supposed. Following Edward III's coup she came to Windsor to spend Christmas 1330 with him,[120] and later travelled freely between her many manors.[121] She continued to use the influence she had to increase her rights and income.[122] What could be more natural than that she should use her influence with the Franciscans to have her lover's body spirited away and buried at a church on one of her own estates? If Edward III, and the world at large, initially believed the traitor interred at the Greyfriars in London, so much the better. The reason why the Coventry Greyfriars were so eager to keep Mortimer's body may, therefore, also be tied up with the reason why it was in Coventry – they were courting royal favour.

A stone carved lordly head sits above the chancel arch in St George's, Orleton. A recent local story says that it depicts Roger Mortimer, 1st earl of March (d.1330), but there is no evidence for this. A Mortimer manor since before the Domesday Book, Orleton was one of the dower properties of Roger's widow, Joan de Geneville, who contributed to the refurbishment of the chancel when the carving was made. Would Joan have paid for a depiction of her executed husband who was commonly believed to have been the lover of the queen? (© Philip Hume)

The list of monuments in the Greyfriars' Church at Coventry, compiled shortly after the Reformation, does not mention Roger Mortimer.[123] As A.R. Martin describes the church of the Franciscan friars at Coventry as 'second only to London in popularity as a burial place',[124] the 164 names preserved seem unlikely to be a full record. The church was rebuilt in 1358, by a grant of Edward the Black Prince, who inherited the manor of Cheylesmore on the death of Queen Isabella,[125] and was itself plundered for stone after the Reformation.[126] The only likely confirmation that this is the last resting place of Roger Mortimer is a bequest to the Coventry Greyfriars of £20 from Catherine, countess of Warwick, in 1369.[127] Catherine was Roger Mortimer's daughter.

The burial of traitors appears to have been greatly influenced by the status of the family from which they came; those owning royal connections being afforded the best provision in preparation for the afterlife. Those from the lower ranks of the nobility were given less consideration, and their families were less able to raise their voices in protest at the treatment they received. A strong heir, of full age, was the best guarantee that a condemned traitor could have of receiving proper burial: it also provided the best chance of retaining or recouping the family lands. A minor heir and a powerful widow probably provided the next best opportunity. Roger Mortimer's lack of an adult heir after 1331 was instrumental in the failure to bury him amongst his ancestors. The Mortimer family fortunes were not restored until that heir had attained adult status and shown his loyalty to the king.

6

Dr Andy King

The Mortimers under arms, 1306–1425

Syr Rosier asur aesawr,	Sir Roger of the azure shield,
Syr Rosier o'r Mortmcr mawr,	Sir Roger of great Mortimer,
Rosier ieuanc, planc plymlwyd,	Young Roger, plank of battle,
Sarff aer o hil Syr Raff wyd,	You are a warlike serpent of Sir Ralph's line
Rhos arglwydd, Rosier eurglaer,	Lord of Rhos, golden bright Roger,
Rhyswr, cwncwerwr can caer ...	Hero, conqueror of a hundred forts ...[1]

THUS wrote the poet Iolo Goch, in a paean of praise probably commissioned for the occasion of the departure of Roger Mortimer, 4th earl of March and earl of Ulster, for Ireland, on Richard II's expedition of 1394–5.[2] This came during a period of unprecedented conflict, following Edward I's invasion of Scotland in 1296, which saw England formally at war with either Scotland or France – and more usually both – until the 1450s and beyond. The nobility as a class were traditionally identified as *bellatores*, 'those who fight', the image which underpins Iolo Goch's poem; they were thus a primary focus of the English Crown's demands for military service. This was also the period which saw the (self-)promotion of the Mortimer family to the highest ranks of the nobility, with the acquisition of their titles of earls of March and Ulster. As such, they led sizeable retinues in the French and Scottish wars, but also had a direct vested interest in campaigning to defend the king's lordship of Ireland, where their estates came under threat from the resurgent Gaelic Irish, and, in Edward II's reign, from the Scots. The military careers of the Mortimers show how war could bring a noble family both social advancement and political disaster; and how

OPPOSITE: A Mortimer knight (© British Library Board, from Legh's *Men of Arms* of *c*.1475–1524 in Sir Thomas Holme's *Book of Armes*, Harley MS 4205 f.045v)

military service could provide a route back from the political wilderness. Their careers thus provide a window into the interplay of war, military service and politics across late medieval Britain, affording a view of the symbiotic relationship between king and noble which underlay it.

ROGER MORTIMER, 1st EARL OF MARCH (c.1287–1330)

Roger Mortimer was knighted by Edward I, alongside the Prince of Wales (the future Edward II), and 300 others, at the so-called 'Feast of the Swans' on 22 May 1306.[3] The knighting was a prelude to his career under arms, for just four days later, he took out letters of protection for himself and 11 followers to serve with the king in Scotland.[4] His service on the subsequent expedition proved a less than glorious debut. The Feast of the Swans had evidently given him a taste for chivalric festivities, for he was one of 22 knights, led by Piers Gaveston the prince's Gascon favourite, who deserted the army to attend a tournament in France. Mortimer's lands were confiscated as a consequence, though they were soon restored.[5]

Roger may have served on the Bannockburn campaign; he certainly took out letters of protection for himself and eight companions in May 1314. If he was indeed present, he seems to have managed to escape the battlefield unharmed.[6] However, Roger's main contribution to the English war effort against the Scots was made in Ireland, where he was one of the most prominent English landholders. Roger had crossed to Ireland shortly before Edward, Robert Bruce's brother, invaded the lordship in May 1315. That December, he was defeated by Bruce at Kells, near his liberty of Trim. The de Lacys, his own tenants, were subsequently accused of abetting the Scots by deserting during the battle.[7] Appointed king's lieutenant in Ireland in November 1316, Roger returned the following April with a large retinue of 150 men-at-arms and 500 archers, paid from his English rather than his Irish revenues. He combined military action with negotiation and conciliation to force the submission of a number of Gaelic lords, bring about a (temporary) degree of unity amongst the English of Ireland and revenge himself on the de Lacys (who were outlawed as traitors). By the time he was recalled to England in May 1318, the English position in Ireland had been greatly strengthened, and Edward Bruce was subsequently killed in battle at Faughart in October.[8]

Roger Mortimer was thus one of the (very) few of Edward's captains who was successful in taking on the Scots; he was well rewarded for this service and

had been closely politically aligned with
the king. And yet, in 1321, after serving
Edward under arms for much of his
reign, Roger took up arms against him
– drawing on the same resources, and
probably leading many of the same men.
Incensed by the rapacious land-grabbing
of the Despensers, Edward's new favourites, which threatened his interests in the
Welsh Marches, Roger was prominent in
the armed uprising of the spring of 1321
which rapidly forced the Despensers into
exile.[9] When Edward raised an army to
subdue the rebels after Christmas, Roger

The grave, at the Hill of Faughart, of Edward
Bruce, killed in the battle of Faughart in
October 1318 (Geograph © Eric Jones)

initially resisted, attacking royal forces to take the town of Bridgnorth. However, he baulked at facing the king himself across a battlefield, and so he came
to Shrewsbury to offer his submission to Edward on 22 January. His prompt
surrender saved his life, but he was imprisoned in the Tower of London, and his
estates were forfeited.[10]

In 1323, Roger escaped the Tower, and fled overseas.[11] In 1326, in conjunction
with Queen Isabella, Edward's disaffected wife, he led what was to be the single
most successful military venture of any of the Mortimers. Crossing the Channel
with a small army, the core of which was 700 men-at-arms raised by the count of
Hainault's brother, he overthrew the king.[12] However, as the de facto head of the
young Edward III's government, Roger was unable to repeat his earlier successes.
In 1327, when he led an army to Weardale, in the bishopric of Durham, to take
on an invading Scottish army, the campaign ended with Edward in tears at the
inability of the English to bring the Scots to battle. Given his shaky political
position, Roger could not risk further unsuccessful campaigns against the Scots;
and so the minority government under his and Isabella's influence agreed a peace
treaty in 1328, widely derided in England as 'the shameful peace'.[13] Roger used
military force to maintain his grasp on power, raising an army to face down
Henry earl of Lancaster's abortive rising in January 1329.[14] He was, however,
unable to protect himself from Edward, who bitterly resented his tutelage and
had him arrested and tried for treason. Roger died on the scaffold in March 1330,
at the age of 43.[15]

Quant le roy an
glois z ses gens
et tout son ost
eurent beu les
fumees des escocois ilz furent
tantost sonner les trompettes
z crier aux armes et comman
der que tout homme se deslo
gast z suyuist les banieres.
Ainsi fut fait et se tira chun
tout arme sur les champs ausi
comme silz voulsissent tantost
combatre. La endroit furent
ordonnees trois grosses batail
les a pie et chascune bataille
auoit deux eles de.v. armures

qui deuoient demourer a che
ual. Et saichez quo disoit
quil y auoit.bm.ᵉ armures
de fer cheualiers z escuyers
z bien.vvv.ᵐ hommes armez
la moitie montez sur petites
haguenees et saust moitie
pietons enuoyez p election
de par les bonnes villes a se
staiges. Et si y auoit bien
vvim.ᵐ archiers apie sans
la ribaudaille. Tout ainsi
comme les batailles furent
ordonnees on cheuaucha tout
rengie apres les escocois z
sendroit des fumees iusqs a

ROGER MORTIMER, 2ND EARL OF MARCH (1328–60)

Edward III chose not to extinguish the Mortimer family, restoring the ancestral estates to Edmund, the first earl's son – who promptly died, in December 1331, leaving a three-year-old son, Roger (later the 2nd earl).[16] Roger first served under arms on the 1346 royal expedition to France, for which he was ordered to array 200 men from his lands in Wales.[17] He was knighted by Edward himself at the first landing, on 12 July, alongside the king's eldest son, Edward of Woodstock, the Black Prince, and he fought at Crécy in the prince's battle.[18] In 1350, Edward brought Roger as one of his companions on his mission to thwart a French attempt to take Calais by bribery.[19] His efforts were lavishly rewarded, with membership

of the newly-founded Order of the Garter, and the restoration of the first earl's estates and title.[20] He continued his service, accompanying Edward on the expedition to France in 1355, and on the expedition to recapture Berwick, at Christmas in the same year, where he witnessed Edward Balliol's surrender of the Scottish kingship.[21] In 1359, Roger crossed to France with a substantial retinue of 300 men-at-arms and 300 archers. He led a quick raid into Normandy, before joining Edward, serving as constable of the army which burned and ravaged its way across France.[22] Roger died of a fever on the campaign, in February 1360, at the age of 31.

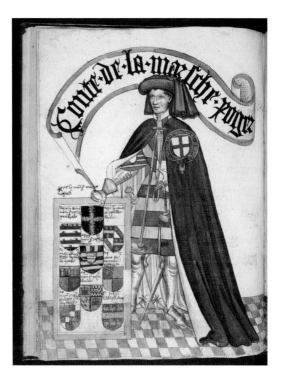

Roger Mortimer, later 2nd earl of March, was one of the founding members of the new Order of the Garter created by Edward III. He is depicted here in his Garter robes (© British Library Board, William Bruges Garter Book, Stowe MS 594 f.015v)

OPPOSITE: Illustration of the stand-off of Stanhope Park in 1327

(© Bibliotheque Nationale de France, *Froissart's Chronicles* (Book 1), FR 2643, f.018r.)

EDMUND MORTIMER, 3RD EARL OF MARCH (1352–81)

Edmund, the 3rd earl, began his military career with the renewed outbreak of Anglo-French war in 1369, commanding a retinue of 60 men-at-arms and 160 archers as part of the reinforcement for the duke of Lancaster's expedition to France.[23] Lancaster's expedition was not notably successful,[24] but Edmund's second experience of military service can only have proved an anticlimax. In February 1372, he indented to serve with 80 men-at-arms and 120 archers on Edward III's projected expedition to Brittany. In July, it was decided to use the forces to mount a naval expedition instead, amid government panic over the English defeat at sea off La Rochelle – but contrary winds prevented most of the fleet from sailing, and the expedition was abandoned.[25]

In August 1374, Edmund contracted to raise a retinue of 400 men-at-arms and 400 archers for another expedition to Brittany, comprising a fifth of the entire army – in keeping with the late fourteenth-century trend for raising armies composed of a few very large retinues.[26] The army sailed in the following April, but achieved little before a truce was sealed, and they returned to England amid recriminations of misconduct and corruption at Edward III's court.[27] The conduct of the war shaped Edmund's political outlook. Discontent over the failure of the Brittany campaign turned him into one of the leading opponents of Edward III's government at the 'Good Parliament' of 1376 – a role which would have been unthinkable for his father.[28] Edmund's disaffection may have been exacerbated by the Crown's dealings with Ireland, in the defence of which he had a direct vested interest, enhanced by his inheritance of the earldom of Ulster from his mother. Already, in January 1373, an Irish parliament, contemplating 'the various misfortunes that there were in the land of Ireland', had requested that the earl of March be sent there, 'with sufficient power'.[29] In the September following, Edward announced that he had ordered the earl to go to Ireland 'as quickly as he can … remaining there for the safe custody and defence of his lands and lordships'; but Edmund did not go.[30] The situation in Ireland continued to deteriorate,[31] and by 1379 the minority government of Richard II was prepared to offer Edmund better terms to serve as king's lieutenant. In June, he sealed an indenture giving him more control over the finances of his office, and promising payment of 20,000 marks (£13,333 6s. 8d.) for three years' service.[32] This would be the first time any of the Mortimer earls had been in Ireland since 1320; and when Edmund crossed the Irish Sea in the spring of 1380, he brought with him a retinue of no less than 200 men-at-arms and 800 archers, perhaps the largest personal retinue commanded by any of the earls of March in this period.[33] He employed them to some effect, obtaining the submission of a number of Gaelic Irish lords, notably Niall Mór Ó Néill, heir of the Uí Néill (O'Neills), the most powerful Gaelic dynasty in Ulster. He also 'treacherously' imprisoned Art na Madhmann Mág Aonghusa (Magennis), lord of Iveagh in Ulster, leaving a legacy of distrust which still lingered when Edmund's son Roger, the 4th earl, came to Ireland in 1394.[34] In 1381, he recaptured the castle of Athlone, to provide a base to restore his authority in Connacht; but he fell ill, and died in December, at the age of 29 – thus, in the words of the chronicler and Mortimer family protégé, Adam Usk, 'depriving [the world] of his nobility'.[35]

Sir Thomas Mortimer (d.1399)

In the aftermath of Edmund's death, his son Roger (the 4th earl) was appointed to replace him as king's lieutenant in Ireland – at the tender age of seven. Clearly, the appointment was nominal, presumably to provide the necessary standing and authority for Sir Thomas Mortimer, an elder kinsman,[36] who was appointed his deputy by a great council in Ireland. As the senior adult male representative of the Mortimer family, Thomas provided a necessary link to the Mortimer military affinity, for it was considered that 'the men-at-arms and archers of the lieutenant's retinue, who were then with the said Sir Thomas, were more likely to remain with Sir Thomas than with anyone else'.[37] The young Roger's lieutenancy ended in June 1383, and Thomas returned to England. Here, he was appointed steward of Roger's lands by the consortium led by Richard, earl of Arundel, which had been granted the wardship of the estate following controversy over Richard II's handling of the minority.[38] Thomas was presumably able to use this position to recruit men for his subsequent military service. In the increasingly fractious atmosphere of Richard's reign, he served with a retinue of four men-at-arms and eight archers on Richard's Scottish expedition of 1385; and with 22 men-at-arms and 80 archers for the defence of London, during the French invasion scare of 1386.[39] He also served on Arundel's successful naval expedition of 1387, with a retinue of 35 men-at-arms and 49 archers.[40] It was probably his connection with Arundel that led Thomas to join with the Appellants in December 1387, taking up arms against the king on their campaign against the royal favourite Robert de Vere, achieving notoriety by killing Thomas de Molyneux, one of Richard's leading Cheshire retainers, at the battle of Radcot Bridge.[41]

Sir Thomas Mortimer fought at the battle of Radcot Bridge, 1387 (© Bibliotheque Nationale de France, *Froissart's Chronicles* (Book 3), FR 2645, f.244r.)

Thomas's opposition to the Crown, presumably initially aroused by Richard's high-handed treatment of the Mortimer lands, was perhaps heightened by Richard's attempt to install his favourite, Robert de Vere, as marquis, and then duke, of Ireland, which threatened the Mortimers' Irish interests.[42] Thomas went to Ireland as Roger's deputy, when the latter was again appointed king's lieutenant in 1393. Thomas' arrival was noted by a Gaelic Irish annalist, and he was soon active, taking custody of hostages from the Uí Néill and the Anglo-Irish Savage family.[43] However, Richard had neither forgotten nor forgiven his rebellion, and Thomas was amongst those appealed for treason in the parliament of 1397. He died an exile in Scotland in 1399.[44]

ROGER MORTIMER, 4TH EARL OF MARCH, EARL OF ULSTER (1374–98)

Roger's arrival in Ireland was delayed – perhaps by controversy surrounding the wardship of his lands – and he eventually crossed with Richard, in October 1394.[45] There was, however, a fundamental incompatibility between the aims of the king and the earl. Richard was determined to reimpose his lordship over the Gaelic Irish lords by bringing them into his allegiance, and then settling disputes between them and the English of Ireland. Roger, on the other hand, was determined to reimpose his lordship over his lands in Ulster and Connacht by force. As a Gaelic chronicler put it, 'the earl of March arrived in Ireland of a purpose to get his rents of the inhabitants'.[46] In particular, Roger was bent on forcing the submission of the Uí Néill. But once the Uí Néill came into Richard's allegiance, Roger would be assailing the king's loyal subjects.[47] Niall Óg Ó Naill, leader of the Uí Néill, summed up the problem from his perspective in a letter to Richard, warning that after his departure, Roger would be able to make 'grievous war' against him, for:

> If I should offer no resistance to him, in forbearance to your royal majesty,
> he will attack me without measure ... yet if I should offer resistance to him,
> my enemies shall say that I am a rebel and traitor against your majesty.[48]

Ó Naill's fears were to prove fully justified when in 1396, just one year after Richard's return to England, Roger led an expedition against him, and burned down Armagh Cathedral – an attack described by a Gaelic Irish chronicler as 'treacherous'.[49] However, Roger's campaign lost momentum, interrupted by the need to return to England in 1397 and again in 1398, as his relations with the king became increasingly fraught.[50] Back in Ireland, he campaigned in Leinster, but was killed in a skirmish at Kellistown in July 1398, at the age of just 24.[51]

SIR EDMUND MORTIMER (1376–1408/9)

The death of the 4th earl left his younger brother, Sir Edmund Mortimer, as the adult male representative of the family's interests during the minority of the earl's six-year-old son. Sir Edmund had been the 4th earl's lieutenant in Ireland, and briefly, king's lieutenant when the 4th earl returned to England.[52] Edmund subsequently came back to England, probably with Richard at the end of July 1399. But immediately he submitted to Henry Bolingbroke.[53]

At the time of Owain Glyn Dŵr's revolt, the Mortimer lands in England and Wales were in the custody of a consortium headed by the earl of Northumberland and his son Sir Henry Percy, who was married to Edmund's sister. It is therefore, perhaps, not surprising that Northumberland named Edmund as the leader of the area around Welshpool in a letter of circa November 1401.[54] The following March, the custody of the Mortimer estates in Radnorshire and Montgomeryshire was transferred to Hugh, lord Burnell.[55] Nevertheless, when

The site of the battle of Bryn Glas 1402, where Sir Edmund Mortimer's Welsh archers changed sides, shooting into the rear of the English army as it charged uphill (© Laura Shepherds Lens Photography, www.laurashepherdslensphotography.com)

the Mortimer lordship of Maelienydd, Radnorshire, was assailed by Glyn Dŵr in June, it was Edmund who led a force to defend it, raising his men from Herefordshire, and from the tenants of Maelienydd. On the 22 June, however, his army was slaughtered in battle at Bryn Glas. He was captured, in part because the Welsh archers he had recruited from Maelienydd defected to Glyn Dŵr on the battlefield and turned on the English.[56]

As a politically-significant prisoner of limited means, Edmund was in an awkward position. Though he was by no means poor, having been generously endowed by his brother with lands worth more than £130 a year, plus annuities of 240 marks (£160),[57] this did not reflect his status as the adult male representative of perhaps the wealthiest noble family in England, and the most important in the Welsh Marches. Glyn Dŵr demanded a ransom of 10,000 marks (£6,666 13s. 4d.) from another of his prisoners, Reginald lord Grey, and Edmund could not afford a ransom on anything like that scale. But while Henry IV was anxious to assist with the raising of Grey's ransom, no such offer was made to Edmund, despite lobbying by the Percys. Henry's reluctance to help may have been rooted in the Mortimers' arguably superior claim to the Crown he had so recently usurped. And so, in October, despairing of being able to raise his ransom, Edmund threw in his lot with Glyn Dŵr, marrying his daughter, and his lands were consequently forfeited.[58] Nothing is recorded of his subsequent military endeavours on behalf of his father-in-law, other than his death during the English siege of Harlech in 1409.[59]

EDMUND MORTIMER, 5TH EARL OF MARCH, EARL OF ULSTER (1391–1425)
Edmund, the 5th earl, spent his teenage years under a cloud of suspicion, as the focus of a number of anti-Lancastrian plots during Henry IV's reign.[60] However, given his grand plans for France, Henry V could not afford to exclude one of his leading nobles, and so Edmund began his military career in 1415, when he led a retinue of 60 men-at-arms and 160 archers on Henry V's expedition to France.[61] The chronicler Thomas Walsingham records that he was one of the many invalided home during the siege of Harfleur, suffering from dysentery.[62] If so, he may have recovered quickly enough to return to fight at Agincourt, for in January and July 1416, two French prisoners of the earl were given licence to return to France to raise their ransoms (it is, though, possible that the prisoners had been captured at the battle by men of the earl's retinue in his absence, and then sold to him).[63] He subsequently served, with a retinue of 300 men-at-arms and 300

archers, on the 1416 naval expedition for the relief of Harfleur, which defeated a French fleet in a singularly sanguinary sea battle off the Seine.[64] He returned to France the following year, serving with the king, with 100 men-at-arms and 302 archers.[65] Henry's new strategy, aimed at the invasion and occupation of Normandy, brought about an evolution of the typical pattern of English military service, necessitating as it did the maintenance of a large permanent army in northern France.[66] Consequently, Edmund campaigned in Normandy continuously thereafter, serving variously as Henry's lieutenant in Normandy, lieutenant of Cotentin and Caen, captain of Mantes and Vire, and at the sieges of Saint-Lô, Rouen and Melun. He only returned to England in February 1421, for the coronation of Queen Katherine.[67] Edmund went back to France with Henry in June, and was at the siege of Meaux and the relief of Cosne-sur-Loire.[68] He returned to England following Henry v's death, whence Henry vi's minority administration dispatched him to Ireland, now a political backwater, appointing him king's lieutenant in May 1423. He crossed the Irish Sea in the autumn of 1424, but died of disease in January 1425, at Trim, at the age of 33.[69]

In one aspect, the Mortimers' military careers were exceptionally unfortunate, for the last four earls all died on campaign, in their late twenties, or early thirties. The 2nd, 3rd and 5th earls died of disease, and the 4th was killed in battle, while Sir Edmund Mortimer died besieged by an English army. The killing of an English earl in combat was unusual. Unlike their French and Scottish contemporaries, the English titled nobility suffered remarkably few casualties in battle in this period. It was less unusual for English noblemen to succumb to the rigours of campaign; for instance, John de Vere, earl of Oxford, died just a month before Roger, the 2nd earl, on the same expedition.[70] By contrast, the fate of Roger, the 1st earl, was comparatively commonplace: he was one of six earls executed between 1322 and 1330. For the Mortimers, military service thus resulted in a series of long minorities, and – with the premature death of the 5th earl – the end of the dynasty, though this probably simply hastened its demise through failure in the male line, a destiny common to many noble families.

Roger, the 2nd earl, was also exceptional in the degree to which military service advanced and enriched him. He died at the zenith of his career, as constable of Edward III's army, marking the apogee of good relations between the Mortimers and the kings of England. Recording his demise, Sir Thomas Gray, who served on the expedition of 1359–60, described Roger as 'the king's closest adviser'.[71]

It was Edward's considered policy to rehabilitate the heirs of the noblemen executed in his father's reign and during his own minority, in order to reunite the political community of the realm.[72] Nevertheless, while Edward generally took a very measured approach to doling out patronage, Roger was conspicuously favoured. His grandfather, the 1st earl, had abused Edward's minority to acquire estates and a title which were forfeited on his execution. Yet by 1354, Edward had restored both the title and the lands (apart from Chirk), annulling his own verdict of treason, and effectively disinheriting the earl of Salisbury of the lordship of Denbigh in the process.[73] Edward evidently entertained a high personal regard for Roger. Indeed, under a king less astute at managing his nobility, he might have been resented as an unpopular royal favourite. However, Roger earned his reward at least partly by his effectiveness as a military commander, over an active career spanning the whole of his adult life.

Frequent military service on expeditions led personally by the king brought opportunities for close personal contact; it was not, however, necessarily sufficient to gain royal favour. The assiduous military service of Edmund, the 5th earl, served to overcome Henry v's distrust, no doubt aided by his revelation of the Southampton Plot.[74] This was reflected in the various offices and captaincies he was appointed to. But only to an extent. Unlike most of Henry's noble captains, Edmund did not receive grants of land in Normandy, nor was he made a knight of the Garter (as the 2nd earl had been). Furthermore, Humphrey of Gloucester's continuing dynastic concerns may have influenced the decision to send him to Ireland after Henry's death.[75] Edmund's appointment effectively isolated him from English politics in a way that service in France – alongside most of the English nobility – could not. Military service did not take place in a political vacuum, nor could it guarantee personal advancement.

Illustration of a Mortimer knight in the Wigmore Abbey chronicle and Brut chronicle (© Hanna Holborn Gray Special Collections Research Centre, University of Chicago Library, Codex Ms 224 f.47v)

In fact, there is little to suggest that any of the earls (with the possible exception of the 2nd earl) made any direct profit out of their military service to the kings of England.[76] Walsingham opined that the royal expedition of 1346–7 – on which Roger made his military debut – yielded so much booty that there were few women in England who did not possess clothes, furs or cushions looted from Caen or Calais. As the captain of a company, Roger would probably have been entitled to a half share of the spoils acquired by his men (though he would in turn have owed half of this to the king).[77] However, his successors would have had fewer opportunities to enrich themselves. The lacklustre 1375 Brittany expedition can have brought the 3rd earl little plunder, while Henry v's strategy of occupation rather than *chevauchée* reduced the scope for pillaging for the 5th earl's men. And Ireland was hardly wealthy enough to offer up an abundance of easily-portable loot – although the 3rd earl did make gifts to Wigmore Abbey of oxen and cows from Ireland, which came into his hands 'as plunder by military fortune'.[78] None of the Mortimer earls appear to have taken any hugely profitable prisoners (although by the same token, none of them suffered capture and ransom themselves).[79] Conversely, Sir Edmund Mortimer suffered the loss of all his lands as a result of his capture and subsequent defection in 1402 – though his nephew, the 5th earl, does seem to have recovered some of these lands.[80]

In fact, providing military service to the Crown was costly. Edmund, the 3rd earl, paid over the odds to acquire the services of at least one of his subcontractors for the retinue he raised in 1374, for the Brittany expedition. He paid an additional *regard* of £51 to the Northumberland knight Sir John Strother, who contracted to provide 30 men-at-arms and 30 archers.[81] And then in 1379, Edmund 'spontaneously' lent Richard £1,000, 'for his expedition of war in Ireland', taking some of the king's jewels as security for the loan – presumably to cover the initial payment of £1,000 specified in

A c.1378–79 seal of Edmund Mortimer, 3rd earl of March (© TNA E 42/195)

his indenture.[82] He subsequently claimed that he spent 20,000 marks (£13,666 6s. 8d.) on his retinue of 200 men-at-arms and 800 mounted archers in the first year of his service in Ireland, and because the Crown had failed to keep up the payments specified in his indenture, he had been obliged to sell off his jewels and plate to pay his men.[83] And his account was not overly inflated; at the standard rates of pay of 1s. a day for men-at-arms and 6d. for archers, he would have had to spend £10,950 a year on his retinue, with additional payments for *regard* for his men-at-arms. Similarly, in the parliament of October 1423, Edmund, the 5th earl, petitioned to have the £642 13s. 6d. which he owed the king offset against the arrears of wages owed to him. The arrears clearly exceeded this sum, probably by a considerable degree.[84]

In effect, the earls were using their landed income to subsidise the king's war effort. Indeed, the expectation that a noble's lands should fund his military service was implicitly understood – and was explicitly expounded during a dispute over the wardship of Roger, the 4th earl, when he was appointed king's lieutenant of Ireland in 1393, while still a minor, aged 19. The earl of Kent, who had custody of his person, requested that Roger be given livery of his lands, with licence to raise loans to the value of a year's revenue 'from his said inheritance', to fund his military service in Ireland. This was opposed by the earls of Arundel, Warwick and Northumberland, who had the custody of Roger's lands in England and Wales – but not on grounds of general principle; rather they were concerned that the proposed arrangements would lead to the 'waste and destruction' of Roger's inheritance. They would willingly countenance the funding of Roger's service from his lands provided that sufficient arrangements were made to prevent such wasting.[85]

In fact, all but one of the Mortimer earls began their military careers before reaching their majority, after receiving seisin of lands to support them in their service. Roger (later the 1st earl) took up arms at the age of 19, taking out letters of protection to serve in Scotland just six weeks after he had purchased the wardship of his own lands from Piers Gaveston.[86] Roger (later the 2nd earl), served in France at the age of 17, having been granted some of his father's estates in 1341. He was subsequently granted custody of the rest as he turned 18, although still a minor, specifically for his 'laudable service'.[87] Edmund, the 3rd earl, likewise took up arms at 17; he took out letters of protection to serve in France in October 1369, having been granted seisin of his wife's considerable inheritance in August and September. He had already been granted custody of his Irish lands the year before, 'so that he find men-at-arms, hobelars and archers for the safe keeping of Ireland and of the premises against the Irish, the king's enemies'.[88] Roger, the 4th earl, first served under arms just after turning 20. Edmund, the 5th earl, was the exception, first taking up arms at 23. This pattern was not untypical of the English nobility,[89] and it is worth noting that the 4th earl's opportunities for military service during his teens were limited by the outbreak of peace in 1389, while the 5th earl's opportunities were limited by Henry IV's lack of trust in him.

Methods of recruitment might change, but, from the perspective of the English Crown, one of the main purposes of the estates of its tenants-in-chief, with their concomitant lordship over men, was to supply the retinues needed to fight its wars. The importance of the Mortimer estates in this respect, with their lands in the fruitful recruiting grounds of the Welsh Marches, is demonstrated by the careers of Sir Thomas Mortimer and Sir Edmund Mortimer during the minorities of the 4th and 5th earl respectively. Neither had full access to the family's landed wealth, and neither was able to raise retinues to match those raised by the earls themselves; but their standing as representatives of the family was still vital in retaining the services of the tenants of the family lands.

As the military service of Roger (later 1st earl) to Edward II had demonstrated – up until his rebellion – the Mortimers' standing as one of the leading English magnate families in Ireland made them an obvious choice as agents of Crown authority there. This standing was hugely augmented by the betrothal, in 1358, of Edmund (six-year-old heir of Roger, the 2nd earl) to Philippa, daughter and sole surviving offspring of Lionel of Antwerp, second surviving son of Edward III.[90] This was a signal honour, earned partly by the 2nd earl's distinguished military service. But there was a strategic imperative to the match: Lionel held the earldom of Ulster by right of his wife, Elizabeth de Burgh (Philippa's mother), and the match strengthened his Irish interests by allying him with the Mortimers. And in the event that Lionel and Elizabeth did not have a son, it provided for the earldom to pass to the Mortimers, giving them an additional incentive to contribute to the defence of the lordship, and to restore English authority in a region where it had deteriorated markedly.[91] Elizabeth died in 1363, leaving her daughter Philippa as her heiress; the marriage to Edmund went ahead in 1368, and so the death of Lionel in the same year left Edmund as earl of Ulster.[92]

Nevertheless, the imperative for the Mortimers to defend their Irish lands did not necessarily accord with the wider strategic interests of the kings of England. It is a revealing indication of the higher priority accorded to France that none of the Mortimer earls served in Ireland under either Edward III or Henry V. This was partly down to circumstance; had Roger, the 2nd earl, not died in France, he would surely have accompanied Lionel to Ireland in 1361, when the latter was appointed the king's lieutenant there.[93] But Lionel was sent to Ireland only after the war with France had apparently been won, following the Treaty of Brétigny of 1360. And the appointment of Edmund, the 5th earl, as king's lieutenant in Ireland in 1423 seems to have been motivated in part by the aim of distancing him from English politics, at a time of renewed dynastic insecurity with the succession of the infant Henry VI.[94]

Coat of arms in Canterbury Cathedral showing
Mortimer quartered with de Burgh
(The Heraldry Society)

Conversely, military service did not necessarily guarantee personal loyalty to the Crown. The careers of the Mortimers exemplify the possible consequences when a powerful magnate's views of what constituted the best royal policy – or indeed their own best interests – were incompatible with the Crown's. While the most dramatic example is provided by the 1st earl, the 4th earl's attack on the Uí Néill and Thomas Mortimer's service with the Appellants serve as a reminder that the military resources of a noble family's landed estate could be used against the king's interests or even turned against the king himself.

Taking up arms to serve under the king earned Roger, the 2nd earl, the restoration of virtually the entire estate amassed by his grandfather, the 1st earl. His grandfather had lost the family lands in the first place by taking up arms *against* the king in 1321–2. But he proved to be that *rara avis*, a successful medieval rebel, making a comeback to lead the only successful invasion of England between 1066 and 1399.[95] He thereby recovered and indeed vastly increased his lands, as well as acquiring his title – although this success should be attributed more to the political collapse of Edward II's regime than to his own martial acuity.[96] Thus, although the 1st earl was gruesomely executed and forfeited his lands, in the long term it was his rebellion which enabled him to establish his family amongst the wealthiest of the English nobility. Arguably, the Mortimer family thus gained as much, if not more, from taking up arms against the king as in his service. However, as a note of caution to would-be rebels, the rebellions of Sir Thomas and Sir Edmund Mortimer were far more typical of those who rose in arms against the king, yielding no great gains and ending ultimately with their ruination.

The poem commissioned from Iolo Goch by Roger, the 4th earl, speaks volumes of the martial self-image of the Mortimers, with its heavy emphasis on the military virtues of the Mortimer lineage. The Mortimer earls would not have made a coldly calculated cost/ benefit analysis of their service under arms. Such service remained a fundamental role of the titled nobility, the *bellatores*, throughout this period. While nobles might on occasion complain bitterly enough about the terms on which they were expected to serve under arms, they never questioned the basic assumption that they should.

7

Dr Paul Dryburgh

Estates and economies of the Mortimer lordships

Lot 260 auctioned by Dominic Winter in Cirencester on 12 October 2022 was a single parchment membrane, 44 x 24cm, written on both sides in medieval Latin. Purchased by the Mortimer History Society, it is now deposited at Herefordshire Archives and Records Centre (HARC).[1] The manuscript carries the account of John Chaundeller, bailiff of the liberty of Roger Mortimer, 4th earl of March (1374–98), and his trustees, keepers of the honor of Wigmore, for the accounting year Michaelmas 1387 to Michaelmas 1388. The manuscript has long been disassociated from its original archive; an almost identical account for 1384–5, that of James Leinthale, was already housed at HARC.[2] A typescript description characteristic of the former curator at the British Library, J.L.M. Gulley, places it within the context of the life of the young earl of March and gives some of its local colour, notably the presence of the customary dues of 'Rapsilver' and 'Solughsilver' in commutation of ploughing and reaping services.[3] Gulley's underwhelmed assessment was that, 'this account roll may thus make a modest addition to our knowledge of Middle English'. Nevertheless, this structured honorial account roll, which includes sections on arrears from the previous year, fixed rents due from land and property in communities surrounding Wigmore, as well as rents no longer collectable, leasing of estates, issues of the manor and from sales of stock,

Detail of the Account Roll for the Honor of Wigmore, 1387–88, purchased by the
Mortimer History Society and deposited at HARC (© Philip Hume)

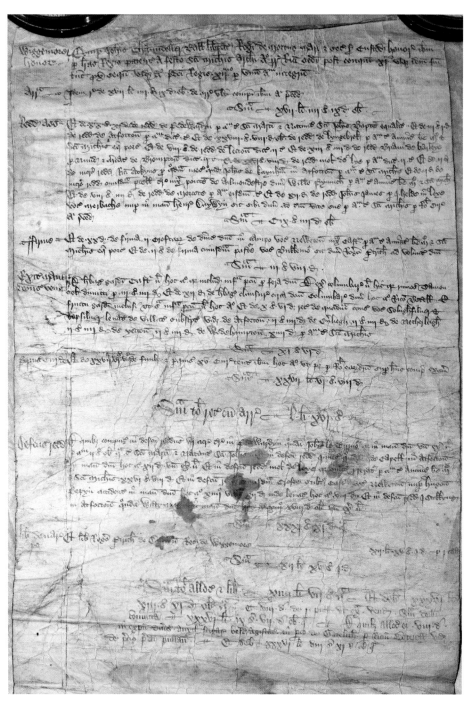

The Account Roll for the Honor of Wigmore, f. 50r (46r), 1387–88, purchased by the
Mortimer History Society and deposited at Herefordshire Archive and Record Centre (© Philip Hume)

perquisites of the honor court and inventories of livestock, gives us valuable information about a late-fourteenth-century marcher estate. It also fills gaps in our knowledge of the lordship which for three centuries had been the hub of the landed economy of one of the most successful and long-lasting noble dynasties in medieval England.

By his accession upon Earl Edmund's untimely death in December 1381, the 4th earl inherited a vast patchwork of lordships, and a title pregnant with pre-tensions to unprecedented authority.[4] The Mortimer lordships were not simply restricted to the family's Welsh marcher power base assertively developed and defended since the eleventh century, and crystallised in the creation of the earldom of March for himself by Roger Mortimer (d.1330) in 1328. This was a title which reflected one man's concerns, ambitions and world view and aimed to assert personal authority over a region and a culture separate from that governed from Westminster.[5] The lordships extended deeper into Wales, across southern England and into Ireland where Roger bore the title of the 6th earl of Ulster, inherited from his royal grandmother.[6] Mortimer lordship was, and had long been, transnational. Over four centuries from the Norman Conquest of England they viewed their estates as a coherent whole despite the variety of legal, cultural and military environments in which they operated. And despite the frequent shockwaves of famine and plague, warfare, the fragility of their hold over estates on the margins of royal and seigneurial authority and loss of royal favour.

While not unique in this transnational profile, the Mortimers were the most prominent and best endowed noble family across these islands and the commit-ment of individual earls to their Irish estates led to all bar the 2nd earl spending considerable time there and the 3rd, 4th and 5th earls dying there.[7] Indeed, the landed estates accumulated by the Mortimers of Wigmore, and their economic potential, fuelled the family's rise from baronial to comital rank and, finally, to the throne. This essay examines that rise through outlining the estates they enjoyed and the strategies of lordship they employed during the Middle Ages. It will assess the varied impact of long, untimely minorities, marital policy and royal favour (and its withdrawal), together with their chameleonic adaptability to the different legal bases of lordship across their dominions. It will also shine a light on the profits of agriculture, the exploitation of seigneurial rights and the market to provide a rounded, broad-brush portrait of the economic props of Mortimer power.

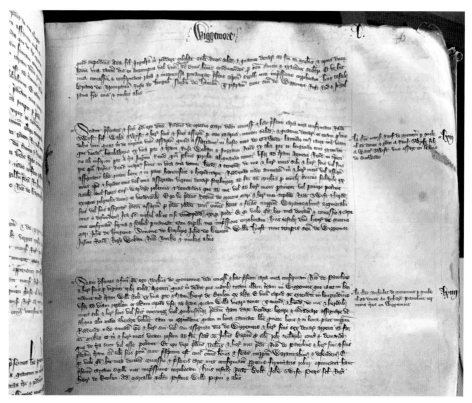

Many of the Mortimer family cartularies are contained in the 'Liber Niger' or Black Book of Wigmore
(© British Library Board, BL Harley MS 1240, f.46r)

These themes have previously been examined in overview: for England by George Holmes; in much greater detail for the Welsh March in the doctoral thesis of Penry Evans and by Rees Davies; for the Irish liberty of Trim by Michael Potterton, and for the broader dominions by Charles Hopkinson and Martin Speight.[8] The sources for such a study are wide-ranging and voluminous. At the core are the family cartularies, most notably the *Liber Niger*, or 'Black Book' of Wigmore, compiled during the 3rd earl's lifetime, which contain copies of hundreds of land transactions.[9] Single-sheet original engrossments and manorial records survive in numerous archival and library collections, often the result of forfeiture or, from 1461, the merger of the Mortimer lands into the Crown estate.[10] Royal inquisitions taken upon the death of a Mortimer lord, and commissions to take their lands into the king's hand upon forfeiture, supplement our knowledge and provide snapshots at moments of crisis.[11] In short, few noble estates are as well documented by their archive as the Mortimers of Wigmore.

Map 2 The locations of the main Mortimer lands in England
by the late fourteenth century (see map on p. 136 for lands
in the Welsh Marches; and on p. 123 for lands in Ireland)

CONQUEST AND SETTLEMENT: 1070S–1230S

Throughout their meteoric rise, Wigmore had been the beating heart of Mortimer lordship. By *c*.1075, Ralph Mortimer (d.1115–27) (son of Roger Mortimer, lord of St Victor-en-Caux in Normandy) had acquired the lofty, dominating castle site, first erected by Earl William fitz Osbern (d.1071) on waste land called 'Merestun', which Gunnfrothr held of King Edward before the Conquest.[12] According to the Domesday Survey of *c*.1086–9, Ralph had two ploughs in demesne and four slaves while the borough rendered an impressive £7. The caput was surrounded by other Herefordshire estates at Downton on the Rock, Burrington, Aston, Elton, Leinthall (Starkes), Lower Lye, Covenhope, Shobdon, Staunton on Arrow and Orleton, several of which appear in our fourteenth-century honorial accounts, as well as at Pilleth in what is now in Radnorshire.[13] During the lifetime of his father who had not apparently adventured with his kinsman King William in 1066, the king gradually endowed Ralph with lands in 12 English counties.[14] These were concentrated in three main areas: the Welsh March, where, alongside the Herefordshire estates, Ralph gained lands in Baschurch, Conditre, Leintwardine and Wrockwardine hundreds (Shropshire), most notably Cleobury, where he had land sufficient for 24 ploughs, a mill and sizeable woodland and whose value had risen by 50% since the Conquest;[15] a Wessex corridor in Hampshire, Berkshire and Wiltshire, centred on Headbourne Worthy by Winchester and Hullavington, formerly of Harold Godwinson;[16] and either side of the Humber Estuary in the East Riding of Yorkshire (concentrated to the north of Hull and in Howdenshire) and Lincolnshire (largely in the north-east of the county in and around Grimsby, but also near the minster town of Stow).[17] Domesday hints at the aggressive nature of the Conquest, an interlineation noting that Ralph held half a virgate of the capital manor of Droxford (Hampshire) 'per vim' ('by force'), and five hides in the manor of Amport (Hampshire). Apparently these were on agreement that a brother of Eadric should hold the land of him for as long as he behaved well, and that if he wanted to sell it would be to no one but Ralph.[18]

However, despite being under half of the entire estate in Domesday and despite the retention of important manors such as Stratfield Mortimer (Berkshire/ Hampshire), the primary focus of the attention of Ralph and his successors for the next two centuries remained the frontier region of the borderlands between England and Wales. The Mortimer lords of Wigmore were active, enthusias-tic participants in the military, diplomatic and legal manoeuvres inherent in English expansion into Wales from the eleventh to the thirteenth centuries.[19] Over several generations the Mortimer lords, their kin and their tenants became embedded in shaping a vibrant, yet violent culture where, as Rees Davies famously remarked, '… to be tired of war in the March was tantamount to a resignation of lordship'.[20] Later lords inherited this tradition. The evolution of the March witnessed moments of aggressive expansion and humiliating retreat, perhaps best witnessed in the struggle for control of Maelienydd in the twelfth century.[21] As John Kenyon outlines above, moreover, castle building played a crucial role in the expansion, consolidation and defence of Mortimer influence, particularly into the Welsh *commotes* of what became Radnorshire.[22] Mortimer rebellions against the Crown in the twelfth century led to confiscation of property but, ultimately, the proximity of individual lords to the person of successive English kings in the thirteenth and fourteenth centuries garnered significant patronage. Land grants and royal 'impotence and permissiveness'[23] allowed the Mortimers to push at the jurisdictional boundaries of the family's holdings, while, as Scott Waugh noted, the marriage alliances between close kin reduced the impact of dowry settlements and kept properties within narrow lines of descent which could subsequently be reconstituted.[24] Each served to extend the landed reach and political profile of the Mortimers of Wigmore.

ROGER MORTIMER (d.1282): CONQUEST, REWARDS FOR SERVICE TO THE CROWN AND MARRIAGE

The effect of this is perhaps best attested in the surviving inquisitions taken in 1304 following the death of Edmund Mortimer, heir to the man justifiably described as he who 'deserves to be remembered as one of the great architects of the late medieval March' – Roger Mortimer (d.1282).[25] At the heart of the lordship remained the castle and town of Wigmore with surrounding hamlets and parks, held in chief by barony for the service of two knights in war in Wales and one knight in war in England. And the manor of Cleobury with its members, also held in chief nominally as an escheat of Roger de Bellême, former earl of Shrewsbury, by service of being steward of all the earl's lands in Shropshire and keeper of Bridgnorth Castle. Appurtenant lands in Radnorshire – Knighton and Pilleth – were held in Welshry, by Welsh law and custom, of the barony of Wigmore in chief. In addition, Roger had also reaped the spoils of war, receiving the Welsh marcher lordships of Ceri and Cedewain from Edward I in 1279 for his support on campaign against Llywelyn ap Gruffudd, and had

Wigmore Castle and its town were the heart of the Mortimers' extensive lands across three countries (© Paul R. Davis)

finally sealed Mortimer control of the heavily-disputed *cantref* of Maelienydd.[26] Another appurtenant *commote* – Gwerthrynion with the site of the castle and town of Rhayader – was regained in a remarkable agreement between Roger and his kinsman, Llywelyn ap Gruffudd, Prince of Wales, on 9 October 1281, with each man offering mutual support in peace and war.[27]

Furthermore, at the height of his influence following the battle of Evesham in 1265, Roger had exploited his close friendship with the Lord Edward, later Edward I, to extract key estates from the shire system of justice and taxation, taking for himself marcher liberties and powers free from Crown interference. These included Wigmore (and its Welshries of Knighton, Norton and Presteigne), Cleobury, Chelmarsh, and their surrounding manors, plus the lordship of Radnor, now on the Welsh side of the border but which had been part of Herefordshire from before Domesday Book.[28]

If military prowess, not to say stamina, was a key facet of the Mortimers' rise, then success in the marriage market was equally important. A glance at the 1304 inquisitions post mortem reveals Edmund held a number of estates which had come to the family with wealthy brides over the previous century. The most transformational of whom was Maud, eldest daughter and co-heiress of William de Braose, who married Roger Mortimer (d.1282) in 1247.[29] A co-parcener, through her mother, of the vast Marshal inheritance in the earldoms of Pembroke and Leinster, Maud extended Mortimer influence in the March, bringing the lordships of Radnor and Narberth, and third parts of each of St Clears and Haverford. This supplemented gains in England: Bridgwater Castle and lands at Milverton and Odcombe (Somerset); a third of the manor of Long Crendon (Buckinghamshire); a share of Newbury (Berkshire); and Awre (Gloucestershire). When added to other English estates held of the barony of Wigmore, such as Bewdley (Worcestershire) and Stratfield Mortimer, and knights' fees in another 21 counties, this territorial expansion – at times gradual, at times rapid – brought the family into the front rank of baronial society. To an extent, though, this only tipped the iceberg. Maud's share of the Marshal inheritance, concluded at Woodstock in May 1247, also included shares in counties Kildare, Kilkenny and Carlow in Ireland.

Ireland became a new frontier and proving ground for Mortimer authority in the later Middle Ages. While the beginnings were inauspicious, the extent and value of the family's burgeoning Irish estates ensured a more consistent presence in their defence. These holdings also established a nexus of new personal, territorial and administrative links on both sides of the Irish Sea during an ensuing century in which bonds forged by other noble houses fractured or shattered.[30] The principal seat of nascent Mortimer power in Ireland was the castle of Dunamase, now in county Laois in the Irish midlands, valued at just over £343 per annum, around a fifth of the total value of Leinster.[31] Perhaps as Roger was underage, the assignment of dower to Countess Margaret, widow of Walter Marshal, went ahead in 1247/8 and apparently involved her bailiffs removing stock and other moveables from Dunamase which Henry III ordered to be restored in April 1249.[32] The volatile state of the English colony in Ireland, with multiple, overlapping frontiers, cultures and jurisdictional claims and already witnessing a contraction of the 'land of peace', did not encourage Roger to venture there unlike some contemporaries.[33] This came despite political currents in England: in December 1264, Roger and other marcher opponents of Simon de Montfort swore to exile themselves to Ireland for a year and a day. Though, as we now

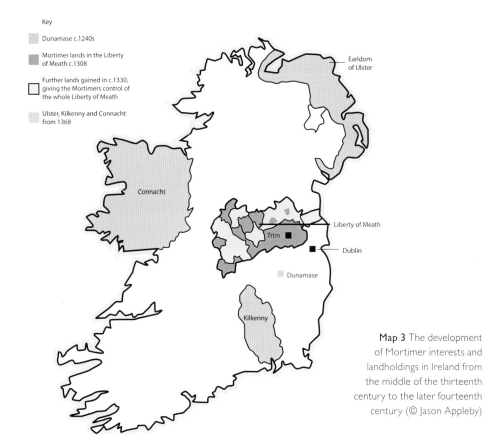

Key

Dunamase c.1240s

Mortimer lands in the Liberty of Meath c.1308

Further lands gained in c.1330, giving the Mortimers control of the whole Liberty of Meath

Ulster, Kilkenny and Connacht from 1368

Earldom of Ulster

Connacht

Liberty of Meath

Trim

Dublin

Dunamase

Kilkenny

Map 3 The development of Mortimer interests and landholdings in Ireland from the middle of the thirteenth century to the later fourteenth century (© Jason Appleby)

know, their disobedience resulted in Mortimer leading the death squad which killed Montfort at Evesham on 4 August 1265.[34] Such inability or unwillingness to establish a personal presence in Dunamase essentially jeopardised that lordship to the point where returns were fragile. Nevertheless, Mortimer's ministers and tenants remained strong enough to take and hold captive Muirchertach Mac Murchadha, king of the Irish of Leinster, a constant thorn in their side, over the winter of 1280–1.[35] This proved a pyrrhic victory: while inquisitions taken in Kildare and Laois following Roger's death in December 1282 showed a lively economy, sizeable tracts of arable land lay waste because of war. The extended value of the estate lay at almost exactly half of its comparable value in 1247 – at £171 7s. 6½d.[36] Maud, Roger's widow, assigned her right to Dunamase to Edmund, their son, in June 1284.[37]

ROGER MORTIMER (d.1330): MARRIAGE AND POWER BRING FURTHER LANDS AND TITLES

Edmund, however, remained stubbornly absent from Ireland. But he kept his eye on the bigger picture and negotiated perhaps the most important match in the family's history (this despite his 1285 marriage to Margaret de Fiennes, a kinswomen of Edward I's queen, Eleanor of Castile).[38] In September 1301, Edmund's son and heir Roger (b.c.1287) married Joan, eldest daughter of Peter, son of Geoffrey de Geneville, lord of Vaucouleurs, Ludlow and Trim and formerly long-time chief governor of Ireland.[39] Not only was Joan heiress (after the confinement of her sisters to Aconbury Priory) to half the marcher lordship of Ewyas Lacy and half of the town of Ludlow, she was also heiress to Trim, which was half of the former de Lacy liberty of Meath. Forty kilometres north-west of Dublin and slightly closer to the mouth of the Boyne, on which it sits, Trim, with its magnificent castle, is at the heart of well-drained, low-lying country.[40] Even following the climatic catastrophe of 1315–18, exacerbating the contemporaneous Scottish invasion of Ireland during which Trim was twice attacked, the lordship was valued at £500 per annum by royal commissioners in the 1320s.[41] This would constitute probably around half of the annual income the Mortimer lord could command in the early fourteenth century. We might therefore see Edmund's demise of 13 April 1300 to Geoffrey and his wife, Matilda – of £120 of land in his Hampshire manors of Stratfield and Worthy Mortimer and in Wigmore and Cleobury for eight years as a pre-nuptial agreement to secure Joan's hand – as part of an attempt to raise the transmarine profile of his inheritance.[42]

Having arranged his granddaughter's marriage in 1301 and having buried his wife three years later, Geoffrey, by now in his seventies, naturally looked to a smooth succession. He had to wait until the tail end of 1307, and the incipient reign of Edward II, for a transition of power to take effect. Though nominally a minor, Roger Mortimer's proximity to the young king and, especially, his favourite Piers Gaveston, in whose wardship he had recently been, enabled him to enter his inheritance early.[43] On Christmas Eve 1307, Geoffrey received licence to divest himself of his Irish estates to Joan and Roger, while he slipped away into retirement at Trim's Dominican friary.[44] This enabled Roger to make reality what had long been elusive – the creation of a transnational Mortimer lordship in three realms. It also provides the best and most sustained contradiction to Robin Frame's broadly justifiable view that, '... although numerous fourteenth-century Englishmen had links with Ireland, for most of them most of the time the Irish dimension of their careers was a thing of low priority'.[45]

To revisit the storied career of Roger Mortimer in narrative detail here would be unnecessary.[46] What is worth emphasising is the singular focus he displayed in defending his rights and exploiting opportunities to expand his territorial and jurisdictional authority on both sides of the Irish Sea, until calamity struck. By such means, he achieved comital rank for the family, and a subsequent reliance by the Crown on the family's transnational status meant that the controversial earldom was not put in abeyance, despite his treason.

Unlike the now largely peaceful condition of Mortimer lordships on the Middle March of Wales, Trim witnessed frontier raiding from rival members of the settler and Gaelic communities on its margins. B.J. Graham has shown that:

> Medieval Meath can be visualised as an area which was constantly under
> attack or threat of attack from the north, west and south-west ... from at
> least the end of the thirteenth century.[47]

Therefore, as Frame noted, 'the maintenance of control required a local presence, local knowledge, and a web of relationships'.[48] Over the dozen years from 1308–20, Roger Mortimer visited Ireland on perhaps as many as six occasions, spending around half of that time there. With Joan by his side for some of that time, it is likely a handful of his 12 children were born in Ireland too. This was an uneasy inheritance, but one which was certainly worth protecting. Legally, the martial and political prowess of Geoffrey de Geneville had bequeathed a situation in which Trim had its own rules for the division of plunder taken in its marches, and its own assize of arms, requiring his tenants to be armed according to their status.[49] The necessity of personal lordship for defence, and a strong personal relationship with his elite military tenants, crystallised in the invasion crisis of 1315–18. During which Edward, brother of Robert Bruce, claimed the kingship of Ireland and attempted to wrest political and military control out of English hands, opening up an Irish front to the Anglo-Scots war underway since the 1290s.

Despite military defeat by Bruce at Kells on 9 December 1315, Mortimer returned as Edward II's 'lieutenant' at the head of a royal army replete with his English tenants at Easter 1317. Two spells as chief governor from 1317–20 enabled the Crown to use Mortimer's local knowledge and connections to launch a successful counter-offensive, which ultimately drove the Scots from Ireland after their defeat by levies from counties Meath and Louth at Faughart on 14 October 1318.[50] We can only speculate how Roger Mortimer's lordship in Ireland might have deepened had his second period in office not been curtailed by the growing threat to Welsh marcher liberties posed by the Despensers from Spring 1320.[51] Might we have seen a more concentrated endowment of his English and marcher adherents to give them a stronger tenurial stake in Ireland?

The civil war of the autumn / winter of 1321/2 made this moot and brought the gradual rise of the Mortimer family of Wigmore to a shuddering halt. Defence of the hard-won marcher liberties against a determined king proved futile. The 'humble submission' of Roger Mortimer and his uncle of Chirk at Shrewsbury on 22 January 1322 avoided a death sentence but not disinheritance.[52] But, while lordship in Ireland required active military engagement to combat multiple threats, it seems that the assertiveness and perceived unjustness of Mortimer lordship in the Welsh Marches, particularly among the Welsh tenantry, engendered resentment and disloyalty, and perhaps contributed to their submission. On 7 January 10,000 Welshmen from Brecon, Maelienydd, Gwerthrynion, Ceri and Cedewain entered Wyre Chase, remaining there for nine days, thereby withdrawing from their lords' campaign against the Despensers.[53] On the day of the Mortimers' surrender, the constable of the royal castle of Montgomery was empowered to receive all those of Ceri and Cedewain who wished to come into the king's peace.[54] On commuting the Mortimers' death sentence for treason to life imprisonment in July 1322, Edward II overlooked a petition from 'the community of Wales' to show uncle and nephew no mercy or the Welsh would be destroyed.[55]

Roger Mortimer of Chirk had acted as royal justice of Wales for an almost unbroken tenure since 1308. This must attest to the perceived brutality of his administration, but the open rebellion of Roger junior's Welsh tenants speaks of a poorly-documented harshness of lordship in the Middle March, where legal and cultural difference could be starkly treated on racial lines.[56]

Only the ingenuity of his escape from the Tower prevented the younger Mortimer being executed in 1323.[57] It also triggered a whirlwind of unpredictable events over a decade which both brought an individual lord to his greatest zenith and threatened to destroy the family. The crashing but bloodless denouement of Edward II's kingship and the turbulence of the minority of his son from 1327–30 need not detain us here.[58] One aspect of Roger Mortimer's rise to national prominence which has received a little less attention, though, is the scale of his territorial ambitions, particularly in Wales, its March and in Ireland.[59] Over four years as the most influential magnate at Edward III's court, Mortimer amassed a vast suite of new estates on the back of pursuit and forfeiture of rivals, access to patronage and legal chicanery. At the Westminster Parliament which opened on 3 February he successfully entered a petition showing his 1322

The Great Seal of Edward III, 1327 (Hereford Cathedral Archives HCA 1327, © Dean and Chapter of Hereford Cathedral)

trial had been erroneous. He had not been allowed to answer the charges, as was his right in peacetime, and had not been tried by his peers.[60] A general pardon and one more specifically relating to his escape from the Tower was issued on 21 February. Just a week later his lands were restored and the resumption of the estates late of Mortimer of Chirk ordered, so that his nephew might succeed him.[61] Mortimer had thus been returned to common law and had re-established the fortunes of his family. His close association with Queen Isabella and almost untrammelled access to the levers of patronage gave free rein to more grandiose ambitions hereafter.

One of his principal motivations was the embedding and expansion of dynastic links throughout the upper echelons of the aristocracy, which, of course, translated into territorial gain for the family. Within weeks of Edward III's accession, Roger had taken commitment of the custody of the heirs of the earldoms of Warwick and Pembroke, and the Audley family of Staffordshire.[62] This allowed him temporary access to the issues of their vast estates and, crucially, to the person of the heir. As Ian Mortimer has shown, these were comital and baronial families with lands and lordships in southern England and the Marches into which Mortimer was later able to marry some of his daughters.[63] More naked acquisitiveness and dynastic rivalry was no doubt behind his receipt of the valuable marcher manor of Stretton (Shropshire), late of the earl of Arundel, whose execution he had engineered 'out of pure hatred', and custody of whose lands on the Marches he received in September 1327. This latter grant also came with custody of the Despenser (formerly Lancaster and de Lacy) castle and lordship of Denbigh on the northeastern March.[64] Elsewhere, Mortimer negotiated with the queen to secure a grant in fee simple of the castle and land of Montgomery with the hundred of Chirbury after her death and the reversion, also in fee simple, of Clifford Castle and the hundred of Chirbury.[65] Several of these grants, though initially overturned by Mortimer's capture and execution late in 1330, did revert to his successors later in the century.

In terms of political and legal authority, not apparently reflected in membership of Edward III's royal council, Mortimer looked to Wales. He was appointed justice within a month of the accession, augmented in June by grant of the custody of the vast and wealthy former de Clare and Despenser lordships of Glamorgan.[66] Over the late summer and autumn of 1328, he secured commitment of the justiceship for life, as well, in May 1330, of an annuity of £500 from the issues of the office.[67] Such grants not only lined his coffers but allowed him to administer royal law and justice in Wales without check. They also realised the ultimate prize of the earldom of March with which he was endowed in late-October 1328.[68] On one level, the choice of title might reflect ancestry from the lords of La Marche in France. At quite another, this was an unprecedented attempt to assert authority over not simply a geographical area but one with distinct legal and jurisdictional independence from the Crown. Such effrontery to marcher sentiment and tradition far exceeded anything Hugh Despenser had attempted, though it was not met with a response as ferocious as that of 1321/2.

Even more than the March of Wales, however, the Mortimer claims over frontier territory also extended to Ireland. During the final year of the minority of Edward III, Roger Mortimer greatly expanded his influence there. The overturning of the sentence against him had led to the restoration of his liberty of Trim in August 1327. In April 1330 Mortimer also succeeded in having the original grant by Henry II of the lordship of Meath, with all jurisdictions and cognisance of all pleas, recited in his favour.[69] This gave him palatine jurisdiction not only over his liberty of Trim but also of the de Verdons' share, which encompassed much of western Meath, and effectively reconstituted one of the great colonial liberties. Additionally, Mortimer received a grant in fee of Athlone Castle and grants of the custody of the lands of the earldoms of Kildare and Louth during vacancies.[70] By his death, Mortimer could lay claim to authority over much of the eastern midlands of Ireland.

Roger Mortimer had over-reached himself. His arrogance, greed and mastery of king and court – as well as the young king's maturity and loyal advisers – brought him down. He had also ridden 'roughshod over family ties and affection' in granting his cousin, heir of Roger Mortimer of Chirk, his estates (bar those of his mother in Brecon and Tedstone Wafer) for life at a token rent, 'in a brazenly cynical act of magnanimity'.[71] Arrested in Nottingham on 19 October and executed at Tyburn on 29 November 1330, Mortimer saw his vast territorial legacy dismantled, at least temporarily.[72] Edward III passed Denbigh to his friend William Montagu in January 1331 and Chirk permanently to the Crown in March.[73] Chirk would, in time, be granted to Richard Fitzalan, the new earl of Arundel, and the principal rival dynasty to the Mortimers in the Middle March. The core of the Mortimer's marcher estates centred on Wigmore and included Maelienydd, Cedewain and Cwmwd Deuddwr, some of which had been entailed upon Roger's son Edmund and his infant bride Elizabeth, daughter of Bartholomew Badlesmere in 1316. Following inquiries in the autumn of 1331, these estates were restored to the couple, along with Roger's property.[74] As so often in the family's history, we can only speculate the extent to which Edmund would have revived its fortunes had he not succumbed to an unknown illness at Stanton Lacy on 16 December 1331. The Mortimer family chronicler, writing in Latin in the 1380s, remembered Edmund as having 'recovered, by sense and probity, the lands awarded to him and his wife which had been unjustly taken from him by the death of his father'.[75]

Worse was to follow. Edmund's untimely death coincided with three long widowhoods which created difficulties for his infant son Roger (b.1328) and his guardians in reconstituting the inheritance. Young Roger's great-grandmother Margaret de Fiennes, widowed in 1304, only died in 1334. Roger's own mother, Elizabeth, took a dower third of the estate enfeoffed upon her and Edmund in 1316, including Wigmore. While his grandmother, the redoubtable Joan, clung to her own inheritance of Ludlow, Ewyas Lacy and the liberty of Trim, despite persistent challenges with regards to the latter from the Dublin Government, eager both for revenue and to suppress lordships outside the shire system in Ireland, and her de Lacy kin. Maintaining a transmarine inheritance proved increasingly problematic as the fourteenth century progressed, not least for an ageing widow. This would be a challenge bequeathed to her grandson and his successors, and one which would witness the deaths of three Mortimer earls in Ireland.[76]

ROGER MORTIMER (d.1360): LANDS RESTORED THROUGH FRIENDSHIP WITH THE ROYAL FAMILY

Edward III was a king to recognise and reward talent. From an early age, Roger Mortimer (b.1328) attracted his attention. Such was his martial prowess, demonstrated in Edward's victorious continental campaigns, notably at Crécy in 1346 where he led 200 men from Wigmore and Radnor – another aspect to the value of their estates to the Mortimers – Roger became a mainstay of the military and chivalric elite distinguished in Edward's creation of the Order of the Garter in 1348.[77] Edward restored Roger to his inheritance incrementally and machinated in his favour. Livery of his lands in Herefordshire and the Marches followed ten days after Crécy. In April 1354, the king in parliament annulled the judgement against his grandfather, claiming disingenuously that the original sentence had been invalid. The correct legal procedures over which, of course, he had presided, had not been observed, in that Mortimer had not spoken in his own defence.[78] Edward then girded Roger with the earldom of March, having seemingly never intended to put this controversial title into permanent abeyance, and restored him to his grandfather's estates. In practical terms, once Joan had died in October 1356, this reunited almost the entirety of his inheritance. Roger took control of Ludlow and the lordship of Maelienydd. His other English manors were returned to him upon the death of his mother Elizabeth the previous June.[79] This was entirely legitimate. Likewise, Edward's commission to Roger of Dover Castle and custody of the Cinque Ports brought him the associated manors of Swanscombe and Erith on the north Kent coast.[80] More dubious was the deal cut with Edward and his kinsman Richard Fitzalan, earl of Arundel, to exclude William Montagu, 2nd earl of Salisbury, from his father's lordship of Denbigh by judgement against him in King's Bench.[81] Roger had married Philippa, the 2nd earl's daughter before 1352, and was able to exploit his personal relationship with the king to override the claims of Montagu – the son of the architect of the 1st earl of March's downfall in 1330 – to make territorial gains in the March.

EDMUND MORTIMER (d.1381): A ROYAL MARRIAGE ADDS EXTENSIVE ESTATES
Edward III was left bereft by Roger Mortimer's unexpected death aged only 31 on campaign at Rouvray on 26 February 1360.[82] With only a seven-year-old heir, Edmund, born in February 1352, another prolonged minority awaited the Mortimer earldom of March.[83] However, in 1358 the king had betrothed young Edmund to Philippa, daughter of his second son Lionel of Clarence. The marriage would eventually take place in 1368, the year of Lionel's death, and overrode an agreement of November 1354 for Edmund to marry Alice, daughter of the earl of Arundel. The king also compensated Roger in £2,000 for the breach of the agreement with Arundel.[84] In 1359 Roger enfeoffed some estates, including Ludlow and Cleobury in Shropshire, upon a group of friends and councillors led by William of Wykeham, bishop of Winchester, to use during his heir's minority, the first of several such enfeoffments employed in the latter half of the century.[85] These arrangements brought the Mortimers into the royal circle of Edward III and made them the 'greatest landholders in England outside of the royal family'.[86] The same can certainly also be said for both Ireland and the Welsh Marches. Philippa was heiress to the widely-dispersed de Clare and de Burgh earldom of Ulster and lordship of Connacht in Ireland, and several of the most valuable lordships in the southern Marches of Wales. By this marriage the Mortimers became arguably the greatest transnational landholding family across these islands in the Middle Ages.

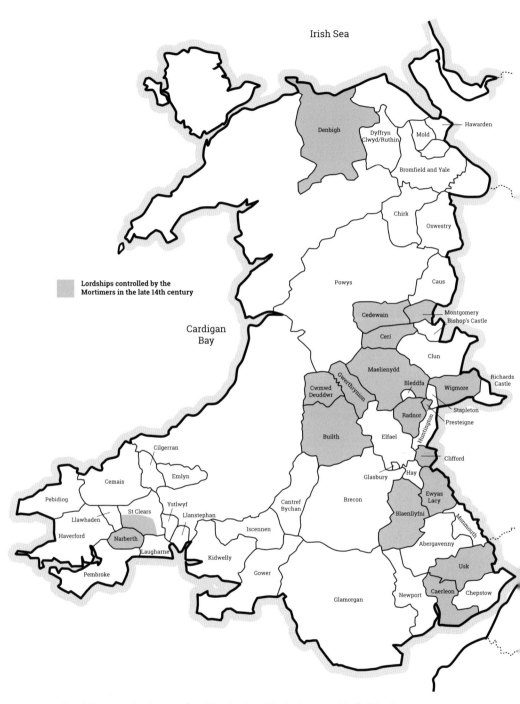

Map 4 Mortimer dominance of the Marcher lordships in the second half of the fourteenth century
(© Jason Appleby)

The extent of the Mortimer family's status and wealth can be gleaned by even a cursory glance at the inquisitions taken in 1382 after the death of Edmund, 3rd earl of March.[87] Alongside the core estates in Herefordshire, Shropshire and the Middle March and others across southern England long in Mortimer hands – such as Worthy and Stratfield Mortimer (Hampshire) and Newbury (Berkshire) – the marriage to Philippa brought estates in East Anglia. These were centred on Meldreth (Cambridgeshire), Great Gransden (Huntingdonshire), Thaxted and Great Barfield (Essex) – held by the courtesy of England – Little Walsingham (Norfolk) and, most valuably and famously of all, the castle and honor of Clare in Suffolk. These gains were richly supplemented by the acquisition of the marcher lordships, castles and manors of Usk, Caerleon and Trellech.[88] One of the most striking aspects of Mortimer lordship was the extent to which lands were now held in trust by feoffees. This was the case, most notably, for the castle and honor of Wigmore, held for life by William Latimer of Danby, Richard Scrope, Nicholas Carew, Peter de la Mare, Mortimer's steward, the clerks John de Bishopstone and Walter de Colmptone, and Hugh de Boraston by an enfeoffment to use of 1379. Similarly, other manors had been demised to the earl's followers, such as Ducklington and Finmere (Oxfordshire) to John Lovell. Enfeoffments such as these attempted to mitigate the problem of minorities and the dispersal of estates through dower.

The valuable castle and honor of Clare in Suffolk came into the ownership of the Mortimers when Philippa, the only daughter of Lionel of Clarence and Elizabeth de Burgh, married Edmund Mortimer, 3rd earl of March. Subsequent Mortimers were benefactors of Clare Priory, which had first been established in 1248, particularly the 5th earl who was buried there (© Paul Dryburgh)

They also coincided with a revival of Mortimer presence in Ireland. The reduction in the size of the colony through the fourteenth century has long been noted.[89] Edward III's plan to endow his second son with an Irish apanage as part of a wider strategy to reassert English transnational lordship had foundered at Lionel's death in 1368. Under the 3rd, 4th and 5th earls of March, however, royal authority mapped onto Mortimer lordship and ambitions, even if somewhat unevenly.[90] In April 1396 the 4th earl wrote to Richard II, a year after the king's expedition during which Roger had assisted in the negotiations preceding the submissions of the kings and community leaders of Gaelic Ireland:

> I do not think to pursue anything which will be against our lord the king
> nor his profit, but, as I think if the thing be well examined, which will be as
> much or more for his profit as for mine ...[91]

All three earls saw stints as the king's lieutenant; commanding large fees, complete control of Irish finances and little accountability to England. Both the 4th and 5th earls were even appointed while minors. All three witnessed military conflict both within and outside Meath as they struggled to establish any tangible authority in the north and west of Ireland. The 3rd and 4th earls would die on campaign; the latter in 1398, apparently clad in Irish dress.[92] Meath and the vast lordships of Ulster and Connacht offered the prospect of significantly supplementing Mortimer coffers. But by 1404 Trim, once valued at £500 a year, could apparently only return £17. Eleven years earlier as the 4th earl received his lands, he received £1,000 to offset the devastation of his estates by Irish rebels and enemies.[93]

THE ECONOMIC BASES OF THE MORTIMERS' WEALTH

In 1393, the Wigmore Chronicle estimated that 40,000 marks had been accumulated in the treasury and that Roger's guardians had performed heroics.[94] Rees Davies calculated that the Mortimer estates in Wales and the March alone accounted for an annual income of *c*.£2,750, at a period when an earl could be comfortably supported on about half that amount.[95] By 1398, a valuation of the 4th earl's Welsh estates for the dower of his widow, Eleanor Holland, estimated a total of £2,345, which excluded Radnor, Gwerthrynion and Narberth.[96] So, while the Irish lordships demanded military intervention to garner returns, such as constructing the bridge spanning the Bann at Coleraine apparently with timber shipped from Usk, the entirety of the Mortimer inheritance remained incredibly valuable.[97] It also remained interconnected and treated holistically, even if at a practical level communications over distance were tricky and individual lordships and manors operated within different economic and legal systems. As a conclusion to this article, we can now turn, briefly, to examining the economic bases of this wealth over three centuries.

The dispersed, transnational nature of the Mortimer estates fostered a mixed economy whose diversity was caused by terrain, climate, access to markets and labour, and navigating the various legal cultures in which each lordship operated. Agriculture and arboriculture underpinned the family's wealth and status. Ralph Mortimer's Domesday lordship included vast tracts of demesne land under plough across England, some of which was reliant on servile labour. At Hullavington in Wiltshire, for example, an estate formerly of Earl Harold, Ralph paid geld for 20 hides and had 14 hides in demesne, with 4 ploughs, 8 slaves and 19 villans. The Cleobury estate in Shropshire had land for 24 ploughs with four ploughs in demesne and 14 slaves, while at Leintwardine in Herefordshire, previously held by King Edward, there was land for 14 ploughs, with 3 ploughs in demesne, 6 oxmen, 10 villans and 8 unfree bordars. It is impossible to determine the extent of Ralph's influence in the early agricultural development of his estates across England – or indeed the veracity of the Domesday Survey – but at Cleobury their value had increased by 50% from pre-Conquest levels by c.1086 and at Leintwardine by 20%.[98] Nevertheless, for the majority of the English estates of the Mortimer family throughout the next two centuries, arable production formed the backbone of the economy, though record evidence for this period is sparse. For much of this time, production was dedicated to stocking the lordly table, but by the end of the thirteenth century there had been considerable commercialisation of the manorial economy.[99] The addition of large East Anglian estates in the fourteenth century hugely supplemented the arable production capacity of the earldom of March and Ulster within England.

In the Welsh Marches, particularly in the upland areas, land proved more marginal for profit drawn from arable farming. Lords came to rely more heavily on the pastoral economy, commutation of rents and services and the profits of marcher justice. Even in Domesday, Shropshire estates at Shirley, Upper Lye and Walford in Conditre hundred and the Edgebolds in Condover, for example, lay waste.[100] As Penry Evans demonstrated in his doctoral thesis, by the second quarter of the fourteenth century seigneurial management of arable farming had to be abandoned in Chirk, Radnor, Norton and Pembridge.[101] More broadly, this trend started before, but was accelerated by the epidemic catastrophe which struck in 1348/9, and then recurred in waves for the remainder of the Middle Ages. Throughout the March and across other Mortimer demesnes, land was leased and compulsory labour services such as ploughing, reaping, weeding and threshing were commuted for money rents.[102] This can be seen in the newly-discovered Wigmore account roll introduced at the start of this chapter. Small parcels of land in Aymestrey, Moorcot and Lye, for instance, are recorded as 'demised', or leased, to named individuals for life at small annual rents payable in two instalments at Lady Day (25 March) and Michaelmas (29 September). In the area around Wigmore Castle itself, some of the instruments of lordly power were also leased. The site of the former dovecote and the herbage of the close around it were leased to Richard Bottrell, then constable, keeper and parker of Wigmore. An apparently curious entry records the receipt by the liberty's bailiff John Chaundeller of 10s. 6d. from a custom called 'Solughsilver and Rapsilver' in Adforton, Upper and Lower Lye and Woodhampton – essentially money payments due in place of the former services of ploughing and reaping within the liberty. This 1387–8 account repeats a commuted service in place since at least 1324.[103]

In general, the fourteenth century witnessed the transition to pastoral farming. Several authors have commented on the large flocks pastured on the Mortimers' estates in the Marches and their entry into this most valuable commodity market. Price lists from the later Middle Ages record the value accorded to wool produced in Herefordshire, particularly.[104] Arable estates transitioned to stock husbandry with granges and manorial centres working to breed animals, shear, sort, weigh and pack wool for the continental and later domestic fine cloth markets. Assessing the total extent of Mortimer involvement in the trade is problematic due to the nature of surviving sources. A manorial centre such as Stanton Lacy, however, appears to have had a flock of around 500 animals in the late fourteenth century, sufficient to produce at least two sacks of wool as well as manure, skins for parchment, cheese and meat.[105] We can undoubtedly compare the earls of March favourably with their relatives of Arundel, whose flocks in the Marches topped 15,000 in 1349 and whose stocks of wool were worth £2,042 in 1376.[106] The Mortimer borough of Ludlow famously developed as one of the centres of the trade in England as a meeting place for merchants and growers.[107]

Direct intervention by Mortimer lords and their predecessors secured Ludlow's position as a local commercial centre, protected and developed by its geography and castle. An undated weekly market and annual fair – at which all manner of goods were traded – are recorded there in 1292. These were held by: Joan, widow of Peter de Geneville, son of Geoffrey; Peter's three daughters – Joan, future countess of March, Beatrice and Matilda; and Theobald de Verdon. On 25 November 1328, the newly-girded 1st earl of March received a charter from Edward III, for himself and his wife, of an annual fair on the same day – the feast of St Katherine – to be held at his manor. These remained in place until Edward IV, himself late earl of March, instituted a Thursday market and Mayday fair for his burgesses of Ludlow.[108] In microcosm, this demonstrates the catalysing effect Mortimer lords could have on local, regional and transnational economies.

The foundation of boroughs with trading privileges and tolls created potentially vibrant urban environments in which trade could flourish and profits be drawn from sale of demesne produce. Market days and fairs, at least in the Marches, appear to have been neatly arranged to prevent clashes. The Domesday borough at Wigmore, valued at £7, had just over 140 burgage plots, a Wednesday market and annual St James (25 July) fair by 1304.[109] The inquisitions taken after Edmund Mortimer's death show likewise that Cleobury included just over 100 plots, whose owners supported a market and annual fair on 14 September, granted to Hugh Mortimer by Henry III in 1226. In Radnorshire, 126 burgesses held 162 plots in Knighton, noted as waste in Domesday, and held a market and annual fair at St Matthew (21 September), granted to Roger Mortimer in 1230. In Old Radnor, 262 burgesses enjoyed a Tuesday market and St Luke's day fair (13 October). The township of Presteigne on the west bank of the River Lugg had a Saturday market and two fairs at the feasts of St Andrew (30 November) and the Nativity of St John the Baptist (24 June) each year, held of the earl of Hereford for an annual render of two marks.[110]

One town that was established by the Mortimers was the aptly named Newtown. This was created by Roger Mortimer (d.1282), after being granted the lordship of Cedewain, when he moved the hillside settlement outside Dolforwyn Castle down into a more economically advantageous position in the valley bottom. Elsewhere, marriage brought the family new urban interests. In Bridgwater in Somerset, for example, Edmund Mortimer (d.1304) died seised of a third of the town, which included burgage rents, shops and stalls, held jointly with his wife. The lordships of Usk and Caerleon boasted substantial boroughs developed by the de Clare earls of Gloucester. By 1381, Usk had a Monday market and fairs at St Luke and around Trinity, while Caerleon had a Thursday market and two fairs at All Saints and around Trinity.[111] In Ireland, moreover, Roger Mortimer (d.1282) bequeathed Newtown (Co. Laois) with 127 free burgages, extended annually with tolls and a tollbooth on ale of £11 11s. 6d.[112] This paints a rather different picture to much of the rest of the extent which displays considerable loss and damage from the incursions of local Irish forces.[113] Trim, however, proved more enduringly fruitful. Its de Lacy founders had developed a wealthy borough with a market and eight-day fair in February from the early thirteenth century, with tolls on wine, hides, cloth, wool, iron, wheat and oats to name but a few commodities traded there.[114] As Roger Mortimer, future 1st earl of March, inherited the liberty in 1307, one of his first acts was to secure a grant of murage – a toll to assist in maintaining the town walls – on a wide range of goods coming into the town on the Boyne from Drogheda (and no doubt overland from Dublin and elsewhere), including such exotic items as figs and raisins.[115] Trim may have seemed a home away from home for a lord used to the English court and the wealthier lordships of the Welsh March.

When granted the lordship of Cedewain with the castle of Dolforwyn, Roger Mortimer moved to the valley bottom the settlement that had been established outside the castle by Llywelyn ap Gruffudd (© Crown copyright 2019 Cadw)

Trim's relatively secure location ensured its fair continued to thrive well into the fifteenth century. By then, its former winter fair had, quite sensibly, been shifted to 14 days from Midsummer. Nevertheless, like Dunamase and Newtown, though to a lesser degree, it remained vulnerable to attack. Towns across the Mortimer dominions were potential targets and some suffered damage in warfare and border raiding. As Helen Watt demonstrated, the war raised by Owain Glyn Dŵr in the early fifteenth century targeted urban centres. The decline in trading in Usk and Presteigne around this time might be attributable to the damage wrought.[116] Similarly, other instruments of lordship could be targeted. Notably mills with associated suit of court, forests and parks with their harsh laws, monopoly on taking of game and their alteration and domination of the landscape. It is noticeable, for example, as mentioned above, that one of the activities of huge numbers of Mortimer tenants to the civil war of 1321/2 was to amass and hunt openly in Wyre Chase.[117]

Mills, of course, are ubiquitous throughout Mortimer manors from Domesday onwards. The overwhelming majority were watermills, such as those at Cleobury, Neen Savage and Meole Brace (Shropshire) and Leintwardine and Much Marcle (Herefordshire). In 1304, Pilleth in the Welshry also operated a fulling mill for cloth production while at Newbury in Berkshire we find a mill for tanning hides.[118] Both grain production for subsistence and profit and revenue from suit of mill proved lucrative. In 1337, £108 could be raised by royal commissioners from Mortimer mills.[119] Of unarguably greater value were the products and profits of the Mortimers' forests and parks. From these stemmed not only timber but rights over pannage (the pasturing of pigs in the forest), game both for the table and as sporting entertainment and a variety of associated produce and privileges that significantly enhanced the economic facets of lordship.[120] Like mills, forests and parks were ubiquitous across the Mortimer lordship, and as Rees Davies sagely noted, 'The lord's claim over the trees of his lordship was at once one of the most extensive and one of the most irksome manifestations of his authority'. Based on the evidence available to him, William Rees argued the forests and chases of Wigmore were much better cared for than many other lordships.[121] This presumably included Wyre Chase around Cleobury, where in Domesday Ralph Mortimer had sufficient woodland to fatten 500 pigs, and the deer park of Gateley close to Wigmore.[122] One of the features of the newly discovered Wigmore account roll is the itemising of stock – mares, foals, draught animals – kept in the park by Richard Bottrell.

Radnor Forest: huge tracts of land lay under forest law in Radnor and Maelienydd
(© Alex Ramsay/ Alamy Stock photo)

By the 1380s this park retained some of its original functions but also may have acted as a breeding station for the 4th earl's horses.

Elsewhere in the March, rights over woodland abounded. Huge tracts of land lay under forest law in Radnor and Maelienydd. As with demesne arable land, however, as the fourteenth century progressed, forests were leased and timber commercialised.[123] Parks could also be found at Cleobury and Radnor, in the latter of which there was no deer in 1304 except in the wood of Clud. Later in the century, across the newly-acquired lordships, the 3rd earl enjoyed parks in Caerleon, Usk, Brimpsfield (Gloucestershire) and perhaps most notably at Southfrith by Tonbridge in Kent, held of the archbishopric of Canterbury, where pannage was due on hundreds of swine.[124] Seigneurial parks dominated the landscape and proved controversial; restrictions on access and arbitrary laws inevitably led to poaching and more violent attacks. As the first year of famine broke in 1315, Roger Mortimer of Chirk and his nephew separately complained of park breaking at Cleobury, Tedstone Wafer, Leintwardine and Arley.[125] This came only two decades after Edmund Mortimer granted his men of Maelienydd, on their complaint of persecution by his and his father's bailiffs, hunting rights in certain areas, and established defined penalties for the taking of beasts illegally.[126]

Other instruments of economic lordship which proved profitable could include fisheries and weirs, such as those granted on the Ithon to Edmund Mortimer's

men of Maelienydd, for which they paid £500, and on the Wye pertaining to the 3rd earl's lordship of Usk.[127] Income from rents, dues and courts formed a significant contribution to Mortimer coffers – the proceeds of what we might term arbitrary justice, such as the wide variety of fines and customs levied across the estates. Their extent and value have been ably dealt with elsewhere.[128]

On 4 March 1461 Edward, earl of March and Ulster ascended the throne as King Edward IV.[129] A Mortimer through his paternal grandmother, Anne countess of Cambridge, Edward's accession finally amalgamated the family's far-flung estates with the Crown estate. And, although disputed over the next two decades, allowed this most ambitious, astute and fortunate medieval dynasty to achieve its destiny. Over almost four centuries the political rise (and fall) of the family had been underpinned by the growth (and loss) of its territorial assets, and its ability to adapt to fluctuating economic and demographic trends, to evolving but not complementary legal environments and to personal and political disasters. Nevertheless, the documentary windfall produced by the management of these estates, both in seigneurial and Crown hands, has yet to be fully exploited, particularly for the fourteenth and fifteenth centuries. As so often in their history, there remains much to be discovered about the Mortimer family; the extent, exploitation and economic value of their estates is perhaps the most important and outstanding.

The surviving medieval tower at Dublin Castle is now known as the Record Tower
(© Mark Reddy, courtesy of the Office of Public Works, Dublin Castle)

8

Patrick McDonagh

A scandal at Mass: the personal networks of Edmund Mortimer, 3rd earl of March

There are two in Munster who destroy us and our goods, namely the earls of
Ormond and Desmond with their followers, who in the end the Lord will destroy.

So sung Richard Wye, bishop of Cloyne in southwestern Ireland, radically altering the preface to mass at an anniversary service being held for Philippa of Clarence, late countess of March, in the chapel at Dublin Castle on 13 December 1380. His fiery attack on two of the leading resident English magnates in Ireland unfolded before Philippa's husband, Edmund Mortimer, lieutenant of Ireland, 3rd earl of March and 5th earl of Ulster (1352–81).[1] This moment appears to have stunned onlookers. Hoping the bishop had gone insane, the earl and his entourage stormed out of the chapel. Nor did Cloyne cease there, continuing his attacks on the earls in subsequent masses over the following days.[2] When confronted by a clerk about whether he sang these words, Cloyne, in a particularly belligerent mood, 'not only admitted but defended it and said he would add more when the time came'.[3] Unsurprisingly, his diatribe caused controversy. Ormond was obviously sensitive to the bishop's accusations as he brought 'a plaint of slander and injury' against Cloyne before William, bishop of Emly and vicar-general of Philip, archbishop of Cashel.[4] These legal proceedings were recorded in a public instrument drawn up by the notary Philip Cadell, clerk of the diocese of Cloyne, on 22 May 1381 (see overleaf).[5]

According to this instrument Cloyne was summoned by the vicar-general to appear before him in the cathedral church of Cashel on 21 February 1381, 'to show cause why he should not be proceeded against for slander and for heresy'.[6] Perhaps unsurprisingly, Cloyne chose not to appear nor did he appear at the later summons on 30 March, 27 April, 14 May and finally on 21 May when final judgement was passed. The charge of heresy, for altering the preface to the mass, was remitted

The excellently preserved 'Cadell's instrument', written in one hand throughout
(image reproduced courtesy of the National Library of Ireland, D.1268)

to the pope. However, the charge of slander was upheld, with major excommunication pronounced against Cloyne.[7] Had Cloyne hoped to discredit Ormond before the earl of March, he had badly miscalculated for the two earls were close allies and enjoyed 'a long affiliation'.[8] This 'long affiliation' materialised in open support for Ormond during the proceedings. On the summons held at Cashel on 27 April Ormond took the opportunity to provide the vicar-general with a notarial instrument in support of his case and the evidence of two witnesses.

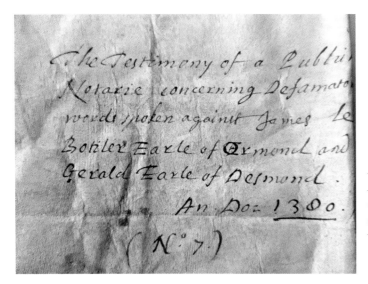

The description on the back of 'Hopton's Instrument' (image reproduced courtesy of the National Library of Ireland, D.1268)

This instrument is of especial significance. Later repeated verbatim within Cadell's instrument of 22 May 1381, the original document has also survived.[9] A small document, it measures 29.2 cm by 19.2 cm. Unlike the superbly-preserved instrument of Cadell, this document is faded, albeit mostly legible, and bears the sign of its author at the bottom. It was composed by the notary Henry Hopton, clerk of the diocese of Hereford, and it provides an additional account of the events of 13 December 1380 that corroborates the version recounted by Cadell. Hopton was a witness to the bishop's actions and when the bishop spoke, he did so according to Hopton 'before all the people and household *of our lord*, Lord Edmund, earl of March'.[10] For the account provided in his instrument, Hopton called upon the testimony of 16 'reverent and discreet men' who had also been present. Naturally, given the event, these were men who had, in varying ways, connections with the Mortimer earl.[11] Their number included eight knights, four esquires and four chaplains who are listed in the following table:

KNIGHTS	ESQUIRES	CHAPLAINS[13]
Sir John Lovell	Walter Bromwich	John Kepeston
Sir John Bromwich	Henry Cornewayle	William Stutvile
Sir Richard Talbot	Leonard Haclyt	John Scherfeld
Sir Thomas Mortimer	William Roure	William Excestre
Sir Ralph Lyngeyn		
Sir Henry Coneweye		
Sir Richard Wythfeld		
Sir Hugh Cheyne		

Table I Henry Hopton's witnesses[12]

A select examination of these 'reverent and discreet men' is the primary focus of this essay.[14] Among them can be found some of the leading figures of the Mortimer affinity during the time of the 3rd earl of March. A study of their careers can serve as a springboard for a wider investigation into the Mortimer affinity and lordship during the late fourteenth century, offering an opportunity – even just for a fleeting glimpse – to see 'the real world of relationships' that underpinned its functioning.[15] Beyond this the study has three outcomes in mind.

Firstly, it aims to redress the historiographical neglect of the Mortimer affinity, despite the existence of an extensive body of evidence to draw upon.[16] Secondly, it will use this prosopographical research to contextualise the political and military activities of the Mortimer earls of March in the late fourteenth century, a period which has been characterised as witnessing the 'ebb-tide' of English political power across the British Isles.[17] Coinciding with this retreat was the gradual disentanglement of tenurial landholding on both sides of the Irish Sea and the emergence of distinctive English aristocracies in England and Ireland.[18] Against this background the Mortimer earls of March made strenuous efforts to implement a vigorous transnational lordship across the 'British Isles'. Their followers, whose careers led them across the Mortimer lordship, were an intrinsic part of this story. Thirdly, this study's focus on an aristocratic affinity is tied up with the current historiographical movement to consider the dominions and realms of the Plantagenet kings of England as a 'Plantagenet Empire'. As part of this discussion the late Professor Mark Ormrod made one important call for action:

One of the things we need most urgently in order to understand the meaning and relevance of relations between the dominions is a concerted prosopography of the Plantagenet Empire.[19]

This *desideratum* should incorporate when feasible the personnel of the major aristocratic and ecclesiastical lordships that extended across the English king's dominions. The Mortimer lordship with its extensive transnational estates in England, Wales, Ireland and Calais aped in miniature the Plantagenet Empire, and an exploratory study of its affinity it is hoped will contribute to the wider endeavour proposed by Ormrod.

It was 'before all the people and household of our lord' that Cloyne launched his attack on the earls of Ormond and Desmond. Our author Henry Hopton, we can safely presume, would have been in a position to know. By 1380 he was a long-standing member of the Mortimer household where he served as a chaplain; it was as a chaplain that he had accompanied the earl on his Breton expedition during 1375 and he had likely been part of his household beforehand.[20] That he was chosen to draw up this instrument in support of Ormond likely indicates the level of trust placed in him. It was not in Edmund's interest to undermine the position of a close ally and powerful resident lord. Less certain is the nature of Hopton's relations with his 16 witnesses, or why they were chosen. As a chaplain himself, his most intimate relationships may have been with the four chaplains who provided testimony.

Of these four, the two most important were John Kepeston and William Stutvile. According to an indenture he made in 1377, Kepeston was the 'clerk of the expenses of the household of my most dread lord the earl of March'.[21] He was the

Stained glass depiction of Edmund Mortimer, 3rd earl of March, in the nineteenth-century west window of St Laurence's, Ludlow (© Philip Hume)

earl's privy expenses clerk (not to be confused with the earl's household treasurer) and consequently enjoyed a close relationship with the earl. On two separate occasions in December 1374, he received £10 from the Mortimer receiver-general in London for the earl's secret use.[22] On 30 May 1378, as the Mortimer household travelled between Royston and Huntingdon (in Cambridgeshire) Kepeston was given 12s. to give in alms to paupers along the way on the earl's behalf.[23] The earl's will, composed at Denbigh on 1 May 1380 just prior to his departure for Ireland, underscores their relationship. Kepeston was left a bequest of 20 marks and was named as one of his executors.[24] Following the earl's unexpected death at Cork on 27 December 1381 at the age of 29, Kepeston received letters from King Richard II under his privy seal commanding him to receive by indenture money from the officials of the Irish Exchequer for the sustenance of the late earl's children who were all in Ireland. However, as Kepeston 'cannot attend to the premises for various reasons' someone else was appointed in his place.[25] Kepeston had returned to England in order to act as one of the earl's executors.[26] He would go on to serve Edmund's son, Roger, 4th earl of March (1374–98), as his privy clerk of expenses in future years.[27] As for Stutvile we know only little. However, even this little is suggestive of his importance. It was Stutvile who wrote out (and witnessed) the earl's will in May 1380.[28] Earlier in 1378 he led a group of the earl's household officials from London to Jedburgh in Scotland in order to provide victuals and carry out preparations in advance of Edmund's arrival. He kept a now-lost account of this work which ran from 15 May to 14 June 1378.[29] Perhaps his most important work was the 89 days he spent between 31 May and 1 September 1375 writing out muniments belonging to the earl.[30] Though we are never told which muniments he was copying, it seems certain the clerk was working on at least one of the three Mortimer cartularies created around this time by the earl's administration, arguably the most significant manuscripts ever produced by the lordship.[31]

The influence these chaplains wielded likely remained restricted to the Mortimer household and relied on personal connections with the earl or other household figures. Of greater social significance were the knights and esquires who had gathered with the Mortimer earl to remember his deceased wife. Among them few would have had the influence and standing of Hopton's first witness, Sir John Lovell. A man of cosmopolitan background, he had, like Chaucer's knight, been on crusade in Prussia and in the eastern Mediterranean, perhaps in 1371 when he went overseas.[32] He was a courtier *par excellence* and later became an important member of the royal household under Richard II.

Such was his perceived identification with the court he was among the members of the household expelled by the Lords Appellant in 1388 following their revolt against the king. Once the king resumed personal power, Lovell was once more deeply involved in the household and government.[33] When Richard II led his expedition to Ireland in 1394, Lovell was part of his retinue, and in 1395 was retained by the king with an annual fee of 200 marks. An adroit politician, he smoothly switched his allegiance to Henry of Bolingbroke during 1399 and would serve as one of the new king's councillors.[34]

Lovell's later adventures made him unique among Hopton's witnesses. However, his earlier career contained one facet which was emblematic of many in Edmund's affinity: service with his father-in-law, Lionel, duke of Clarence (1338–68). Lovell had accompanied the duke to Italy in 1368, where Lionel unexpectedly died that same year.[35] Following the duke's death Lovell made a natural progression into the service of his son-in-law. His high standing (and personal rank) within the Mortimer affinity is suggested by his presence as the leading witness in Hopton's instrument and in two acts of the earl in 1375.[36] He headed the witnesses in a quitclaim made to the earl of land in Dorset and Gloucestershire in 1374.[37] Additionally, he was among the witnesses to the earl's charter in November 1374 granting a portion of his estates in trust.[38] A sign of the earl's favour can likewise be seen in the gift of a doe which was brought from the manor of Thaxted in Essex to London for Lovell.[39] Lovell's own territorial holdings were in southern England, especially in Oxfordshire and Wiltshire.[40] In a further token of munificence Lovell was granted for life the custody of the manors of Ducklington and Finmere in Oxfordshire.[41]

Consequently, he may have had reason – personal and material – to lament Edmund's own unexpected death. Although he predominantly moved in royal circles after Edmund's death, Lovell did not completely sever his connection with the house of Mortimer. It is surely not without significance that he was one of the mainpernors for Thomas Holland, earl of Kent and the king's half-brother, when Holland was granted the marriage of Edmund's son and heir Roger for the sum of 6,000 marks.[42] Simon Walker has noted that among his children were two sons named Robert and Thomas.[43] A Robert Lovell was issued with letters of protection in May 1397 for service in Ireland with Earl Roger,[44] while 35 years after Cloyne's diatribe a Thomas Lovell accompanied Edmund, 5th earl of March (and grandson of the 3rd earl of March), to the siege of Harfleur in 1415. Unlike the earl however, Thomas would be among the participants at the battle of Agincourt that year.[45] It is tempting to equate both of these men with John Lovell's sons. Given his own personal standing, it is of little surprise that Lovell brought his own retinue to Ireland and among its members was another of Hopton's witnesses, Sir Richard Wythfeld.[46] A Gloucestershire knight and professional soldier, Wythfeld had served in a number of theatres of war throughout the 1370s including previously in Ireland.[47] His presence among the witnesses in Hopton's document is an excellent demonstration of how the Mortimer affinity – particularly the military retinue component of the affinity – was itself composed of smaller affinities that complemented each other.

Following Lovell in the witness list and of similar importance was Sir John Bromwich. Like Lovell, he had accompanied Lionel of Clarence to Italy in 1368 and was additionally a beneficiary of the duke's will, receiving a destrier (war horse) which was called 'Gerfacon' (Gyrfalcon).[48] Unlike Lovell, and more in keeping with other members of the Mortimer affinity, Bromwich had a background in the English border counties of the Welsh March. His wife Elizabeth was the widow of Sir Richard Talbot, and through her dower lands Bromwich was a transnational landowner – albeit on a much smaller scale than Earl Edmund – with estates in England and Ireland.[49] Following Lionel's death he entered the service of the young Earl Edmund. In May 1371 Bromwich was pardoned the forfeiture of his Irish estates – forfeited as he had not come to Ireland or sent someone to defend them – as he had been in the service of Lionel in Lombardy and afterwards with Edmund in France and England.[50] This means that Bromwich must have accompanied Edmund on his first military campaign to France in 1369 in an expeditionary force led by the earl of Warwick.[51]

Just as Lovell headed the list of witnesses in Hopton's instrument and Edmund's two known acts of 1374 so too does Bromwich follow him as second witness. He was among the witnesses of the quitclaim made in 1374 by Katherine de la Pole to Edmund and Philippa of the manors of Marshwood Vale in Dorset and Brimpsfield in Gloucestershire, which had been granted to Katherine by Lionel.[52] He also had positive relations with the earl's mother, Philippa [Montagu], the dowager countess of March. In her will she described Bromwich as 'my dearest and good friend in God'.[53] In October 1379, prior to his departure to Ireland, he enfeoffed the countess (along with others) of his manor of Eaton Tregoz in Herefordshire and the moieties he held in two manors in Northumberland.[54] The trust Mortimer placed in Bromwich is most apparent during his lieutenancy of Ireland. On 28 June 1379, Edmund made an indenture with the king to serve as the lieutenant of Ireland for three years commencing the day he arrived.[55] From this moment preparations were set into motion that culminated in Edmund's actual arrival in May 1380. In the interim it was agreed that Bromwich would be appointed justiciar of Ireland and sent ahead of the earl leading a company of 40 men-at-arms and 120 archers.[56] During the preparations for his own expedition Bromwich sealed an indenture for life service in peace and war with the earl. This took place on 18 October 1379 at Hereford, and Bromwich was granted a generous fee of 100 marks from the Welsh marcher manors and lordships of Clifford and Glasbury.[57]

It was probably on 26 November 1379 when Bromwich arrived in Ireland, as he would later order the officials of the Irish Exchequer in March 1380 to pay the arrears of his fee from that date until 26 February.[58] On 8 December he presided over a meeting of the royal council in Dublin which resulted in the grant of a subsidy.[59] His actions over the following months remain mostly obscure. In April 1380 he was at Trim where he attested the appointment of Sir Ralph Poley as steward of the liberty of Meath (by letters patent transmitted by Edmund).[60] Poley was a Norfolk knight and an old comrade of Bromwich with an illustrious career in Ireland behind him.[61] A member of Lionel's army of the 1360s he established himself as a figure trusted by the earl.[62] He can be seen serving as the steward of the liberty of Kilkenny in December 1365.[63] A letter from January 1369 from the archbishop of Armagh reveals that he was then the

An aerial view of Kilkenny Castle, where Sir Ralph Poley served as Steward (© Office of Public Works, Kilkenny Castle)

current steward of the liberty of Ulster.[64] Later in July the Irish Exchequer was ordered to pay him wages (if not previously paid) for his past service as Lionel's justice in Connacht.[65] Returning to Bromwich, his military stature can be seen in the run up to the anniversary service for Philippa. In October and November 1380, he was sent with four knights, 91 men-at-arms and 258 mounted archers to counties Kilkenny and Tipperary to suppress a local 'lineage' called the Tobins who were at open war.[66] By sending Bromwich here, Edmund was also availing of Bromwich's own networks of support, as he had estates in Jerpoint, county Kilkenny. That Bromwich had built up his own links in Ireland is suggested by his appointment in 1378 of John Yonge, abbot of Jerpoint, as one of his attorneys in Ireland.[67]

Also at the mass with which we begun this paper were two family members of Bromwich – his step-grandson Sir Richard Talbot and his brother Walter Bromwich.[68] Walter had also made a career in Edmund's service and made an indenture for life service in peace and war with the earl on 4 April 1373 at Hereford. In return, Walter was granted an annuity of 20 marks from the manor of Mansell Lacy in Herefordshire.[69] This indenture came three months after Edmund was granted livery of the remaining bulk of his paternal inheritance including Mansell Lacy on 6 January 1373.[70] It indicates the earl's willingness to utilise his inheritance to reward and cultivate his following. Walter certainly was able to avail of the earl's good graces for in May 1379, at Edmund's supplication, Walter was exempted for life from being put on a range of official – and doubtless onerous – positions such as assizes and juries or being made sheriff or justice of the peace.[71] He probably accompanied the earl during the Normandy campaign in 1369 and the abortive naval campaign of Edward III while he is known to have accompanied him to Brittany in 1375 and to Ireland in 1380.[72]

Following Edmund's death Walter returned to England and in May 1382 had his annuity from Mansell Lacy confirmed.[73] Later in November 1382 he was committed the keeping of the manor of Mansell Lacy until the 4th earl came of age.[74] Walter's son Thomas continued his family's service to the Mortimers and was one of the men-at-arms in Sir Thomas Mortimer's retinue in the naval expedition led by the earl of Arundel in 1387.[75] The retinue rolls for the 4th earl's campaigns in Ireland have not survived so it is impossible to say if he went to Ireland like his father and uncle. As for John Bromwich, after the earl's death in 1381 he returned to England. The surviving estate accounts for these years suggest he no longer played any role in the Mortimer estates, though he still stayed in touch with old comrades. One of the men who accompanied him on his voyage to Ireland in late 1379 was Walter Brugge, a former follower of Duke Lionel and a former treasurer of the liberty of Ulster under Edmund.[76] During the minority of the 4th earl Brugge would become the receiver-general of the Mortimer estates in England, Wales and the Marches, a role which involved much travelling. In the midst of one of these journeys he saw fit after leaving Gloucester on 31 May 1386 to spend the night at Hampton where he had dinner with Bromwich.[77] Perhaps it was on official business. Or perhaps it was a social call for two men whose shared experiences in the service of Lionel and Edmund had created a bond between them.

The witness to the Hopton instrument with perhaps the most experience of Ireland was Sir Henry Coneweye.[78] By the time of the Mortimer expedition to Ireland in 1380 he had a career on the island stretching back almost 20 years. He had accompanied Duke Lionel back in 1361 and subsequently made a career on its military frontiers.[79] Coneweye would appear in the retinue roll of Lionel's replacement, William of Windsor, in 1371 along with a Robert Coneweye, perhaps a relation.[80] Military life in the Irish colony was no sinecure and in November 1370 Coneweye was awarded £20 in compensation for the loss of horses (allegedly worth £40) while fighting the Gaelic Irish in Windsor's company.[81] During this time he established positive relationships with John Bromwich and William of Windsor and would be appointed as both men's attorneys in Ireland in May 1371 and August 1372 respectively.[82]

At what moment Coneweye entered the orbit of the Mortimer earl is unknown, but with a history of service to his father-in-law and some relationship to Bromwich, Coneweye probably had little difficulty doing so. Given his long service in Ireland, it must have been for his knowledge and experience of conditions in the colony and on the frontiers that made him valuable in the earl's eyes. When Coneweye made an indenture for life service in peace and war with the earl in 1381, it referred to an earlier indenture for the same service for which Coneweye had received 50 marks annually for life from the marcher lordships of Clifford and Glasbury.[83] This earlier indenture has not survived; however, a surviving receiver's account for this lordship (and others) from 1377/8 includes payment of this annuity.[84] Though the account does not indicate when this annuity was granted, it does at least provide us with our earliest date to locate Coneweye membership of the Mortimer affinity.

On the face of it, we know very little of Coneweye's actions in Ireland. We know he accompanied the earl and was in attendance during Countess Philippa's anniversary service.[85] The only other fact we know is that he made a new indenture for life service with the earl on 1 August 1381.[86] This indenture is rich with information and informs us that Coneweye had been knighted by the earl and was to continue in his life service to him in the estate of a bachelor. Coneweye was now one of the earl's bachelors which likely indicates his increased importance in the Mortimer household. Additionally, Coneweye surrendered his previous annuity of 50 marks and in return was now granted an annuity of £40 from the lordship of Cedewain. This indenture carries greater significance than it would at first glance. Though the dating clause of the indenture does not include the location where it was made, we know from elsewhere that on 1 August 1381 Edmund was at Athlone, which lies on the River Shannon – then separating the liberty of Meath from Connacht.[87] That day, two writs were issued by the Irish Chancery: one concerning the appointment of Thomas O'Cathissy (or O'Casey) to be constable of Athlone Castle; and the second, dated at Athlone, granting this constable 20 marks 'for his labours and expenses

Athlone Castle, County Westmeath (1650s, attributed to Jan Peeters I, Flemish, 1624–c.1677
© National Gallery of Ireland: NGI.2007.1)

in recapturing the castle of Athlone' from the Gaelic Irish.[88] The exact date of Athlone's capture is unknown but on 22 July Edmund was at Castledermot in Kildare and it was during this gap, perhaps on 1 August itself, that Athlone was taken.[89] That Coneweye's indenture dates from this time must surely imply that he had played a significant role in its recapture. Given his extensive experience of Irish military conditions he seems likely to have been one of the earl's principal military advisors in Ireland.

Following Edmund's death in December 1381 Coneweye drifted away from the Mortimer family. He secured a confirmation of his annuity of £40 from the earl with one change: he would now receive it from the marcher lordship of Denbigh in North Wales rather than from the lordship of Cedewain in the central Marches.[90] If Coneweye's toponymic surname related to him personally (rather than some distant ancestor) it indicates that he might have come from Conwy in North Wales. His later career seems to have been largely restricted to North Wales. During the invasion scare in the summer of 1385 Coneweye and his household garrisoned Rhuddlan Castle in Flintshire. In June in the same summer, for otherwise unknown good service rendered to Edward III and Prince Edward [Edward of Woodstock, the Black Prince], he was granted the keeping of the castle after the death of the current keeper with a fee of 40 marks from the issues of the Principality in North Wales.[91] However, this grant would be revoked later the same month.[92] He made possibly his last trip to Ireland in 1386 as part of the retinue of John Stanley, deputy of Robert de Vere, then marquess of Dublin and lieutenant of Ireland.[93] Hereafter, Coneweye remains associated with Rhuddlan. It was as mayor and constable of the castle that he witnessed a property transaction within Rhuddlan in April 1397.[94] On 17 November 1397 he was granted the constableship for life with an annual fee of £40.[95] Later, during the reign of Henry IV, he was issued with a letter of protection – still described as constable of Rhuddlan Castle – to stay in the company of Henry, prince of Wales, 'on the safe keeping of the castle'.[96]

Our focus now turns to two witnesses to the Hopton instrument who would be leading personalities within the Mortimer affinity for the next two decades: the esquire Leonard Haclyt (or Hakeluyt) and Sir Hugh Cheyne.[97] Hakeluyt came from a Herefordshire family of Welsh origin that had long-standing traditions of service to the Mortimer family.[98] His father Edmund had followed this tradition and was a member of the affinity of the 2nd earl of March and had been the steward of Trim during the 1350s. The dangers of frontier life were all too real for the elder Hakeluyt and he was imprisoned by local malefactors during his stewardship.[99] An earlier Edmund Hakeluyt (perhaps Leonard's grandfather) had accompanied Roger of Wigmore to Ireland in 1317 and was appointed escheator of Ireland in 1318.[100] Leonard was thus continuing a long family tradition yet he did not restrict his service solely to the usual patrons of his family. In 1373 he was a member of the retinue of John Montfort, duke of Brittany, as part of the great chevauchée through France led by Montfort and the duke of Lancaster.[101] Leonard's first known connection with the Mortimer earl was in November 1374 as he prepared to travel with Edmund's retinue to Brittany.[102]

In common with the majority of Hopton's witnesses little is known of Hakeluyt's actions in Ireland at this time. Nonetheless, he must have impressed Edmund for on 1 September 1381 he was granted an annual annuity of £10 from the manors of Erith and Swanscombe in Kent.[103] Following the earl's death, Hakeluyt, unlike our previous witnesses, is known to have remained in Ireland. In the ensuing emergency the chancellor of Ireland, John Colton, was appointed as justiciar of Ireland on 10 January 1382.[104] This was only a short-term expedient and on 24 January the deceased earl's son and heir, Roger, was appointed as the new lieutenant.[105] As the new Mortimer earl was seven years old, real power lay

Trim Castle, the administrative centre of the liberty of Meath (© Hugh Wood)

in the hands of his uncle Sir Thomas Mortimer (another of Hopton's witnesses) who was formally appointed his deputy on 3 March 1382.[106] It must have been due to Thomas' authority that Hakeluyt was appointed steward of Trim on 8 March 1382.[107] That his father had previously held the position must have had influence on his appointment, and it may be that Hakeluyt knew something of the liberty from stories told by his father. It is not clear how long Hakeluyt held the stewardship of Meath, but it may have finished with the end of the new Mortimer lieutenancy in 1383.

On his return to England, he remained involved with the administration of the Mortimer lordship. On 10 March 1386 he made an indenture with the receiver-general of the late earl's executors, Roger Nasshe. It recorded that he had received from Nasshe muniments, indentures and writings made by Robert Stepulton with his son Robert, and the latter's wife Cecily, regarding their marriage and inheritance.[108] A roll of expenses for the receiver-general of the Mortimer estates from late 1387 records that Hakeluyt received his annuity of £10 by the hand of the receiver of Wigmore from part of the farm of the manor of Oddingley in Worcestershire.[109] The receiver's account for Wigmore for 1390/1 reveals that Hakeluyt was the farmer of this manor.[110] Instead of taking his annuity from the manors of Erith and Swanscombe in Kent, he was instead farming the manor of Oddingley. It was probably therefore worth more than the £10 he accounted for but perhaps more importantly it was closer to his estates in Herefordshire and Somerset.[111]

Hakeluyt was a significant figure in local society in both Herefordshire and Somerset. He represented the former in parliaments during 1385, 1388 and 1394,[112] while he would stand for Somerset in the reign of Henry IV during 1404 and 1406.[113] Of these, his election in February 1388 for the upcoming Merciless Parliament was the most significant. In late 1387 a group of magnates known as the Lords Appellant successfully led a revolt against the king and scattered a royal army. In 1388 they set about purging the royal household and in the Merciless Parliament would execute some of the king's favourites.[114] One of the prominent figures of this rebellion was Sir Thomas Mortimer.[115] Whether Hakeluyt participated in the rebellion is unknown, but his election must have been influenced by his identification as a known supporter of the Mortimer family.

His service for the family continued into the majority of the 4th earl of March and he accompanied the young Earl Roger to Ireland in 1394 as one of his knights.[116] In July 1397 the earl granted him an annuity of £20 from the

Herefordshire manor of Much Marcle, in which he called Hakeluyt his bachelor.[117] The same month Hakeluyt was appointed as one of the earl's attorneys to safeguard his interests in England having returned from Ireland with the earl around April.[118] His appointment as attorney was repeated again March 1398 as the earl prepared to depart to Ireland for the last time where he would die in battle that July.[119] A rare record of his actions as attorney has been preserved in the receiver's account for the lordship of Denbigh for 1397/8. On 26 April 1398, with the earl en route to the sea to set sail, Hakeluyt was at Denbigh with his fellow attorney Sir Kynard de la Bere where they made an indenture with Milo Daunsore. Daunsore was described as a former servant of Earl Edmund and was given alms on account of his poverty, which were to be paid annually from the lordship of Denbigh.[120] He was probably the same individual as the Milo Dancere who was owed 20s. of his fee from the account of the 3rd earl's wardrober back in 1376/7.[121] Hakeluyt may have personally known him – or at least remembered him – from that time.

The last of the witnesses discussed in this chapter will be Sir Hugh Cheyne.[122] Long before he is known to have entered the orbit of the Mortimer earls of March Cheyne had forged a career in royal service. It was as the king's yeoman that he was granted an annuity of 10 marks at the Exchequer in September 1358, while later in December 1365 he was called the king's esquire when he was granted the keeping of the royal castle in Shrewsbury for life.[123] In early 1369 he was preparing to set sail to Aquitaine to serve with Prince Edward and must have witnessed the outbreak of war with France later that same year.[124] We next catch sight of Cheyne in 1373 – now a knight – as he was preparing once more for service in France, probably as a member of the expedition being led by the duke of Lancaster.[125] Cheyne's links with the royal household may have served as the pathway to his service with Edmund Mortimer, whose wife Philippa was the eldest grandchild of the king.

However, it is possible their association owes more to geographical proximity. A later accord made by Cheyne for the marriage of his granddaughter and heir willed that the young couple would receive his manor of Cheney Longville in Shropshire and several other manors in Worcestershire.[126] Cheney Longville appears to have been Cheyne's favourite residence, and in September 1394 he was granted licence to crenellate his manor house there.[127] The manor also lay some ten miles from Ludlow which was one of the more important Mortimer powerbases in the March of Wales. One manor not mentioned in the marriage

Grange Farm (Wigmore Abbey remains): a watercolour by Louisa Puller, 1941, looking down on the remains of Wigmore Abbey, which was heavily patronised by the 3rd earl, set among the buildings of Grange Farm (Catalogue of Drawings in the 'Recording Britain' Collection given by the Pilgrim Trust to the V&A Museum published by the V&A Museum, Prints, Drawings and Paintings Department, 1951 E.1582–1949)

accord but certainly held by Cheyne at least in 1379 was Bitterley in Shropshire. Cheyne also held the advowson of the church there and granted this advowson (but not the manor) to the abbey of Wigmore. Wigmore was the Mortimer family mausoleum and heavily patronised by Edmund, and Hugh must have been familiar with it. An inquisition taken of Bitterley manor and advowson revealed that Cheyne held them of the barony of Ludlow (which at that time was held by trustees of Edmund).[128]

In common with all of our witnesses, the precise moment Cheyne entered into the service of the Mortimers will remain unknown. His first known association with Edmund dates to late 1374, getting ready to sail in the earl's retinue for an expedition to Brittany.[129] He was certainly valued by the young earl for on 2 November 1376 he was retained for life service in peace and war. For his services he was to receive an annuity of 40 marks for life from the manor and town of Ludlow.[130] Another sign of his importance is his inclusion among the witnesses to the making of Edmund's will at Denbigh on 1 May 1380 just before they departed for Ireland.[131] This was not Cheyne's first visit to Ireland for in

May 1377 he had received letters of protection to go there on the king's service.[132] What he was doing in Ireland remains a mystery but it must have been related to the Mortimer earl. Similarly to practically all our witnesses, we know nothing of his activities during Edmund's expedition other than his presence at Philippa's anniversary mass. He was, however, likely to have been in the earl's company when Edmund unexpectedly died at Cork on 27 December 1381. In the state of emergency which ensued Cheyne was appointed keeper and steward of the liberty of Ulster in January and was sent north with 33 archers 'for the restoration of the peace between the English and Irish'.[133] He spent six weeks in the liberty when on 8 March 1382 he was appointed steward of Ulster by the new lieutenant, Earl Roger Mortimer.[134]

How long Cheyne remained as steward of Ulster is unclear, but he had returned to England by June 1382.[135] Surprisingly, despite not being one of the earl's original executors he had now become one of their number. Back in 1374 Edmund had put a number of his estates (including the manor and town of Ludlow) in trust, which following his death were transferred to his executors.[136] These executors sent two letters from Ludlow on 26 June 1382 to the receiver of Radnor which reveals Cheyne's inclusion. As the earl's executor he possessed some authority within the substantial estates held in trust and some of his various commands can be seen in a collection of ministers' accounts for the marcher lordship of Radnor during 1382/3.[137] The receiver's account for the lordship of Radnor for 1384/5 reveals that not only was Cheyne steward of the lordship, he was also described as being the steward of all the lordships in the hands of executor. He was in effect the chief steward of the executors.[138] This position would have given him great influence across the March of Wales and English border counties.

During the minority of the 4th earl of March, the rest of the Mortimer estates in England and Wales were being held in trust by a group of magnates which included the young earl. The chief steward of these estates was his uncle Sir Thomas Mortimer. Together both Thomas and Hugh would have acted as the practical representatives of the child earl until his majority. His influence and authority must go some way to explain Cheyne's election as a representative for Worcestershire in February 1388 for the infamous Merciless Parliament and later for Shropshire in September 1388 for the follow-up parliament held at Cambridge.[139] Though he had previously been elected in parliaments held in 1378 and 1379, his election to the two parliaments of 1388 must have been heavily influenced by the revolt of the Lords Appellant in late 1387 discussed earlier. Whether Cheyne actively took part or not is unclear, but he did think it wise to later secure a pardon for his support.[140] His public identification with the Mortimer family probably led to his two elections that year. Despite his history of service to Edward III and Prince Edward his service to the Mortimer family appears to have been the primary focus of his loyalty.

His position smoothed the way for his son John Cheyne to follow him into Mortimer service. John first appears in the Mortimer accounts in October 1393 as he delivered £30 from the receiver of Wigmore to the receiver-general at Westminster.[141] John accompanied his father in the Mortimer retinue which set out for Ireland in the autumn of 1394, and both would be leading figures in the young earl's affinity.[142] John's importance only becomes clear in 1398. In January 1398 Earl Roger attended the Shrewsbury Parliament, which was the continuation of the 'Revenge Parliament' held at Westminster back in September 1397.[143] During this former parliament the king had executed the earl of Arundel and sentenced the earl of Warwick to exile. Among the men appealed of treason was the earl's uncle Thomas Mortimer who Roger had conspicuously failed to deliver up to the king. During a moment of real danger – both politically and personally – Roger entered Shrewsbury surrounded by knights wearing his colours of red and white (perhaps an allusion to the banner of St George) and was greeted by crowds wearing hoods in the same colour.[144] This all cost a great deal of money and a slip of allowances belonging to the bailiff of Wigmore borough during this time included the bailiff travelling to Shrewsbury to transport gold at John's command.[145] Additionally, during March the receiver of Denbigh would pay a Welsh valet for riding from Denbigh to Conwy, Beaumaris and Caernarfon, to find ships for the passage of Cheyne and others of the earl's retinue about to travel to Ireland in March on the earl's business.[146] Cheyne was clearly in command of this force and was going ahead of the earl who would not depart till the end of April.

The elder Cheyne's importance during the brief majority of Earl Roger can be seen in an indenture for life service in peace and war he made with the earl in Ireland on 20 October 1397.[147] The agreement included the clause that Hugh was retained to be of the earl's council and his faithful councillor for life. Should the earl die before Hugh, he would be on the council of Roger's heir and serve no other person saving his allegiance. For this service Hugh was granted an additional 20 marks to be paid from the manor of Ludlow. Though the immediate context of this indenture was a successful military campaign launched against the O'Byrnes in the Wicklow mountains, the earl's premonition proved correct.[148] The following year on 20 July 1398 the earl was killed in a minor skirmish at Kellistown, county Carlow. According to the family chronicler he had ridden far ahead of his men while dressed as an Irishman when he was suddenly surrounded and killed by the O'Byrnes, not knowing who he was.[149]

For Hugh Cheyne his faithful service to the Mortimer family ultimately ended in tragedy. Not because of the earl's untimely death but because of those who died with him. According to a later set of Irish annals: 'A battle was given to the English by O'Byrne and O'Toole, in which the Earl of March was slain, and the English were slaughtered.'[150] Among the slain appears to have been Hugh's son John for on 5 August escheators in

The seal of Roger Mortimer, 4th earl of March, on a grant to William Boteller of land in County Meath on 23 November, 1397 (image reproduced courtesy of the National Library of Ireland, D.1364)

Herefordshire and Shropshire were ordered to take the lands which he held by right of his late wife Margery of Earl Roger into the king's hand.[151] John's death was a huge blow for Hugh and when he negotiated the marriage of John's daughter Elizabeth with Edward Cheyne of Beckford, one of the conditions of the marriage was that Edward was to carry Hugh's arms completely after his death, and that Hugh's arms and surname were to be maintained and sustained as if to a true male heir of Hugh.[152]

His personal loss was accompanied by a loss of status. When Richard II was overthrown by Henry of Bolingbroke in 1399 Cheyne was viewed with suspicion because of his Mortimer connections. Despite having been granted the constableship of Shrewsbury Castle by Edward III for life in 1365, the new king granted the life constableship to one of his esquires in November 1399.[153] It would not be until 22 May 1403 that Cheyne was able to secure a confirmation of his annuities from Ludlow granted by Earls Edmund and Roger.[154] Shortly afterwards, on 6

June, he was granted the custody of the castle and town of Ludlow with a fee of 40 marks.[155] That they were confirmed can probably be explained by both the continuing crisis of the revolt of Owain Glyn Dŵr and the influence of Henry 'Hotspur' Percy. Percy was the son of the earl of Northumberland, and was also husband to Elizabeth Mortimer, daughter of the 3rd earl of March. Though Percy was not among Hopton's witnesses, both Percy and Cheyne witnessed the 3rd earl's will in 1380 and must have known each other.[156] It was perhaps not a coincidence that a month later Percy launched his rebellion against Henry IV. Raising an army in Cheshire, he marched south into Shropshire towards Shrewsbury where the young Henry of Monmouth – the future Henry V – was in residence.[157] Cheyne's appointment may have been made with an eye to having a known Mortimer supporter holding Ludlow. All the same, the Percy revolt was over too soon – with Percy defeated and killed at the battle of Shrewsbury – to know with certainty what Cheyne would have done. He had lost much already in the service of the Mortimers; would he have been willing to lose more? He had much to reflect on in his final days and was dead by 5 August 1404 when one of Henry IV's esquires, Roger Acton, was granted the constableship and custody of Ludlow Castle.[158] Perhaps fittingly Cheyne was buried at Ludlow.[159]

The day of 13 December 1380 promised to be a solemn occasion for those within the Mortimer household. Many of Henry Hopton's witnesses would have known the late countess of March and perhaps regretted her early death. Perhaps none more so than her husband Edmund. It is conceivable that when the bishop of Cloyne hijacked this mass for sordid political manoeuvring some in the Mortimer household were genuinely angered by his words and willing to testify against his actions. Earlier, I commented on the uncertainty regarding why these particular 16 individuals testified; and it still remains a mystery if they were asked (or commanded) to testify or did some volunteer? What is less uncertain is the importance of the majority of these witnesses. When the earl of Ormond requested support from the Mortimer earl, the leading members of his household and affinity came forward. When Hopton asked Lovell or Bromwich to recount their memory of the day's events, he was calling upon men who held the ear of the earl and likely held great sway over him. Many of them represent that solid core of followers who surrounded Edmund and were regularly in his company. Many of the witnesses we have examined (and others there was not space to study here) originated from the English counties bordering the Welsh

167

Marches, emphasising the continual legacy of the Mortimer family's origin as marcher barons. That the Mortimers had grown beyond the March and border counties can be seen in such men as Lovell who was by no means atypical in this respect among the wider affinity.

Service under the Mortimer earls during this period was akin to 'imperial' service that spanned the Mortimer's transnational 'empire'. Ireland was one of the primary theatres of Mortimer activity during the late fourteenth century, with large volumes of men and money being funnelled into the defence of Mortimer claims on the island. This activity can be traced in the careers of large swathes of the Mortimer affinity – no better illustrated than the presence of our witnesses in the royal chapel of Dublin Castle to honour the memory of Countess Philippa. Their careers saw them active in different regions across the Mortimer transnational lordship which served to unify the estates as one functioning entity.

This contribution to a 'concerted prosopography of the Plantagenet Empire' also highlights a different aspect of the careers of Hopton's witnesses.[160] Few, if any, of these men had careers solely in the service of the Mortimer earls. Their lives led them down avenues where they exercised power amid different forums of authority. This can be seen in Lovell's guise as a royal courtier, Coneweye's time as a constable of a castle in North Wales, or in Cheyne and Hakeluyt's experiences as parliamentarians. Just as their careers across the Mortimer 'empire' fostered a shared understanding of the extent of the earl's lordship and played a unifying role, so too their other experiences fostered a greater awareness of the dominions of the Plantagenet kings of England. For all the variety and discordances in the late fourteenth-century Plantagenet world, the careers of Hopton's witnesses underscore the essential wider unity of that world.

As a final comment, this chapter bears the weight of being an exploratory work. It only offers a partial redress to the historiographical neglect of the later Mortimer affinity. Hopton's witnesses were all important household figures and so this work has provided a much-needed study into the household during the time of the 3rd earl. They were not however the totality of the Mortimer affinity. Power radiated from this centre to the regions of the lordship and was exercised by local agents in such arenas as the liberty of Meath and the honor of Clare. A more far-ranging study of the Mortimer affinity will need to adopt a regional approach, but it is a study that can rely on a much-neglected corpus of surviving manuscript sources.[161]

9

Professor Chris Given-Wilson

Family support: minority and the Mortimer inheritance, 1380–1425

B ETWEEN 1354 and 1425, the earldom of March was held by four members of the Mortimer family, none of whom lived beyond the age of 33: Roger (d.1360, aged 31); Edmund (d.1381, aged 29); Roger (d.1398, aged 24); and Edmund (d.1425, aged 33). Throughout these 71 years, therefore, there were around 33 years during which the earldom was held by an active adult earl and 38 years when it was held in wardship for a minor. And not just any minor, but a succession of boys with an emerging and plausible claim to be the next king of England.

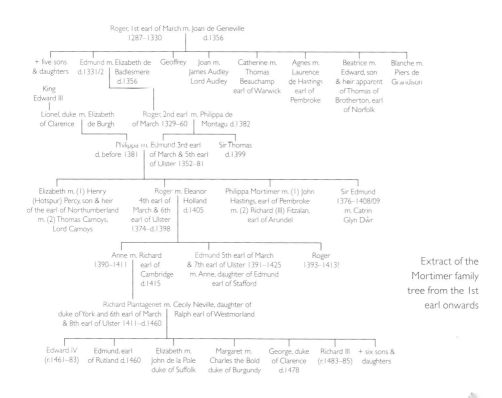

Extract of the Mortimer family tree from the 1st earl onwards

Even for the greatest inheritances, minorities were widely regarded as periods of jeopardy, when estates might be asset-stripped and heirs married off in the interest of those to whom the king happened to have granted the wardship of either the lands or the heir or both. Continuity of service and patronage was lost. Ambitious rivals circled for prey. The questions which this paper poses are, firstly, to what extent was the Mortimer inheritance preserved from predators during these successive periods of minority, and secondly, by what means was this done? It focuses principally on the relatives, by blood and by marriage, legitimate and illegitimate, of the successive Mortimer heirs, and their role in maintaining not just the inheritance itself but also the Mortimer claim to the throne. The history of the Mortimers between the 1360s and the 1420s is not so much the history of its earls as the history of a clan. Firstly, however, something needs to be said about the evolution of medieval English wardship.

For tenants-in-chief – those who held their land directly from the king, as almost all great nobles did – the wardship and marriage of an underage heir fell to the Crown, and between the twelfth and the early fourteenth centuries kings often exploited their rights ruthlessly: King John was notorious for it, but he certainly wasn't alone. Kings habitually sold their rights of wardship and marriage to the highest bidder, or granted them to favourites. Exploitation of the assets was common, and minors often had to pay large sums to regain their inheritances. When Roger, lord Mortimer, sometimes described as the 1st baron Mortimer, came of age in 1252, he paid £1,333 to Henry III to, in effect, buy back his lands. The wardship of Roger the 1st earl (d.1330), was granted to Edward II's notorious favourite Piers Gaveston, and according to the Wigmore chronicle he had to pay £1,666 to redeem it, which was considerably more than the annual value of his estates at the time.[1]

By the mid-fourteenth century, however, views on wardship were changing, and property law was becoming more complex. In October 1339, in return for granting a substantial tax for the war, the lords in parliament asked that:

> the wardship of lands which fall into the hands of the lord king because of the minority of the heirs might henceforth be delivered to the next blood relation of the said heirs, rendering to our lord the king the extent of the said lands.[2]

In the Good Parliament of 1376, the commons reminded Edward III of this 'statute' – although whether it had ever actually been passed as a statute is unclear – and repeated the request, this time specifying that wardships should be granted to 'the nearest kinsmen of the said heirs to whom the inheritance cannot descend'. The final clause was an important qualification, designed to prevent other potential or collateral heirs from taking advantage of a situation in which the underage heir apparent might not be able to mount an effective defence against a fraudulent guardian with much to gain. The king approved the petition, 'saving entirely to him his regality'.[3] This clearly left him some latitude.

If these petitions are an indication of the way views on wardship were evolving, there were also more direct methods by which landholders might seek to protect their heirs' inheritances, for it was also around this time that the enfeoffment to use became common among the nobility. The enfeoffment to use – or 'use' – was essentially a trust, whereby a landholder could grant his lands, or as many or few of them as he wished, to a group of feoffees, or trustees, usually reliable friends or councillors, with instructions as to what to do with them after his death. Since these grants were made in fee simple, the landholder was not therefore the legal holder of the lands at his death, so the Crown was deprived of its right to wardship of the lands (though not the marriage). His feoffees could continue to administer the estates during his heir's minority and grant them to the heir when he came of age. By such means, the noble estate could theoretically become an undying corporation.

Yet enfeoffments to use needed to be licensed, and much therefore depended on the attitude of the king. Before the mid-fourteenth century, kings were generally reluctant to licence great magnates to create them, but Edward III was less restrictive, and the Mortimers were among those who benefitted from his tolerance.[4] Thus when Earl Roger died in 1360, many of his lands were enfeoffed in a use which he had set up in 1359, and the king respected these arrangements, so that when his son Edmund came of age in 1373, his inheritance passed to him almost undisturbed.[5] Richard II, however, was less sympathetic to such arrangements, so that when this Edmund died in December 1381, leaving a seven-year-old son, Roger, as his heir, and having only created an enfeoffment to use for a minority of his estates, it was not long before the king drew up charters granting the custody of part of his estates to a group of his courtier-knights.[6] What followed demonstrated just how much attitudes had changed during the fourteenth century, because when he sent these charters into the chancery to be issued, his chancellor, lord Scrope of Bolton, refused to seal them, arguing that they contravened 'the custom of the realm'.[7] Richard was furious and dismissed Scrope from the chancellorship, but he was forced to give way, and the charters were never issued. Instead, the March inheritance was placed in the hands of a consortium of nobles, headed by the earls of Arundel, Northumberland and Warwick, all of whom were related by marriage to the young heir and who administered them largely through the late earl's own ministers. According to the Wigmore Chronicle, they not only maintained them impeccably but accumulated a surplus of £25,000 over ten years, all of which was duly handed over to Roger when he came of age in 1394. If the sum is unverifiable, the message is clear. Nobles such as Northumberland, Arundel and Warwick were well aware of what might happen to their own heirs and inheritances if Richard was allowed to turn the clock back in such fashion. No longer could a king expect to treat great inheritances like Christmas presents – or at least not a king who was still only 15 years old and still feeling his way towards kingship. Yet Richard II did still turn a profit from the March inheritance, for he sold Roger's marriage to his half-brother Thomas Holland, earl of Kent, for £4,000.[8] An enfeoffment to use could protect lands, but it could not protect the person of the heir from royal exploitation. In October 1388, Roger duly married Holland's daughter Eleanor.

The earls of Warwick became close allies of the Mortimers following the marriage of Catherine Mortimer to Thomas Beauchamp, 11th earl of Warwick. TOP: their magnificent burial effigy in St Mary's, Warwick (Photo: Andy Marshall © St Mary's Collegiate Church, Warwick). ABOVE: The arms of Thomas Beauchamp dimidiated with those of Catherine Mortimer, above their tomb in St Mary's, Warwick (© St Mary's Collegiate Church, Warwick)

In February 1394, when he was still 19 and technically underage, Roger was granted livery of his estates in order to fund his campaigns in Ireland. It was in Ireland, therefore, that he spent most of the next four years, acting, as his father had, as the king's lieutenant, and it was in Ireland, like his father, that he died on 27 July 1398, killed in battle against the Irish at Kellistown, aged just 24. There is nothing to indicate that he had enfeoffed to use any of his lands, and it is not impossible that Richard II had withheld permission for him to do so. The two men were never close, and there were rumours that the king and his magnate-courtiers not only coveted Roger's great estates but may even have been planning to arrest him.[9] At any rate, Richard lost no time in parcelling out Roger's lands after his death. His Anglo-Welsh properties were placed in the custody of the newly-created dukes of Aumale and Exeter, and the earl of Wiltshire, with power to replace all Roger's existing ministers; excess profits were to contribute to the expenses of the new queen, the seven-year-old Isabel of France. His Irish lands were given to the duke of Surrey to fund his lieutenancy of Ireland.[10] These arrangements lasted only a year, however, until the deposition of Richard II in 1399, an upheaval which also ushered in a new era in the history of the Mortimer family.

Three times in 40 years, then – in 1360, 1381 and 1398 – an earl of March had died leaving a seven-year-old-boy as his heir, yet on each occasion, despite some alarms, the great Mortimer inheritance was preserved more or less intact until the boy came of age. This was not fortuitous, nor was it primarily because of the new late medieval attitude to wardship, although that undoubtedly helped, especially during the 1381–94 minority. It was also due to the efforts of brothers, uncles, wives, sisters and kinsmen, by blood or marriage, of the heir. Inter-marriage was, of course, always important for the forging of connections between great magnate families – those to whom an heir might look for support in a crisis – and the marriages made by Mortimer women were crucial in this respect. From the 1350s to the 1370s, the great families with which the Mortimers had been most closely associated were the earls of Northampton, Warwick, and Arundel, partly as a result of marriage alliances and partly through comradeship in arms in the war against France.[11] By the early fifteenth century, the orbit within which they circulated had shifted. The Arundels were still there, but it was the Percy earls of Northumberland and the ducal house of York who were now their closest allies among the higher nobility. It was partly marriages and partly political circumstances which had caused this shift.

One connection in particular was to prove transformative: the marriage of Elizabeth, older sister of Roger (d.1398) to Henry Percy, 'Hotspur', the eldest son of the earl of Northumberland. This took place in 1379, when Hotspur was 15 and Elizabeth was eight, and established a link between the two families which would have an enduring impact on the politics of the time. It was Northumberland, Arundel and Warwick, all of whom were related by marriage to the Mortimers,[12] who were mainly responsible for overseeing the administration of the inheritance between 1383 and 1394, and as already noted they did so admirably. Not surprisingly, Roger nominated Northumberland as chief executor of his will, and

Statue at Alnwick castle of Henry Percy, 'Hotspur', who married Elizabeth Mortimer, the eldest sister of Roger Mortimer, 4th earl of March (Detail from original © Nick Goonan, Scenic Photos Ltd)

within six months of his usurpation Henry IV had granted Northumberland and Hotspur the wardship of the entire Mortimer inheritance.[13] Naturally they derived considerable profit from this, but they also ensured that the young Edmund's rights were upheld, even in relatively minor matters.[14] They certainly took their responsibilities seriously – in fact, as it turned out, rather too seriously. No one had done more than the Percys to ensure the success of Henry's revolution in 1399, and their rewards were enormous, but when they fell out with the new king and rebelled *en masse* against Henry IV in 1403, their avowed aim was to replace him with the young Edmund Mortimer. To justify their rebellion, they made several allegations: they claimed, for example, that when they joined Henry at Doncaster in July 1399, they had made him swear upon holy relics not to seize the throne 'if anyone could be found who was worthier of the Crown than he was' – surely a reference to the Mortimer claim. This, they said, Henry agreed to do.[15] They also claimed that, once Richard II had been captured and brought back to Westminster, and it became clear that Henry did indeed plan to claim the throne himself, they had protested, but since Henry had already persuaded them to send their retainers home, there was nothing they could do about it. Nevertheless, Hotspur claimed to have refused to attend Henry's coronation.

Depiction of Henry Bolingbroke claiming the Crown in Jean Creton's 'La Prinse et mort du roy Richart'
[Book of the Capture and Death of King Richard II] (© The British Library Board, Harley MS 1319 f.057r)

What underlay the Percys' claims in 1403 was, of course, their fundamental and devastating assertion that it was their ward, Edmund, not Henry IV, who had the better claim to be Richard II's successor and should therefore be king. That Edmund was the primogenitary heir to the childless Richard is undeniable; whether that made him the rightful heir is arguable, and to say so openly was a dangerous game. From the moment of Henry IV's usurpation in 1399, he knew very well that there were a fair number of people who thought that Edmund should have become king, but his reaction to such rumours was both sensible and consistent: he pretended not to have noticed. For Henry IV, 'Don't Mention the Mortimers' was elevated almost to the status of an article of faith, and it was certainly a test of loyalty, often with fatal consequences.

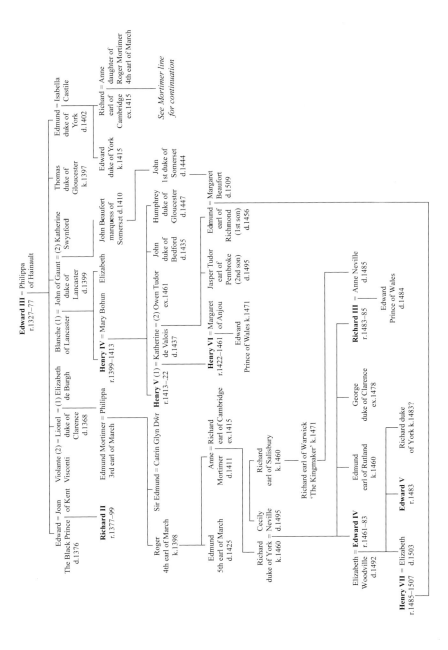

Edward III = Philippa
r.1327–77   of Hainault

Edward = Joan | Lionel (2) = (1) Elizabeth | John of Gaunt = (2) Katherine | Elizabeth | Thomas | Edmund = Isabella
The Black Prince | of Kent | Violante | duke of | de Burgh | Blanche (1) = | duke of | Swynford | | duke of | duke of | Castile
d.1376 | | Visconti | Clarence | | of Lancaster | Lancaster | | | Gloucester | York
| | | d.1368 | | | d.1399 | | | k.1397 | d.1402

Richard II | Edmund Mortimer = Philippa | **Henry IV** = Mary Bohun | John Beaufort | Edward | Richard = Anne
r.1377–99 | 3rd earl of March | r.1399–1413 | | marquess of | duke of York | earl of | daughter of
| | | | Somerset d.1410 | k.1415 | Cambridge | Roger Mortimer
| | | | | | ex.1415 | 4th earl of March

Roger | Sir Edmund = Catrin Glyn Dŵr | **Henry V** (1) = Katherine = (2) Owen Tudor | John | Humphrey | John | *See Mortimer line*
4th earl | | r.1413–22 | de Valois | ex.1461 | duke of | duke of | 1st duke of | *for continuation*
of March | | | d.1437 | | Bedford | Gloucester | Somerset
k.1398 | | | | | d.1435 | d.1447 | d.1444

Edmund | Anne = Richard | **Henry VI** = Margaret | Jasper Tudor | Edmund = Margaret
5th earl | Mortimer | earl of Cambridge | r.1422–1461 | of Anjou | earl of | earl of | Beaufort
of March | d.1411 | ex.1415 | k.1471 | | Pembroke | Richmond | d.1509
d.1425 | | | | | (2nd son) | (1st son)
| | | Edward | | d.1495 | d.1456
| | | Prince of Wales k.1471

Richard | Cecily | Richard | | George
duke of York = Neville | earl of Salisbury | | duke of Clarence
d.1460 | d.1495 | k.1460 | | ex.1478

| | Richard earl of Warwick | Edmund = Anne Neville
| | 'The Kingmaker' k.1471 | Richard III | d.1485
| | | r.1483–85

Elizabeth = **Edward IV** | Edmund | Richard duke | Edward
Woodville | r.1461–83 | earl of Rutland | of York k.1483? | Prince of Wales
d.1492 | | k.1460 | | d.1484

Henry VII = Elizabeth | **Edward V**
r.1485–1507 | d.1503 | r.1483

Descendants of Edward III, showing the Mortimer/York descent from his second surviving son, Lionel

176

As to the Percys' retrospective claims about their conduct in 1399, these are almost certainly disingenuous. Between 1399 and 1402 they had no compunction about accepting a cascade of favours from Henry. By the winter of 1402–3, however, Henry had come to realize the folly of placing so much power in Percy hands and began to withdraw his favour. This, allied to specific policy disagreements, is what led them to rebel in July 1403, whereupon they decided to reshape the history of their role in Henry's usurpation. Edmund was still only 11, and if they could put him on the throne instead of Henry IV, their power would be almost unchallengeable. In fact, as is well known, it could not have ended worse for them. Hotspur was killed at the battle of Shrewsbury (21 July 1403), his uncle Thomas was captured and executed, and Northumberland's power was broken. Although he rebelled again in May 1405, once again declaring that Edmund should be king, his revolt was brutally suppressed and he was driven into exile.

By this time, however, the House of York had stepped in – a development which requires explanation. Edmund of Langley, the first duke of York who died in 1402, is said to have had three children. Firstly, Edward (b.1373), his eldest son and heir, a slippery character much favoured by Richard II in his later years, whose loyalty to the Lancastrian regime was often questioned. Secondly, a daughter, Constance (b.1375); she married Thomas Despenser, another of Richard II's favourites, who lost his life trying to restore Richard to the throne in January 1400. Thirdly, Richard of Conisburgh, who was not born until 1385 and was probably not Edmund's son but the product of a liaison between his wife, Duchess Isabella, and John Holland, the king's half-brother.[16]

Richard of Conisburgh has been described as weak and foolish, and his short life is really only known for two things. The first is his marriage to Anne Mortimer, the sister of Edmund (d.1425) – a momentous marriage indeed, for it produced Richard duke of York, progenitor of the Yorkist dynasty, and established the link between the houses of March and York which would ultimately, in 1461, justify the Yorkist usurpation of the throne. Yet the marriage between Richard of Conisburgh and Anne Mortimer did not take place until 1408, whereas at least some members of the House of York were actively supporting the Mortimer claim to the throne by 1405 at the latest. By this time, Edmund Mortimer was 13 and his younger brother – another Roger – was 11. In later times, under Richard III or the Tudors, the boys might well have been quietly done away with in the Tower, but Henry IV chose to treat them, if not generously, at least humanely. As teenagers, they were brought up in the royal household along with the king's own younger children, who were almost exactly the same age, under the surveillance of his most trusted retainers – men such as Sir Hugh Waterton and Sir John Pelham. In effect, they were state prisoners, usually at either Windsor or Berkhamstead, with around £300 a year allocated for their maintenance.[17]

Yet Windsor was no more secure as a royal residence 600 years ago than it appears to be now, and in February 1405 a sympathetic locksmith at the castle was persuaded to make a set of duplicate keys and the two boys were smuggled out. The plan was to take them to Wales, but they only got as far as Cheltenham before being recaptured. The locksmith, having metaphorically lost his head, now literally did so, but Henry IV evidently regarded Edmund and Roger as too young to be culpable. However, they were watched more closely from then on, and moved about more frequently, to foil any further plots.

What is interesting about this episode for present purposes is that the person behind their kidnap in 1405 was Constance of York, duke Edmund's daughter. Her motivation is unclear. Was she seeking revenge for her husband's death five years earlier? Were she and her brothers picking up the baton forfeited by the Percys and plotting to establish a dynasty which might be more sympathetic to their ambitions? When she was tried before the king's council, she not only accused her elder brother, Edward, of instigating the plot, but also testified that, a few weeks earlier, Edward had been planning to climb over the wall of Eltham Palace while Henry IV was celebrating Christmas there and assassinate him in his sleep. This seems fanciful, but there can be no doubt that others were implicated to varying degrees and they may well have included Edward. In the event, Henry IV locked both Edward and Constance away for several months but then released them. They were lucky. Henry did not believe in executing women, and he was prepared to take his cousin Edward's word on several occasions, despite some of his supporters advising him not to. In the end, though, Henry's clemency was repaid: Edward lived until 1415 and died at Agincourt, fighting for Henry V.

The second thing that Richard of Conisburgh is famous for is his participation in the so-called 'Southampton Plot' of July 1415 – indeed it has been claimed that he, rather than his fellow conspirators, Henry lord Scrope and Sir Thomas Grey, was probably its principal promoter. The aim of the plotters was to kill Henry V and put Edmund Mortimer on the throne, but it was a fiasco. Edmund himself, whom they had tried to involve, declined the chimerical offer of a crown on his head in favour of keeping it attached to his neck, unmasked

Portchester
Castle
where the
'Southampton
Plot' was
revealed to
Henry V
by Edmund
Mortimer, 5th
earl of March
(© Andy King)

the plotters to the king, and Henry had no hesitation in executing all three of them. What is more interesting is the question of why Richard of Conisburgh was prepared to risk (and lose) his life by trying to put Edmund on the throne. That his marriage was a significant factor is self-evident – after all, Edmund was his brother-in-law.[18] He also felt hard done by, not without reason. Having had good expectations of promotion – or at least some land – under Richard II, he was treated shabbily both by his own family (his nominal father, the first duke of York, barely acknowledged him, and his siblings did little for him) and, more significantly, by the Lancastrian regime. Even in 1414, when Henry V finally created him earl of Cambridge, he was not granted any land to maintain his new dignity.

Yet the bond that may well have induced Richard to align himself with the Mortimer cause had been established more than a decade earlier, when he was 19 and involved in the fighting in the Welsh Marches against Owain Glyn Dŵr and his followers. Of particular significance, it has been argued, was the comradeship-in-arms that he formed at that time with Edward Charlton, lord of Powys (d.1421). Charlton was one of the leading Marcher lords and, since 1399, the husband of Earl Roger Mortimer's widow, Eleanor.[19] How influential this friendship was in drawing Richard into the Mortimer orbit is a matter of conjecture. Yet it is not easy otherwise to explain how a landless, untitled, almost certainly illegitimate and unquestionably resentful cadet of a family widely suspected of plotting against the Crown, managed in 1408 to secure the hand of Eleanor's daughter Anne, a young woman who might one day become the sister of the king of England. It was, at any rate, a clandestine marriage – perhaps a love match – but if so, it was star-crossed, because in 1411, after just three years, Anne died, though not before giving birth to a daughter, Isabel, and a son, Richard, the future duke of York.

Whether all this adequately explains the evident desire of Edward, Constance and Richard to overthrow the Lancastrian dynasty in favour of the Mortimers is a matter of judgement. It is equally possible that Edward, a well-practiced schemer and an unpopular character who had once been a great favourite of Richard II's, may have harboured hopes of taking the throne for himself, for it was alleged in the parliament of 1399 that Richard II had declared that he would like Edward to succeed him.[20] He was, after all, like Henry IV, Richard's first cousin. In other words, it's quite likely that he was using the Mortimer claim for his own ends. That was what seemed to happen to young Edmund – he became a pawn in the intrigues of others who had a grudge against the Lancastrians.[21] Yet these intrigues did at least mean that his claims were not forgotten.

Constance is one example of a woman who played a conspicuous part in the Mortimer story. Eleanor, Roger's widow, is another – the mother of the young Edmund, his brother Roger, Anne and another daughter, also called Eleanor. The date of her remarriage to Edward Charlton is not certain, but it was certainly before June 1399, because Adam Usk, that busybody and Mortimer protégé, tells us that in late July 1399, when Edward and Eleanor were at their castle of Usk and heard that Henry Bolingbroke had invaded England, they initially planned to oppose him. This is what the intrepid chronicler says:

> Also there [at Bristol, on 29–30 July 1399] was the compiler of this present work, and it was through his influence that peace was made between Duke Henry and the lordship of Usk, his birthplace, which the duke had intended to ravage on account of the resistance which the lady of that place, the king's niece, had planned there. This compiler also arranged for Sir Edward Charlton, who was then that lady's husband, to be retained by the duke; and he got all the people of Usk, who had been brought together at Monsturri in order to oppose the duke, to go back to their homes, to their great relief.[22]

Usk Castle, part of the de Burgh inheritance that came to the Mortimers, was one of the dower properties held by Eleanor, the widow of Roger, the 4th earl. It was also the birthplace of the chronicler and Mortimer protégé, Adam Usk (© Paul R. Davis)

What Usk does not say, unfortunately, is on whose behalf Edward and Eleanor were planning to resist Henry. The conflict of loyalties faced by Eleanor in 1399 was acute. As the daughter of Thomas Holland, Richard II's half-brother, she was indeed Richard II's niece; yet as Earl Roger's widow, she is unlikely to have had benevolent feelings towards the king. On the other hand, was she prepared to see her sons' rights be airbrushed out of history by the usurpation of a Lancastrian king, or would she stand up for them? In other words, were she and Charlton planning to resist Henry in order to keep Richard on the throne, or on behalf of the seven-year-old Edmund Mortimer? Since Richard had been issuing bare-ly-veiled threats against the House of Mortimer for the past two years, the latter seems more likely. And if Eleanor was indeed trying to stand up for her sons, it is the only strictly contemporary piece of evidence we have for anyone trying to do anything to uphold their rights in 1399 – and not just anyone, of course, but good old Mum.

By this time, however, the Lancastrian juggernaut was virtually unstoppable, and once Henry had made himself king, and especially once Eleanor's father, Thomas Holland, had been killed trying to restore Richard II to the throne in January 1400, she must have realised the futility of further resistance. Instead, she lived discreetly with her new husband, enjoying her substantial dower and the company of her two daughters, until October 1405, when she died, appar-ently in childbirth.[23]

The long minorities of successive earls did not merely magnify the significance of the marriages of the Mortimer women, they also placed great responsibilities on those to whom it fell by default to assume the leadership of the House of March. That meant not just relations by marriage, but also younger sons, legitimate or otherwise – and three in particular: Sir Thomas, Sir Edmund and Sir John.

Thomas Mortimer was the illegitimate son of Roger, the 2nd earl (d.1360).[24] Although his illegitimacy barred him from the inheritance, in almost every other respect he was recognised as a full member of the family. For example, the consortium of earls to whom the wardship of the estates was granted in 1383 appointed him as head of the council entrusted with the administration of the lands – and, as noted above, he appears to have performed his duties exceptionally well. He also acted as marshal of the young Earl Roger's household in the 1380s, as a result of which he established many contacts with the earl of Arundel.[25] It was probably through these contacts with Arundel and his followers that in 1387 Sir Thomas, fearing that the inheritance was under threat, joined the duke of Gloucester and the earls of Arundel and Warwick in opposition to Richard II. He was one of the commanders who routed the royalist army at the battle of Radcot Bridge in December 1387. For this he incurred the undying enmity of the king, and ten years later, when Richard revenged himself on his enemies, Thomas was appealed of treason, along with Gloucester, Arundel and Warwick, and ordered to appear for trial in Parliament within three months. Fortunately for him he was in Ireland at the time, with his nephew Earl Roger, so the king had to content himself with sending a mandate to Roger to arrest Thomas and send him to Westminster. Had he done so, Thomas would undoubtedly have been executed for treason. As for the earl, this was clearly a calculated test of his loyalty: 'Perhaps the earl of March will be unable to capture him,' Richard remarked slyly to one of his cronies. 'I shall wait, therefore, until I hear what has been accomplished.'[26] Earl Roger did his best to protect his uncle, and Thomas made his escape to Scotland, where he was hunted down and killed in the spring of 1399. He had certainly done his bit to defend the Mortimer inheritance, and deserves to be better-known.

After the upheavals of 1398–99, things became complicated. Earl Roger was dead, Sir Thomas was dead, Henry IV had usurped the throne and Edmund was only eight. It was time for another uncle to step forward, and this time it was Roger's legitimate younger brother, Sir Edmund Mortimer. Sir Edmund had been treated generously by his elder brother, and held several sizeable Marcher lordships, including Narberth and St Clears. He now became the foremost defender of the Mortimer family interest. Adam Usk, that lifelong Mortimer protégé, calls him *dominus meus* – my lord.[27] However, it was the Percys to whom the wardship of the great majority of the lands had been entrusted. Fortunately, Sir Edmund seems to have got on well with the Percys, and especially with Hotspur. Like them, he initially supported Henry IV, or at least gave the impression of doing so. When Glyn Dŵr's revolt broke out in 1400, he and Hotspur were often to be found together campaigning against the Welsh.

It has been suggested that this is the effigy of Sir Edmund Mortimer in St Nicholas' Church, Montgomery, though recent work has cast doubt on this
(© Philip Hume)

Like the Percys, however – and partly, no doubt, because of his friendship with Hotspur – he soon began to turn against Henry. Cause and effect are difficult to disentangle at this point, but the sequence of events was as follows. In June 1402, Glyn Dŵr led a raid across the border in central Wales. Edmund raised a local force to oppose him, but the result was not only a Welsh victory but also the capture of Edmund, who was led away by Glyn Dŵr to Snowdon.[28] The expectation was that he would be ransomed, and this is what Hotspur and his father told the king he ought to do. But Henry IV was suspicious: rumours began to circulate that Edmund had colluded in his own capture, and Henry believed them. He not only refused to ransom Edmund, but began seizing his lands and declaring him to be disloyal. Whether the king was correct, or whether it was Henry's distrust that turned Edmund against him, by November matters had come to a head. Edmund married Catrin, Glyn Dŵr's daughter, and wrote to his supporters encouraging them to rebel against Henry IV. If Richard II was still alive, he declared, he was the rightful king; if not, then the young earl of March should be king.

Sir Edmund remained allied to Glyn Dŵr for the rest of his life. He supported the Percy rebellion in 1403, and three years later, acting presumably on behalf of his nephew, put his name to the celebrated 'Tripartite Indenture', whereby he, Glyn Dŵr and the earl of Northumberland vowed to dethrone the Lancastrian

Harlech Castle where Sir Edmund Mortimer died defending it for Owain Glyn Dŵr (© Paul R. Davis)

usurper and divide England and Wales between them. By this time, however, the Welsh revolt was becoming a lost cause, and by 1409, when Harlech Castle was recaptured by the English, it was effectively over. Sir Edmund died during the siege of Harlech, possibly of starvation. His wife Catrin and their children were captured and consigned to the Tower of London, where they also died, apparently of the plague.

Despite his miserable fate and personal failure, Edmund's defiance of Henry iv had important consequences. The Mortimer name certainly added legitimacy to Glyn Dŵr's revolt; it also ensured that the Mortimer claim to the English throne continued to be remembered. More important still was Sir Edmund's legacy, which was to foster a sense of common purpose between the Mortimer family and the people of Wales. It's easy to forget that, to the native Welsh, the Mortimers had started out as conquerors in the name of the English Crown, and to some extent they were still the enemy from without who had become the enemy within. This is not to say that they lacked support among the native Welsh, many of whom (including the young Owain Glyn Dŵr) found gainful employment with Marcher lords. Nor did they lack Welsh ancestry, for in the early thirteenth century Ralph Mortimer had married Gwladus Ddu, the daughter of Llywelyn the Great, which gave the Mortimers not just a princely Welsh bloodline but also a historic claim to represent the Welsh people. On the other hand, it was still with the English Crown and Marcher interests that they habitually sided – until, that is, Sir Edmund threw in his lot with Glyn Dŵr. Edmund continued to be remembered by the Welsh as a hero: songs about his prowess were sung at feasts, and stories circulated of the lurid portents that accompanied his birth.[29] Looking further ahead, to the Wars of the Roses, when Lancastrian territorial dominance and Tudor ancestry should have ensured Wales's loyalty, memories of Sir Edmund meant that the Yorkists could point to their own Welsh ancestry and attachment to the Welsh cause, an important factor in balancing out Welsh allegiance to Lancastrian and Tudor kings.

Exactly who Sir John Mortimer was has always been something of a puzzle, now happily resolved by Ian Mortimer, who has shown that he was a distant cousin of the earls descended from the Mortimers of Chirk. But although he claimed kinship with the Mortimers he was far too distantly related to be treated with the same generosity as Sir Thomas had been.[30] He thus had to make his own way, which he did, mainly as a soldier, until 1418, when he was imprisoned for making seditious remarks about King Henry v. Most of the remaining six years of his life were spent in the Tower. According to his accusers, he had alleged that Henry v had no right to the throne, that his wars against France were doomed and that the earl of March should be king. His crime thus falls under the general heading of 'treason by words', a grey area at this time. It was rendered even more nebulous in this case since the principal evidence for the prosecution came in the form of a conversation reported by Mortimer's jailer in the Tower, William King, who was under considerable pressure to provide damning evidence, not least because he had allowed Sir John to escape and make his way to Wales in 1422, although he was quickly recaptured. According to William King:

> [Sir John Mortimer] said the earl of March was a dawe [idiot], yet the greatest, noblest and worthiest in blood in this land … that if truth were known, he should be king, and he [Sir John] should be his heir, but if the earl of March would not take up the rule of the realm and the Crown, he would do so, because he was the next heir.[31]

Sir John was finally executed in 1424, a controversial decision even at the time, for little was proved against him, and parliament had to pass a retrospective Act to secure his conviction. The real significance of his story is to demonstrate the continuing danger to the Lancastrian dynasty from relatives and supporters of the Mortimers and the continuing insecurity of the Lancastrians in the face of that threat.[32] A quarter of a century after Sir John's death, the rebel Jack Cade adopted the pseudonym 'John Mortimer' as his *nom de guerre* when he led an insurrection against the government of Henry VI.

Less than a year after Sir John's death, in January 1425, Earl Edmund, for whose right to be king of England so many people had risked and lost their lives during the past quarter of a century, also died, like his father, and like his grandfather, in Ireland, apparently of the plague. He was 33 years old and, since he was childless and his younger brother Roger had died in about 1413, he was the last earl of March of the line of Mortimer of Wigmore. Emasculated by his ancestry, he had lived a cautious and unremarkable life. Despite his royal blood, he was never openly acknowledged as a member of the royal family. His coming of age was delayed beyond his 21st birthday – Henry IV said he had forgotten how old Edmund was! – and he was never granted the sort of offices, titles, honours or responsibilities (such as membership of the Order of the Garter, or a dukedom) to which his birth entitled him.[33] In February 1415, when Edmund married Anne, the daughter of the earl of Stafford, without royal permission, Henry V imposed a fine of £6,666 on him – the largest fine for such an offence since the notorious amercements of King John's reign 200 years earlier. It was probably intended to destroy Edmund's ability to attract supporters to his cause, for £6,666 amounted to twice his annual income. What is more, he actually had to pay it, which he did by mortgaging 45 manors in England and some of his Welsh lordships.[34] Yet he served Henry V faithfully, holding a number of respectable if not sufficiently pre-eminent military commands, and managed to maintain a low profile. He made no move, either in 1413 when Henry IV died, or in 1422 when Henry V died, to promote his own claim to the throne. Yet still suspicions lingered, and it may be that the decision to send him to Ireland at the beginning of Henry VI's reign was an attempt to get him out of the way. If so, it was unexpectedly successful. Ireland always seemed to be a graveyard for the Mortimer earls of March.

OPPOSITE: A depiction of Henry V in Hoccleve's *Regement of Princes*. The author, Hoccleve, is presenting a copy to the king (© The British Library Board, Royal MS 17 D VI f.040r)

ye and noble prince excellent
My lord the prince, my lord gratious
I humble seruaunt and obedient
vnto your estate hye and glorious
Of whiche I am full tendir and full ielous
me recomaunde vnto your worthynesse
With hert entier and spirite of mekenesse

The temptation for Edmund to raise a rebellion to press his claims must have been enormous – and so, apparently was the pressure. In part, this was a matter of honour: by the standards of the time, it was almost a moral imperative for individuals as much as for nations not to relinquish their claims without a fight. Friends, relatives and spiritual confidants urged him to rebel. When he didn't, they called him a coward, or accused him of shaming his lineage. It is easy enough for modern historians to sneer at what they characterise as spinelessness or vacillation,[35] but if Edmund had decided to take a chance, he would almost certainly have lost his head, and his family would have lost everything – estates, titles, claims. Instead, he chose to remain – for a young man of such great birth – almost unnaturally inconspicuous, which meant that it was others who often seemed to take the leading role in keeping the Mortimer family's claims alive: uncles, brothers-in-law, wives, widows. And, despite all the alarms, minorities and insinuations of the previous 50 years or so, these descended intact to his 13-year-old nephew Richard of York, and we know what, in the fullness of time, he did with them.

Whether this would have happened without the support of uncles, wives, widows, brothers-in-law and siblings (both legitimate and illegitimate) is questionable. In many ways, the story of the Mortimers between 1380 and 1425 is not so much the history of its earls as the history of a clan. In some cases, the alliances made at this time were ephemeral – for example, with the Percys, who were consistently Lancastrian during the Wars of the Roses. In other cases, however, the results of their efforts were of lasting significance. The Welsh connection certainly became more important, and the alliance with the House of York was, of course, pivotal. Their efforts also meant that the element of continuity which was so vital for a family constantly jeopardized by minorities was maintained. Collectively, the Mortimer clan and its allies in the years between 1380 and 1425 had refused to allow the rights inherent in the name of Mortimer simply to fade away, despite the attempts made by Henry IV and Henry V to airbrush it out of history.

10

Dr Ian Mortimer

Who was Sir John Mortimer?

IN a revealing book chapter published in 1995, Edward Powell drew historians' attention to the extraordinary circumstances of the death of Sir John Mortimer of Bishop's Hatfield, Hertfordshire, who was executed in late February 1424.[1] In short, this man was arrested on suspicion of treason in October 1418 and subsequently spent most of the rest of his life in prison, on Henry v's personal instructions. This was directly in contravention of clauses 39 and 40 of Magna Carta, which read:

> [39:] No free man is to be arrested, or imprisoned, or disseised, or outlawed, or exiled, or in any other way ruined, nor will we go against him or send against him, except by the lawful judgment of his peers or by the law of the land. [40:] We will not sell, or deny, or delay right or justice to anyone.[2]

On 14 February 1424, Mortimer's gaoler at the Tower of London, William King, gave evidence to Parliament that Sir John had uttered some seditious words to him about 15 days earlier. This included a statement to the effect that if Sir John could escape and reach Wales, he would raise an army there with the earl of March, whose heir he was, and either set the earl on the throne or, if the earl would not serve, take the throne himself. Parliament was then persuaded to change the law temporarily, so that a suspected traitor who escaped from gaol should be automatically deemed guilty of treason, regardless of whether he was guilty of the original offence. It appears that William King was then instructed to help Sir John escape, which he did on 23 February. Sir John was recaptured, injured, in Tower Lane, immediately outside the castle.[3] Two days later he was led before the mayor of London and a jury to enquire further into the truth of the matter and the following day his case was heard in Parliament. He was found guilty of breaking the newly-created law

Sir John Mortimer was arrested and imprisoned in contravention of clauses 39 and 40 of Magna Carta
(Salisbury Cathedral © Ash Mills)

The Tower of London, from which Sir John Mortimer escaped twice: in 1422 and 1424
(photograph © Joseph Gilbey, Unsplash)

and sentenced to be drawn, hanged, beheaded and quartered. He was probably executed the same day. The law was then allowed to lapse. Thus Sir John Mortimer – a man with almost no wealth, whose supposed crime was never heard in court – was imprisoned illegally by Henry v and subsequently judicially murdered by the government of the infant Henry vi.

Powell was principally interested in the event as a legal matter, illustrating developments in the law of treason and the implications for the security – or, rather, the vulnerability – of the Lancastrian dynasty. Thus he did not go into the question of who Sir John was in any depth. Nor did Sarah Stockdale in her PhD on treason in the fifteenth-century royal family.[4] The reason is that Sir John is a very shadowy character. His parentage is unknown and he is otherwise of little historical consequence. He only appears in the spotlight due to his long imprisonment, his trials and his execution. However, his identity is important. It makes a great deal of difference to our understanding of the Lancastrian dynasty's security or vulnerability whether he was a charlatan, a bastard son of one of the Mortimers of Wigmore, a member of a different Mortimer family or a legitimate heir to the earl of March and a real threat. That he was no mere impostor is indicated by his status as a knight and the extraordinary measures the government took to kill him, not to mention the large amounts spent on his incarceration. But otherwise, the question remains open. Was Parliament spurred into action by a false understanding of his lineage, simply going on the strength of his name? Was this man a bastard, as Powell presumed? Or was he truly the earl of March's heir?

It is impossible to prove how Sir John was related to the Mortimers of Wigmore. No document of the types usually employed to establish family connections in the magnate class mentions him. Rather this chapter builds on Powell's work in six ways. First, it tackles the all-important task of distinguishing between Sir John and his namesakes, of whom there were several. Next, it highlights links between Sir John and the Mortimers of Wigmore. Third, it discusses his influential supporters. Fourth, it narrows down the possibilities as to how Sir John might have been connected to the Mortimers of Wigmore. Fifth, it shows how a number of assumptions have distorted the picture of his death. Finally, it points to the political context of the Mortimer claim to the throne to suggest that the reasons he was killed were very different from those supposed by historians to date.

Powell was unaware of the number of John Mortimers there were in the early fifteenth century. Several of these were described as 'esquire', which makes the task of distinguishing between them harder. In addition to our man, there was Sir John Mortimer (1391–1415) of Edvin Loach, Martley and Tedstone Wafer, who, according to his inquisition *post mortem*, was slain on the battlefield at Agincourt.[5] Then there was the John Mortimer esquire who served as a man-at-arms in the navy of Richard Fitzalan, earl of Arundel, in 1387 and 1388.[6] According to Powell, one John Mortimer esquire was captured by the French on his way back from the duchy of Aquitaine in 1401 and held there until he was ransomed in 1406, Henry IV paying £20 of his ransom and describing him as 'our esquire'. Powell assumes that he was the same man as the John Mortimer who served in the Calais garrison under John Beaufort, earl of Somerset, in 1407 and returned to England in 1414.[7] But in July 1410, one John Mortimer was given £10 to pay to Sir Thomas Beaufort, admiral, towards his men's wages, and in November 1413 he or another man of the same name had letters of protection on his departure for France.[8] There were at least three John Mortimers on the Agincourt campaign: one was an archer with the duke of York.[9] Another travelled to Agincourt as a knight in the company of Thomas Fitzalan, earl of Arundel. The third, not knighted, went on that same expedition with Sir John Baskerville.[10] In 1417 a man-at-arms called John Mortimer served in France with Sir Richard Arundel.[11] Our Sir John Mortimer, meanwhile, was commissioned to guard the south coast in February 1417 and so was probably a different individual.

Civilian records list at least six John Mortimers flourishing in the first quarter of the fifteenth century. Besides Sir John himself, there was John Mortimer of Castle Bromwich, who was pardoned in 1405 by Henry IV for assisting in a murder.[12] There was also John Mortimer, the illegitimate son of Roger Mortimer (d.1402) of Edvin Loach, who held a farm from his father in Herefordshire.[13] One John Mortimer of Warminster was commissioned to collect the tenth and the fifteenth for the county of Wiltshire in 1416.[14] Fifth, there was John Mortimer of Kent, who in 1412 held lands in Cliffe, Kent, which had been held by his Mortimer forebears in that county since the thirteenth century.[15] Sixth, there was the John Mortimer of Northamptonshire, who held half a fee in Ufford from the dowager countess of Kent in 1411.[16] The problem is that the military references could be connected with any of the above men. Alternatively, they might relate to one of the John Mortimers who lived beyond 1424. These include: the John Mortimer esquire who shared a loan with Reginald Braybrook from 1405 until the 1430s; the John Mortimer esquire who witnessed the will of the duke of Bedford in 1435; the John Mortimer of Berkshire, who in 1426 was a juror giving information at the inquisition *post mortem* of John, earl of Huntingdon; and John Mortimer esquire, MP (d.1446), who was lord of the manor of Grendon, Northants, and Eakley in Stoke Goldington, Bucks. We cannot assume that, just because Sir John Mortimer had a military role, all references to John Mortimer esquire serving in France relate to him.

St Etheldreda's Church, which dates from the thirteenth century, is the parish church of Bishop's Hatfield where Sir John Mortimer owned property (© Pete Seaward)

We have three ways of identifying references to the judicially murdered man. One is through mention of his time in gaol and his trials. Another is the identity of his wife, Eleanor Rossall or Russell, whose petition to the council about her husband's incarceration survives. The third is his ownership of property in Bishop's Hatfield, Hertfordshire, which is partly described in his inquisition *post mortem*. Using records that mention one or more of these elements we can start to rebuild his core career with confidence. It may well be that other records also relate to him, especially before 1415. However, in a quest to identify Sir John with certainty, we cannot entertain sources that are open to doubt.

The earliest definite references to him are found in connection with his wife, Eleanor Rossall. She was the elder of the two daughters of Sir Walter Rossall and his wife Beatrice (who had previously been married to Sir Thomas Cobham). The two girls became their parents' coheiresses, their elder brother, John Rossall, having been killed at the battle of Shrewsbury in 1403 fighting against the Lancastrians. Eleanor was probably born in 1377 as she is described as being aged 26 (and her sister 22) in her brother's inquisition *post mortem*, dated 31 December 1403.[17] She was at that time the widow of Nicholas Dagworth (d.1402) of Blickling in Norfolk, having married him in 1395 but having borne him no children. Richard II had granted her a pension of £40 per year and Henry IV confirmed this, giving her also the Nottinghamshire manors of Mansfield and Linby, up to the value of 40 marks a year, for life.[18] In 1404 she petitioned the king for the recovery of her rights in the manors of Rossall, Yagdon and Sleap (all in Shropshire).[19] In May 1406 she received from her mother Beatrice and her mother's husband, Sir John Prendergast, her mother's interest in Hunmanby in Yorkshire.[20] She was still described as a widow in April 1407 when she sold part of the manor of Blickling which she had previously been assigned in dower.[21]

Eleanor was thus 32 years of age in 1409, which is probably when she married John Mortimer esquire.[22] He was not described as a knight at the time. Nor was he a knight in a fine dated 3 November 1413, by which three trustees granted 'John Mortimer esquire' and Eleanor a moiety of the manor of Hunmanby in the county of York and a moiety of the manors of Rossall, Yagdon and Sleap in the county of Shropshire, to be inherited by their heirs.[23] On 24 April 1415 the Issue Rolls of the Exchequer record a payment of £60 to Eleanor, formerly the wife of Sir Nicholas Dagworth to whom King Richard had granted £40 per year, which was handed to John Mortimer, her husband. Still he was not described as a knight. However, on 12 May 1416, as Sir John Mortimer, he and Eleanor made an agreement with Eleanor's sister, Alice, and her husband, Philip Englefield esquire, to divide the Rossall inheritance. Sir John and Eleanor would have the Yorkshire manor of Hunmanby and Philip and Alice would have the Shropshire manor of Rossall.[24] This shows Sir John was knighted between 24 April 1415 and 12 May 1416.

We can narrow this date range further. As mentioned above, three men called John Mortimer served on the Agincourt campaign: one man-at-arms who was already knighted, another man-at-arms who travelled in the company of Sir John Baskerville, and an archer, who presumably would have been too low in status for knighthood.[25] The man who travelled in the company of Sir John Baskerville was knighted on the campaign, at Pont-Rémy in mid-October 1415.[26] This was Sir John Mortimer of Edvin Loach and Kyre Wyard, who was killed at Agincourt on 25 October.[27] This may be deduced from Sir Thomas Camoys's settlement, made at his manor of Trotton on 22 July 1415, before setting out on the campaign. One of Sir Thomas's trustees was Sir John Mortimer. As this man was a knight before the campaign and was still alive when Sir Thomas Camoys died in 1421 (as made clear in Sir Thomas's inquisition *post mortem*), he cannot have been the John Mortimer knighted at Pont-Rémy in October 1415 or the Sir John Mortimer killed at Agincourt later that month.[28] It follows that Sir Thomas Camoys's trustee was the only other Sir John Mortimer recorded at this time – the subject of our present enquiry. Sir John was thus knighted between 24 April and 22 July 1415. It also follows that the three men who received letters of protection to accompany Sir John Mortimer on the campaign were under the command of our Sir John. These were William Spicer of Orford, Suffolk; John Strange, citizen and barber of London; and Thomas atte Wood of Canterbury, yeoman.[29]

In February 1417, as John Mortimer of Bishop's Hatfield, our man was commissioned to defend the coast with 150 men and 300 archers for six months. The overall commander was Sir Thomas Carew. Sir Thomas Camoys and Sir John Pelham were ordered to inspect Sir John's men at Winchelsea.[30] But within a year, things had started to go wrong. In February 1418 he was required to be loyal to the king on penalty of payment of £1,000. At the same time, several men were made to stand surety for his good behaviour, binding themselves to pay £100 or, in the case of Sir Thomas Hoo of Bedfordshire, £200.[31] Things went from bad to worse. It was alleged that in the summer of 1418 Sir John uttered some ill-advised comments at St Albans – to the effect that he wished the king were as poor as he was, and that if he were with the king of France

Kenilworth Castle where Sir John Mortimer was first imprisoned in 1418 (© Paul R. Davis)

and had 500 men at his disposal, he would drive Henry out of Normandy.[32] He was arrested and locked up initially in Kenilworth Castle. From there he was brought south in December on the orders of the duke of Bedford (the keeper of the realm in the king's absence) to be imprisoned in the Tower of London.[33] Meanwhile, on 22 November 1418, an inquisition *post mortem* was initiated into the extent of his estates in Herefordshire and the Welsh Marches.[34] Strikingly the writ refers to him as dead. The jurors met and deliberated at Bromyard on 27 April 1419, whereupon they reported that Sir John Mortimer held no lands in Herefordshire.

Sir John Mortimer was not charged with any crime. He was left to languish in the Tower. In February 1420 he was forced to find more sureties that he would be 'a true prisoner to the king within the Tower of London and not depart hence without his special licence'.[35] His wife Eleanor's income of £40 was cut off. Twice in 1421 she had to ask that it be restored, the first time in July and again in November.[36] It may well have been this shortage of money that caused Sir John to sell the manor of Ludwick in the parish of Hatfield, which he owned in conjunction with Alice, countess of Oxford, in early May 1421.[37] Meanwhile, the conditions in which he was held worsened. He himself petitioned the Commons to ask the Lords to persuade the king to release him from the Tower, where he was being held in irons, in May 1421.[38] The response from the king was to put the matter to the Lords. Another petition was then submitted by Sir John, that he be allowed to state his case before the king so that he might be released 'as he has found pledges in Chancery from nine citizens of London that he would keep the peace, and from others for his loyalty and good behaviour.'[39] His wife Eleanor similarly petitioned the king's council to allow Sir John to be held in a room above ground and be allowed to go out under guard, as he had been when first imprisoned at the Tower.[40]

On 18 April 1422 Sir John escaped from the Tower together with four other men, including Thomas Payn, an erstwhile secretary of the Lollard knight Sir John Oldcastle (who had been executed in 1417). On 28 April the government ordered the bishops of the southern counties to act with local magistrates to keep the peace.[41] Two days later messengers were sent 'to each county of England and the Marches of Wales' to instruct the sheriffs and the captains of all the ports to arrest Sir John.[42] He was tracked down and captured in Wales by John Petit.[43] Henry Botolf was paid 6s 8d for bringing the news of Sir John's recapture to the government at Southampton. Sir John was indicted on 15 May 1422, almost as soon as the news arrived.[44] He was charged with conspiring with Thomas Payn to bring about the death of the king; of having feloniously escaped from the Tower with the king's enemies; and of plotting to enter the service of the French to attack English ships. Sir John pleaded not guilty. The jury agreed. The government laid a heavy burden on them to reconsider their verdict. The jury remained adamant he was not guilty.

Sir John should then have been released. However, the government sent him back to the Tower. On 20 May he was indicted on a different charge, of speaking treasonable words. This was soon dropped. No further legal action was taken, probably due to the fear that a jury would again find him innocent. He continued to be held without charge, being transferred from the Tower to Pevensey Castle on 29 May 1422, where he was guarded by Sir John Pelham. The cost of his maintenance was put at 4s per week for him and 3s per day for his guard of six men, a total of £1 5s per week.[45] The sum paid was slightly more than this: £1 6s 8d, the same as 'the Bastard of Bourbon', a French military commander also in Pelham's custody.[46] He remained in Sir John Pelham's custody until 30 June 1423, when he was returned to the Tower at a cost of £9.[47]

Sir John Mortimer was transferred to Pevensey Castle in May 1422,
and imprisoned there until June 1423 (© Paul R. Davis)

Whether or not Sir John ever uttered the treasonable words repeated by William King of Ryedale, Yorkshire, his gaoler, to Parliament on 14 February 1424 is open to doubt. The official record simply states that he escaped with William King's help in return for a sum of money.[48] He was executed not because of what he was reported to have said but for escaping from the Tower while suspected of treason and thus breaking the temporary law designed to convict him without the need for a trial. William King's report of his treasonable words is only significant in that it persuaded Parliament to agree to change the law for this purpose.

The chronicle written by an anonymous citizen in London is by far the fullest account of these proceedings.[49] According to this source, William King persuaded Sir John that he was his friend. At the same time, King reported to the deputy lieutenant of the Tower, Robert Scott, that he suspected Sir John of being disloyal. Scott charged him to encourage Sir John to speak freely and to report any treasonable words he uttered. William King subsequently asked Sir John what he would give if he helped him escape from the Tower. Sir John promised him '£10 in his purse, a haburion and a doublet, and £40 of land by yere' for life. He further promised that, within six months of his escape, he would make William a knight and 'give him as much land as any baron in England has'. On being asked by King what he would do after his escape, Sir John is supposed to have said that he would go into Wales to join the earl of March and that he would:

> make arise xl Ml. men in Walis and England and on the bordres of Walis. And he seid he wolde fere the Duke of Gloucestre and smyte of his hedde and al the Lordes heddes. And specially the Bisshoppis hedde of Wynchestre, for Mortymer wolde pley w[ith] his money. And he seid also that therle of the March was but a dawe, save that he was the grettist, noblist, and worthiest blode of this land. And this William seid, Save the kynges blode. And this Mortymer seid, that therle of the March shulde be kyng, if he had right and trouth; And he shulde be his here. And if therle of the March wolde not take the Rule of the Realme and the Crowne, this Mortymer seid that he wolde take vpon hym the Rule and the Crowne, for he was next heir therto. Also the same William askid of Mortymer at the same tyme, if he myght not haue his purpose and holde his way into Walis, to what place that he wolde goon ellis. And Mortymer seid that he wolde goon [go on] vnto the Dolphyn in ffraunce, for there he knewe wele he shuld haue releffe, and retinewe of xx Ml. people to bryng hym to his purpose, and that he shulde be right welcome to the Dolphyn. And al thes matiers the seid William wol prove vpon the same Mortimer w[ith] his body, or elles as the Lordes and Comons of this present Parliament wol awarden. Which John Mortymer, after that the Statute aforeseid was enactid, he escapid out of the tour wilfully and was taken ageyne. And by auctorite of the Parliament he was dampned to be drawen and hanged as for a treitour.[50]

It is unclear whether Sir John was simply 'drawn and hanged' as this chronicle suggests. The official parliamentary record states that he was sentenced to be:

> led to the aforesaid Tower and then drawn through the aforesaid city up to the gallows at Tyburn and be hanged on the gallows in that place and stretched out on the ground and his head cut off and his intestines burnt, and his body divided into four parts, and his head placed on the gate of London Bridge, and the said four parts of his body be put separately on the other four gates of London, and that his goods and chattels lands and tenements shall be forfeited to the lord king.[51]

Sir John Mortimer's body was buried at St John's Hospital, Clerkenwell
(St John's Gate: Image © Museum of the Order of St John, London, LDOSJ 6296.1.)

The Chronicle of the Greyfriars of London agrees that he was 'draune and hongyd
and behedyd and qwarterd for treson', although it gives the day as 22 February.[52]
Gregory's Chronicle likewise states that he was 'draw[n]e, hangyd and quartered'
and that his body was buried at St John's hospital, Clerkenwell, and his heart at
the church of the Greyfriars beside Newgate. Both elements of his resting place
are verifiable. The register of the monuments of the Greyfriars' church specifies
that his heart was buried beneath a stone carved with his name in the nave.[53] His
widow asked in her will, dated 1428, that she be buried alongside his body in the
church of St John of Jerusalem, Clerkenwell.[54] If Sir John was quartered, he was
soon gathered up and buried in two prestigious churches.

Five months later, a writ was issued to enquire into his lands in Hertfordshire.
This revealed that:

> He held no lands, tenements, rents or services the day of his forfeiture. By
> his charter dated at Hatfield, 24 June 1423, and shown to the jurors, and
> described as John Mortymer esquire, he granted all his lands, tenements,

rents and services which he had in Bishop's Hatfield parish and elsewhere in the county, to Henry bishop of Winchester, John Bassyngbourne esquire, William Westyngton esquire, William Shakeville esquire, Thomas Hunt of Linby, Thomas Grantham, parson of Bramfield Church, and John Seward, their heirs and assigns. The feoffees were seised on the day of his forfeiture and are still. The lands and tenements contained in the charter comprise the following. Annual values: the messuages, nil; each acre of arable 2d.; each acre of meadow 6d.; and each acre of wood nothing after enclosure.[55]

The lands in question amounted to five messuages and 100 acres forming the estate called Watership and other parcels of land amounting to less than 100 acres in Hatfield itself; a messuage with 54 acres in Digswell; and a messuage and just over 100 acres in the parish of Bramfield. Given that the first-named trustee was the bishop of Winchester and John himself is described therein as an 'esquire', and further considering that he was in custody at Pevensey on the day that this charter was supposedly sealed in his name at Hatfield, the charter in question has probably been incorrectly dated. The *Victoria County History* for Hertfordshire indeed dates it to 1413, not 1423.[56] Thus when he sold his manor of Ludwick in 1421, he was left with nothing. He had already granted away his other estates to the abovementioned feoffees.

So who was this man who, with no lands, was able to incur the wrath of the Lancastrian government?

The first thing we have to note is just how much effort went into keeping him in prison despite the fact he apparently could not be charged with any crime. Parliament was persuaded to be complicit in a plot to kill him judicially. The total cost of his custody easily exceeded £300. It is clear that he was widely assumed to be a scion of the Mortimer family of Wigmore. The government presumed in 1418 he had estates in the heartlands of the Mortimer family – Herefordshire and the Marches of Wales. As soon as he escaped from the Tower in 1422, he made his way straight to Wales, just as William King said that he would do again in 1424. Although no great admirer of Edmund Mortimer, 5th earl of March, he saw him as the legitimate heir to the throne. He was not just a Mortimer by name, he was of their affinity.

In support of this, Sir John's supporters were Mortimer adherents. As noted above, he was the first-named trustee in Sir Thomas Camoys's settlement of his estates in July 1415. Sir Thomas at that time was married to Elizabeth Mortimer, the eldest sister of the 4th earl of March. Moreover, Sir Thomas was a reliable, experienced and trusted man – about to command the left wing of the English army at Agincourt. He was not the sort of person likely to trust someone who would lie about being a member of his wife's family.

Sir John's other supporters are equally significant. The witnesses of his and Eleanor's settlement of the Rossall estates in 1416 include Sir William Fulthorpe, Sir Ralph Yver, Sir Adam Peshale MP, Sir Richard Lacon MP, David Holbache MP, William Poynour esquire and John de Aske esquire. Sir Adam Peshale MP was married to the widow of Sir Henry Mortimer of Chelmarsh. Sir Richard Lacon MP, sometime sheriff of Shropshire, and David Holbache, a justiciar of South Wales, were close associates of Peshale. Both were adherents of the earl of Arundel. The list of men vouching for Sir John Mortimer in 1418 included Sir William Palton, who would be elected MP for Somerset in 1422; and Richard Clitherowe esquire of Yorkshire, MP. Both of these men had connections to the Lollard knight and political agitator, Sir John Oldcastle. Palton had supported Sir Thomas Brooke in 1414, when Brooke was accused of conspiring with Oldcastle, and Clitherowe's son, Roger, had married Oldcastle's daughter. The fact that Sir John Mortimer escaped from the Tower in 1422 with another Oldcastle supporter, Thomas Payn, may be a coincidence or it might indicate that Sir John too had Lollard sympathies. However, such inclinations had not stopped him being knighted in 1415 nor prevented his commission in February 1417. It also needs to be remarked that Palton and Clitherowe were not rebels but highly-respected men. So too was a third supporter in 1418, Sir Thomas Hoo, who served alongside Sir Thomas Camoys at Agincourt. The other two sureties were John Wele MP and Philip Englefield of Essex. Wele was a close associate of Sir Richard Lacon and David Holbache, and, like those men, a retainer of the earl of Arundel. According to the *History of Parliament*, he had had the safekeeping of the widow and daughters of Sir Edmund Mortimer after their capture in 1409. Englefield was presumably Sir John's brother-in-law. The reputations of all these men and that of Sir Thomas Camoys should incline us to take Sir John's standing as similarly respectable.

The same impression is given when we consider his supporters in 1420. First and foremost among these was the Irish peer, James Butler, 4th earl of Ormond. His wife, Joan de Beauchamp, was related in two ways to the Mortimer earls of March, being both a second cousin of Roger Mortimer, 4th earl of March (through her mother) and his second cousin once removed (through her father). Like Roger Mortimer, the earl of Ormond had served as Lord Lieutenant of Ireland. Ormond's father had fought alongside Roger and his brother Sir Edmund in Ireland. Sir John's other supporters in 1420 were all MPs. William Esturmy of Wolf Hall was 12 times an MP. In addition, his daughter Maud was married to Roger Seymour, the great-nephew of the famous Speaker of the House of Commons, Sir Peter de la Mare, steward of Edmund Mortimer, 3rd earl of March. Sir John Beaufo was the MP for Northamptonshire in 1420. Richard Lacon has already been mentioned. The last supporter, John ap Harry, was MP for Herefordshire in 1406, 1407 and 1410, and sheriff of the county in 1399. He had also stood surety for Sir John Oldcastle, with whom he had been a comrade in arms.[57] He was steward of the Mortimer lordships of Builth and Dinas during the minority of Edmund Mortimer, 5th earl of March, and subsequently half the Mortimer lordship of Ewyas Lacy. When Roger Mortimer of Tedstone Wafer had died in 1402, ap Harry had been given the custody of the family estates and the wardship of his heir. According to the *History of Parliament*, he was the steward of the earl of March's Usk estates at the time of his supporting Sir John Mortimer. There is no getting away from the fact that Sir John Mortimer was supported by men who were closely connected to the Mortimer earls of March. If some of them had connections with Oldcastle too, it was because Oldcastle himself had interests in the region where the Mortimers were most powerful.

Given his supporters' connections with the earls of March, it is significant that Sir John's final trial and execution was undertaken just as the earl of March himself clashed with the Lancastrians. The earl had long been viewed with suspicion. He had been kept in custody with his younger brother Roger throughout Henry IV's reign. In 1415 he was privy to a supposed plot initiated by the earl of Cambridge, his brother-in-law, to put him on the throne. Thus when Henry V died, March was seen once more as a dangerous figure by the late king's brothers. He responded without tact: arriving in London to attend Parliament in October 1423 with an enormous entourage, far larger than Henry V had permitted him to have. He set up house at the bishop of Salisbury's London residence and handed out food daily to the people.[58] This both threatened and angered the Lancastrian lords. On 14 February 1424 – the same day that William King told Parliament that Sir John supported the earl of March's claim to the throne – orders were issued to gather ships to take the earl of March to Ireland so he could take up his position as Lord Lieutenant of Ireland in person.[59] He was effectively banished. Thus the fate of Sir John Mortimer was bound up with that of the earl of March: a public spectacle aimed at all supporters of the Mortimers.

All this gives us good reason to believe that Sir John Mortimer was a member of the Mortimer family of Wigmore. We cannot help but note also that he received a high-status heart burial in one royal church and his body was interred in another. This is a mark of high respect for a man with no land who was executed for treason. His heart burial at the Greyfriars' church is probably not a coincidence given that Roger Mortimer, the 1st earl of March, had also escaped from the Tower, had also been executed for treason at Tyburn and had also been temporarily laid to rest in the Greyfriars' church. Historians have accordingly linked Sir John to the main line of the Mortimer family for centuries.[60] They have taken William King's evidence about Sir John's supposed claims at face value and have assumed that he must have been a male-line descendant of either the 3rd earl of March or the 4th earl (as any earlier descents would not have implied a claim to the

Sir John Mortimer's heart was buried at the church of Greyfriars beside Newgate. At the time, the Franciscan monastic church was the second largest in London; after it was destroyed in the Great Fire of London of 1666, it was rebuilt as Christ Church Greyfriars to the designs of Sir Christopher Wren. Much of the church, except for the Tower, was destroyed by bombs during the Second World War, and the ruins are now a public garden (© John Fleming)

throne). But apart from that anonymous London chronicle, there is no indication that Sir John ever claimed to have a royal connection. All we know is that his government-appointed gaoler reported that Sir John said these seditious things, at the government's request, in the context of the government trying to persuade Parliament that Sir John was dangerous and should be executed without trial. This is hardly an unbiased account of Sir John's own views.

We also need to bear in mind that there is good evidence from a variety of sources to demonstrate that Sir John was not of the main line of the family. The *Fundatorum Historia* – the history of the Mortimer family of Wigmore, written in the 1390s with an emphasis on the right of the family to the throne – states that the 4th earl of March only had two sons: Edmund Mortimer, the 5th earl, born in 1391, and his brother Roger, born in 1393. The latter was stated to have died without offspring (*obit etiam sine prole*) and to have been buried at Stoke Priory.[61] That there were no other brothers is shown by the references to just two Mortimer boys while they were under house arrest during the reign of Henry IV.[62] Henry IV's signet letters similarly name only two boys.[63] Had there been another brother, he too would have been politically sensitive and placed in safe keeping. When the two brothers were released and knighted at Henry V's accession, no third brother was with them; only Edmund and Roger were named as receiving robes.[64] No contemporary document suggests Sir John was the brother of the earl of March. Nor did the earl vouchsafe to guarantee Sir John's good behaviour in 1418 or 1420, which one might have expected if he was his brother. Lastly, Sir John's marriage to Eleanor – a widow with only a modest income and a small inheritance – was not of the status that one would expect if he was so closely related to the earls of March. In short, all the direct evidence conflicts with the theory that Sir John was a son of the 4th earl of March.

He was not a son of the 3rd earl either. The *Fundatorum Historia* names all four of the earl's children and gives their birthdates but it does not mention John. The four are all similarly named in their father's will, which does not mention John. The 4th earl made plentiful provision for his brother, Sir Edmund Mortimer, but he never made any grants to a John Mortimer. The chronicler Adam Usk, a Mortimer family protégé, also named all four children of the third earl but did not mention John. Nor, in describing the family of Sir Edmund Mortimer (1376–1409), who married Catrin Glyn Dŵr in 1402 or 1403 and had three daughters and a son, Lionel, by her, does he mention a son John.[65] It is theoretically possible that Sir Edmund had married another woman before Catrin Glyn Dŵr but, again, as Sir Edmund was the

Memorial to Catrin Glyn Dŵr, wife of Sir Edmund Mortimer (© John Fleming)

earl of March's son and descended from Edward III, we would expect to see significant evidence of his match with a bride from an equally noble and landed family. Not a trace of any earlier marriage has come to light despite a comprehensive search of all the relevant calendars. Furthermore, the inquisition *post mortem* covering Sir Edmund's estates in Dorset in 1418 specifically mentions that he had no heirs of his body.[66] Had Sir John been his illegitimate son, or a bastard son of the earls of March, he would have been barred from inheriting anything – lands, titles or a claim to throne. In such circumstances he would have posed no risk to the Lancastrian dynasty and it would not have been necessary to persuade Parliament to change the law so he could be executed without trial.

It remains theoretically possible that Sir John was descended from an earlier Mortimer of Wigmore – the 1st earl of March, one of his sons, or the 2nd earl – and that he was indeed the heir to the earldom of March but not to the Mortimer claim to the throne. In this case, the danger to the Lancastrians would have been not that Sir John was himself of royal blood but that, if the earl of March died and Sir John inherited the Mortimer titles and any estates entailed on the male line, he would be in a good position to advance the claims of the young Richard, duke of York, as a rival to the Lancastrians. However, the Mortimers' estates and titles were not entailed on the male line, as shown by their inheritance by the 5th earl of March's heir general, the duke of York, in 1425. In any case, he was not a legitimate descendant of one of the earls of March. The Mortimer family of Wigmore is exceptionally well documented in the fourteenth century – not only in the *Fundatorum Historia* but also the mass of official records of the kingdom. Although Sir Thomas Mortimer (d.1399) is not mentioned in either the family chronicle or the will of his father's widow, Philippa, countess of March, prompting historians to suspect he was illegitimate, he appears regularly in other documents – his brother's will, his brother's grants to augment his estate, and official appointments – so that we are left in no doubt that he was the younger brother of the 3rd earl of March.[67] No such references appear to any John Mortimer. Nor do we find any reference in the official records to Sir Thomas marrying before he made an advantageous match with Alice Poynings, widow of lord Bardolf, in 1386. Nor is there any reference to him having any children. A generation earlier, the 2nd earl of March did have a younger brother, called John, but we are informed by the author of the *Fundatorum Historia* that he died as a boy. Nothing more is known of him. In the previous generation two sons of the first earl of March, John and Roger, died without heirs.[68] The descendants of the earl's other son, Sir Geoffrey Mortimer, did survive in France until the sixteenth century but when the 5th earl died in 1425, they were not recognised as being entitled to any titles or estates. After a comprehensive search of all the published calendars, online catalogues and relevant chronicles, it appears that the only legitimate male-line descendant of the 1st earl of March alive in 1418 was Edmund Mortimer, the 5th earl of March, and his rightful heir was his nephew and heir general, the young duke of York.

This leaves us with what, on the face of it, looks like a conundrum. Sir John Mortimer was close to the Mortimers of Wigmore and very much of their affinity but, at the same time, not one of them. In order to resolve this, it is necessary to take a different approach. Rather than look for connections between Sir John and the main line of the family – which is a methodology susceptible to confirmation bias – we should investigate his own background. Was there a Mortimer family in Hertfordshire, where he lived? The answer is that there probably was.

The founder of the Mortimer family of Great Bromley, Essex, was one Nicholas Mortimer, who acquired a moiety of Great Bromley by marriage.[69] Nicholas originally came from Hertfordshire. One 'Nicholas Mortymer of Hertfordshire' is mentioned in conjunction with two London merchants and other Hertfordshire men in a writ to the sheriff of Hertford in May 1412.[70] As his successor as lord of Great Bromley, David Mortimer esquire (d.1494), sold lands in Bishop's Hatfield and Essenden in Hertfordshire in 1466, it seems likely that Nicholas was David's father and his roots lay in that part of the county.[71] David's son and heir, Robert Mortimer (d.1485), died fighting at Bosworth alongside John Howard, duke of Norfolk, whose daughter Isabel he married.[72] The significance of this is that the Mortimers of Great Bromley also bore the *barry of six, or et azure* arms of the Mortimers of Wigmore. Robert Mortimer differenced them with three nails on the escutcheon.[73] Sir John Mortimer of Hertfordshire and his contemporary, Nicholas Mortimer of Hertfordshire, both believed they were related to the Mortimer earls of March and both owned land in Bishop's Hatfield. It would be a huge coincidence if they were not brothers or first cousins.

Nothing has hitherto been written about the Mortimers of Bishop's Hatfield for the good reason that they have left few traces in the documentary record. One Richard Mortimer appears in a fine dated 1375 along with John de Ludwick and others as a tenant of the manor of Tewin, which is five miles from Hatfield.[74] He was also a tenant at will of the manor of *Lokkelebery* or Lockleys in the parish of Welwyn, about two miles from Hatfield, where he was reported

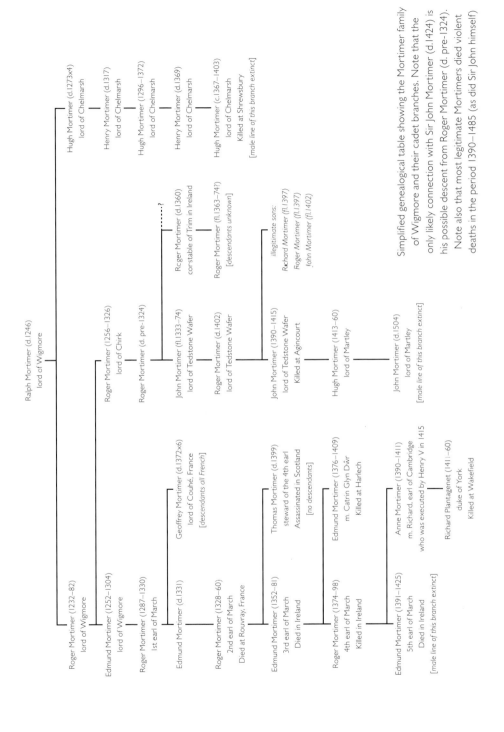

Ralph Mortimer (d.1246)
lord of Wigmore

Roger Mortimer (1232–82)
lord of Wigmore

Hugh Mortimer (d.1273x4)
lord of Chelmarsh

Edmund Mortimer (1252–1304)
lord of Wigmore

Roger Mortimer (1256–1326)
lord of Chirk

Henry Mortimer (d.1317)
lord of Chelmarsh

Roger Mortimer (1287–1330)
1st earl of March

Roger Mortimer (d. pre-1324)

Hugh Mortimer (1296–1372)
lord of Chelmarsh

Edmund Mortimer (d.1331)

Geoffrey Mortimer (d.1372x6)
lord of Couhé, France
[descendants all French]

John Mortimer (fl.1333–74)
lord of Tedstone Wafer

Roger Mortimer (d.1360)
constable of Trim in Ireland

Henry Mortimer (d.1369)
lord of Chelmarsh

Roger Mortimer (1328–60)
2nd earl of March
Died at Rouvray, France

Roger Mortimer (d.1402)
lord of Tedstone Wafer

Roger Mortimer (fl.1363–74?)
[descendants unknown]

Hugh Mortimer (c.1367–1403)
lord of Chelmarsh
Killed at Shrewsbury
[male line of this branch extinct]

Edmund Mortimer (1352–81)
3rd earl of March
Died in Ireland

Thomas Mortimer (d.1399)
steward of the 4th earl
Assassinated in Scotland
[no descendants]

John Mortimer (1390–1415)
lord of Tedstone Wafer
Killed at Agincourt

illegitimate sons:
Richard Mortimer (fl.1397)
Roger Mortimer (fl.1397)
John Mortimer (fl.1402)

Roger Mortimer (1374–98)
4th earl of March
Killed in Ireland

Edmund Mortimer (1376–1409)
m. Catrin Glyn Dŵr
Killed at Harlech

Hugh Mortimer (1413–60)
lord of Martley

Edmund Mortimer (1391–1425)
5th earl of March
Died in Ireland
[male line of this branch extinct]

Anne Mortimer (1390–1411)
m. Richard, earl of Cambridge
who was executed by Henry V in 1415

John Mortimer (d.1504)
lord of Martley
[male line of this branch extinct]

Richard Plantagenet (1411–60)
duke of York
Killed at Wakefield

Simplified genealogical table showing the Mortimer family of Wigmore and their cadet branches. Note that the only likely connection with Sir John Mortimer (d.1424) is his possible descent from Roger Mortimer (d. pre-1324). Note also that most legitimate Mortimers died violent deaths in the period 1390–1485 (as did Sir John himself)

208

for having allowed a house to fall down and having sold five marks of timber without permission in 1387.[75] A generation earlier, in 1348, one Hugh Mortimer was serving in the household of Sir William de Ludwick, lord of Ludwick and Digswell in Bishop's Hatfield, Hertfordshire.[76] The manor of Ludwick descended from Sir William to John Ludwick MP (d.1411), who died with land in Welwyn and Tewin, as well as Digswell and Ludwick.[77] The reversion of these lands was to John Perient, from whom Sir John Mortimer held his land in Digswell before 1413. The manor of Ludwick and all the Ludwick family lands in Hatfield came to John Bassingbourne esquire, who conveyed them to Sir John Mortimer and Alice, countess of Oxford, prior to their quitclaiming them to John Perient in 1421.[78] It seems highly likely that Sir John Mortimer was the heir of this minor family who, in their coat of arms, preserved a memory of their connection with the Mortimers of Wigmore. That the arms were *azure et or* rather than *gules et or* indicates that they believed they were descended from the Mortimers of Wigmore or those of Chirk and Tedstone Wafer, not Chelmarsh. Given the lack of connections between the Wigmore Mortimers and Sir John, let alone the other Hertfordshire Mortimers, the likelihood is that the Mortimers of Hertfordshire were descended from the Mortimers of Chirk. It is possible that Hugh Mortimer who served Sir William Ludwick in 1348 was a brother of John Mortimer of Tedstone Wafer (fl.1333–74?) and his brother Roger Mortimer of Chirk (d.1360), the sons of Roger Mortimer of Chirk (d.pre-1324) and the grandsons of Roger Mortimer (1256–1326), the builder of Chirk Castle and the uncle of the 1st earl of March. Certainly Sir John's ability to count on the support of John ap Harry in 1420 points to a connection with Roger Mortimer of Tedstone Wafer (d.1402).

This would make Sir John Mortimer a very peripheral figure in the Mortimer family. However, to emphasise the peripherality would be to fall into the trap of assuming that he was executed on account of his lineage. This was not necessarily the case. If we consider the wider picture of the Mortimer family in the fourteenth century, we see that the various houses – of Wigmore, of Chelmarsh and of Chirk and Tedstone Wafer, together with their younger sons – all acted as part of the same faction. Sir Roger Mortimer of Chirk (d.1360) and his son of the same name acted as custodians of Trim on behalf of their second and third cousins, the earls of March.[79] The elder of these two Chirk Mortimers acted as the attorney in Ireland for Joan, dowager countess of March, his father's cousin's widow, in 1338.[80] He did the same thing for Henry Mortimer, lord of Chelmarsh, his second cousin once removed, in 1341.[81] Similarly, Sir Hugh Mortimer of Chelmarsh and John

Mortimer of Tedstone Wafer were trustees of the estate of the heir to the earldom of March in 1341.[82] The young earl was Sir Hugh's second cousin twice removed and John's second cousin once removed. The 3rd earl of March borrowed £500 from Roger Mortimer of Tedstone Wafer, his fourth cousin, which he still owed at the time of his death in 1381. In 1394, when Roger Mortimer, 4th earl of March, went to Ireland with the king, he was accompanied by his uncle, Sir Thomas Mortimer (d.1399), and his fourth cousin twice removed, Hugh Mortimer of Chelmarsh (d.1403), as well as John Rossall (d.1403), the brother of Sir John's future wife.[83] The earl was also accompanied by one Sir Thomas Carew, who may have been the admiral who sailed with Sir John Mortimer in 1417. In this context of service to the main family by all the Mortimers bearing the arms of the Mortimers of Wigmore, it is perhaps significant that in 1417, Nicholas Mortimer of Hertfordshire – Sir John's probable brother or cousin – served in France in the company of Edmund Mortimer, earl of March.[84]

The seal of Roger Mortimer of Chirk, lord of Penketlyn (d.1326), and the first of the Mortimers of Chirk, affixed to the Barons' Reply to Pope Boniface VIII, (also showing the seals of Thomas de Multon, lord of Egremont, and John Lestrange, baron of Knokyn) (© The National Archives, Feudal Lords, de Walden Library 1301, C20)

In pulling all of these threads together, it seems highly likely that Sir John Mortimer was a distant cousin of the earls of March, being descended from a minor family descended from a younger son of the Mortimers of Chirk which held a few farms in Hertfordshire. His name and distant connections may well have brought him to prominence, resulting in his marriage to the sister of a Mortimer retainer, John Rossall, and eventually his knighthood. But that prominence made him vulnerable. When his loyalty was suspected, his name made him a powerful symbol. When in prison, he became a hostage whom the earl of March had no willingness to defend. And when the Lancastrians needed to send a message to the earl of March and the public at large, he was at their mercy. In this way, his execution can be seen not as a sign of the Lancastrians' weakness but as one of their strength. Almost the entire Mortimer faction was wiped out

in the years 1398–1425 and the Lancastrians played a major part in their exter-
mination. After Roger Mortimer, 4th earl of March, was killed in an ambush
in Ireland in 1398, his uncle Sir Thomas was tracked down and assassinated in
Scotland by Warin fitz Fulk le Cook of Cheshire, who was later rewarded for
the service.[85] Hugh Mortimer of Chelmarsh was slain at Shrewsbury in 1403.
Sir John Mortimer of the Chirk/ Tedstone Wafer line was killed at Agincourt.
The subject of our present study was judicially murdered in 1424. The last of the
Mortimers, Edmund, 5th earl of March, was sent to Ireland at the same time
and died there within the year, reportedly of plague. The Lancastrians may have
been fortunate in some of these deaths but they certainly engineered others.
Even the countess of Oxford, with whom Sir John held Ludwick, fell foul of
the Lancastrian government, losing all her lands in October 1421, ostensibly for
marrying without the king's permission. Her husband, the London merchant
Sir Nicholas Thorley, was locked up in the Tower and only released in February
1424, the same month that Sir John Mortimer was tried and executed.[86] Henry v
might have come down to us via Shakespeare as 'the golden boy of the fifteenth
century' (to quote Anne Curry) but that is not how he appears from a Mortimer
perspective.[87] Sir John Mortimer was not imprisoned because he himself had a
claim to the throne. He was imprisoned by Henry v and judicially murdered by
the Lancastrians as an example to all those who believed the earl of March was
the rightful king – including the earl of March himself.

Anne Mortimer's descent from Lionel Duke of Clarence and her marriage to Richard of Conisburgh are depicted in this detail from a political poster from c.1461. The whole poster is shown on p. 222 (© The British Library Board, Harley MS 7353 f.001r)

11

Dr J.L. Laynesmith

Anne Mortimer's legacy to the House of York

Edward III's youngest grandson, Richard of Conisburgh (or York), was left no estates by his father, was excluded from positions of authority by successive kings and was executed for treason in 1415. Yet his only son – Richard duke of York – was eventually declared heir to the kingdoms of England and France, two of Conisburgh's grandsons were crowned king at Westminster and the modern royal family are his descendants. Both the motivation for Richard of Conisburgh's fatal treason and the eventual success of his descendants were rooted in his marriage to Anne Mortimer, sister of the last Mortimer earl of March.

This chapter explores the significance of Anne's legacy for the House of York; both in providing legitimate and legendary dynastic claims to kingship, and in transmitting the right to the Mortimer family estates which provided a powerbase to make good on those claims. It focusses primarily on the manuscripts created to celebrate and communicate the House of York's royal heritage. These range from assertions of Richard duke of York's right to the Castilian throne in documents that were created on his (previously Mortimer) lands at Clare, to pedigrees, leaflets and chronicle dedications setting out Edward IV's claim to all the Crowns of Britain. It is suggested that much of the propaganda inspired by Mortimer family history and legend was not centrally driven but was created by the king's subjects. Earlier historians have tended to present all of these dynastic narratives as attractive propaganda opportunities for Edward, but it is argued here that some were not welcomed by all of Edward's subjects. The chapter concludes that the Mortimer family's stories and iconography provided a significantly more impactful legacy for their royal descendants than is commonly appreciated.

ANNE MORTIMER

Anne Mortimer was the eldest daughter of Roger Mortimer, 4th earl of March, and of Eleanor Holland, daughter of Thomas, 2nd earl of Kent. Anne was only nine when Earl Roger died in 1398.[1] Shortly afterwards, Eleanor Holland remarried but she too died in 1405, leaving Anne and her sister Eleanor in the custody of their stepfather, Edward Charlton, lord of Powys. This does not seem to have been a happy arrangement since the sisters petitioned Henry IV the very next year, complaining that they were 'destitute of all their parents and friends and have not wherewithal to maintain themselves'.[2] In May 1406 Henry IV gave instructions for them to be paid £100 a year from the revenues of their mother's properties, which were now in Lord Charlton's hands. Although their stepfather did make payments, their income was still a matter of controversy in January 1408.[3] This sense of neglect may have been a motive behind Anne's politically explosive marriage later that year.

Anne would have been well aware that her father had been considered a potential heir to Richard II because he was descended from Richard's oldest uncle, Lionel duke of Clarence. Lionel's only child had been a daughter, Philippa, who married Edmund Mortimer, 3rd earl of March, in 1468. Because the subsequent Mortimers were thereby descended from Edward III through a woman, and because the eldest male at the time that Richard II was overthrown was not quite nine years old, it was easy to ignore their potential claim in 1399 and to accept the eldest son of Lionel's younger brother, John duke of Lancaster, as Henry IV. Nonetheless, in 1405, another of Edward III's grandchildren, Constance of York (Richard of Conisburgh's elder sister), kidnapped Anne's two brothers, apparently in an attempt to use them to oust Henry IV from the throne. So Anne had good reason to resent both her small income and her marginal position, living in north Wales. She was presumably also aware that the Lancastrian king would be keen to ensure that she and her offspring could not pose the threat to his family that her brothers did, and so was likely to marry her off into a loyal family of lower status than her own.

In the spring of 1408 Anne seized the chance to determine her own destiny by secretly marrying another discontented descendant of Edward III: Richard of Conisburgh. The couple knew that such a marriage was within forbidden degrees of kinship. But they were able to secure absolution in retrospect, through a temporary separation and penance, so that their children were considered legitimate.[4] Anne died sometime before 1414, possibly as a consequence of complications at the birth of her second surviving child, and only son, in September 1411. In 1414 Henry V gave her (now remarried) widower the title earl of Cambridge, but not the estates needed to uphold such status. It seems to have been resentment at his continuing marginalised position that prompted the newly-made earl to try to take advantage of Henry V's Agincourt campaign to play kingmaker. Richard of Conisburgh's plot was chaotic and ill-conceived. His choice of replacement kings was a pretender claiming to be Richard II (although both the pretender and Richard II were already dead), or Anne's brother, Edmund earl of March, who soon thought better of the scheme and revealed it to the king. Richard of Conisburgh was executed as a consequence, but his son was allowed to inherit the duchy of York after Conisburgh's elder brother, Duke Edward, died at Agincourt a couple of months later.[5]

RICHARD DUKE OF YORK

Anne Mortimer's son, the orphaned Richard duke of York, was brought up by loyal Lancastrians, married to a daughter of Joan Beaufort, countess of Westmorland, and began a career in royal service. Three months after accompanying Henry VI to his coronation in France, York was given livery of his lands. The estates he inherited from his York uncle were extensive but also, to quote T.B. Pugh, 'burdened with debt and dowagers'.[6] However, his Mortimer uncles had also died without children and York's inheritance from this half of his family made him one of the wealthiest nobles in the country. These properties ranged from a townhouse in Calais to the castles at Bridgwater, Clare, Denbigh, Usk, Wigmore and Ludlow, and included lands in more than 30 counties.[7] In 1445 Henry VI granted York's three-year-old heir, Edward, the Mortimer title 'earl of March'. This was probably at York's request in order to strengthen his attempts to secure a French royal bride for Edward, a scheme that foundered when York's position as King's Lieutenant in Normandy was not renewed.[8] Through the 1440s there is no indication that York had any interest in drawing attention to his potential rights to the English throne through his Mortimer lineage to Lionel duke of Clarence. Indeed, he seems to have been much more interested in laying claim to the throne of Castile as a consequence of his descent from Pedro the Cruel's younger daughter, Isabel duchess of York.[9]

Two of the surviving texts that draw attention to York's interest in Castile were produced at Clare in Suffolk. The castle at Clare was part of the inheritance that Elizabeth de Burgh had brought to her marriage to Lionel duke of

Clarence. The couple were buried at the Augustinian priory there and successive Mortimer family members were generous patrons both to this and the nearby house of Stoke-by-Clare which Edmund 5th earl of March re-founded as a house for secular priests in 1415. As lord of Clare, Richard duke of York and his family benefitted from the exceptional literary culture there. In 1445, his sister, Isabel, commissioned a 'Life' of St Mary Magdalene from one of its inhabitants, Osbern Bokenham. In the prologue to this work, celebrating his patron's family, Bokenham asserted that the right to 'the royal tytle of spayne' to 'The duk of York, syr Rychard, is come,/Wych god hym send, yf it be hys wyl'.[10] The other text with a Castilian link was produced the same year – it was an edition in Latin and English of Claudius Claudianus' poem 'On the Consulate of Stilicho'. The original version was a panegyric on a Roman consul written in 400 AD. As Livia Visser-Fuchs has demonstrated, the Clare author 'turned the Stilicho text into a long, consistent ode to York's virtuous life and a proclamation of the certainty that, whatever his problems at the time the translation was made, his reward would follow'.[11] Within this, the author's strikingly free translation of a speech by the allegorical figure of Spain seems to turn the figure's words into a plea to rule that land. Fifteenth-century nobles and gentry commonly shared their books within their social circle and such texts were habitually read aloud, especially at mealtimes, thereby spreading their audience further. It is difficult to guess what York's friends might have made of the lavish praise given to him in these works, but it is not impossible that they contributed to the popular assumption of Richard duke of York's fitness for authority that was to prove political dynamite a few years later.

In 1456 a more personal document was created for the duke of York at Clare: a 'Dialogue … at the grave of Dame Joan of Acre'. This poem, in parallel Latin and English versions, celebrated the patrons of Clare priory from Richard de Clare to Joan of Acre (daughter of Edward I) and, via the de Burgh earls of Ulster and Philippa of Clarence, to the earls of March and York's own children.[12] Vibrantly painted coats of arms along the length of the roll reinforced the message of the family's illustrious heritage. The duke and duchess of York also owned an edition of the *Legenda Aurea* that was translated/ rewritten by Osbern Bokenham.[13] This last was only recently discovered and there may well have been other works connecting the family with Clare that have not survived. The evidence we have does not suggest a centre of culture on a par with Humphrey duke of Gloucester's quasi-court at Greenwich, but Clare was definitely

On this genealogy of Edward IV tracing his lineage from the Creation, his claim to the throne of Castile and Leon is personified in the figure third from the left. From the Chronicle of the History of the World from Creation to Woden, with a Genealogy of Edward IV (© Free Library of Philadelphia, Lewis E 201)

at the heart of a local network of literary-minded patrons.[14] York's status as lord there can only have enhanced his image as a cultured prince.

It was also thanks to York's de Burgh/ Mortimer inheritance that he was the most obvious candidate to be appointed Lieutenant of Ireland in 1447, because he was earl of Ulster. In 1449 he decided to travel to Ireland himself, rather than governing through a deputy, quite possibly because he wanted to distance himself from the court clique whose policy in France he disagreed with. The following year, in Kent, Jack Cade adopted the name John Mortimer in a rebellion whose demands included greater political influence for the duke of York. No evidence survives to indicate that York had any part in instigating the rebellion, and the only indication that his maternal genealogy was being referenced as a justification for usurpation lies in contentious 'prophecy' literature.[15] Nonetheless, the use of the Mortimer name clearly alarmed those close to Henry VI. When York tried to return to court, the king's officers prevented him from making landfall at Beaumaris, accusing him of treason. York consequently sailed around the coast to his own marcher lordship of Denbigh and was able to make his way south through the Marches to Ludlow Castle.[16] This magnificent fortress, acquired by the 1st earl of March through his marriage to Joan de Geneville, was one of York's principal homes and it was here that he set up an independent household for his eldest sons, Edward and Edmund.

In the parliament that followed York's return to England, one of his lawyers, Thomas Young, asked Henry VI to name an heir. Young was apparently encouraging the king to select York, although the precise details were not recorded on the Parliament Rolls.[17] The situation was complicated because the dukes of Exeter were descended from Henry IV's sister and the dukes of Somerset from one of his originally illegitimate Beaufort half-brothers, so both families were more closely related to Henry VI than York was, but in potentially compromised lines compared with York's own from Edmund duke of York. Parliament was dissolved and Young was sent to the Tower. It is impossible to know when York seriously began to consider using the royal claim through his mother instead. Through the 1450s he repeatedly asserted his loyalty to Henry VI, demanding only that he be given due influence in the king's councils, and twice seizing the opportunity to be protector and defender of the realm. But as the decade closed, relations between York and the court party broke down dramatically. In October 1459 York and his allies were routed by the king's forces at Ludford Bridge and he fled into exile in Ireland.

When York returned to England a year later, it was to set out his claim through Anne Mortimer to a superior right to the throne than Henry VI's. This was a revolutionary approach. In the early Middle Ages there had been an acknowledgement that 'kings are to be lawfully chosen by the priests and elders of the people, and are not to be those begotten in adultery or incest'.[18] In common with English law for inheriting property and land, the heir to the throne was always assumed to be a close relative of the king. A custom of primogeniture was gradually adopted, although even after the Conquest it was ignored by (or for) William Rufus, Henry I, Stephen and John. Where the succession might not be entirely clear, kings tended to declare their preferred successors. So, having lost all but one of his sons, Edward I appointed his eldest daughter as heir should her only brother die without children. This arrangement would ensure that an heir of Edward I's body would follow him, not his younger brother. In contrast to this acceptance of female heirs, Edward III created an entail favouring John of Gaunt's children over Philippa of Clarence's. Ignoring this, Richard II seems to have considered that he might choose an heir from among his cousins.[19] When Henry IV attempted to exclude his female heirs, presumably trying to pre-empt later Mortimer challenges, he was forced to back down because the English kings' claims to the French throne depended on their descent from Edward III's mother. In practice, once a king was dead, it was still the 'priests and elders' whose acceptance was crucial to successful kingship, as the Empress Matilda had found to her cost.

Richard duke of York's assertion that primogeniture took precedence over the pragmatism of the status quo was probably a narrative of political convenience that was designed to allow the lords to depose an inept king, rather than York's sincerely held ideology.[20] Unfortunately for him, Parliament was not as eager to remove Henry VI as York had assumed. It was argued that their oaths of loyalty to Henry VI, earlier entails, and Acts of Parliament all took precedence over York's genealogy. York naturally mustered counter-arguments to these.[21] Eventually a compromise was reached in the Act of Accord which disinherited Henry VI's own son in favour of Richard duke of York as his heir. Neither party were satisfied, and further bloodshed was inevitable. York himself was killed only a few weeks later at the battle of Wakefield, but his son Edward earl of March was triumphant first at the battle of Mortimer's Cross, where he had been able to recruit in his family's marcher heartlands, and then, decisively, at Towton on Palm Sunday 1461. The teenage Edward seems to have benefitted from the fact that he was not tarnished by his father's long association with discontent and rebellion. But his supporters must also have been reassured that his very significant inheritance, much of it from his predecessors as earls of March, meant that as king he should be cushioned from the straitened finances that had plagued Henry VI. As Edward now sought to woo over those not yet weary of Lancastrian rule, a three-fold strategy of justification for his kingship emerged that drew from different aspects of his Mortimer inheritance.

EDWARD IV – HEIR OF CLARENCE

Edward IV's first parliament set out his claim to the English throne using the same arguments about his descent from Lionel duke of Clarence that his father had done. In the months since he had been acknowledged as king – and over the next few years – a variety of bills, posters, pamphlets and genealogical scrolls were created disseminating this information. As the variety of formats used to convey Edward's claim suggests, while some must have emanated from Edward IV's own circle, many were produced outside the court, either by supportive subjects who were keen to ensure Edward stayed on the throne, or by persons eager to demonstrate their loyalty to the new regime – and gain something thereby. The clearest example of the latter was the chronicler John Hardyng who wanted to encourage English conquest of Scotland and to provide advice on good governance. He had already dedicated a previous version of his work to Henry VI and began one that celebrated the Yorkist claim through the duke of Clarence as early as 1460. Hardyng, who was in his eighties, seems never to have finished the chronicle which includes an introductory dedication to the duke of York and a concluding dedication to Edward IV. Nonetheless, it was clearly popular and quite widely disseminated because at least 12 complete copies survive (as well as some extracts) witnessing five different attempts to complete the gaps Hardyng had left. The manuscripts we have range in quality from elegant parchment volumes with illuminated initials to an undecorated paper volume compiled by five different scribes.[22]

Despite this range, not every literate subject could afford such volumes. A much briefer work of propaganda that focussed purely on Edward's claims to the three thrones of England, France and Castile (and the duchy of Normandy) survives in two manuscripts in the British Library, headed:

> This brief tretys compiled for to bringe people oute of doute that haue not
> herd of the Cronicles of the lineall descenste vnto the Crowne of England
> and of Fraunce of Castell and of Legeons [Leon] and to the Duchie of
> Normandie sith that it was first conquest made.[23]

It began with the birth of Rollo, here called 'Rouland', first duke of Normandy and gave a short account of each duke and then king up to Edward III before explaining the relative claims of his son's offspring. Edward IV's claims first through Lionel to Edward III's inheritance, and then through Isabel duchess of York to Castile were laid out. It concluded by clarifying Edward III's claim to

France as well.[24] This was a work that could be easily disseminated and collected by members of the gentry and urban elites and perhaps originated in Edward's immediate circle.[25]

An alternative means of communicating this message that has survived in rather more copies is the diagrammatic genealogy with accompanying commentaries. Some of these genealogies were in rolls, others codices and some, uniquely in Edward IV's reign, a combination of the two: the accordion book.[26] The production of royal genealogies had been popular for some decades before Edward's accession. Many of those produced prior to 1461 were likely designed to reinforce the Lancastrian claim to the throne, while others were probably more generally educational. A few seem to have been produced for major noble families, showing their own place in royal, Biblical and legendary history.[27] Kathleen Scott has noted that one scribe created more than 20 of the surviving genealogy manuscripts in the period from the birth of Henry VI's son to the early part of Edward IV's second reign.[28] After 1461, Edward of Lancaster was omitted, and the descendants of Lionel duke of Clarence and Edmund duke of York were included so that Anne Mortimer's marriage to Richard of Conisburgh could be displayed.[29] In later versions the scribe expanded this further by including the

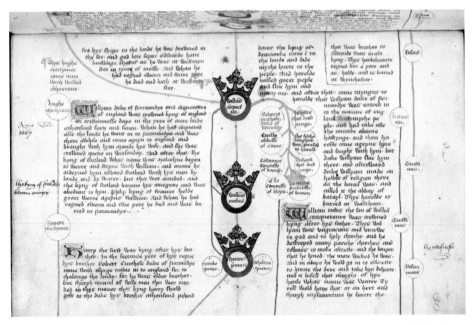

Early members of the Mortimer family were included in royal genealogies from the later 1460s like this accordion genealogy from about 1467 (Oxford, Bodleian Library MS. e Musaeo 42 f.30r)

Mortimer ancestors of Philippa of Clarence's husband as far back as Hugh Mortimer who 'come inne with William Conquerour'.[30] This did not add to the message of Edward's legitimacy as king, but perhaps indicates a desire to assure readers that all his ancestry was illustrious, particularly after his controversial marriage to Elizabeth Woodville. It also points to the wider purpose of such manuscripts as works of reference designed to be as encyclopaedic as possible.

Possibly the most elaborate surviving statement of Edward's descent from Lionel duke of Clarence is BL Harley MS 7353 (also known as *the Edward Poster*), which was perhaps created at the Dominican priory in Gloucester.[31] The centre of this manuscript depicts key moments in Edward IV's story in parallel with comparable Biblical stories (for instance, Edward's flight across the Channel escaping Henry VI's army is beside an image of the infant Moses in his basket in the river evading Pharoah's soldiers). At the top are two panels – in one are prophets and precedents for Edward's claim gathered around the figure of *ratio* (reason/rule) enthroned. On the other Edward IV is depicted enthroned upon a wheel of fortune whose turns have been stopped by *ratio*. The message of these images seems to be that the logical order of things has been restored and this is justified in a genealogy that resembles a rose bush in the lower half of the poster. It looks much like a Jesse Tree – probably deliberately evoking comparison with Christ's lineage to emphasise the implications of Edward IV as divine saviour that the images in the middle

The *Illustrated Life of Edward IV*, or the *Edward Poster* (© The British Library Board, Harley MS 7353 f.001r)

of the poster suggest. In the centre of the rose bush, Richard II is shown falling sideways as his blossom is being cut from the branch by a sword-wielding Henry IV. A ghostly figure of the adult Moses stands on Richard II's branch. He is admonishing Henry IV by reminding him of the story (in Numbers 27) of the daughters of Zelophehad whom Moses had determined should inherit from their father because he had no sons. Gilbert Foliot, abbot of Gloucester, had used the same Old Testament passage centuries earlier in defence of the Empress Matilda's queenship, although in the fourteenth century the Dominican Thomas Waleys argued that this was relevant only to private families, not the throne.[32] Waleys's work, a commentary on *The City of God*, was widely read but the Gloucester Dominicans, or whoever designed this poster, were apparently too pragmatic to let that interfere with current political need. They were not alone: John Hardyng had appealed to the same Mosaic precedent in his *Chronicle* dedication for Edward's father.[33] No lawgiver was greater than Moses so his must have seemed the strongest authority to invoke to assert Philippa and Anne's right to pass on their royal inheritance to Edward IV.

The case of the daughters of Zelophehad was, however, rather different from that of Philippa of Clarence's descendants since Philippa's father had predeceased Edward III. There were various precedents in England and neighbouring realms of preference given to a living son over an older line grandson in such circumstances.[34] In 1399, Henry IV as Edward III's grandson was clearly closer to the throne on this model than Edmund Mortimer had been – the grandson of a granddaughter. The parliamentary decision to accept York's claims in the 1460 Act of Accord was very likely motivated more by hope of achieving peace in the short term than a strong conviction of his superior right to the throne. With Henry VI still at large and Queen Margaret working hard to build support to reinstate him, it made sense for Edward IV to find additional material to justify his right to the throne that he had just seized.

EDWARD IV – HEIR OF BRUTUS AND ARTHUR'S LEGACY

Edward IV's Mortimer ancestry provided just such an alternative as a result of the 1st earl of March's great grandfather's marriage to Gwladus Ddu in about 1228.[35] Gwladus was a daughter of Llywelyn the Great and aunt of the last independent Prince of Wales. While Edward was growing up at Ludlow Castle, he must have been aware of the legendary implications that this marriage had accrued for the Mortimers. There is a colourful fourteenth-/ fifteenth-century manuscript, now at the University of Chicago, which is likely to have played a key part in educating the House of York about the legendary potential of their Mortimer relations. The manuscript includes several genealogies showing Gwladus's descent from Cadwaladr, the quasi-legendary last king of the British. One of these genealogies, which traces the Mortimer lineage through the legendary Trojan founder of Britain (Brutus) to Adam, even claims to include King Arthur's maternal grandfather.[36] Most late medieval English genealogical chronicles of British kings closely followed the names in Geoffrey of Monmouth's *History of the Kings of Britain* and so focussed less on blood descent than on who succeeded whom.[37] By contrast, drawing on various Welsh traditions, this genealogy claimed to present a bloodline descent, between Brutus, Arthur and Cadwaladr, and on from Cadwaladr to Llywelyn ab Iorwerth and his daughter Gwladus to the Mortimer family.[38]

The compilation of texts in the Chicago University manuscript sets out the Mortimer family's 'royal' lineage, their illustrious history and their rights to various contested estates.[39] As Mary Giffin has argued, it appears to have been compiled specifically to advance the Mortimer family's claim to the English throne.[40] It begins with a copy of an early thirteenth-century Anglo-Norman chronicle of Wigmore Abbey, so was perhaps originally created there. This is followed by a Latin chronicle of Britain that is heavily based on genealogies and king lists, including a genealogy from Brutus to Llywelyn that mentions Gwladus Ddu's marriage to Ralph Mortimer. After this there is a summary of kings, largely based on Geoffrey of Monmouth, from Brutus to Beohtric of Wessex leading into an annotated genealogy from King Alfred's family through to Henry v. In this Philippa of Clarence is the only one of Edward iii's granddaughters whose children are included, dominating the page and pushing John of Gaunt's family line to the bottom. All of these works serve as context for a very similarly structured genealogy/ chronicle of the Mortimer family which is generally called the Wigmore *Fundatorum Historia* (history of the founders of Wigmore Abbey). It was written in stages from 1262/3 to 1415 and includes paternal and maternal genealogies for Gwladus Ddu on some of the most ornate and colourful pages of the book.[41]

There are various early fifteenth-century insertions to the original chronicle text, some of which draw attention to Richard duke of York's rights to the Mortimer inheritance, thereby keeping alive a memory of this potential alternative royal lineage. At some time between 1424 and 1444 shields for York and his wife

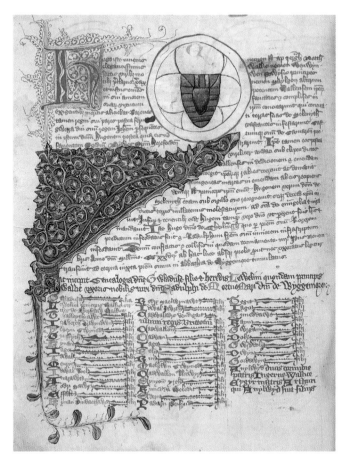

Gwladus Ddu's descent from King Arthur's maternal grandfather was depicted in this late fourteenth-/ early fifteenth-century manuscript which seems to have been created to present the Mortimer family's right to the English Throne. The Wigmore Abbey chronicle and Brut chronicle (© Hanna Holborn Gray Special Collections Research Centre, University of Chicago Library, Codex MS 224 f.51v)

wcrc added onto the end.[42] After these, there are incomplete drawings of three more shields executed with much greater skill than the previous illustrations and it is these that I would suggest indicate that the manuscript had come into the possession of Edward IV's family. Above the shields are images of two men and, in between them, a woman. Although Giffin identified both the images of men as Edward IV, I would argue that the first man is actually Richard duke of York. Giffin convincingly identifies the woman as Cecily duchess of York and through-out the book double-page spreads have depicted husbands to the left and wives to the right so that it would be highly illogical for her son to be to Cecily's left here.[43] Moreover, the man in the last image has a youthfully slender face and shoulders, shoulder-length hair and a floriated sceptre, whereas the man opposite Cecily is clearly in middle age and holds only a rod or staff of office. This is probably the closest we have to a portrait of Richard duke of York since all other images of him are more stylised. The quality of the drawing is strongly reminiscent of that in the Beauchamp Pageant and so may be the work of a professional commissioned by the lord of Wigmore. This means that, even if the manuscript originated at Wigmore Abbey, it is likely that at some point in the early fifteenth-century it was given to the Mortimer family or their York heirs. Below the image of Richard duke of York, his supporters are the lion of Mortimer and a hart for Richard II. There is no surviving evidence that York used this combination of supporters in life, but it may be that he had adopted them in 1460 when assuming the royal arms, abandoning his York falcon but retaining the Mortimer lion which represented his dynastic link to Richard II.[44] In this manuscript it is Duchess Cecily whose arms maintain the York link with two falcons as her supporters. Edward IV's shield is supported by another lion, this one guardant, and another unequivocally Mortimer beast, the black bull of Clare (or Clarence).[45]

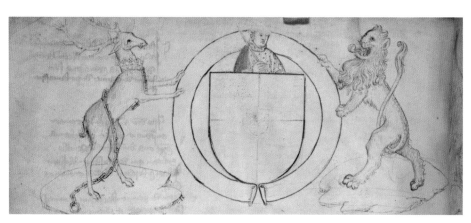

This image of Richard duke of York was one of the last additions to the Chicago University manuscript celebrating the Mortimer family's royal claims. His arms are supported by the Mortimer white lion and Richard II's white hart. The Wigmore Abbey chronicle and *Brut* chronicle (© Hanna Holborn Gray Special Collections Research Centre, University of Chicago Library, Codex MS 224 f.62v)

The 'evidence' of the Mortimer ancestry in this manuscript gave Edward IV obvious opportunities for enhancing his image. Ever since Geoffrey of Monmouth had completed his *History of the Kings of Britain*, English kings had been attempting to harness the glamour of Arthur's legend to enhance their own authority.[46] In the wake of their marriage into Welsh royalty, it appears the Mortimer family may have been attempting to do the same, although, as Paul Dryburgh cautions, we cannot know at what time the earliest version of this Arthurian pedigree for the Mortimers was drawn up.[47] The *Fundatorum Historia* describes a magnificent

Round Table tournament at Kenilworth organised by Gwladus Ddu's son, Roger, in 1279. Mary Giffin suggests that the tournament revealed this Roger Mortimer's hopes for supremacy in Wales following the death of his cousin, Llywelyn the Last.[48] Yet Round Table tournaments did not have to be dynastically inspired – the earliest seems to have been one held by the de Lusignans in Cyprus in 1223 and they were popular across northern France and the Low Countries in the later thirteenth-century.[49] As Chris Given-Wilson observes, the late fourteenth-century author of the *Fundatorum Historia* looks to have been embellishing his description of the Kenilworth tournament in order to present the Mortimers as 'quasi-fictional heroes of romance, fitting progenitors of such a great family'.[50] Consequently, it is perhaps safest to conclude only that fourteenth-/ fifteenth-century readers of the *Fundatorum Historia*, such as the young Edward earl of March, would have seen this tournament as proof of a long tradition of appreciating Arthurian connections in the Mortimer family. This perspective would have been reinforced by knowledge of the 1st earl of March's Round Table that was held at Wigmore in 1329. This was part of Earl Roger's wider programme of cultivating Arthurian culture during his brief period of power after ousting Edward II.[51]

Shortly after Gwladus Ddu's son's Round Table tournament at Kenilworth, Edward I had arranged his own at Nevin. Perhaps, as Giffin suggests, this was partly a riposte to Mortimer, but it also followed on from the king's participation in a reburial of Arthur at Glastonbury in 1278 that was meant to discourage Welsh resistance to his rule.[52] Half a century later, having ousted the 1st earl of March from power, Edward III also adopted the trappings of Arthuriana. As Mark Ormrod observes, it was his subjects who tended to present Edward as 'Arthur *redivivus*' whereas the king himself, perhaps cautious of the scorn that Roger Mortimer had garnered for emulating Arthur at Wigmore, preferred to adopt the guise of one of Arthur's knights.[53] Unhelpfully, this was eventually to complicate the Mortimer family's relationship with Arthur still further. Edward III regularly reprised the guise of Sir Lionel that he had been given at the Wigmore tournament (it was a name drawn from the *Prose Lancelot*) and he eventually gave that name to one of his own sons. Edward III compounded this Arthurian identity for his third son when he gave Lionel the title duke of Clarence. As Leo Carruthers has pointed out, other dukedoms created at the time were based on real places and usually involved upgrading earldoms, whereas the duke of Clarence is a character in several Arthurian stories, presumably chosen as a pun on Lionel's recent acquisition of the honour of Clare.[54]

mortimere Erle of þ marche next Righte
full eire proclamed to kyng Richard in the
xxj. yere of his Reyne. be lawefull successi
and a doughtr. Alice weded to Sir Henr̄ Perc̄
and thei had issue Henr̄ Erle of Northūbl̄
þ deid at seint Allwins. in þ yere of oū lord. 1ca

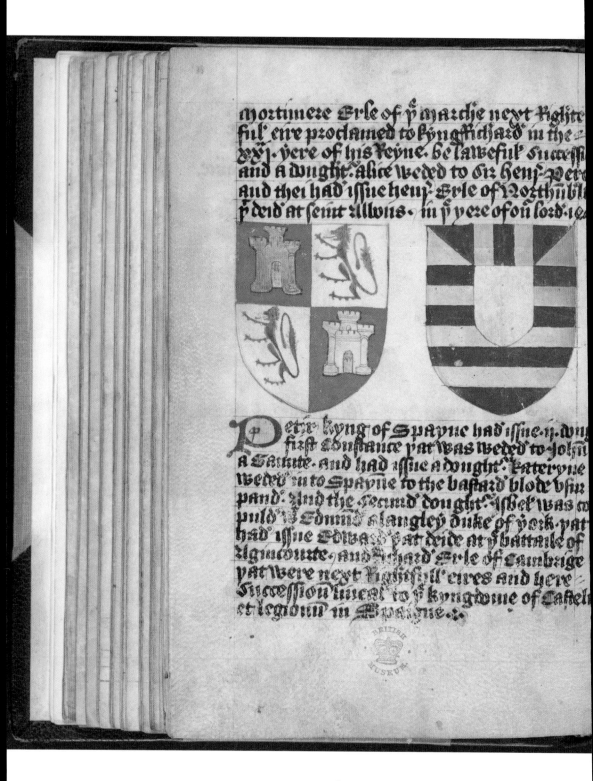

Peter kyng of Spayne had issue. ij. doug
first Cōstance þat was weded to John
a Gaūte. and had issue a doughtr. Kateryne
weded in to Spayne to the bastard blode vsur
pand. And the secund doughtr. Isbell was w
puld w̄ Edmūd of langley duke of york þat
had issue Edward þat deide at þ battaile of
Agincourte. and Richard Erle of Caunbrige
þat were next Rightfull eires and yere
Succession lineall to þ kyngdume of Castell
et legioūn in Spayne.

Carruthers notes that a duke of Clarence also features in *Sir Gawain and the Green Knight*, a poem composed after Lionel of Antwerp's death. This contributes to his argument that the poem was composed under the patronage of Lionel's Mortimer descendants.[55] If Carruthers is correct, it suggests there was a late fourteenth-century earl of March who was disgruntled by his exclusion from ducal titles compared with his royal cousins and was harking back to his own family's old ducal title.[56] Henry IV was possibly aware of this, hence his decision to award that title, somewhat randomly, to one of his own sons in 1412, even though the honour of Clare remained with the Mortimer family. Very occasionally the pageantry of Lancastrian kingship also made reference to Arthur.[57] With Edward IV's accession, this tug of war over Arthur's legacy could finally be resolved. Yet Edward seems to have been even more keen to present himself as heir to Arthur's Trojan ancestor, Brutus.

John Hardyng's *Chronicle* had identified Richard duke of York as heir to Brutus's claims across Britain purely because of his descent from English kings.[58] The tradition of the Mortimer family's direct lineal descent provided material to expand on. One example that used this is a colourful pamphlet preserved in BL Cotton Vespasian E vii which was emblazoned with the royal arms of England and Spain, the invented arms of Cadwaladr and the Mortimer arms. It is the 'British History' equivalent of the descent from Rollo pamphlet described above and it explains in succinct prose that the 'blod and rightfull eires of Brute' continued down to Gwladus Ddu and through the Mortimers to Edward IV, 'kyng of Brutayne, Fraunce and Spaigne'.[59] An elegant genealogy in Egerton MS 1076 celebrated the Mortimer family a little differently. This opens with three lines of descent for Edward IV – from King John, St Louis and, to the left of those, from 'Roger Mortimer that weddede the Heyre of Brute'.[60] There are several mistakes in the Mortimer line (including calling both Gwladus and Philippa's husbands Roger) which suggest that this is yet another instance of an affirmation of Edward's lineage that was not created by the king's immediate circle.

In a survey of genealogies of Edward IV preserved in the British Library and the College of Arms, Sydney Anglo observed that the majority included some reference to Edward's 'British History' through the Mortimer family.[61] Work by Kathleen Scott and Maree Shirota on specific types of genealogies from a wider range of libraries suggests that, in fact, the 'British History' was not quite so prevalent in fifteenth-century royal genealogies as Anglo claimed.[62] Nonetheless, the many manuscripts that Anglo did identify does suggest that, despite the scepticism

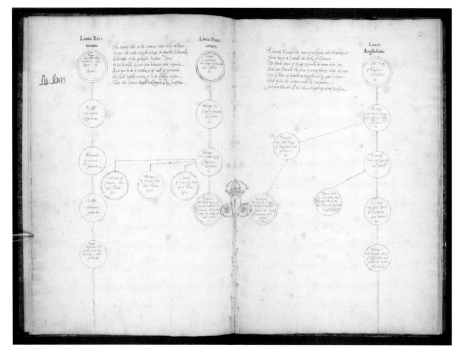

This eighteenth-century codex was most likely copied from a fifteenth-century genealogy for Edward IV that similarly began with lines from King John, St Louis and Gwladus's Ddu's marriage into the Mortimer family. It sets out Edward IV's right to the throne so clearly that, according to its author, only those who were 'wittless, or of will so frowarde' could fail to accept his claim (© The British Library Board MS Egerton 1076 ff. 001v-2r)

for Geoffrey of Monmouth's tales expressed by generations of chroniclers, many of Edward's subjects valued this narrative of descent from Brutus. Whether they truly believed it, or simply enjoyed the way it wrote their own present into an entertaining myth of the past, must remain another unknown. For Edward himself, and some of his subjects, there was an additional, almost Messianic, dimension to this story of British descent. But it was also highly problematic.

Edward IV – heir of Cadwaladr and the Red Dragon
Geoffrey of Monmouth's *History of the Kings of Britain* had claimed that the last British king, Cadwaladr, left Britain for Brittany during a plague and that when he planned to return an angelic voice told him

> God did not want the Britons to rule over the island of Britain any longer, until the time came which Merlin had foretold to Arthur. The voice commanded Cadwaladr to go to Pope Sergius in Rome, where, after doing

penance, he would be numbered among the saints. It said that through his blessing the British people would one day recover the island, when the prescribed time came, but that this would not happen before the British removed Cadwaladr's body from Rome and brought it to Britain.[63]

The future British victory prophesied by the angel came to be linked with an earlier passage in Geoffrey's work where Merlin interprets a battle between red and white dragons as a metaphor for the British and Saxons respectively. Geoffrey seems to have been drawing these prophecies from earlier Welsh prophetic tradition. He complicated the story of the dragons so that although the red returned after long absence and the seeds of the white died, it is possible to interpret it as a prophecy of the Norman triumph with support from the descendants of the red dragon exiled to Brittany, thereby cancelling the implied threat of a later 'British' invasion.[64]

Historians of the late medieval and early modern uses of this prophecy have tended to skate over its complex reception before 1460 and presented it only as an attractive opportunity for affirming Edward IV's legitimacy.[65] I would suggest that the red dragon prophecy was as much a problem that Edward's propagandists needed to take control of as it was an opportunity, and that this explains why the red dragon was never a common emblem for the House of York. Elements of the prophecy survived in various formats and its mixed reception is especially evident in the chronicle-style reworkings of Geoffrey of Monmouth's story. Wace, who was writing in Normandy in the 1150s, avoided interpreting the dragon fight in his Anglo-Norman version of the tale.[66] He also abbreviated the story of divine prophecy to Cadwaladr and made the British return more strongly contingent on recovering Cadwaladr's body, something which must by 1150 have

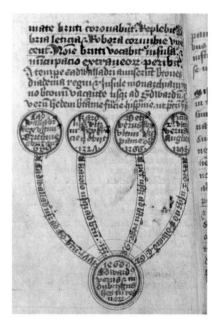

This diagram, in a collection of prophecies from 1465, sums up Edward IV's status as heir to Cadwaladr, Charles IV of France, Pedro of Castile and Richard II. (Oxford, Bodleian Library, MS. Bodl. 623, f.014v)

232

seemed impossible. Laȝamon, who lived not far from the Welsh border and finished his Middle English *Brut* in 1225, did not even link the red and white dragons with the British and Saxons. He was, however, much more explicit than Geoffrey about the promise to Cadwaladr of a future 'British' victory and the golden age that this would bring in: 'then shall in Britain bliss become rife; fruits and weathers prosperous, after their will'.[67] He concluded his chronicle by observing that this promised British victory 'came not, be it henceforth as it may; happen what happen, happen God's will!'.[68] Laȝamon was perhaps directly familiar with some of the same legends that had inspired Geoffrey and aware that the Welsh still hoped for such a victory.

It was Wace's Norman approach that proved the more influential version of events in England.[69] The earliest version of the immensely popular *Prose Brut* that evolved from it completely omitted Cadwaladr's story and amended the story of the dragons so that the white dragon and the Saxons were the unequivocal victors.[70] This remained the dominant version of the *Brut* story thereafter.[71] Yet fragments of Geoffrey's story of Cadwaladr and the dragons were reintroduced into some versions from the fourteenth century. The genealogical chronicle in the Wigmore manuscript includes an angel telling Cadwaladr to go to Rome, but omits the crucial clause 'until the time came which Merlin had foretold to Arthur' and the subsequent promise of a British return.[72] In context it seems likely that this Wigmore writer was drawing from a similarly abbreviated original that had been framed to acknowledge a tradition involving Cadwaladr but to avoid elements that were uncomfortable for English readers.[73] Nonetheless, from about the time of Edward II's fall, some Middle English versions of the *Brut* chronicle had started to reinclude the angel's prophesy to Cadwaladr in full from Geoffrey's *History*.[74] This timing was perhaps linked to new interpretations of the so-called 'Prophecies of Merlin'.

The prophecies associated with the dragons' battle had been circulating widely across Europe separately from the rest of Geoffrey's narrative, often in compilations with other prophetic literature. Successive medieval scholars attempted to make sense of them in terms of contemporary political events and extra prophecies were incorporated into them. Anglo-Norman French translations were made in the thirteenth century and over 300 medieval manuscript copies of the prophecies survive today.[75] Victoria Flood has suggested that Geoffrey's original creation of the Merlin prophecy was intended to flatter Robert of Gloucester whose territorial influence overlapped with much of the focus of the prophecies.[76] (Many of the same properties were later in Mortimer hands or close to their lands.) In King John's reign elements of Geoffrey's text were reworked into the 'Prophecy of the Eagle' as a critique of John's kingship and the loss of Normandy.[77] Likewise the crises of Edward II's reign and defeat prompted a reworking known as the 'Six Kings' which was often inserted into the *Brut* as a prophecy from Merlin to Arthur.[78] The promised hero of the 'Six Kings' was the boar of Windsor, who was very clearly Edward III. Many variants developed through the fourteenth and early fifteenth centuries, some affirming and others opposing first Richard II and then Henry IV.[79] Flood has examined the use of these motifs in Percy propaganda at the opening of the fifteenth century and suggested they were later repurposed in the Welsh Marches as proto-Yorkist material.[80] In the mid-1390s the poet Iolo Goch had linked Roger Mortimer with the dragon prophecy in a poem that looked for a saviour from Richard II's tyranny: 'It is prophesied that it will be our dragon who will make the action this year: from the head of the lion with the valiant sword, one akin to Gwynedd will be crowned'.[81] Similarly suggestive, a version of the prophecy *When Rome is removed* in a Welsh manuscript of the mid 1450s replaced the usual final statement with 'out of brawe keynde blode of brutus then/ the ryght schall to the ~~lyne of brutus~~ lyne of gwladus'.[82] The crossing out suggests the extent to which Gwladus's line was understood to be interchangeable with Brutus's and the hope that it was destined for the throne.

Jonathan Hughes has argued that the intellectuals around Edward earl of March were able to use these traditions to ignite in him the heroic confidence in his own destiny that enabled him to emerge so brilliantly from the disaster of his father's death.[83] Yet Edward must also have been aware of opposing traditions. John Hardyng, who was very familiar with the Percy family and had written in anticipation of Richard duke of York's accession, dismissed the idea of a Welsh line reclaiming the English Crown as 'vayne fantasye'.[84] For Hardyng, who despised the Welsh as much as he did the Scots, the idea of a Welsh saviour would not have been palatable. Moreover, Hardyng must have known that many incarnations of the prophecy imagined a future in which Britain was divided in three.[85] This was likely fuelled both by Welsh resentment of English rule and the ambitions of the Tripartite Indenture between Owain Glyn Dŵr, Sir Edmund Mortimer, and Henry Percy, earl of Northumberland, in 1405.[86] This division was the opposite of the quasi-imperial ambitions that Hardyng imagined for a king who was heir of Brutus simply by virtue of taking the English throne.

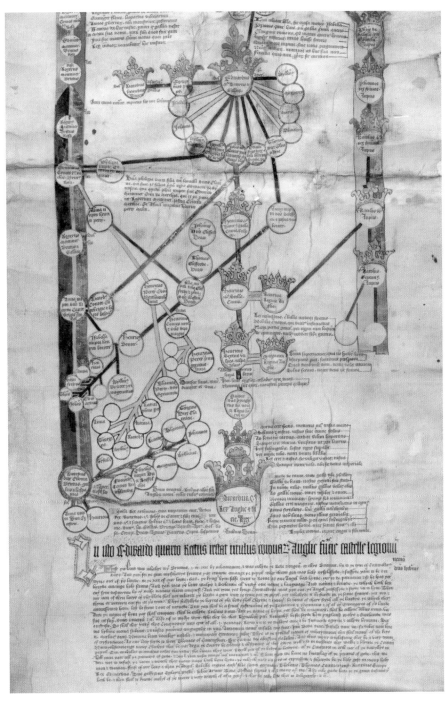

This genealogical roll from 1461 demonstrates that Edward IV's accession was the fulfilment of the prophecies of Merlin about the red and white dragons (© The British Library Board Add. MS 18268A)

The same uneasiness about this tradition perhaps explains its absence from the Edward IV poster associated with the Gloucester Dominicans – a multitude of other prophecies of Edward's accession are referenced in the top panel of this poster, but there is no sign of Cadwaladr.[87] At about the same time that Hardyng was writing, Robin Ddu of Anglesey completed an ode to Owen Tudor following his death at Edward's hands in the aftermath of the battle of Mortimer's Cross. In this the poet promised that there would still be 'victory of the red dragon over the dishonoured white'.[88] To Robin Ddu, Edward earl of March was a Saxon descendant of the white dragon, and it was the Tudors who embodied the red. The traditions surrounding Cadwaladr's heir and the prophecy of the red dragon were thus a contested and complex inheritance from many traditions which needed to be harnessed and controlled to Edward IV's needs.

This was done most effectively in BL Additional MS 18268A, a vellum roll that traces three lines of descent for Edward IV from the British (beginning with Cadwaladr's grandfather), Frankish and Saxon kings, and incorporates both the claim to Castile and Edward's lineage through Lionel duke of Clarence. At the very top it explains in Latin that the white dragon was defeated by the red in the year 1461. The words *Rubius Draco* are written over and over beside the British/ Welsh line and *Albus Draco* beside the Saxon/ English. The prophecy is explained in English at the foot of the page in much more detail. Unsurprisingly, there is no mention of Cadwaladr's body being moved from Rome. Instead, the prophesied time would be when the island's inhabitants had fallen into the 'same synnys' for which Cadwaladr and his people had been driven out, presumably meaning civil war and its attendant evils as a result of a sick king. Moreover, the angel continues by promising that Cadwaladr's heirs will recover 'all ye landys ye which they antecessowrs have lost beforne', and so govern England, Wales and Scotland as Brutus had done. It is not impossible that this roll emanated from Edward IV's immediate circle. However, this ambition for Scottish conquest and the prominent inclusion of the Percy family's descent from Philippa of Clarence and the 3rd earl of March may indicate that it was created by someone connected with the Percy family. They were perhaps consciously repurposing the earlier mythology discussed by Flood into a document more palatable to the new regime at the same time as reminding Edward IV that, despite their Lancastrian loyalties, the Percys were a family he should honour.

This dragon prophecy genealogy may have been used by the creator of the most striking genealogy of all: Philadelphia Free Library MS European 201.[89]

There seems little doubt that this roll was created specifically for Edward IV to depict him as he wished to be seen in the early years of his reign.[90] It is known as the *Coronation Roll*, or simply the *Edward IV Roll*, and makes full use of every element of Edward's Mortimer and Plantagenet legacies.[91] It is 479 cm long, brilliantly coloured, rich in gold detail, lavishly decorated with badges, shields and banners, and scattered with lines of Biblical texts and later 'prophetic' literature. The roll begins with a picture of Edward himself on horseback. The heraldry on his horse's trapper is that of the kingdoms he claimed – England, France, Castile and Leon – and set on this is an escutcheon of blue with three gold crowns which was, according to some fifteenth-century texts, the arms of Brutus.[92] Edward's British ancestry was consequently as immediately apparent as his royal aspirations. The roll provides a narrative of the ultimate triumph of dynastic rights despite being long in abeyance which all served to negate the impact of the fact that Edward's most obvious claim to kingship had been overlooked through so many generations.

The combination of images and texts, as Kathleen Scott observes, 'promote the idea that Edward had been destined to kingship since the Creation'.[93] Beneath Edward IV, one roundel encloses God in a sunburst at the moment of Creation. Below Him are Adam and Eve, and their line leading to Noah. A division of lines from Noah's grandson leads in one branch to the Trojans (and on to the Britons and the Franks) and in another to the Saxons. Previous genealogies of English kings had most commonly set the Trojan/ British/ Welsh line to the far right, even if the accompanying text mentioned the tradition that the descent from Noah was older. This roll makes the dynastic superiority of the British, with their Trojan and Roman connections, visually obvious by setting the British line on the left. In an age when it was commonplace to describe current events through comparisons with Roman history, this connection with Roman authority also added kudos to Edward's position. In order to include every king named by Geoffrey of Monmouth there is a somewhat confusing double line from Brutus which finally resolves with Cadwaladr. The Wigmore manuscript could have provided a conveniently shorter lineage from Brutus to Arthur's mother and Cadwaladr, but Edward opted for a pedigree that was familiar to English audiences and focussed on those who had actually ruled rather than on blood lineage.

This genealogy does lay claim to the red dragon prophecy through Edward's Welsh lineage – the names of Cadwaladr's descendants are frequently accompanied by the words 'Brutus' or *rubeus draco* and Gwladus Ddu's marriage to Ralph

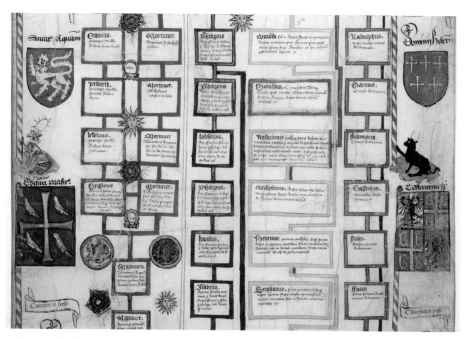

Mortimer family members are outlined in red on the Edward IV Roll. Roundels of red and gold dragons where the Mortimer line joins the royal house of Wales refer to the Prophecy of the Dragon which Edward IV claimed to fulfil. From the *Chronicle of the History of the World from Creation to Woden, with a Genealogy of Edward IV* (© Free Library of Philadelphia, Lewis E 201)

Mortimer is marked with red and gold dragons in roundels to draw attention to this point in the line. However, this narrative is trumped by the much more prominent paintings a little further up the scroll of seven worthies representing Edward's seven titles of prince of Wales, duke of Cornwall, king of France, of England, and of Castile and Leon, duke of Aquitaine and duke of Normandy (see image on p. 217). Below these figures the lines of the dukes of Normandy and Aquitaine, counts of Anjou, the Mortimers and the de Clare ancestors of Elizabeth de Burgh are introduced to the genealogy. The last of these provides yet another opportunity to celebrate inheritance through the female line as well as explaining Edward's title to the earldom of Ulster. Curiously the Mortimer line is distinct from all the others because, until the marriage with Philippa of Clarence, each entry is headed with the same name – Mortimer – rather than the given names which head every entry in the other lines (the given names of the Mortimers appear in smaller letters below their surname). In contrast to the red dragon genealogy or Hardyng's chronicle, this roll is more circumspect about aspirations to lordship in Scotland. No doubt claiming a right to Scottish

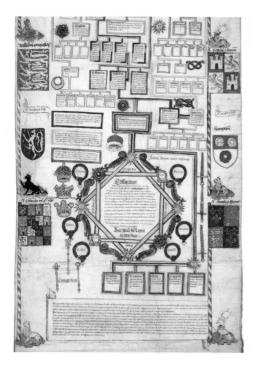

At the top of this section of Philadelphia, Lewis E 201 Anne Mortimer and her siblings are framed in gold and blue to indicate their descent from Edward III as heirs of England and France. Below Anne, Richard of Consiburgh's frame includes a deep red for his Castilian descent. Around Edward IV himself these colours are interlaced with a square of scarlet, white and green, reintroducing the colours used earlier for his Mortimer, Irish and Welsh/ British descent respectively. In the lower half of the manuscript the banners are all supported by either the white lion of March, the black bull of Clare or Richard II's white hart. From the *Chronicle of the History of the World from Creation to Woden, with a Genealogy of Edward IV* (© Free Library of Philadelphia, Lewis E 201)

kingship would have been impolitic at a time when Edward was trying to persuade the Scots not to support the Lancastrians, but the creator of this roll perhaps also recognised that such a claim was so tenuous that it could only serve to undermine the credibility of the other lines of descent that Edward claimed. Instead, he simply added in a note beside Edward I that John Balliol had paid homage to that king at Newcastle.

Gradually the multitude of lines resolve themselves in the offspring of Anne Mortimer and Richard of Conisburgh, with Edward's name at the centre, surrounded by emblems of his royal claim: ostrich feathers, garters, crowns, swords and sceptres. The genealogy is decorated throughout with Edward's badges: the rose-en-soleil above all, but also sunbursts and fetterlocks. At least 20 of the 54 banners and shields along the margins related directly to the Mortimer family or their British lineage.[94] In the lower half of the scroll, each banner is supported by one of Edward IV's beasts – the Mortimer white lion, Richard II's white hart or the black bull with golden horns of Clare. Such prestige pieces as this manuscript would only ever be seen by a small audience but these emblems, succinct allusions to the king's Mortimer heritage, were scattered liberally across England in woodwork, glass and heraldic paintings.

Edward IV: Mortimer emblems

As Michael Siddons has argued, the white lion was likely first adopted by Edmund Mortimer, 3rd earl of March, in homage to his father-in-law, Lionel duke of Clarence.[95] The origins of the black bull with golden horns are more opaque since its earliest surviving identification with Clare is a 1460/61 list of badges of the duke of York. It may not be a coincidence that the black bull with golden horns was also linked with King Arthur.[96] Both the lion and the bull were used as supporters for Edward IV's arms. His mother, Cecily, eventually came to use the combination of a white hart and a Mortimer lion that appears in the University of Chicago Wigmore manuscript for her husband.[97] The emblem most closely associated with Edward IV, however, has become synonymous with the House of York and the county of Yorkshire, despite being another legacy from Anne Mortimer and the earls of March: the white rose.

Roses were common emblems in the fourteenth and fifteenth centuries and the earliest Mortimer use was very likely not governed by a particular colour. The dragon prophecy genealogy ascribes the rose to Hugh Mortimer and his descendants. It is likely that the roll's creator was backdating its use too far, but certainly in 1461 we must assume that the rose was understood to be a Mortimer emblem. A widely-copied list of the duke of York's badges recorded that 'the bages that he beryth by the Castle of Clyfford is a Whyte Roose'.[98] Roger Mortimer, 1st earl of March had taken this castle into his possession in August 1330, not long before he was deposed by Edward III.[99] Two decades later, Clifford Castle was among the many properties eventually returned to the earl's grandson in the 1350s and so it came into the House of York's possession in 1425. However, the *Coronation Roll* suggests a different Mortimer descent for the rose – Maud de Braose, wife of Gwladus Ddu's son, Roger, is marked *prima rosa*, 'the first rose'. Richard duke of York had

In the 1470s Cecily Duchess of York paired the Mortimer Lion with Richard II's White Hart on her Great Seal (© Society of Antiquaries of London)

included a rose on one of his earliest seals and it appears in white on some of his manuscripts, including the *Consulatu de Stilicho*.[100] Fred Hepburn has plausibly suggested that it was the prophecy of the red dragon and the white that then inspired Henry Tudor to balance Edward IV's white rose by adopting a red rose for his own family. The invention of the Tudor rose firmly identified the white rose in the popular imagination with the House of York, yet the Wars of the Roses might more accurately be described as a conflict between the families of Lancaster and Mortimer, than of Lancaster and York.[101]

CONCLUSION

Anne Mortimer's descent from Lionel, duke of Clarence, was the *sine qua non* of the House of York's claim to precedence over the Lancastrian dynasty. But it was only by adding her brother's estates to their existing titles and lands that the York family occupied a sufficiently powerful position to take advantage of that lineage. Many of the Mortimer family properties remained in royal hands long after, and both the Mortimer white lion and the black bull of Clarence are among the heraldic beasts still used by the modern royal family. The Mortimer legacy for the House of York went beyond the tangible effects of a historic bloodline and wealth. The literary culture at Clare in the 1440s and '50s enhanced Richard duke of York's position. And through the 1460s the legends associated with Gwladus Ddu's family were effectively harnessed to strengthen Edward IV's image, despite controversy over their credibility and a risky association with a divided Britain. Perhaps the most significant of all the threads of Anne Mortimer's legacy was that, when Edward IV successfully established his sovereignty on the basis of descent through Anne and Philippa, he ensured that the English Crown would never be constrained, as the French was, by the exclusion of women. Ironically it was another claimant to the red dragon prophecy, Henry Tudor, who next made effective use of this in a claim that rested not only on his mother but also his future wife, Edward IV's daughter. It would be more than five centuries before a queen regnant finally succeeded in pushing this to its logical conclusion so that women could inherit the English throne on equal terms with their brothers.

~

ABBREVIATIONS

BBCS	*Bulletin Board of Celtic Studies*
BIHR	*Bulletin of the Institute of Historical Research*
BJRL	*Bulletin of the John Rylands Library*
CACCW	*Calendar of Ancient Correspondence concerning Wales*
CCR	*Calendar of Close Rolls*
CDS	*Calendar of Documents Relating to Scotland*
CFR	*Calendar of Fine Rolls*
CIM	*Calendar of Inquisitions: Miscelleaneous*
CIPM	*Calendar of Inquisitions Post Mortem*
CPR	*Calendar of Patent Rolls*
EETS	Early English Text Society
EHR	*English Historical Review*
Foedera	*Foedera, conventiones, litterae et cujuscunque generis acta publica*, 4 vols in 7 parts (London: Record Commission, 1816–69)
HMSO	Her Majesty's Stationery Office
IHS	*Irish Historical Studies*
JBS	*Journal of British Studies*
JMH	*Journal of Medieval History*
JMHS	*Journal of the Mortimer History Society*
ODNB	*The Oxford Dictionary of National Biography*, ed. H.C.G. Matthew and B.H. Harrison, 60 vols (Oxford, 2004–); online at: www.oxforddnb.com
PMLA	*Proceedings of the Modern Language Association of America*
PRIA	*Proceedings of the Royal Irish Academy*
PROME	*Parliament Rolls of Medieval England, 1275–1504*, ed. P. Brand, A. Curry, C. Given-Wilson, R. Horrox, G.H. Martin, W.M. Ormrod and J.R.S. Phillips, 16 vols (Woodbridge: Boydell & Brewer, 2005)
RCAHMW	Royal Commission on Ancient and Historic Monuments of Wales
RLC	*Rotuli Litterarum Clausarum in Turri Londoniensi Asservati*
Rot. Parl.	*Rotuli Parliamentorum*
Rot. Scot.	*Rotuli Scotiae*
RS	Rolls Series
TRHS	*Transactions of the Royal Historical Society*
VCH	Victoria County History of England

NOTES

1. Mortimer women, dynastic power and the Welsh frontier, *c.*1066–1282
Dr Emma Cavell

1 *The Ecclesiastical History of Orderic Vitalis,* ed. Marjorie Chibnall, 6 vols (Oxford, 1969–80),
   iv, 87–9.
2 *Calendar of Documents Preserved in France, 918–1206,* ed. J.H. Round (London, 1899), no. 1264.
   The Mortimers' kinship with William the Conqueror is set out in Ian Mortimer, 'The
   chronology of the de Mortimer family of Wigmore, *c.*1075–1185, and the consolidation of a
   Marcher lordship', *Historical Research,* 89 (2016), 613–35, 614 and idem, 'An Outline Genealogy
   of the Mortimers' on the Mortimer History Society website: https://mortimerhistorysociety.
   org.uk/the-mortimers/mortimer-genealogies/ [last accessed 10/2/2023]. See also Katherine
   Keats-Rohan, 'Aspects of Robert of Torigny's genealogies revisited', *Nottingham Medieval
   Studies,* 37 (1993), 21–7, 24. Kinship between Stephen count of Aumale and the Conqueror is
   mentioned in a charter, dated 1115, issued by Count Stephen to the monks of St Lucian of
   Beauvais: *Early Yorkshire Charters,* ed. William Farrer and C.T. Clay, 12 vols (Edinburgh and
   Wakefield, 1914–65), iii, no. 1304.
3 P.M. Remfry, 'The Early Mortimers of Wigmore', *Foundations,* 3 (2011), 404–8, 405–6. Cf
   Farrer's explanation for Eustace FitzJohn's possession of Mortimer territory in *Early Yorkshire
   Charters,* iii, v.
4 *Chartes de l'Abbaye de Jumièges v. 825 à 1204,* ed. J.-J. Vernier, 2 vols (Rouen, 1916), i (A.D.
   825–1169), no. 37. The original is Archives Départementales de Seine-Maritime, Normandy, 9
   H 1739/1. The couple's crosses, which are almost certainly autograph, are visible at the head
   of the witness list. A photograph of the charter is available through the AD de Seine-Maritime
   official website: https://www.archivesdepartementales76.net/ [last accessed 17/1/2023]. Thank
   you to my colleague, Professor Daniel Power, for alerting me to this online repository.
5 *Cal. Docs France,* no. 1264.
6 Mortimer, 'The chronology of the de Mortimer family of Wigmore', 631; Daniel Power, *The
   Norman Frontier in the Twelfth and Early Thirteenth Centuries* (Cambridge, 2004), 368, 370 n. 21.
7 *Ecclesiastical History of Orderic Vitalis,* vi, 281. Thank you to Daniel Power for providing me
   with this reference.

8   For Hugh's death, in old age, as a canon of Wigmore, see the short Latin chronicle of the
    Mortimers of Wigmore published by William Dugdale under the title *Fundationis et
    Fundatorum Historia*: William Dugdale, *Monasticon Anglicanum*, ed. J. Caley et al., 6 vols
    (London, 1846–9), vi (i), 348–55, and the sets of annals (1066–1306) and chronicle extracts
    (1360–77) published together as *The Wigmore Chronicle 1066–1377. A Translation of John Ryland
    Manuscript 215, ff.1-8 and Trinity College, Dublin, MS.488, ff. 295–9*, ed. P.M. Remfry (2013),
    20. For Hugh's likely retirement, around 1181, and the transfer of his lands to his son, see: *Pipe
    Roll*, 27 Henry II, 2, 4, 17, 19. For the possible existence of an older brother, see Mortimer,
    'The chronology of the de Mortimer family of Wigmore', pp. 620–1 and idem, 'Outline
    Genealogy' https://mortimerhistorysociety.org.uk/the-mortimers/mortimer-genealogies/
    [last accessed 10/2/2023]

9   R.W. Eyton, *Antiquities of Shropshire*, 12 vols (London, 1854–60), ii, 205n.

10 Belmeis's 1138/9 charter granting Ruckley in Tong to Buildwas Abbey is printed in full Eyton,
    Antiquities, ii, 202. For charters concerning the Lilleshall canons see, for example: Shropshire
    Archives, Shrewsbury, 6000/16290; *The Cartulary of Lilleshall Abbey*, ed. Una Rees
    (Shrewsbury, 1997), no. 18; *Mon. Ang.*, vi, 262.

11 Mortimer, 'The chronology of the de Mortimer family of Wigmore', 632.

12 See the Anglo-Norman *Chronicle* of Wigmore Abbey, likely compiled between c.1185 and after
    1252, published in *Three Anglo-Norman Chronicles*, ed. Peter T. Ricketts (Manchester, 2011),
    5–19, 10–11. See also *Ludlow Castle. Its History and Buildings*, ed. Ron Shoesmith and Andy
    Johnson (Almeley, 2000), 31–3.

13 For Roger's imprisonment following the murder of Cadwallon, see the Anglo-Norman
    Chronicle, 15. The killing itself is in *Brut y Tywysogyon or The Chronicle of the Princes. Peniarth
    MS 20 Version*, ed. T. Jones (Cardiff, 1952), 72 and *The Historical Works of Ralph de Diceto*, ed.
    William Stubbs, 2 vols (1876), i, 437. For Roger's capture in Normandy and destruction of
    Wigmore Abbey, see *The Wigmore Chronicle*, 30. The *Fundationis et Fundatorum Historia*
    erroneously places the burning of the abbey in 1221.

14 *Rot. Lit. Claus.*, i, 34, 46b, 47.

15 *Rot. Lit. Claus.*, i, 65b, 85b.

16 Following the loss of Normandy in 1204, Isabel's eldest brother, who held the family estates,
    chose to remain in the allegiance of the king of France. Isabel bought Lechlade (with
    Longbridge) in 1205 and Oakham in 1207, at a total cost of 600 marks: *Rot. Lit. Claus.*, i, 30b,
    97; *Pipe Roll*, 6 John, 148; *Rot. Ob. et Fin.*, 209.

17 Sethina Watson, 'A mother's past and her children's futures: female inheritance, family and
    dynastic hospitals in the thirteenth century', in *Motherhood, Religion, and Society in Medieval
    Europe, 400–1400. Essays presented to Henrietta Leyser*, ed. Leslie Smith and Conrad Leyser
    (Farnham, 2011), 213–49, 238.

18 See David Carpenter, 'A noble in politics: Roger Mortimer in the period of baronial reform
    and rebellion, 1258–1265', in *Nobles and Nobility in Medieval Europe: Concepts, Origins, and
    Transformations*, ed. Anne J. Duggan (Woodbridge, 2000), 183–203.

19 Anglo-Norman *Chronicle*, 16. The concluding portion of narrative, in which this story is told,
    was written down only after Isabel's death in c.1252. In contrast to the rest of the narrative,
    which was penned around 1200, this section is concerned with the relationship between Roger
    Mortimer (d.1214) and Wigmore Abbey.

20 Anglo-Norman *Chronicle*, 17.

21 Watson, 'A mother's past and her children's futures', 238–43.

22 *The Wigmore Chronicle*, 35; 'Annales of Tewkesbury' in *Annales Monastici*, ed. H.R. Luard, 5 vols (1864–9), i, 42–182, 69; *Reading Abbey Cartularies*, ed B.R. Kemp, Camden Society, 4th ser. 33, 2 vols (1987), ii, 235; *CPR*, 1225–32, 171; *Excerpta Rot. Fin.*, i, 166; *CCR*, 1242–1247, 450.

23 *The Beauchamp Cartulary Charters 1100–1268*, ed. Emma Mason, Pipe Roll Society, n.s. 43 (London, 1980), xxiii.

24 Watson, 'A mother's past and her children's futures', 238.

25 Anglo-Norman *Chronicle*, 17; *Fundationis et Fundatorum Historia*, 350–2. See also *CChR*, 1226–57, 296 and the 'Black Book of Wigmore': London, British Library, MS Harley 1240, f. 44v.

26 Watson, 'A mother's past and her children's futures', 241. Hugh's heart and viscera were interred in Reading Abbey: *Reading Abbey Cartularies*, ii, no. 1072.

27 BL, MS Harl. 1240, f. 48v (44v).

28 Watson, 'A mother's past and her children's futures', 241–2.

29 Brock Holden, *Lords of the Central Marches. English Aristocracy and Frontier Society 1087–1265* (Oxford, 2008), 84.

30 David Crouch, 'The complaint of King John against William de Briouze', in *Magna Carta and the England of King John*, ed. Janet S. Loengard (Woodbridge, 2010), 168–79, 171, 177.

31 *CCR*, 1231–4, 230, 421, 500; 1234–7,128, 299; 1237–42, 44, 66, 154, 269; *CPR*, 1225–32, 501; 1232–47, 80.

32 E.J. Dobson, *The Origins of Ancrene Wisse* (Oxford, 1976), 308.

33 Liz Herbert McAvoy, *Medieval Anchoritisms. Gender, Space and the Solitary Life* (Woodbridge, 2011), 97; A.K. Warren, *Anchorites and their Patrons in Medieval England* (Berkeley, 1985), 165–6, 175–7. See also Tom Licence, *Hermits and Recluses in English Society, 950–1200* (Oxford, 2011), 106–7.

34 Chapter 11 in this volume by J.L. Laynesmith, specifically 213.

35 *Brut y Tywysogyon. Peniarth*, 101–2. Note that William de Braose was the son of Gracia Brewer and not Llywelyn's daughter Gwladus.

36 BL, MS Harley 1240, f. 57; *CCR*, 1242–7, 484.

37 *Cal. Inq. post mortem*, ii, no. 446.

38 For details of Maud's extensive inheritance, see Emma Cavell, 'Periphery to core: Mortimer women and the negotiation of the king's justice in the thirteenth-century March of Wales', *Mortimer History Society Journal*, 2 (2018), 1–19, 3–4.

39 TNA, Kew, C(ommon) P(leas) 25/1/283, no. 378; British Library, London, Egerton Roll 8723, m. 3d.

40 The earl of Arundel is recorded in 1295 as having a brother, John: *Calendar of Ancient Correspondence concerning Wales*, ed. J.G. Edwards (Cardiff, 1935), 144.

41 *CCR*, 1268–72, 512; *Cal. Inq. post mortem*, i, no. 812.

42 *CFR*, 1272–1307, 309, 440.

43 See e.g. 'Annals of Tewkesbury', 179; 'Annals of Dunstable', in *Annales Monastici*, iii, 3–408, 227; *Flores Historiarum*, ed. H.R. Luard, 3 vols (London, 1890), ii, 486.

44 Carpenter, 'A noble in politics', 201.

45 *The Metrical Chronicle of Robert of Gloucester*, ed. W.A. Wright, 2 vols (1866–8), ii, 757–8.

46 *Metrical Chronicle*, 758; *De Antiquis Legibus Liber: Cronica Maiorum et Vicecomitum Londoniarum*, ed. T. Stapleton, Camden Soc., 34 (1846), pp. 75–6. For further chronicle references to Montfort's death and the treatment of his corpse, see Emma Cavell, 'Intelligence and intrigue in the March of Wales: noblewomen and the fall of Llywelyn ap Gruffudd, 1274–82', *Historical Research*, 88 (2015), 1–19, 7, n. 31.

47 TNA, S(pecial) C(ollections) 1/11, no. 47 and printed in *Cal. Ancient Correspondence*, 29.

48 TNA, SC 1/22, no. 69 and printed in *Cal. Ancient Correspondence*, 111.

49 *Annales Cambriae (A.D. 444–1288)*, ed. J.W. ab Ithel (London, 1860), 100; *Brut y Tywysogyon. Peniarth*, 110, 112; 'Annals of Waverley', 370; *Cal. Ancient Correspondence*, 94.

50 For evidence of the positive relationship between Isabel and her father see Emma Cavell, 'Aristocratic widows and the medieval Welsh frontier: the Shropshire evidence', *Transactions of the Royal Historical Society*, 17 (2007), 57–82, 75–7 and idem, 'Intelligence and intrigue', 4.

51 For fuller details of Isabel's interests in the Fitzalan lands, see Cavell, 'Aristocratic widows and the medieval Welsh frontier', 57–82.

52 TNA SC 8/219, no. 10925; *CPR*, 1272–81, 309, 404; Cavell, 'Aristocratic Widows', 73.

53 For a full breakdown of Fitzalan's possessions, including Isabel's dower therein see *CR*, 1268–72, 505–15.

54 See e.g. *The Wigmore Chronicle*, 53.

55 *CFR*, 1272–1307, 171.

56 *Cal. Ancient Correspondence*, pp. 130–1, 171–2.

57 *CCR*, 1279–88, 171, 198.

58 *CPR*, 1281–92, 38; *Cal. Welsh Rolls*, 257.

59 Cavell, 'Periphery to core', generally.

60 For a brief outline of the royal courts to which Maud and Isabel had access, see Cavell, 'Periphery to Core', esp. 7–8.

61 In the lands of William de Braose: their mother Eve Marshal (d.1246); Gwladus Ddu (d.1251), widow of Reginald de Braose; and Joan de Redvers widow of William Brewer junior. In the Marshal estates: Eleanor 'of England' (d.1275), sister of Henry III, widow of William Marshal junior and wife of Simon de Montfort; Marjorie of Scotland (d.1244), widow of Gilbert Marshal; Margaret de Quency (d.1266), widow of John de Lacy, hereditary constable of Chester, and of Walter Marshal; Maud de Bohun (d.c.1252), widow of Anselm Marshal and wife of Roger de Quency, earl of Winchester; and Maud de Lacy (d.1289), daughter of John de Lacy and Margaret de Quency above, and widow of Richard de Clare, earl of Hertford and Gloucester (son and heir of Isabel Marshal).

62 *CLR*, 1245–51, 147; *CCR*, 1242–7, 415; D.A. Carpenter, *The Struggle for Mastery. Britain 1066–1284* (London, 2003), 363.

63 *CCR*, 1237–42, 190, 350; 1242–7, 484; *CPR*, 1232–47, 326; 1247–58, 8, 156.

64 *CPR*, 1272–81, 12; TNA, K(ing's) B(ench) 27/12, m. 12d.

65 TNA, KB 26/159, m. 1d.

66 *CPR*, 1247–58, 41. See also G.H. Orpen, *Ireland under the Normans, 1169–1333*, 4 vols (Oxford, 1911–20), iii, 77.

67 *CCR*, 1247–51, 70–1, 156–7, 294, 366. Margaret's dower is detailed in L.J. Wilkinson, *Women in Thirteenth-Century Lincolnshire* (Woodbridge, 2007), 53–4.

68 See, for example, TNA, KB 27/92, m. 21; KB 27/94, mm. 28d, 45.

69 The arrangements are set out in Cavell, 'Aristocratic Widows', 76.

70 *CCR*, 1279–88, 262; Cavell, 'Aristocratic Widows', 76.

71 *The Welsh Assize Roll, 1277–1282*, ed. J.C. Davies (Cardiff, 1940), 277, 296. The plea reappeared at the common bench in 1280: TNA, CP 40/36, m. 53d; CP 40/38, m. 35; CP 40/41, m. 29d; CP 40/42, m. 88d.

72 For example: TNA, KB 26/208A, m. 25d; KB 26/208B, m. 7; KB 27/31, m. 17d; KB 27/33, m. 8d; KB 27/41, m. 24; KB 27/42, m. 11d; KB 27/45, m. 15; KB 27/47, m. 8; KB 27/49, m. 13d; CP 40/5, m. 14; CP 40/7, m. 9d; CP 40/9, m. 10; CP 40/21, m. 64; CP 40/26, m. 146d. See also Cavell, 'Aristocratic Widows', 61–2.

73 TNA, CP 40/50, m. 26; CP 40/51, m. 12.

74 See Linda E. Mitchell, 'Noble widowhood in the thirteenth century: three generations of Mortimer widows, 1246–1334' in *Upon my Husband's Death: Widows in the Literature and Histories of Medieval Europe*, ed. Louise Mirrer (Ann Arbor, 1992), 169–90, 176–8.

75 TNA, SC 1/19, no. 130.

76 TNA, SC 1/19, no. 131; *Recueil de lettres Anglo-Francaises, 1265–1399*, ed. F.J. Tanquerey (Paris, 1916), no. 70.

77 *CCR*, 1296–1302, 73.

78 *CCR*, 1279–88, 200, 205, 205. In about 1297 Maud also sent a formal petition, apparently dealt with by the Exchequer, concerning outstanding sums of money owed to her: TNA, SC 8/312/E26.

79 TNA, SC 8/219/10925; *CPR*, 1272–81, 309, 404; Cavell, 'Aristocratic Widows', 73.

80 Roger Mortimer was rewarded for his services in the war around this time: Cavell, 'Aristocratic Widows', 79.

81 TNA, SC 8/62/3077.

2. The Mortimers and their Welsh tenantry: some observations
Dr David Stephenson

1 In general, lowland regions of the March, which emerged as focal points of English manorial and proto-urban settlement, will not be the focus of this study.

2 B.P. Evans, 'The Family of Mortimer' unpublished PhD thesis, University of Wales, 1934; R.R. Davies, *Lordship and Society in the March of Wales 1282–1400*, (Oxford: Clarendon Press, 1978) – though Davies did not focus on the Mortimer lordships in the same way in which he examined, say, the de Bohun and Bolingbroke rule in Brecon lordship, a subject which had formed the basis of his doctoral thesis.

Other notable works include Speight and Hopkinson, *The Mortimers, Lords of the March* (Almeley: Logaston Press, 2002); J.J. Crump, 'The Mortimer family and the Making of the March,' in M.C. Prestwich, R.F. Frame and R.H. Britnell (eds.), *Thirteenth Century England* VI (Woodbridge, 1997), 117–26; Paul Dryburgh, 'The Career of Roger Mortimer, first earl of March c.1287–1330' (unpublished PhD thesis, University of Bristol, 2002); Philip Hume, *The Welsh Marcher Lordships Vol. 1: Central and North* (Logaston Press, 2021), and in general the impetus provided by the development of the Mortimer History Society, to the influence of which the present volume bears witness.

3 Davies, *Lordship and Society*, 40 notes that in the case of the Mortimers of Wigmore, minorities lasted for 46 years of the fourteenth century.

4 Ibid., 40–3.

5 Huw Pryce (ed.) *The Acts of Welsh Rulers, 1120–1283*, (Cardiff: University of Wales Press, 2005), no. 113.

6 Ibid., 252, where Pryce builds on an idea put forward by Paul Remfry. It is clear that Madog had the support of at least some of the *optimates* of Maelienydd, and it is possible that his presence in Maelienydd by May 1212 may have resulted less from an agreement with Roger Mortimer, and more from the latter's inability to dislodge him.

7 J. Beverley Smith, 'The Middle March in the Thirteenth Century' *BBCS* 24 (1970) 77–94, esp. 89–93. Hywel was noted as steward of Roger Mortimer 1277, while Philip ap Hywel was steward to Edmund in 1297. See David Stephenson, *Patronage and Power in the Medieval Welsh March: One Family's Story* (Cardiff: University of Wales Press, 2021), 19, 34–5.

8 Dryburgh, 'The career', 215 notes the 'constant shuttling between his Welsh and Irish estates' of Roger Mortimer (d.1330) in his early career, and that 'he could voyage to Ireland safe in the knowledge that his uncle of Chirk would be attending to his interests on the March.'

9 Ibid., 59.

10 Davies, *Lordship and Society*, 84. The livery as given in one Wigmore chronicle (Dugdale, *Monasticon Anglicanum* VI, (1) 352, was green with the right hand (glove) yellow.

11 Hopkinson and Speight, *The Mortimers*, 119.

12 *Calendar of Inquisitions, Miscellaneous*, II, 170. The record relates to Welsh forces which had deserted from Mortimer service, but is none the less significant as an indication of the size of the levies.

13 Thomas Jones (ed. and trans.) *Brut y Tywysogyon – Red Book of Hergest Version* (Cardiff: University of Wales Press, 1955), 252–3

14 David Stephenson, 'The chronicler at Cwmhir abbey, 1257–63: the construction of a Welsh chronicle', in R.A. Griffiths and P.R. Schofield (eds.), *Wales and the Welsh in the Middle Ages* (Cardiff: University of Wales Press, 2011).

15 *Eodem anno in uigilia sancti andree apostoli per industriam hominum de maelenit captum deuastatum fuit castellum de keuenellis. Eodem etiam die captum fuit castellum de bledvach et destructum.* The text as quoted here is that of the edition of Henry Gough-Cooper in the website of the Welsh Chronicles Research Group: http://croniclau.bangor.ac.uk/documents/AC%20B%20first%20 edition.pdf (accessed 30 September 2022). The castle and lordship of Bleddfa were held by Hugh Mortimer, a close ally of Roger: see Hume, *Welsh Marcher Lordships*, 149.

16 J.G. Edwards (ed.), *Calendar of Ancient Correspondence concerning Wales* (Cardiff: University of Wales Press, 1935), 131.

17 Ibid.

18 It is unclear whether the £500 payment was exacted in relation to both grants, or whether it applied simply to the hunting rights granted in the second charter. For the 1297 Maelienydd charters see *Calendar of Patent Rolls 1291–1301*, 290–1.

19 *Calendar of Close Rolls, 1296–1302*, 107.

20 Penry Evans, 'Family of Mortimer' 375, dates the charters, granted on the morrow of Holy Trinity, to 27 June, but the morrow of Holy Trinity in 1297 fell on 10 June.

21 For discussion of that episode see Stephenson, *Patronage and Power*, 34–5.

22 *Calendar of Ancient Correspondence*, 101.

23 The point is emphasised by Davies, *Lordship and Society*, 60.

24 It is clear that both Philip ap Hywel and his brother Master Rees/ Rhys maintained consistently close relations with the Mortimer family. See Stephenson, *Patronage and Power*, chapters 3 and 4, passim. In addition, Dryburgh, 'The Career', (quoting BL MS Harleian 1240, ff.39v., 40r.) 190, n.298, notes that Philip witnessed 'two charters of Roger Mortimer in 1316 and 1319': cf ibid., 72 n. 22.

25 Evans, Family of Mortimer', 509. It is probable that *tebeset* is to be identified as Tempseter in the western part of Clun lordship, a territory adjoining the border with Maelienydd.

26 For the most recent examination of these risings see David Stephenson '"The Malice and Rebellion of Certain Welshmen": The Welsh Risings of 1294–1295', in Adrian Jobson, Harriet Kersey and Gordon McKelvie (eds), *Rebellion in Medieval Europe* (Boydell, forthcoming).

27 BL Harleian MS 1240, f. 58. For further discussion see Dryburgh, 39, 189.

28 Evans 'Family of Mortimer', 476 notes that the grievances of the Welsh community of Maelienydd 'were but temporarily allayed by these charters … since forty years later a host of fines and amercements were still being levied there.' But the charters did not promise or attempt to remove 'fines and amercements', but expressly provided for them, albeit in a regulated and more reasonable form: see 30–31 above.

29 *Calendar of Ancient Correspondence*, 81.

30 BL Harleian MS 1240, ff. 67–8.

31 Evans, 'Family of Mortimer', 482

32 *Lordship and Society*, 47.

33 *Calendar of Inquisitions Miscellaneous*, II 295–6. For a partial restoration of the rights of the Welsh community under the Arundel lords of Chirk in the following years (in exchange for very substantial payments) see Evans, 'Family of Mortimer', 481, Davies, *Lordship and Society*, n.22, and for context and full details Llinos Beverley Smith, 'The Arundel charters to the lordship of Chirk in the fourteenth century, *BBCS* 23 (1969) 153–66.

34 Notwithstanding the fact that the lord's demesne around Pilleth had been leased out by the later fourteenth century: Hopkinson and Speight, *The Mortimers*, 151. The symbolic associations of a site might endure beyond its immediate use or possession.

35 See 12–13 above.

36 The phrase is that of Rees Davies, *Lordship and Society*, 61, here with specific reference to the situation in the lordship of Chirk.

37 See D.R. Johnston (gol.) *Gwaith Iolo Goch* (Caerdydd: Gwasg Prifysgol Cymru, 1988), poem XX.

38 Roger's pedigree went back to the union of Gwladus Ddu, daughter of Llewelyn ab Iorwerth, and Ralph Mortimer of Wigmore, the Syr Raff of line 4 of the poem.

39 Ibid., poem VIII, l.96. It should be noticed, however, that there is some uncertainty as to whether the lines of the poem to Glyn Dŵr, in which the phrase appears, are part of the original composition or a rather later addition; see Gruffydd Aled Williams, 'More than "skimble-skamble stuff": the medieval Welsh poetry associated with Owain Glyndŵr', *Proceedings of the British Academy*, 181 (2012) 1–33, at 27. That uncertainty does not damage the point being made here.

40 Compare the verdict of Dryburgh, 'The Career', 230, on the first earl of March that 'He was a harsh landlord who, conversely, repeatedly found himself able to rely on the loyalty of his men …'.

3. THE CASTLES OF THE MORTIMERS: AN OVERVIEW
Dr John R. Kenyon

1 D. Stephenson, 'Rhyd yr Onen Castle: politics and possession in western Arwystli in the later twelfth century', *Montgomeryshire Collections* 94 (2006), 15–22.

2 P. Hume, *On the trail of the Mortimers in the Welsh Marches*. New edition (Eardisley: Logaston Press, 2022). See also C. Hopkinson and M. Speight, *The Mortimers, lords of March* (Almeley: Logaston Press, 2002 – especially chapter 10).

3 L. Butler and J.K. Knight, *Dolforwyn Castle, Montgomery Castle* (Cardiff: Cadw, 2004).

4 P. Hume, *The Welsh Marcher lordships 1: central and north* (Eardisley: Logaston Press, 2021).

5 For details of several publications on the conservation of Wigmore, as well as the works by Paul Remfry on the castle and its owners, see J.R. Kenyon, *Castles, town defences and artillery fortifications in the United Kingdom and Ireland: a bibliography 1945–2006*, 183–84 (Donington: Shaun Tyas, 2008).

6 S. Rátkai, *Wigmore Castle, north Herefordshire: excavations 1996 and 1998* (London: Society for Medieval Archaeology, 2015 – Monograph 34). The report includes a chapter on the history and architecture of the castle by C. Davidson Cragoe, 5–34. Other publications to note that appeared after the bibliography cited in note 4 include R. Shoesmith, *Castles & moated sites of Herefordshire*, revised edition, 288–301 (Almeley: Logaston Press, 1996). Also, the summary of the site visit to the castle during the Castle Studies Group's annual conference in April 2016: *Castle Studies Group Journal* 30 (2016–17), 76–94. This last publication contains two reconstruction drawings, with different perspectives, and there is one in Shoesmith.

7 Rátkai (note 6), 238.

8 Ibid., 14, 22.

9 Ibid., 10; *Castle Studies Group Journal* 30 (2016–17), 78.

10 R. Higham, *Shell-keeps revisited: the bailey on the motte?* [S.l.] (Castle Studies Group, 2015). Also available on the CSG's website. Royal Commission on Historical Monuments England, *An inventory of the historical monuments in Herefordshire. 3. North-west*, 205–8 (London: HMSO, 1934).

11 L.B. Larking, 'Inventory of the effects of Roger de Mortimer at Wigmore Castle and Abbey, Herefordshire', *Archaeological* Journal 15 (1858), 354–62.

12 C. Davidson Cragoe, 'Historical and architectural overview', in Rátkai (note 6), 29–31.

13 R. Shoesmith and A. Johnson (eds), *Ludlow Castle: its history & buildings*. Extended edition (Almeley: Logaston Press, 2006; first published 2000). W.H. St J. Hope's paper remains of great value, with one of the earliest uses of colour phased plans: 'The castle of Ludlow', *Archaeologia* 61 (1908), 257–328.

14 A.D.F. Streeten, 'Monument preservation, management & display', in Shoesmith and Johnson (note 13), 117–22.

15 See the two chapters on the north range by R.K. Morriss and the late M.W. Thompson in Shoesmith and Johnson (note 11), 155–66, 167–84. Thompson preferred a date ranging from 1250 to 1280 for the solar and hall, but this author supports the Morriss theory of post-1280. On the rooms adjacent to the Pendover Tower, see a recent report for the Powis Estate by R. Cook of ArchaeoDomus: *Pendover Tower & Tudor lodgings, Ludlow Castle, Shropshire* (Lampeter: ArchaeoDomus Archaeological & Heritage Services, 2021).

16 Thompson (note 15), 172.

17 P. Remfry and P. Halliwell, 'St. Peter's Chapel & the court house', in Shoesmith and Johnson (note 13), 201–4.

18 A. Brooks and N. Pevsner, *Herefordshire (The buildings of England)*, 392–93. London: Yale University Press, 2012.

19 J.A.A. Goodall, 'The baronial castles of the Welsh conquest', in D.M. Williams and J.R. Kenyon (eds), *The impact of the Edwardian castles in Wales*, 155–65 (Oxford: Oxbow Books, 2010). See also the same author's *The English castle, 1066–1650* (London: Yale University Press, 2011).

20 R. Turner and C. Jones-Jenkins, 'The history and digital reconstruction of Holt Castle, Denbighshire', *Archaeologia Cambrensis* 165 (2016), 241–82.

21 A. Taylor, *The Welsh castles of Edward I*, 43. London: Hambledon Press, 1986.

22 Goodall, *The English castle* (note 19), 244; see also Goodall's paper on Alnwick: 'The early development of Alnwick Castle, c.1100–1400', in J. Ashbee and J. Luxford (eds), *Newcastle and Northumberland: Roman and medieval architecture and art*, 232–47 (Leeds: Maney for the British Archaeological Association, 2013 – Conference transactions 36).

23 N. Ludlow, 'The castle and lordship of Narberth', *Journal of the Pembrokeshire Historical Society* 12 (2003), 5–43. The writer is indebted to Neil's paper, as well as a site visit, for this piece on Narberth.

24 P.M. Remfry, *The castles and history of Radnorshire.* Revised edition. [S.l.]: Castle Studies Research & Publishing, 2008.

25 D.M. Brown and A. Pearson, *Cefnllys Castle, Radnorshire.* Aberystwyth: RCAHMW, [2006]. See https://coflein.gov.uk/en/archive/6180112/. A PDF of the report can be accessed and downloaded via a link at the bottom of the site entry for Cefnllys Castle (NPRN 96530) on Coflein, here: https://coflein.gov.uk/en/site/96530/. See also A.E. Brown, 'The castle, borough and park of Cefnllys', *Transactions of the Radnorshire Society* 42 (1972), 11–22. That one of the sites may have been built by the Welsh has been suggested (Remfry, ibid.), a theory disregarded by the present writer.

26 J.G. Edwards, *Calendar of correspondence concerning Wales*, 94. Cardiff: University Press Board, 1935.

27 R. Suggett, *Houses & history in the March of Wales: Radnorshire 1400–1800*, 37–38 (Aberystwyth: RCAHMW, 2005).

28 A.E. Brown (note 25), 19.

29 R.A. Brown, H.M. Colvin and A.J. Taylor, *The history of the king's works. 2. The Middle Ages*, 624 (London: HMSO, 1963).

30 Ibid. In that year the various editions of the Chronicle of the Princes record that 'Roger Mortimer came with a host to Maelienydd. And he built a castle in the place called Cymaron and drove away the two sons of Cadwallon.' *Brut y Tywysogyon or the Chronicle of the Princes. Peniarth Ms. 20 version*, 75 (Cardiff: University of Wales Press, 1952). See also J.J. Crump, 'The Mortimer family and the making of the March', in M. Prestwich, R.H. Britnell and R. Frame (eds), *Thirteenth century England VI: proceedings of the Durham conference 1995*, 117–26 (Woodbridge: Boydell Press, 1997).

31 *Ancient Monuments Board for Wales Annual Report* 38 (1991–2), 16.

32 For the town in particular, see R. Silvester, 'New Radnor: the topography of a medieval planned town in mid-Wales', in N. Edwards (ed.), *Landscape and settlement in medieval Wales*, 157–64 (Oxford: Oxbow Books, 1997 – Monograph 81).

33 R.R. Davies, *The revolt of Owain Glyn Dŵr*, 260 (Oxford: Oxford University Press, 1995).

34 L. Butler and J.K. Knight (note 3).

35 L. Butler, 'Dolforwyn Castle: prospect and retrospect', in J.R. Kenyon and K. O'Conor (eds), *The medieval castle in Ireland and Wales: essays in honour of Jeremy Knight*, 149–62 (Dublin: Four Courts Press, 2003).

36 R. Williams, 'Early documents relating to Dolforwyn Castle, Newtown, etc.' *Montgomeryshire Collections* 28 (1894), 145–64. Butler and Knight (note 2), 15. See also Butler (note 35), 154–62 for a study of the distribution and access of the Llywelyn/ Mortimer buildings.

37 Brown, Colvin and Taylor (note 29), 743. Butler and Knight (note 3).

38 L.A.S. Butler, *Denbigh Castle, Denbigh town walls, Lord Leicester's Church, St Hilary's Chapel, Denbigh Friary*. Revised edition (Cardiff: Cadw, 2007). W. J. Hemp, 'Denbigh Castle', *Y Cymmrodor* 36 (1926), 64–120.

39 Butler, ibid., 14. Hemp, ibid., 83.

40 J.K. Knight and A. Johnson (eds), *Usk Castle, priory and town* (Almeley: Logaston Press, 2008).

41 S.C. Priestley and R.C. Turner, 'Three castles of the Clare family in Monmouthshire during the thirteenth and fourteenth centuries', *Archaeologia Cambrensis* 152 (2003), 9–52: 20.

42 Ibid., 16.

43 R.J. Silvester, Castell Blaenllynfi, Brecknock: a Marcher castle and its landscape', *Archaeologia Cambrensis* 153 (2004), 75–103. R.F. Walker, 'Bwlchyddinas Castle, Breconshire, and the survey of 1337', *Brycheiniog* 31 (1998–9), 19–30.

44 B. Smith, 'Transitional lordship and the Plantagenet empire: the Mortimer lords of Wigmore, 1247–1425', *Welsh History Review* 29 (2018), 27–50: 35. See also A.R. Hayden, *Trim Castle, Co. Meath: excavations 1995–8*. Dublin: Stationery Office, 2011. See pages 18–21 for the role of the Mortimers at Trim in the chapter contributed by Seán Duffy. See also K. O'Brien and J. Fenlon, *Trim Castle, Co. Meath* (Dublin: Dúchas, the Heritage Service, 2002).

45 T. McNeill, *Castles in Ireland: feudal power in a Gaelic world*, 192 (London: Routledge, 1997). O'Brien and Fenlon (ibid.), 50.

46 R.K. Morris, 'Review article: Goodall, John, *The English castle*', *Transactions of the Ancient Monuments Society* 56 (2012), 129–36, 130.

47 Rátkai (note 6), chapter by S.J. Linnane, 34–73.

48 L. Butler, 'Dolforwyn Castle, Montgomery, Powys. First report: the excavations 1981–1986', *Archaeologia Cambrensis* 138 (1989), 78–98; idem, 'Dolforwyn Castle, Montgomery, Powys. Second report: the excavations 1987–1994', *Archaeologia Cambrensis* 144 (1995), 133–203. Dr Lawrence Butler died in 2014, and the third report, on the final excavations, has not been published, requiring work on the plans, and the finds were to be examined in detail in a fourth report but see Butler (note 35), 153–54 and the section on material evidence in the two interim reports. I am grateful to Dr Sian Rees, formerly of Cadw, for the state of play re the final two reports.

49 J.K. Knight, 'Excavations at Montgomery Castle. Part III. The finds: other than metalwork', *Archaeologia Cambrensis* 143 (1994), 139–203: 162–65.

50 Ibid., 179–83 for the glass, 196–203 for Graeme Lawson's study of the musical instrument remains. The glass is published in colour in the guidebook to the castle (Butler and Knight – note 3, 17).

51   J.K. Knight, 'Excavations at Montgomery Castle. Part II. The finds: metalwork', *Archaeologia Cambrensis* 142 (1993), 182–242. The author's report on the excavations themselves appeared in *Archaeologia Cambrensis* 141 (1992), 97–180.

52   TNA E 154/1/11B. Larking (note 11); Rátkai (note 6), 26. Ian Mortimer made use of this survey in his *The greatest traitor: the life of Sir Roger Mortimer* (London: Jonathan Cape, 2003), 116–20.

53   R. Williams, 'Early documents relating to Dolforwyn Castle, Newtown, etc.', *Montgomeryshire Collections* 28 (1894), 145–64: 151–3.

54   TNA E 372/179, rot. 22d, .2. I am grateful to Dr Paul Dryburgh for providing the correct reference to this document in The National Archives, and to Dr Jeremy Ashbee who very kindly translated the survey for me. The original document is included in D.A. Harding's M.Phil. thesis, 'The regime of Isabella and Mortimer, 1326–1330', University of Durham, 1985, Appendix 3.

55   I wish to thank Jeremy Ashbee, Will Davies, Paul Dryburgh, Neil Guy, Philip Hume, Christine Kenyon and Bill Zajac who assisted me in a variety of matters. Will's comments on the castles in Radnorshire were invaluable and various suggestions have been incorporated into my text. Of course, any errors are mine alone.

4. The escape of Roger Mortimer from the Tower of London, 1323
Dr Laura Tompkins

1   The main accounts of Mortimer's life are: R.R. Davies, 'Mortimer, Roger, first earl of March (1287–1330), regent, solider, and magnate', *Oxford Dictionary of National Biography* (2008); P.R. Dryburgh, 'The Career of Roger Mortimer, first earl of March (c.1287–1330)' (Unpublished PhD Thesis, University of Bristol, 2002); I. Mortimer, *The Greatest Traitor: The Life of Sir Roger Mortimer, 1st Earl of March, Ruler of England, 1327–1330* (London, 2003).

2   TNA, E 163/24/12, printed in J.C. Davies, *The Baronial Opposition to Edward II, its Character and Policy* (Cambridge, 1918), 565; *CPR, 1321–24*, 249; *1327–30*, 141–3; *The Anonimalle Chronicle, 1307 to 1334: From Brotherton Collection MS 29*, ed. W.R. Childs and J. Taylor (Leeds, 1991), 110–11.

3   A. Gransden, *Historical Writing in England II: c.1307 to the Early Sixteenth Century* (London, 1982), 4–7.

4   *Johannis de Trokelowe et Henrici de Blaneforde, Monachorum Sancti Albani, Necnon Quorundam Anonymorum, Chronica et Annales*, ed. H.T. Riley (London, 1866), 145–6.

5   For discussion of Blaneford's inaccurate dating to 1324, see E.L.G. Stones, 'The Date of Roger Mortimer's Escape from the Tower of London', *English Historical Review*, 66 (1951), 97–8.

6   J. Taylor, *English Historical Literature in the Fourteenth Century* (Oxford, 1987), ch. 6 'The French Prose *Brut* and Its Continuations', and app. 1 'The Long Continuation of the Prose *Brut* (1307–1333)'; *Anonimalle*, 15–17; Gransden, *Historical Writing*, 73–6.

7   *The Brut or The Chronicles of England*, ed. F.W.D. Brie (London, 1906), 231. Spelling and grammar modernised.

8   This was probably because Segrave was a former retainer of Lancaster: J.R. Maddicott, *Thomas of Lancaster, 1307–1322. A Study in the Reign of Edward II* (London, 1970), 48, 51, 54, 59, 61.

9   *Anonimalle*, 3–20.

10   Ibid., 114–17.

11 *Chroniques de London*, ed. G.J. Aungier, Camden Society, 28 (London, 1844), 46–7.

12 Gransden, *Historical Writing*, 17–22; J.R.S. Phillips, *Edward II* (London, 2010), 8–9.

13 *Flores Historiarum*, ed. H.R. Luard (London, 1890), iii, 217. Biblical quotes or allusions italicised. Translation adapted from Gransden, *Historical Writing*, 20.

14 *Chronicles of the Reigns of Edward I and Edward II*, ed. W. Stubbs, 2 vols (London, 1882–3), I, 305–6.

15 Gransden, *Historical Writing*, 25–9. The author of the *Annales Paulini* also had factual knowledge of an inquisition held in Portsmouth regarding the escape, discussed in further detail below.

16 *Adae Murimuth Continuatio Chronicarum*, ed. E.M. Thompson (London, 1889), 40; *Vita Edwardi Secundi: The Life of Edward II*, ed. W.R. Childs (Oxford, 2005), xxii, 127.

17 *CCR, 1323–27*, 13–14.

18 *Chronicon de Henrici Knighton vel Cnitthon Monachi Leycestrensis*, ed. J.R. Lumby, 2 vols (London, 1889–95), I, 429; Gransden, *Historical Writing*, 159–60.

19 *CPR, 1327–30*, 498–9.

20 *Ibid.*, 240.

21 *Ibid.*, 14.

22 *Brut*, 231.

23 *Flores*, iii, 217.

24 Phillips, *Edward II*, 440 n. 148.

25 *Flores*, iii, 217.

26 *Anonimalle*, 116–17.

27 Dryburgh, 'Roger Mortimer', 86–9.

28 *Blaneforde*, 138–9.

29 *CPR, 1321–24*, 314. Spelling of place names modernised.

30 *Ibid.*, 349.

31 Phillips, *Edward II*, 440.

32 *CCR, 1323–27*, 13–14.

33 Stones, 'Roger Mortimer's Escape', 98 n. 7.

34 Phillips, *Edward II*, 441.

35 *Annales Paulini*, 306.

36 *CFR, 1319–27*, 242.

37 G.A. Williams, *Medieval London: From Commune to Capital* (London, 1963), 293.

38 *Ibid.*, 297–9; C.M. Barron, *London in the Later Middle Ages* (Oxford, 2004), 26–7.

39 *CPR, 1321–24*, 342.

40 *Anonimalle*, 45, 117; *Chroniques*, 47.

41 Williams, *Medieval London*, 286–90; Barron, *London*, 17, 33.

42 *CCR, 1318–23*, 723.

43 Dryburgh, 'Roger Mortimer', 89.

44 *CCR, 1323–27*, 13–14.

45 Phillips, *Edward II*, 441.

46 *CCR, 1323–27*, 189, 195–6.

47 Phillips, *Edward II*, 452–4.

48 e.g. Conway Davis, *Baronial Opposition*, 107; *Vita Edwardi Secundi Monachi Cuiusdam Malmesberiensis*, ed. and trans. N. Denholm-Young (London, 1957), p. xiii, n. 1; W. Hepworth

Dixon, *Her Majesty's Tower*, 5th edn (London, 1869), 50; C.G. Harper, *The Tower of London: Fortress, Palace, and Prison* (London, 1901), 131; R. Davey, *The Tower of London* (London, 1910), 108–9; R.J. Minney, *The Tower of London* (New Jersey, 1970), 55–9; N. Jones, *Tower: An Epic History of the Tower of London* (London, 2011), 58–9, 309–11.

49 T. Borman, *The Story of the Tower of London* (London, 2015), 56–7.

50 Dryburgh, 'Roger Mortimer', 85–6.

51 TNA, SC 1/37/45.

52 Mortimer, *Greatest Traitor*, 129–30, 284 n. 20.

53 F.D. Blackley, 'Isabella and the Bishop of Exeter', in T.A. Sandquist and M.R. Powicke (eds.), *Essays in Medieval History Presented to Bertie Wilkinson* (Toronto, 1968), 220–4.

54 N.M. Fryde, *The Tyranny and Fall of Edward II, 1322–1326* (Cambridge, 1979), 147; Phillips, *Edward II*, 489–90.

55 K. Warner, *Isabella of France: The Rebel Queen* (Stroud, 2016), 161–2.

56 Ibid., 161; Phillips, *Edward II*, 490.

57 Warner, *Isabella of France*, 161.

58 A.C.N. Borg, 'The State Prison', in *The Tower of London: its Buildings and Institutions*, ed. J. Charlton (London, 1978), 86; J. Ashbee, 'The Structure and Function of the White Tower, 1150–1486', in *The White Tower*, ed. E. Impey (London, 2008), 149–50.

59 For an overview of the development of the building works at the Tower of London in the Middle Ages, see R.A. Brown, H.M. Colvin, and A.J. Taylor, *The History of the King's Works*, 6 vols (London, 1963–82), ii, 706–29.

60 E. Impey & G. Parnell, *The Tower of London: The Official Illustrated History* (London, 2000), 32–8.

61 J. Ashbee, 'The Tower of London as a Royal Residence, 1066–1400' (Unpublished PhD Thesis, Courtauld Institute of Art, 2006), 114–65; S. Thurley, 'Royal Lodgings at the Tower of London 1216–1327', *Architectural History*, 38 (1995), 37–46; G. Parnell, *Book of The Tower of London* (London, 1993), 27–32; Impey and Parnell, *Tower of London*, 26–8.

62 *CLR, 1226–40*, 166; *1240–5*, 62.

63 Ashbee, 'Royal Residence', 166–91; Thurley, 'Royal Lodgings', 46–51.

64 Ashbee, 'Royal Residence', 193–5; Thurley, 'Royal Lodgings', 51–3.

65 *Munimenta Gildhallae Londoniensis: Liber Albus, Liber Custumarum, et Liber Horn, Vol. II, Part I*, ed. H.T. Riley (London, 1860), 409.

66 TNA, E 101/468/20, f. 9r; E 101/469/7, mm. 3–5.

67 TNA E 101/469/7, mm 8–11.

68 Ashbee, 'Royal Palace', 196–9, 206–7.

69 *Blaneforde*, 145.

70 e.g. Harper, *Tower of London*, 131; Jones, *Tower*, 310–11.

71 *Blaneforde*, 146.

72 Ashbee, 'White Tower', 150. The location is described as a turret in the king's lodgings, which by this stage probably referred to the Lanthorn Tower, but could have also feasibly meant the Wakefield.

73 Ashbee, 'Royal Palace', 206 (Fig 7.3); Thurley, 'Royal Lodgings', 50 (Fig. 10).

74 Ashbee, 'Royal Palace', 108–9, 146.

75 From an early stage of its existence the ground floor of this block was used to house the royal wardrobe, with the king's great chamber situated above. Either space could have feasibly been used to house Mortimer by the time of his imprisonment.

76 e.g. Hepworth Dixon, *Her Majesty's Tower*, I, 33; Harper, *Tower of London*, 131; Davey, *Tower of London*, 109; Minney, *Tower of London*, 57; Jones, *Tower*, 311; Mortimer, *Greatest Traitor*, 131; B.A. Harrison, *The Tower of London Prisoner Book, 1100–1941* (Leeds, 2004), 3. Harrison also states that Mortimer swam across the Thames, but this appears to be a misinterpretation of Mortimer crossing the river by water.

77 TNA E 101/469/7, mm. 5–7; K.J. Mears, *The Tower of London: 900 Years of English History* (Oxford, 1988), 46.

78 Brown, Colvin and Taylor, *King's Works*, ii, 724.

79 TNA, E 371/85, m. 15; E 101/531/17; Phillips, *Edward II*, 506–8.

5. THE EXECUTION AND BURIAL OF ROGER MORTIMER, 1ST EARL OF MARCH (1287–1330)
Barbara Wright

1 M.C. Prestwich, *Edward I* (New Haven and London, 1997), 297.

2 R.W. Kaeuper, *War, Justice and Public Order* (Oxford, 1988), 230; J.G. Bellamy, *The Law of Treason in England in the Later Middle Ages*. (Cambridge, 1970), 22, 24–7; M. Strickland, 'Treason, Feud and the Growth of State Violence: Edward I and the "War of the Earl of Carrick", 1306–7', in *War, Government and Aristocracy in the British Isles, c.1150–1500. Essays in Honour of Michael Prestwich*, ed. C. Given-Wilson, A. Kettle and L. Scales (Woodbridge, 2008), 84–113.

3 For recent research in this area see also M. Strickland, '"All brought to nought and thy state undone": treason, disinvestiture and disgracing of arms under Edward II', in *Soldiers, Nobles and Gentlemen: Essays in Honour of Maurice Keen*, ed. P. Coss and C. Tyerman (Woodbridge, 2009), 279–304; D. Westerhof, 'Deconstructing Identities on the Scaffold: The Execution of Hugh Despenser the Younger, 1326', *Journal of Medieval History* 33 (2007), 87–106.

4 F. Pollock and F.W. Maitland, *The History of the English Law before the Time of Edward I*, 2 vols (2nd edn: Cambridge, 1898; reprinted 1968), 505.

5 P.R. Dryburgh, 'The Career of Roger Mortimer, 1st Earl of March (c.1287–1330)' (Unpublished PhD Thesis, University of Bristol, 2002), 112–13.

6 For biographical treatment of Roger Mortimer see, principally, I. Mortimer, *The Greatest Traitor. The Life of Sir Roger Mortimer, 1st Earl of March, Ruler of England, 1327–1330* (London, 2003). For his analysis of the trial and execution see 237–43.

7 Recently analysed in M. Raven, 'Parliament and the Trial of the "Peers of the Land" in Henry of Lancaster's Revolt, 1328-29', Institute for Historical Research, Parliaments, People and Politics Seminar, 16 February 2021, available online: https://thehistoryofparliament.files. wordpress.com/2021/01/parliaments-politics-and-people-parliament-and-the-trial-of-the-peers-of-the-land-in-henry-of-lancasters-revolt-1328-29-2.pdf

8 *CCR, 1327–1330*, 528.

9 For Edward's childhood see W.M. Ormrod, *Edward III* (New Haven and London, 2011), 1–89.

10 K. Warner, 'The Adherents of Edmund of Woodstock, Earl of Kent, in March 1330', *English Historical Review* 126 (2011), 779–805.

11 Ian Mortimer has speculated on the queen's possible pregnancy with Mortimer's child in 1329: Mortimer, *Greatest Traitor*, 221–4, 227.

12 Hugh Turplyton, Richard de Monemue [Monmouth] and William Dey: see *CPR, 1330–4*, 53, 69, 74, 82, 172; *CPR, 1338–40, 4.*

13 Bellamy, *The Law of Treason*, 27–8, 41–2.

14 *Rotuli Parliamentorum*, ed. J. Strachey et al., 6 vols (London, 1787), ii, 52–3.

15 Pollock and Maitland, *History of the English Law*, 500.

16 R.C. Finucane, 'Sacred Corpse, Profane Carrion: Social Ideals and Death Rituals in the Later Middle Ages', in *Mirrors of Mortality*, ed. J. Whaley (London, 1981), 49–50.

17 Bellamy, *The Law of Treason*, 27.

18 J.R. Maddicott, *Thomas of Lancaster, 1307–1322. A Study in the Reign of Edward II* (London, 1970), 311–12.

19 *Statutes of the Realm* (London, 1810), 319–20; A. Tuck, *Crown and Nobility, 1272–1461*, (Oxford, 1986), 156; E.R.H. Ivamy, *Mozley & Whiteley's Law Dictionary*, 10th edn (London, 1988), 478; W.R.J. Barron, 'The Penalties for Treason in Medieval Life and Literature', *Journal of Medieval History* 7 (1981), 187–202 (189).

20 W.A. Morris, *The Medieval English Sheriff to 1300.* (Manchester, 1968), 233–4.

21 T. Madox, *History of the Exchequer* (London: 1711), 255–6; C. Johnson (trans.), *Dialogus de Scaccario.* (London, 1950), 88n.

22 *Rot. Parl.*, ii, 53. *CCR, 1330–3*, 109.

23 R.B. Pugh, *Imprisonment in Medieval England.* (Cambridge, 1968), 210–11, 238.

24 'die Jouis in vigilia sancti Andree a turri usque calafurcia detrahitur et hora suspenditur vespertina': BL Cotton MS Nero A. iv, ff.59v–6or (*Llandaff Chronicle*); *Chronica Adami Murimuthensis, 1303–1346*, ed. T. Hog (London: Sumptibus Societatis, 1846), 65; *Cronica Adae Murimuth et Roberti de Avesbury*, ed. E.M. Thompson (London: Rolls Series 93, 1889), 285; *Chronique de Ricard Lescot (1328–1344): Continuation (1344–1364)*, ed. J. Lemoine (Paris: 1896), 21–2.

25 *Rot. Parl.*, ii, 55.

26 BL Cotton MS Nero A. iv, ff.59v–6or; *Murimuth*, ed. Hog, 65; 'Bridlington Chronicle' in *Chronicles of Edward I and Edward II*, ed. W. Stubbs, 2 vols (London: Rolls Series 76, 1882–3), II, 101–2; *Chronicon de Lanercost, 1201–1346*, ed. J. Stevenson (Edinburgh: Maitland Club, 1839), 266; *Anonimalle Chronicle, 1307–1334*, ed. W.R. Childs and J. Taylor, Yorkshire Archaeological Society Record Series 147 (Leeds, 1987), 142–5; *Eulogium Historiarum*, ed. F.S. Haydon, 3 vols (London: Rolls Series 9, 1858–63), iii, 201; University of Chicago MS 224, f.56; *Chronica Monasterii S. Albani*, ed. H.T. Riley, 7 vols (London: Rolls Series 28, 1863–76), i, Historia Anglicana, 193.

27 *Calendar of Chancery Warrants, 1: Privy Seals, 1244–1326* (London, 1927), 76.

28 Bellamy, *The Law of Treason*, 24–6.

29 *Livere de Reis de Brittanie e le Livere de Engleterre (Chroniques de Sempringham)*, ed. J. Glover (London: Rolls Series 42, 1865), 322–3; *Polychronicon Ranulphi Higden, Monachi Cestrensis: together with the English translations of John Trevisa and an unknown Writer in the Fifteenth Century*, ed. C. Babington and J.R. Lumby, 9 vols (London: Rolls Series 41, 1865–1886), 266; 'Ypodigma Neustriae' in *Chronica Monasterii S. Albani*, vii, 175; *Annales Monastici,* ed. H.R. Luard, 5 vols (London: Rolls Series 36, 1864–9), ii, 'Waverley', 400; iii, 'Dunstable', 293–4; 'Bermondsey', 466; iv, 'Worcester', 488–9; *Chronicon Henrici Knighton, Vol. 1, 959–1336*, ed. J.R. Lumby (London: Rolls Series 92, 1889), 277; *Chronicle of England by John Capgrave*, ed. F.C. Hingeston (London: Rolls Series 1, 1858), 166; Pollock and Maitland, *History of the English Law*, 501.

30 R.R. Davies, *The Age of Conquest: Wales 1063–1415* (Oxford, 1991), 380–1.

31 Bellamy, *The Law of Treason*, 30–1.

32 For the full background to the Anglo-Scots war, see F.J. Watson, *Under the Hammer. Edward I and Scotland, 1286–1307* (East Linton, 1998).

33 A.E. Middleton, *Sir Gilbert de Middleton* (Newcastle: 1918), 58–9; Bellamy, *The Law of Treason*, 46–7.

34 For which see J.R.S. Phillips, *Edward II* (New Haven and London, 2010), 397–9.

35 *Lanercost*, 245; *Murimuth*, ed. Thompson, 36; *Murimuth*, ed. Hog, 37; C. Moor (ed.), *Knights of Edward I*, Harleian Society 80, 5 vols (London: Harleian Society, 1929).

36 *Murimuth*, ed. Thompson, 35; 'Annales Paulini', in *Chronicles of Edward I and Edward II*, i, 301.

37 Bellamy, *The Law of Treason*, 49.

38 Ibid., 52–3; Phillips, *Edward II*, 433–4.

39 For which see N.M. Fryde, *The Tyranny and Fall of Edward II, 1322–1326,* particularly 63–68 (Cambridge, 1979).

40 *Anonimalle*, 131; *Bridlington*, 87; *Lanercost*, 256; *Murimuth*, ed. Thompson, 49.

41 *Anonimalle*, 130–1; *Annales Paulini*, 321; *Knighton*, 436.

42 The best modern account is Westerhof, 'Deconstructing Identities'.

43 *Lanercost*, 265; *Murimuth*, ed. Thompson, 59–60 and Appendix, 253–7; Warner, 'The Adherents of Edmund of Woodstock'.

44 Kaeuper, *War, Justice and Public Order*, 230.

45 For analysis and references see Phillips, *Edward II*, 397–9, 408–11, 433–4.

46 T.F.T. Plucknett, 'The Origins of Impeachment', *Transactions of the Royal Historical Society*, 4th series, 24. (1942), 47–71 (61–2); Bellamy, The Law of Treason, 53–4.

47 T.S.R. Boase, *Death in the Middle Ages* (London, 1972), 113.

48 Finucane, 'Sacred Corpse', 49.

49 Gwenllian, daughter of Llywelyn, died a nun at Sempringham in 1337: Davies, *Age of Conquest*, 361; *cf. CPR, 1327–30*, 21. Owain, son of Dafydd was still confined at Bristol on 21 October 1320: *CCR, 1318–23*, 267.

50 Bellamy, *The Law of Treason*, 31.

51 For a more recent discovery relating to the fate of Wallace's corpse, John R. Davies, 'The execution of William Wallace: Saint Bartholomew's Eve, Monday 23 August 1305', *Breaking of Britain: Cross-Border Society and Scottish Independence 1216–1314*, available online at: http://eprints.gla.ac.uk/87808/7/87808.pdf.

52 *CCR, 1327–30*, 404.

53 *Calendar of Papal Letters, Vol.2, 1305–1342*, ed. W.H. Bliss (London, 1895), 349.

54 *The Brut: The Chronicles of England*, ed. F.W.D. Brie, Early English Text Society Old Series 131 (London, 1960), 240; W. Dugdale, *The Baronage of England* (London: 1675; reprinted, Hildesheim: 1977), 393.

55 *CCR, 1330–3*, 175.

56 Finucane, 'Sacred Corpse', 49.

57 *Anonimalle*, 142–3; *Chronica Monasterii de Melsa, 1150–1506*, ed. E.A. Bond, 3 vols (London: Rolls Series 43, 1866), ii, 359–60; *Knighton*, i, 453; 'Historia Anglicana', in *Chronica Monasterii S. Albani*, i, 193.

58 R.B. Pugh, 'The Knights Hospitallers as Undertakers', *Speculum* 56 (1981), 566–74, (566–7).

59 *CCR, 1323–27*, 72.

60 *Bridlington*, 101–2; *Lanercost*, 266.

61 *Murimuth*, ed. Hog, 45.

62 *Anonimalle*, 144–5.

63 *Historia Anglicana*, 193.

64 BL MS Cotton Nero A. iv, ff. 59v–60r.

65 University of Chicago MS 224, f. 56r, quoted in *Monasticon Anglicanum*, ed. W. Dugdale, 8 vols (London, 1846–52), vi, 352.

66 *Murimuth*, ed. Hog, 65.

67 *Visitations by the Heralds in Wales*, ed. M.P. Siddons, Harleian Society NS 14 (London, 1996), 85 records some of the monuments in Wigmore Abbey, but none for Roger.

68 *Chronicle of the Grey Friars of London*, ed. J. Gough, Camden Society 53 (London, 1852), 4–6; *Monumenta Franciscana, Vol. 2*, ed. R. Howlett (London: Rolls Series 4, 1882, 152; C.L. Kingsford, *The Grey Friars of London* (Aberdeen, 1915), 70–177; E.B. Shepherd, 'The Church of the Friars Minor in London', *Archaeological Journal* 59 (1902), 238–87 (pp. 258–87).

69 A.G. Little, 'The Constitution of Provincial Chapters of the Minorite Order', in *Essays in Medieval History presented to T.F. Tout*, ed. A.G. Little and F.M. Powicke (Manchester, 1925), 249–67, (267).

70 *Monasticon Anglicanum*, viii, p.1531; H. Owen and R.B. Blakeway, *History of Shrewsbury* (London, 1825), ii, 460; A.J. Gaydon (ed.), *Victoria County History: Shropshire, Vol. 2.* (London: Institute of Historical Research and Clarendon Press, 1973), 89–90.

71 'Mortimer, Roger', *The Dictionary of National Biography*, 22 vols (London, [1917]; now available online with a new biography by Professor Sir Rees Davies, https://www.oxforddnb.com/display/10.1093/ref:odnb/9780198614128.001.0001/odnb-9780198614128-e-19354).

72 T. Wright, *The History and Antiquities of Ludlow.* (Ludlow, 1826; reprinted, Manchester, 1972), 224.

73 *Foedera*, ii, 828.

74 *CCR, 1330–3*, 403.

75 *CPR, 1330–4*, 213.

76 *CPR, 1330–4*, 13.

77 *CCR, 1330–3*, 65–6; *CPR, 1330–4*, 57; TNA C 145/112, nos 1, 21.

78 *CCR, 1330–3*, 99, 105; TNA E 372/177, rot. 46.

79 *CCR, 1330 3*, 110, 111.

80 Ibid., 269.

81 *Rot. Parl.*, ii, 62.

82 *CCR, 1330–3*, 345–6, 350; BL MS Harleian 1240, f. 43r. Conviction for a felony only permitted the king to retain the lands for a year and a day, whereupon they were to be returned to the tenant-in-chief. The post-1352 charge of treason allowed the lands to be kept in perpetuity: Bellamy, *The Law of Treason*, 80.

83 *CPR, 1330–4*, 193.

84 *Complete Peerage*, ix, 284–5; E.B. Fryde, D.E. Greenway and others, *Handbook of British Chronology*, 3rd edn (London: Royal Historical Society, 1986), 557.

85 TNA E 101/333/4; *cf. CPR, 1330–4*, 193.

86 University of Chicago MS 224, f. 56v.

87 *CFR, 1327–37*, 292: *cf. CIPM*, vii, no.387.

88 TNA SC 8/173/8638. Trim had been taken into the king's hand on 26 November 1331 by Anthony de Lucy, Justiciar of Ireland, under orders to confiscate all grants of land made during the regency. Joan's grant, dated 23 August 1327, was not, however, a grant by the regency but a restoration of her title to Trim which had been erroneously confiscated by a writ of *quo warranto* in 15 Edward II [1321–2].

89 TNA SC 8/61/3027, clause 3.

90 *CCR, 1330–3*, 489-490.

91 *CPR, 1327–30*, 159.

92 *CCR, 1330–3*, 503.

93 *CPR, 1330–4*, 380.

94 TNA SC 8/61/3027, clause 4.

95 TNA C 81/191/5599; *CFR, 1327–37*, 325.

96 *CFR, 1327–37*, 339.

97 TNA SC 8/61/3027, clause 2.

98 *CPR, 1330–4*, 87. G.W. Watson, 'Geoffrey de Mortemer and his Descendants', *The Genealogist*, n.s. 22 (1906), xiii, 1–16, (3).

99 R. Perry, *Edward II: Suddenly, at Berkeley* (Wotton-under-Edge, 1988), 95. The issue of Edward II's 'murder', 'death' and possible 'survival' has become controversial, with much heat being generated alongside a little light. The debate is crystallised in I. Mortimer, *Medieval Intrigue. Decoding Royal Conspiracies* (London, 2010), 1–44, 61–108, 109–52, 153–74; A. King, 'The Death of Edward II Revisited', *Fourteenth Century England IX*, ed. J.S. Bothwell and G. Dodd (2016), 1–22; J.R.S. Phillips, 'Some Afterthoughts on Edward II', in *People, Power and Identity in the Late Middle Ages. Essays in Memory of W. Mark Ormrod*, ed. G. Dodd, H. Lacey and A. Musson (London, 2021), 285–304. Further evidence relating to Berkeley Castle can be found in *Edward II: His Last Months and Monument*, ed. J. Barlow, R. Bryant, C. Heighway, C. Jeens and D. Smith, The Bristol and Gloucestershire Archaeological Society (Bristol, 2015).

100 variously Ogle, Ocle, Okele, Oakley.

101 Perry, *Edward II*, 96–100.

102 Fryde, *Tyranny and Fall*, 206.

103 C. Daniell, *Death and Burial in Medieval England, 1066–1550.* (London, 1997), 92.

104 M.E. Giffin, 'A Wigmore Manuscript at the University of Chicago', *National Library of Wales Journal* 7 (1952), 316–25, (322).

105 Though the *Llandaff Chronicle* (BL MS Cotton Nero A. iv, f. 59v) also promulgates Shrewsbury as the location, and was written *c*.1338.

106 Giffin, A Wigmore Manuscript', 316; *Monasticon Anglicanum*, vi, 344–55; J.C. Dickinson and P.T. Ricketts, 'The Anglo-Norman Chronicle of Wigmore Abbey', *Transactions of the Woolhope Society* 39 (Hereford, 1969), 413–46. Digital images of the Wigmore Chronicle (the so-called Fundatorum Historia, edited by Dugdale and now University of Chicago MS 224) can be viewed online: https://www.lib.uchicago.edu/e/scrc/findingaids/view.php?eadid=ICU.SPCL.MS224

107 TNA SC 8/61/3027, clause 2.

108 P. Binski, *Medieval Death: Ritual and Representation.* (London, 1996), 57.

109 *Proceedings before the Justices of the Peace, Edward III to Richard III*, ed. B.H. Putnam (London, 1938), 408–9; *Melsa*, i, 356; *Charters and Records of Hereford Cathedral*, ed. W.W. Capes (Hereford: Cantilupe Society, 1908), xxx, 44.

110 R.C. Finucane, *Miracles and Pilgrims: Popular Beliefs in Medieval England.* (London, 1977), 33; B. Ward, *Miracles and the Medieval Mind: Theory, Record and Event, 1000–1215.* (London, 1982), ch.7, 'The Shrines that Failed', 127–31.
111 J.R.H. Moorman, *A History of the Church in England* (London, 1973), 106; M. Brett, *The English Church under Henry I.* (Oxford, 1975), 227.
112 A.G. Little, *Franciscan Papers, Lists, and Documents.* (Manchester, 1943), 137.
113 Little, *Franciscan Papers*, 230, 240–1; Moorman, *A History of the Church in England*, 106.
114 Little, *Franciscan Papers*, 34–7.
115 Shepherd, 'The Church of the Friars Minor in London', 241–2; Kingsford, *The Grey Friars of London*, 163–5.
116 A.R. Martin, *Franciscan Architecture in England* (Manchester, 1937), 63.
117 *CPR, 1327–30*, 96.
118 Robert de Montalt died on Tuesday, 26 December 1329 (*CIPM*, vii, 335–6). Emma, his widow, died in 1332 (*CCR, 1330–3*, 447, 580). Cheylesmore was annexed to the Duchy of Cornwall (subject to Isabella's life interest) in 1337: *CChR*, iv, 432; *CCR, 1337–9*, 287, quoted in A.A. Dibben, *Coventry City Charters.* Coventry Papers (Coventry, 1969), 2, 16. In Queen Isabella's inquisition post mortem Cheylesmore is described as being held by Edward, the Black Prince, by grant of the king (*CIPM*, x, 359).
119 S. Menache, 'Isabelle of France, Queen of England – A Reconsideration', *Journal of Medieval History* 10 (1984), 107–24 (122).
120 *CPR, 1330–4*, 36.
121 *Register of Edward the Black Prince* [hereafter *BPR*], *Vol.4 (England), 1351–1365* (London, 1933), 165; *CPR, 1334–8*, 129–30, 474, 551; *CPR, 1338–40*, 95, 114, 467, 524.
122 R.H.C. Davis, *The Early History of Coventry*, Dugdale Society Occasional Paper, 24 (Stratford-upon-Avon, 1976), 9; A and E.A. Gooder, 'Coventry before 1355; Unity or Division? The Importance of the Earl's Half', *Midland History* 6 (1981), 1–38, (27).
123 BL MS Harleian 6033, ff. 17–19.
124 Martin, *Franciscan Architecture in England*, 66–7.
125 *BPR*, iv, 272; *CPR, 1377–81*, 286.
126 A. Munden, *The Third Spire*, Coventry and Warwickshire Historical Association Pamphlets 17 (Coventry, 1991), v.
127 N.H. Nicolas, *Testamenta Vetusta*, 2 vols (London, 1826), 78.

6. The Mortimers under arms, 1306–1425
Dr Andy King

1 Iolo Goch, *Poems*, ed. and trans. Dafydd Johnston (Llandysul, 1993), 82.
2 For more on Iolo Goch's praise poem, see David Stephenson in chapter 2 of this volume (21).
3 For the Feast of the Swans, see Constance Bullock-Davies, *Menestrellorum multitudo: Minstrels at a Royal Feast* (Cardiff, 1978), ix–xli. Mortimer's career is analysed in depth by Paul Dryburgh, 'The Career of Roger Mortimer, First Earl of March (*c.* 1287–1330)', unpublished PhD thesis (University of Bristol, 2002). It is difficult to separate the career of Roger Mortimer of Wigmore from his like-named uncle of Chirk (1256–1326), as they are not always distinguished in Crown records.

4   Grant G. Simpson and James D. Galbraith (eds), *CDS, v (Supplementry)* (Edinburgh, 1988), no. 2600. For Mortimer retinues in this period: David Simpkin, 'The Mortimer Retinue for War, 1277–1421', *JMHS* 3 (2019).

5   J.S. Hamilton, 'Edward II: Favourites, Loyalty, and Kingship', in *Ruling Fourteenth Century England*, ed. James Bothwell, Rémy Ambühl and Laura Tompkins (Woodbridge, 2019).

6   Simpson and Galbraith (ed.), *CDS, v*, no. 2973; and see Dryburgh, 'Career of Roger Mortimer', 39. The notion that Mortimer was captured at Bannockburn stems from a misreading by Antonia Gransden of the 'Continuation' of Trivet (it was actually Roger de Monthermer); *Nicolai Triveti Annalium continuatio*, ed. Anthony Hall (Oxford, 1722), 16; *Antonia Gransden, Historical Writing in England II: c.1307 to the Early Sixteenth Century* (London, 1982), 9.

7   *Chartularies of St. Mary's Abbey, Dublin*, ed. John T. Gilbert, 2 vols (London: Rolls Series, 1884, ii, 344–5, 348, 407–16; Dryburgh, 'Career of Roger Mortimer', 41–7.

8   *Foedera, conventiones, litterae et cujuscunque generis acta publica*, 4 vols in 7 parts (London: Record Commission, 1816–69) [hereafter *Foedera* (RC)], II, i, 301–2 (calendared in *CPR 1313–17*, 563–4); *CPR 1313–17*, 574–5; Paul Dryburgh, 'Roger Mortimer and the Governance of Ireland, 1317–1320', in *Ireland and the English World in the Late Middle Ages*, ed. Brendan Smith (Basingstoke, 2009), 89–102.

9   For which see J.R.S. Phillips, *Edward II* (New Haven and London, 2010), 363–409.

10 Phillips, *Edward II*, 366–9, 373–94, 402–4; Dryburgh, 'Career of Roger Mortimer', 73–5, 80–6.

11 As explored in greater detail in this volume by Laura Tompkins. See chapter 4 of this volume (59).

12 *Istore et croniques de Flandres*, ed. Kervyn de Lettenhove, 2 vols (Brussels, 1879–80), i, 334; Phillips, *Edward II*, 40, 479–519; Dryburgh, 'Career of Roger Mortimer', 88–90, 98–108.

13 Dryburgh, 'Career of Roger Mortimer', 113–21, 124–7; Clifford J. Rogers, *War Cruel and Sharp: English Strategy under Edward III, 1327–60* (Woodbridge, 2000), 10–26.

14 Dryburgh, 'Career of Roger Mortimer', 129–32; W. Mark Ormrod, *Edward III* (London and New Haven, 2011), 74–8.

15 As explored by Barbara Wright in this volume. See chapter 5 of this volume (81).

16 *CPR 1330–4*, 193; *CIPM*, vii, no. 387; G.A. Holmes, *The Estates of the Higher Nobility in Fourteenth-Century England* (Cambridge, 1957), 14.

17 George Wrottesley (ed.), *Crecy and Calais* (London, 1898), 69. For his career, see Matt Raven, 'The Loyal Mortimer: The Career of Roger Mortimer, 2nd Earl of March', *JMHS* 2 (2018).

18 *Chronicon Galfridi le Baker de Swynebroke*, ed. E.M. Thompson (Oxford, 1889), 79; 'Chronicle of Saint Omer', in *The Battle of Crécy: A Casebook*, ed. Michael Livingston and Kelly DeVries (Liverpool, 2015), 102–3.

19 *Chronicon Galfridi le Baker*, 104; Ormrod, *Edward III*, 325–7.

20 See below, at 113

21 'Robertus de Avesbury', in *Chronica Murimuth et Avesbury*, ed. E.M. Thompson (London: Rolls Series, 1889), 247–8; TNA, E 159/140, Brev. Mich., rot. 32; *Rotuli Scotiae*, ed. D. Macpherson, 2 vols (London, 1814–19), i, 797–8; Rogers, *War Cruel and Sharp*, 292–304, 334–40.

22 TNA, E 101/393/11, fol. 79v.; *Sir Thomas Gray: Scalacronica (1272–1363)*, ed. Andy King, Surtees Society 209 (2005), 170–1; Rogers, *War Cruel and Sharp*, 391–416.

23 TNA, C 76/52, m. 5; E 403/438, mm. 28 (5 July), 35 (28 Aug.); *Issue Roll of Thomas de Brantingham*, ed. Frederick Devon (London, 1835), 473, 486; James Sherborne, 'Indentured Retinues and English Expeditions to France, 1369–80', *EHR* 79 (1964), 720–3.

24 Jonathan Sumption, *The Hundred Years War III: Houses Divided* (London, 2009), 35–44.

25 TNA, E 403/444, m. 28 (8 Mar.); E 403/446, mm. 3 (24 Apr.), 25 (14 July); Sumption, *Hundred Years War III*, 131–56; Mortimer's indenture is printed in *Sir Christopher Hatton's Book of Seals*, ed. L.C. Loyd and D.M. Stenton (Oxford, 1950), 164–5.

26 TNA, E 364/10, rot. 73; Sherborne, 'Indentured Retinues', 730; Andrew Ayton, 'Military Service and the Dynamics of Recruitment in Fourteenth-Century England', in *The Soldier Experience in the Fourteenth Century*, ed. Adrian R. Bell et al. (Woodbridge, 2011), 9–59.

27 Sumption, *Hundred Years War III*, 213–38; George Holmes, *The Good Parliament* (Oxford, 1975), 37–56.

28 Holmes, *Good Parliament*, 101, 150–3.

29 The documents are printed in Maude V. Clarke, 'William of Windsor in Ireland, 1369–1376', *PRIA*, 41 (1932–4), 99, 107–8 (quotes at 99).

30 *Foedera* (RC), III, ii, 990.

31 A.J. Otway-Ruthen, *A History of Medieval Ireland* (2nd edn, London, 1980), 309–13.

32 Printed in Dorothy Johnston, 'Chief Governors and Treasurers of Ireland in the Reign of Richard II', in *Colony and Frontier in Medieval Ireland*, eds Terry Barry, Robin Frame and Katherine Simms (London, 1995), 113–15.

33 TNA, SC 8/125/6231.

34 *Annals of the Kingdom of Ireland, by the Four Masters*, ed. John O'Donovan, 2nd edn, 7 vols (Dublin, 1856), iv, 676–9 (quote at 676–7); *Annals of Ulster*, ed. W.M. Hennessy and B. MacCarthy, 4 vols (Dublin, 1887–1901), iii, 4–5; Brendan Smith, *Crisis and Survival in Late Medieval Ireland* (Oxford, 2013), 70–1.

35 *The Chronicle of Adam Usk 1377–1421*, ed. C. Given-Wilson (Oxford, 1997), 46–7. Edmund's service in Ireland is analysed by Smith, *Crisis and Survival*, 69–74; and Simon Egan, 'A Task too great for One Dynasty? The Mortimer Earls of March, the de Burgh Inheritance and the Gaelic Nobility *c.*1370–*c.*1425', *JMHS* 4 (2020), 11–12.

36 Thomas' relationship to the fourth earl is not clear; he may have been illegitimate; James L. Gillespie, 'Thomas Mortimer and Thomas Molineux: Radcot Bridge and the Appeal of 1397', *Albion* 7 (1975), 161–73, at p. 162; see also the section by C. Given-Wilson in chapter 9 of this volume (169), particularly fn. 24.

37 *CPR 1381–5*, 88; *CIRCLE: A Calendar of Irish Chancery Letters, c. 1244–1509*, Patent Roll 5 Ric. II, no. 39; Close Roll 5 Ric. II, no. 65, available online at https://chancery.tcd.ie/content/welcome-circle.

38 Holmes, *Estates of the Higher Nobility*, 77; Alastair Dunn, 'Richard II and the Mortimer Inheritance', in *Fourteenth Century England II*, ed. Chris Given-Wilson (Woodbridge, 2002), 159–61; Mark King, 'Richard II, the Mortimer Inheritance and the March of Wales, 1381–84', in *Fourteenth Century England VIII*, ed. J.S. Hamilton (Woodbridge, 2014), 95–118.

39 TNA, E 403/508, m. 16 (30 June); E 403/515, m. 9 (9 Nov.).

40 TNA, C 76/71, m. 10; E 101/40/33, m. 10. For the expedition, Sumption, *Hundred Years War III*, 593–4, 603–6.

41 *The St Albans Chronicle: The* Chronica maiora *of Thomas Walsingham*, ed. John Taylor, Wendy R. Childs and Leslie Watkiss, 2 vols (Oxford, 2003–11), i, 838–9; Gillespie, 'Thomas Mortimer and Thomas Molineux', 838–9; Dunn, 'Richard II and the Mortimer Inheritance', 161–3.

42 Anthony Tuck, 'Anglo-Irish Relations, 1382–1393', *PRIA*, 69 (1970), 15–31, at 23–7.

43 *A Roll of the Proceedings of the King's Council in Ireland 1392–93*, ed. James Graves (London: Rolls Series, 1877), 255–60; 'Mac Carthaigh's Book', in *Miscellaneous Irish annals*, ed. Séamus Ó hInnse (Dublin, 1947), 149; *CIRCLE*, Close Roll 17 Ric. II, nos 62–4.

44 'Richard II: September 1397, Part 1', *PROME*, ed. C. Given-Wilson et al. (London, 2005), item 19; *Adam Usk*, ed. Given-Wilson, 26–7, 30–1; *Foedera, conventiones, litterae et cuiucunque generis acta publica*, ed. Thomas Rymer, 20 vols (London, 1704–35), viii, 82 (calendared *CPR 1396–9*, 574); Gillespie, 'Thomas Mortimer and Thomas Molineux', 170–3.

45 See below, at 115

46 *The Annals of Clonmacnoise*, ed. Denis Murphy (Dublin, 1896), 316.

47 Dorothy Johnston, 'Richard II and the Submissions of Gaelic Ireland', *IHS* 20 (1980), 1–20, at 17–20; Dorothy Johnston, 'The Interim Years: Richard II and Ireland, 1395–9', in *England and Ireland in the Later Middle Ages*, ed. James Lydon (Dublin, 1981), 175–95; Simon Egan, 'Richard II and the Wider Gaelic World: A Reassessment', *JBS* 57 (2018), 221–52, at 248–9.

48 Edmund Curtis, *Richard II in Ireland, 1394–5* (Oxford, 1927), 135 (my translation).

49 'Mac Carthaigh's Book', ed. Ó hInnse, 157.

50 *CPR 1396–9*, 147, 184–5; *Foedera*, viii, 21 (calendared in *CCR 1396–9*, 221–2); *Adam Usk*, ed. Given-Wilson, 38–41.

51 Brendan Smith, 'Dressing the Part in the Plantagenet Empire: The Death of Roger Mortimer, Earl of March and Ulster, in 1398', in *The Plantagenet Empire*, ed. Peter Crooks, David Green and W. Mark Ormrod (Donington, 2016).

52 *CPR 1396–9*, 58, 62, 147; *CPR 1399–1401*, 81. For Sir Edmund's career: T.F. Tout, revised by R.R. Davies, 'Mortimer, Sir Edmund (1376–1408/9)', *ODNB*; see also C. Given-Wilson in chapter 9 of this volume (169).

53 *Historia Vitae et Regni Ricardi Secundi*, ed. G.B. Stow (Pennsylvania, 1977), 154–5.

54 *CFR 1399–1405*, 22; Michael Livingston and John K. Bollard (eds), *Owain Glyndŵr: A Casebook* (Liverpool, 2013), 60–1, 311.

55 *CFR 1399–1405*, 155.

56 J.E. Lloyd, *Owen Glendower* (Oxford, 1931), 51–2; see also D. Stephenson in chapter 2 of this volume (21).

57 *CCR 1396–9*, 351; *CPR 1396–9*, 428; *CPR 1401–5*, 176, 256, 266.

58 'Henry IV: September 1402', *PROME*, item 13; *Adam Usk*, ed. Given-Wilson, 158–61; *Continuatio eulogii: The Continuation of the Eulogium Historiarum, 1364–1413*, ed. Chris Given-Wilson (Oxford, 2019), 114–45, 118–19; *St Albans Chronicle*, ed. Taylor, et al., ii, 336–9; R.R. Davies, *The Revolt of Owain Glyn Dŵr* (Oxford, 1995), 179–80.

59 *CPR 1401–5*, 176, 256, 267, 389, 474; Frederick Devon (ed.), *Issues of the Exchequer* (London, 1837), 295; *Adam Usk*, ed. Given-Wilson, 160–1.

60 Ralph Griffiths, 'Mortimer, Edmund, Fifth Earl of March and Seventh Earl of Ulster (1391–1425)', *ODNB*. For a – somewhat jaundiced – overview of Edmund's career, T.B. Pugh, *Henry V and the Southampton Plot of 1415*, Southampton Records Series 30 (1988), 77–85.

61 TNA, E 101/45/5, m. 4.

62 Walsingham, ed. Taylor, et al., ii, 672–3. At least 33 of Edmund's men were invalided home from Harfleur: TNA, E 101/44/30, no. 1, m. 6.

63 *Foedera*, ix, 362; 'French Rolls, Henry v', *Forty-Fourth Annual Report of the Deputy Keeper of the Public Records* (London, 1883) [hereafter DKR], 576. For the transfer of prisoners, Rémy Ambühl, *Prisoners of War in the Hundred Years War: Ransom Culture in the Late Middle Ages* (Cambridge, 2013), 111–15.

64 'William Gregory's Chronicle of London', in *The Historical Collections of a Citizen of London in the Fifteenth Century*, ed. James Gairdner, Camden Society, new series, 17 (1876), 114; TNA, E 101/70/1, no. 569 (my thanks to Dr Gary Baker for supplying a photo); Anne Curry, 'After Agincourt, What Next? Henry V and the Campaign of 1416', in *The Fifteenth Century VII*, ed. Linda Clark (Woodbridge, 2007), 32–8; Jonathan Sumption, *The Hundred Years War IV: Cursed Kings* (London, 2015), 485–99.

65 TNA, C 76/100, m. 21; E 101/51/2, m. 7.

66 Adrian R. Bell, Anne Curry, Andy King, and David Simpkin, *The Soldier in Later Medieval England* (Oxford, 2013), 264–8.

67 'Norman Rolls', *41st DKR*, 690, 700, 719, 792; 'Norman Rolls', *42nd DKR*, 324; Walsingham, ed. Taylor, et al., ii, 754–5; 'William Gregory's Chronicle', 139; 'Chronique de Normandie', in *Henrici Quinti, Angliæ regis, gesta, cum Chronicâ Neustriæ, gallicè*, ed. Benjamin Williams (London, 1850), 181–2, 191, 204, 231, 241, 257.

68 'French Rolls', *44th DKR*, 625; 'Chronique de Normandie', pp. 207, 260; Walsingham, ed. Taylor, et al., ii, 770–3.

69 *Foedera*, x, 282–5 (calendered, rather meagrely, in *CPR 1422–9*, 96); *Proceedings and Ordinances of the Privy Council of England*, ed. N.H. Nicolas, 7 vols (Record Commission, 1834–7), iii, 49; 'De actibus tempore regis Henrici Sexti', *Incerti scriptoris Chronicon Angliæ de regnis trium regum Lancastrensium*, ed. J.A. Giles (London, 1848), 6.

70 Anthony Tuck, 'Vere, John de, seventh earl of Oxford (1312–1360)', *ODNB*. For noble mortality rates on campaign, Bell, et al., *Soldier in Later Medieval England*, 27–30.

71 *Scalacronica*, ed. King, 173–4.

72 Ormrod, *Edward III*, 93–6.

73 'Edward III: April 1354', *PROME*, items 8–12; Holmes, *Estates of the Higher Nobility*, 13–17; Richard Partington, 'The Nature of Noble Service to Edward III', in *Political Society in Later Medieval England*, ed. Benjamin Thompson and John Watts (Woodbridge, 2015), 74–92, 85–6.

74 *Adam Usk*, ed. Given-Wilson, 254–5; Pugh, *Henry V and the Southampton Plot*, 61–2.

75 Robert Massey, 'The Lancastrian Land Settlement in Normandy and Northern France, 1417–1450', unpublished PhD thesis (University of Liverpool, 1987), 62; and see above at 112

76 For a survey of the profitability of military service, G.L. Harriss, *Shaping the Nation: England 1360–1461* (Oxford, 2005), 133–5.

77 *Thomas Walsingham, quondam monachi S. Albani, Historia Anglicana*, ed. H.T. Riley, 2 vols (London, Rolls Series, 1863–4), i, 272; A. Ayton, *Knights and Warhorses: Military Service and the English Aristocracy under Edward III* (Woodbridge, 1994), 124–37.

78 'Wigmore Chronicle', in William Dugdale, *Monasticon Anglicanum*, new edn, 6 vols in 8 parts (London, 1817–30), VI, i, 353.

79 The two men ransomed by Edmund, the 5th earl, after Agincourt do not appear to have been of any very great status; see note 63 above.

80 *CPR 1396–9*, 428; *CPR 1401–5*, 176; *CIPM*, xxii, nos 486, 488, 490, 501.

81 Woodhorn, Northumberland Archives, ZSW 4/42; Simon K. Walker, 'Profit and Loss in the Hundred Years War: The Subcontracts of Sir John Strother, 1374', *BIHR* 58 (1985), 100–6.

82 *CPR 1377–81*, 390; Johnston, 'Chief Governors and Treasurers of Ireland', 114.

83 TNA, SC 8/125/6231; printed in *Documents on the Affairs of Ireland before the King's Council*, ed. G.O. Sayles (Irish Manuscripts Commission, 1979), 253–4.

84 'Henry VI: October 1423', *PROME*, item 28. The debt was the residue of the 10,000 marks he had offered the king for the right to his own marriage.

85 The documents are printed in 'Translation of a French Metrical History of the Deposition of King Richard the Second', trans. John Webb, *Archaeologia* 20 (1824), app. ii, 246–8. See also Tuck, 'Anglo-Irish Relations', 28–31.

86 'Wigmore Chronicle' 351; *CPR 1301–7*, 244; *CCR 1302–7*, 377. The inquisitions post mortem on his father give Roger's date of birth variously as 25 April or 3 May 1287: *CIPM*, iv, no. 235.

87 *CFR 1337–47*, 246; Wrottesley (ed.), *Crecy and Calais*, 159; *CCR 1346–9*, 101, 199.

88 *CPR 1367–70*, 114; *CCR 1369–74*, 55–6; TNA, C 76/52, m. 5. His wife Philippa, the daughter of Lionel of Antwerp, received her inheritance at the age of 14, as was customary for married heiresses: Sue Sheridan Walker, 'Proof of Age of Feudal Heirs in Medieval England', *Mediaeval Studies* 35 (1973), 306–23, at 307.

89 Bell, et al., *Soldier in Later Medieval England*, 25–7.

90 Ormrod, *Edward III*, 391.

91 Brendan Smith, 'Transnational Lordship and The Plantagenet Empire: The Mortimer Lords of Wigmore, 1247–1425', *Welsh History Review* 29(1) (2018), 27–50, at 37.

92 G.E. Cockayne, et al., *The Complete Peerage*, rev. & ed. Vicary Gibbs (13 vols, London, 1910–59), viii, 445–6.

93 Ormrod, *Edward III*, 424–5.

94 Pugh, *Henry V and the Southampton Plot*, 84; and see above, 112, 113.

95 Unless the arrival of Henry FitzEmpress (the future Henry II) in England in January 1153 should be counted as a successful invasion.

96 Paul Dryburgh, 'For Queen and Country: The Interim Administration of Queen Isabella and Edward of Windsor, October-December 1326', in *English Medieval Government and Administration. Essays in Honour of J.R. Maddicott*, ed. Nigel Saul and Nicholas Vincent, Pipe Roll Society NS 65 (Woodbridge, 2023), chapter 17.

7. Estates and economies of the Mortimer lordships
Dr Paul Dryburgh

1 For the auction see https://www.dominicwinter.co.uk/Auction/Lot/lot-260---herefordshire-account-roll-account-roll-of-honour-of-wigmore-1387-88/?lot=384564&so=0&st=&sto=0&au=802&ef=&et=&ic=False&sd=0&pp=48&pn=6&g=1. At the time of writing no archival reference had been attributed.

2 Rotherwas, Herefordshire Archive and Record Centre, A 31/25.

3 My thanks to Chris Albury for this information. A cursory check of the catalogues of The National Archives, National Records Scotland and the National Library of Wales reveals many manuscripts purchased from Dr Gulley. His doctoral thesis, 'The Wealden landscape in the early seventeenth century and its antecedents', was submitted in 1960 (https://discovery.ucl.ac.uk/id/eprint/1317520/).

4 Discussed by Patrick McDonagh in chapter 8 below.

5 Mortimer, Ian, *The Greatest Traitor. The Life of Sir Roger Mortimer, 1st Earl of March, Ruler of England, 1327–1330* (London: Constable, 2003), 214–15. For an overview of the Welsh March see Davies, R.R., 'Colonial Wales', *Past & Present* 65 (1974), 3–23; idem, *Lordship and Society in the March of Wales, 1282–1400* (Oxford: Clarendon Press, 1978). For Ireland see Frame, R.F., *Colonial Ireland, 1169–1369* (2nd edn, Dublin: Four Courts Press, 2012). For a comparative assessment see Davies, R.R., 'Frontier Arrangements in Fragmented Societies: Ireland and Wales', in *Medieval Frontier Societies*, ed. R. Bartlett and A. Mackay (Oxford: Clarendon Press, 1996), 77–101.

6 Davies, R.R., 'Mortimer, Roger, fourth earl of March and sixth of Ulster (1374–1398)', *ODNB*.

7 Smith, Brendan, 'Transnational Lordship and the Plantagenet Empire: The Mortimer Lords of Wigmore, 1247–1425', *Welsh History Review*, 29(1) (2018), 27–50.

8 Holmes, G.A., *The Estates of the Higher Nobility in Fourteenth-Century England* (Cambridge: CUP, 1957), *passim*; Evans, B.P., 'The Family of Mortimer' (unpublished PhD thesis, University of Cardiff, 1934), 355–485; Davies, *Lordship and Society, passim*; Potterton, Michael, *Medieval Trim: History and Archaeology* (Dublin: Four Courts Press, 2005); Hopkinson, Charles & Speight, Martin, *The Mortimers: Lords of the March* (Almeley: Logaston, 2002), 141–64.

9 BL, Harley MS 1240; Additional MS 6041; Egerton Rolls 8713–30. For analysis see Wright, Barbara, *Why Make Back-Up Copies? The Mortimer Cartulary and the Technological Revolution* (Otley: Flower Press, 2010).

10 There is no single inventory of Mortimer manuscripts. For records of individual manors in England and Wales, consult the Manorial Documents Register: https://discovery. nationalarchives.gov.uk/manor-search. Many forfeited muniments, rentals, surveys and manorial accounts, can be found in the series SC 6, SC 11 and 12 at The National Archives. A number of relevant manuscripts remains in private hands, notably the Harley archive at Brampton Bryan.

11 These records are discussed in the analysis below.

12 Lewis, C.P., 'Mortimer, Roger de (fl.1054–*c*.1080)', *ODNB*.

13 TNA, E 31/2/1, ff. 180r–v, 183v.

14 Lewis, C.P., 'Mortimer, Ralph de (*c*.1080–after 1115)', *ODNB*.

15 TNA, E 31/2/1, ff. 257r–260v.

16 ibid., ff. 41r–72v.

17 ibid., ff. 325r, 380v–382r (Yorkshire); 360r–363r (Lincolnshire). See Dalton, P. *Feudal Politics in Yorkshire 1066–1154*, (unpublished PhD thesis, University of Sheffield, 1990), Table 2 following 9 & 28 and map.

18 ibid., ff. 41v, 45v.

19 For the earlier history of the family, see Mortimer, Ian, 'The Chronology of the de Mortemer Family of Wigmore, *c*.1075–1185, and the Consolidation of a Marcher Lordship', *Historical Research* 89 (2016), 613–35. What follows is a severely telescoped account of an incredibly complex history best dealt with in Davies, R.R., *Age of Conquest: Wales, 1063–1415* (Oxford: OUP, 2000), 3–107, 271–307, and Stephenson, David, *Medieval Wales, c. 1050–1332: Centuries of Ambiguity* (Cardiff, 2019), 7–120. See also Hume, P.R., *The Welsh Marcher Lordships, I: Central & North* (Eardisley: Logaston, 2020), 57–100.

20 Davies, *Lordship and Society*, 69.

21 Hopkinson & Speight, *Lords of the March*, 142; Hume, P.R., 'The Mortimers and Radnorshire (part 1): the Conquest of Maelienydd', *Journal of the Mortimer History Society vol. 3* (2019); 'The Mortimers and Radnorshire (part 2): Marriage and Inheritance – Radnor and Elfael', *vol 4 (2020)*.

22 See chapter 3 above.

23 Davies, *Lordship and Society*, 24.

24 Waugh, S.L., *The Lordship of England: Royal Wardships and Marriages in English Society and Politics, 1217–1327* (Princeton: Princeton University Press, 1988), 39–44.

25 TNA, C 133/114, no. 8, printed in *CIPM*, IV, no. 235, 157–66; quote at Davies, *Lordship and Society*, 26.

26 *Davies, Age of Conquest*, 322, 337.

27 ibid., 343.

28 *CChR, 1257–1300*, 61 (9 November 1266); *Placita de Quo Warranto temporibus Ed. I, II and III in curia receptae scaccarij Westm. asservata*, ed. W. Illingworth (London: Record Commission, 1818), 675, 677, 681; *Rotuli Hundredorum temp. Hen. III & Edw. I in turr' Lond' et in curia receptae scaccarij Westm. asservati*, 2 volumes (London: Record Commission, 1812–18), ii, 90–1, 108; *Calendar of Ancient Correspondence Concerning Wales*, ed. J.G. Edwards (Cardiff: Cardiff University Press, 1935), 101–2; TNA, E 159/67, rots 48, 68; *CCR, 1251–3*, 220.

29 Crump, J.J., 'Mortimer, Roger (III) (1231–82)', *ODNB*; Davies, R.R., 'Kings, lords and liberties in the March of Wales, 1066–1272', *Transactions of the Royal Historical Society*, 5th ser., 29 (1979), 41–61.

30 Hartland, Beth, 'Reasons for leaving: the effect of conflict on English landholding in late thirteenth-century Leinster', *Journal of Medieval History* 32 (2006), 18–26; Frame, R.F., 'Aristocracies and the Political Configuration of the British Isles', in idem, *Ireland and Britain, 1170–1450* (London: Hambleton, 1998), 151–70.

31 *A New History of Ireland, II: Medieval Ireland, 1169–1534*, ed. Art Cosgrove (Oxford: Clarendon Press, 1987), 168.

32 *CCR, 1247–51*, 71 (22 July 1248), 152 (5 April 1249).

33 Frame, *Colonial Ireland*, pp. 74–80; idem, 'The "Failure" of the First English Conquest of Ireland", in *Ireland and Britain*, 1–14; *New History of Ireland*, 241.

34 Frame, R.F., 'King Henry III and Ireland: the Shaping of a Peripheral Lordship', *Ireland and Britain*, 31–57; idem, 'Ireland and the Barons War', *Ireland and Britain*, 59–69; Maddicott, J.R., *Simon de Montfort* (Cambridge, 1996), 307–8; Laborderie, O., Maddicott, J.R. & Carpenter, D.A., 'The Last Hours of Simon de Montfort: A New Account', *EHR* 115:461 (2000), 378–412. Montfort's order for the marchers' exile came in spite of a conciliar plan for an expedition to Ireland in the early weeks of 1265: *CCR, 1264–8*, 35.

35 Duffy, Seán, 'Irish and Welsh responses to the Plantagenet empire in the reign of Edward I', in Crooks, P., Green, D. & Ormrod, W.M. (eds), *The Plantagenet Empire, 1259–1453* (Donington: Shaun Tyas, 2016), 150–68, at 156.

36 TNA, C 133/32, no. 7, mm. 15–16d; printed in *Inquisitions and Extents of Medieval Ireland*, ed. Paul Dryburgh and Brendan Smith, List & Index Society 320 (Kew, 2007), no. 54, 29–31. The accuracy of inquisitions post mortem is disputed so, given Mortimer appears to have abandoned the lordship before his death, we might question the buoyancy of the valuation: Otway-Ruthven, A.J., 'The medieval county of Kildare', *Irish Historical Studies [IHS]* 11, no. 43 (1958–9), 181–99, at 184; Holford, M.L., '"Notoriously unreliable": the

valuations and extents [Fifteenth-century Inquisitions *Post Mortem*]', *The Fifteenth-Century Inquisitions Post Mortem*, ed. M.A. Hicks (Woodbridge, 2012), 117–44.

37 BL, Egerton Rolls 8723, m. 3d.

38 Manchester, John Rylands Library [JRL], Latin MS 215, f. 6v; printed in Evans, 'Family of Mortimer', 507; with commentary in Mortimer, *Greatest Traitor*, 11, 270.

39 JRL, Latin MS 215, f. 8r; printed in Evans, 'Family of Mortimer', 511. For Geoffrey, see Hartland, Beth, 'Vaucouleurs, Ludlow and Trim: the role of Ireland in the career of Geoffrey de Geneville (*c*.1226–1314), *IHS* 32, no. 128 (November 2001), 457–77.

40 Potterton, *Medieval Trim*, 17.

41 ibid., 93–5. For the Bruce invasion see Duffy, S., *Robert the Bruce's Irish Wars: the Invasions of Ireland, 1306–29* (Stroud: Tempus, 2002).

42 *CIPM*, IV, no. 235; *CCR, 1302–07*, 170–1.

43 Dryburgh, P.R., 'The Career of Roger Mortimer, 1st Earl of March (*c*.1287–1330)', (unpublished PhD thesis, University of Bristol, 2002), 22–7.

44 *CPR, 1307–13*, 33; BL, Harley MS 1240, f. 114v; Add. MS 6041, f. 45r. Roger received livery of his Irish lands as a 'special favour' from the new king on 15 December: *CCR, 1307–13*, 15.

45 Frame, R.F., *English Lordship in Ireland, 1318–1361* (Oxford: Clarendon Press, 1982), 7.

46 See Mortimer, *Greatest Traitor*.

47 Graham, B.J., 'Anglo-Norman Settlement in County Meath', *PRIA* C 75 (1975), 223–48, quote at 233.

48 Frame, R.F., 'Power and Society in the Lordship of Ireland 1272–1377', *Past & Present* 76 (1977), 3–33.

49 Frame, 'Power and Society', 15–16; *Calendar of the Gormanston Register*, ed. James Mills and M.J. McEnery (Dublin, 1916), 181–2.

50 Dryburgh, P.R., 'Roger Mortimer and the Governance of Ireland, 1317–20', in *Ireland and the English World in the late Middle Ages: Essays in Honour of Robin Frame*, ed. Brendan Smith (Basingstoke, 2009), 89–102; idem, '"The Mortimer has taken great pains to save and keep the peace": crown, city and community during the Bruce invasion and its aftermath', *Medieval Dublin XVII*, ed. Seán Duffy (Dublin, 2019), 224–38.

51 Dealt with in most detail by Davies, J.C., 'The Despenser War in Glamorgan', *TRHS*, 3rd series 9 (1915), 21–64. For Mortimer's participation see Mortimer, *Greatest Traitor*, 99–115.

52 Dryburgh, 'Career', 82 and references.

53 *Calendar of Inquisitions Miscellaneous (Chancery) preserved in the Public Record Office*, 8 vols (London, 1916–2003), II: *1307–49*, no. 682, 170.

54 *CPR, 1321–4*, 51.

55 *Calendar of Ancient Petitions Relating to Wales from the thirteenth to the sixteenth century in the Public Record Office London* (Cardiff, 1975), [6], no. 255; *Rotuli Parlamentorum*, ed J. Strachey et al (London, 1767), I, 384, 400.

56 Davies, R.R., 'Race Relations in Post-Conquest Wales: Confrontation and Compromise', *Transactions of the Honourable Society of Cymmrodorion* (1974-5), 32–56; also, see chapter 2 above by David Stephenson for a more detailed analysis of the Mortimers' relationship with their Welsh tenants and gentry.

57 Discussed with fascinating new detail by Laura Tompkins in chapter 4 above.

58 Fryde, N.M., *Tyranny and Fall of Edward II, 1322–1326* (Cambridge: CUP, 1979); Mortimer, *Greatest Traitor*, 116–241; Phillips, J.R.S., *Edward II* (New Haven and London: Yale University Press, 2010), 410–576.

59 For what follows see Dryburgh, 'Career', Appendix II, 258–60.

60 BL, Harley MS 1240, ff. 38r–40v; *CPR, 1327–30*, 14.

61 *CFR, 1327–37*, 28.

62 ibid., 20; *CPR, 1327–30*, 22. The grant of the Hastings custody was further extended on 16 March 1329: ibid., 377.

63 Mortimer, *Greatest Traitor*, Appendix 2, 319–24.

64 *CChR, 1327–41*, 55, which also includes the lordships of Oswestry and Clun. For Stretton see *CPR, 1327–30*, 192 (22 November 1327); BL, Harley MS 1240, f. 45r (20 September 1330).

65 BL, Add. MS 6041, f. 31v (16 April 1330); *CPR, 1327–30*, 546 (8 August 1330).

66 *CFR, 1327–37*, p. 19; *CPR, 1327–30*, 125.

67 *CPR, 1327–30*, 299, 317, 327, 528, 535

68 Mortimer, *Greatest Traitor*, 206, 294 n. 22.

69 Dublin, National Archives of Ireland, RC 8/15, 586–9; Potterton, *Medieval Trim*, 94, 97; Wood, 'Muniments', 313 and Appendix, deed ix.

70 BL, Harley MS 1240, ff. 115v, 116r, 124r.

71 Davies, *Lordship and Society*, 46–7; *CPR 1327–30*, 141–3; BL, Harley MS 1240, f. 43v. In August 1359, John Mortimer, Chirk's grandson, quitclaimed Blaenllynfi, Bwlch-y-dinas, Narberth and a third of St Clears to the second earl and the lordship of Chirk to the earl of Arundel: Harley MS 1240, ff. 43v, 50.

72 Mortimer, *Greatest Traitor*, 214–15.

73 *CChR, 1327–41*, 210; *CPR, 1330–4*, 109. On 2 December 1331, the castle, honor and land of Chirk were committed to royal keepers: *CFR, 1327–37*, 290.

74 *CIM, 1307–49*, no. 1137, 281; *CCR, 1330–3*, 345–6, 350; *CPR, 1330–4*, 193; BL, Harley MS 1240, ff. 43r, 67r; Add. MS 6041, f. 16r.

75 University of Chicago MS 224, f. 56v. There is a single letter which described Edmund as 'formerly earl of March' but this appears to be in error: *CFR, 1327–37*, 239. For the inquisition into Edmund's lands taken after his death see TNA, C 135/29, no. 5, printed in *CIPM*, VII, no. 387, 278–80.

76 TNA, C 81/191/5599 (17 June 1332); SC 8/61/3027; *CPR, 1330–4*, 257; *CFR, 1327–37*, 325 (16 September 1332), 339 (12 December 1332), 344 (29 January 1333). For Trim see; TNA, C 47/10/19, no. 7, m. 4, overturned on appeal in King's Bench in 1328: KB 27/273 (Trinity 1328), rot. 128; *Documents on the Affairs of Ireland Before the King's Council*, ed. G.O. Sayles (Dublin: Irish Manuscripts Commission, 1979), 151–2, 279; Potterton, *Medieval Trim*, 94–5; Wood, 'Muniments', Appendix, deed iv; TNA, C 260/42/2A. For petitions from Hugh de Lacy in 1332 see TNA, SC 8/243/12105, 12108; 238/11877. For the challenge to Joan's tenure in the late 1340s, and her attempts to divest herself of her Irish lands, see TNA, C 81/320/18448–9 (16 June 1347); C 260/58/24 (7 April 1347); *Rot. Parl.*, ii, 222; *CCR, 1346–9*, 253–4, 311–12, 314; Wood, 'Muniments', 321–2.

77 Davies, R.R., 'Mortimer, Roger (vi), second earl of March (1328–1360), magnate', *ODNB*; Ormrod, *Edward III*, 261–467; Barber, R., *Edward III and the Triumph of England* (London: Allen Lane, 2013), 226–450. For Crécy see *The Chronicle of Geoffrey le Baker of Swinbrook*, ed. Richard Barber (Woodbridge: The Boydell Press, 2012), *sub anno* 1346.

78 *PROME*, V, 95–101; BL, Harley MS 1240, ff. 65r–66r; Hopkinson & Speight, *Lords of the March*, 110.

79 TNA, C 135/133/28; *CIPM*, X, no. 291.

80 *CFR, 1347–56*, 433. Roger received a 300-mark annuity, for which see Raven, Matt, 'The Loyal Mortimer: the Career of Roger Mortimer, second earl of March', *JMHS* 2 (2018), 51–71, 67–8.

81 TNA, KB 27/367, rots 20–21; *CCR, 1354–60*, 50–1; *PROME*, V, 95–101. For discussion see Given-Wilson, Chris, *The English Nobility in the Middle Ages* (London: Routledge, 1996), 39; idem, 'Richard II, Edward II, and the Lancastrian Inheritance', *EHR* 109 (1994), 555–6. Montagu petitioned for restoration of his lordship upon Mortimer's death in 1360: TNA, SC 8/15/735.

82 Ormrod, *Edward III*, 467. Inquisitions post mortem for Earl Roger can be found at TNA, C 135/133/27; /154/1; *CIPM*, XV, no. 640.

83 University of Chicago MS 224, f. 58v.

84 ibid., f. 57v; Davies, *Lordship and Society*, 55. For comment on the marriage see Ormrod, W.M., 'Edward III and his family', *Journal of British Studies* 26 (1987), 398–422, at 409. For livery of the inheritance in Ireland despite Edmund's minority see *CPR, 1367–70*, 114. For the Arundel marriage see *CCR, 1354–60*, 92–4; TNA, E 403/394, mm. 28, 33; E 404/6/36 (28 January, 33 Edward III). I owe these references to Matt Raven.

85 *CPR, 1358–61*, 266–7; BL, Harley MS 1240, f. 48v; Holmes, *Estates of the Higher Nobility*, 45–6; see chapter 9 below by Chris Given-Wilson for a discussion of the use of enfeoffment in the period.

86 Given-Wilson, *Nobility*, 42.

87 TNA, C 136/20; *CIPM*, XV, nos 534–71.

88 The IPM for Roger Mortimer, fourth earl of March, from 1398 adds a detailed extent for the manor and chase of Cranborne in Dorset, similarly brought to Edmund by the Clare marriage: TNA, C 136/104–5; *CIPM*, XVII, nos. 1184–1232.

89 Frame, 'Power and Society', 3–8, 25–6.

90 A point made recently by Brendan Smith in his 'Transnational Lordship'. See also Potterton, *Medieval Trim*, 106–12; Smith, Brendan, *Crisis and Survival in Late Medieval Ireland* (Oxford: OUP, 2013), 73–4, 86–7.

91 Johnston, Dorothy, 'The interim years: Richard II and Ireland, 1395–1399', in James Lydon (ed.), *England and Ireland in the Later Middle Ages: Essays in Honour of Jocelyn Otway-Ruthven* (Dublin: Irish Academic Press, 1981), 175–95, quote at 181.

92 Davies, 'Mortimer, Roger, fourth earl of March and sixth of Ulster', *ODNB*; Curtis, Edmund, *Richard II in Ireland, 1394–5, and submissions of the Irish chiefs* (Oxford: Clarendon Press, 1927); Johnston, Dorothy, 'Chief governors and treasurers of Ireland in the reign of Richard II', in Barry, Terry, Frame, Robin & Simms, Katharine (eds), *Colony and Frontier in Medieval Ireland: Essays Presented to J.F. Lydon* (London: Bloomsbury, 1995), 97–115.

93 Potterton, *Medieval Trim*, 107, 111. For Roger's livery see *CPR, 1391–6*, 284, 375.

94 University of Chicago MS 224, f. 59v; Holmes, *Estates of the Higher Nobility*, 19, n. 2. In December 1387, carts laden with £1400 had travelled from Wigmore to London under armed escort: BL, Egerton Rolls 8730.

95 Davies, *Age of Conquest*, 402–3.

96 Davies, *Lordship and Society*, 196; TNA, SC 11/23.

97 University of Chicago MS 224, f. 58r; TNA, SC 6/1184/22.

98 TNA, E 31/2/1, ff. 72r–v, 260r. A 'hide' is defined as 'primarily, the amount considered adequate for the support of one free family with its dependants; at an early date defined as being as much land as could be tilled with one plough in a year': *Oxford English Dictionary*, online: https://www.oed.com/view/Entry/86719.

99 Davies, *Lordship and Society*, 110–11.

100 TNA, E 31/2/1, ff. 260r–v.

101 Evans, 'Family of Mortimer', 450–1, quoting TNA, SC 6/1236/5.

102 Bailey, Mark, *After the Black Death: Economy, Society and the Law in Fourteenth-Century England. The Ford Lectures for 2019* (Oxford: OUP, 2020), esp. chs 6 & 7; Hopkinson & Speight, *Lords of the March*, 155.

103 Evans, 'Family of Mortimer', 444; TNA, SC 6/1236/18.

104 Davies, *Lordship and Society*, 118–19; Hopkinson & Speight, *Lords of the March*, 163–4. For the wool trade, see Bell, A.R., Brooks, C. & Dryburgh, P.R., *The English Medieval Wool Market*, c.1230–1327 (Cambridge: CUP, 2007), 47, 49.

105 Evans, 'Family of Mortimer', 453.

106 Davies, *Lordship and Society*, 118.

107 Faraday, M.A., *Ludlow, 1085–1660: a social, economic and political history* (Chichester: Phillimore, 1991).

108 *Placita de Quo Warranto*, I, 678; *CChR, 1327–41*, 94; *CChR, 1427–1516*, 156; *Gazetteer of Markets and Fairs in England and Wales to 1516*, ed. Samantha Letters: https://archives.history. ac.uk/gazetteer/gazweb2.html.

109 TNA, E 31/2/1, ff. 180r–v, 183v.

110 *CIPM*, IV, no. 235; *Gazetteer of Markets and Fairs*, under Cleobury Mortimer, Knighton, Radnor.

111 *CIPM*, XV, nos 534–71.

112 *Inquisitions and Extents of Medieval Ireland*, no. 54, 30.

113 Discussed in Ó Cléirigh, Cormac, 'The problems of defence: a regional case study', in Lydon, J.F. (ed.), *Law and Disorder in Thirteenth-Century Ireland: The Dublin Parliament of 1297* (Dublin: Four Courts Press, 1997), 25–56.

114 Potterton, *Medieval Trim*, 67, 143–50.

115 *CPR, 1307–13*, 70. The fourth earl secured a further murage grant in 1393.

116 Watt, E.H., '"On Account of the Frequent Attacks and Invasions of the Welsh": The Effect of the Glyn Dŵr Rebellion on Tax Collection in England', in *The Reign of Henry IV: Rebellion and Survival, 1403–1413*, ed. Dodd, G. & Biggs, D. (York: York Medieval Press, 2008), 48–81.

117 *CIM, 1307–49*, nos 682, 170.

118 *CIPM*, IV, no. 235.

119 TNA, SC 6/1209/6; Davies, *Lordship and Society*, 128.

120 Mileson, S.A., *Parks in Medieval England* (Oxford: OUP, 2009).

121 Davies; *Lordship and Society*, 123; Rees, William, *South Wales and the March, 1284–1415: a social and agrarian study* (Oxford: OUP, 1924), 111.

122 TNA, E 31/2/1, f. 260r.

123 Hopkinson & Speight, *Lords of the March*, 157.

124 *CIPM*, IV, no. 235; XV, nos 534–71.

125 *CPR, 1313–17*, 323.

126 *CPR, 1292–1301*, 290–1. This is the second of two charters inspected and confirmed by Edward I, the former granting them particular legal rights and freedom from unjust persecution.

127 ibid.; *CIPM*, XV, nos 534–71,

128 For the March Rees Davies' *Lordship and Society* remains indispensable.

129 Horrox, Rosemary, 'Edward IV', *ODNB*.

8. A SCANDAL AT MASS: THE PERSONAL NETWORKS OF EDMUND, 3RD EARL OF MARCH
Patrick McDonagh

1 There is a discrepancy in the earl's year of birth. The *Fundatorum Historia* says Edmund was born 'on the eve of the Purification of the Blessed Virgin Mary A.D. 1351' [New Style dating: 1 February 1352]. However, the rubricator also says this is the 25th regnal year of King Edward III. As that year began on 25 January 1351, the correct year by that reckoning would be 1351. Historians have followed the New Style dating: George Holmes, 'Mortimer, Edmund, third earl of March and earl of Ulster (1352–1381)', *ODNB* (https://doi.org/10.1093/ref:odnb/19342).

2 *Calendar of Ormond Deeds: Volume II, 1350–1413 A.D.*, ed. Edmund Curtis (Dublin, 1934), 169. The bishop of Cloyne was a Carmelite friar. The episode is contextualised in Peter Crooks, *Factionalism and Noble Power in English Ireland, c.1361–1423* (University of Dublin, unpublished PhD thesis, 2007), 127–8, 134.

3 *Ormond Deeds II*, 171.

4 Ibid., 169. For commentary, A.J. Otway-Ruthven, *A History of Medieval Ireland* (New York, 1968; 1980), 314.

5 This instrument was calendared almost 90 years ago by Edmund Curtis in *Ormond Deeds II*, 168–71. A transcription appears on pp. 172–9.

6 Ibid., 169.

7 This would not be the end of Cloyne. He reappears at an emergency council meeting in January 1382 following the unexpected death of the earl of March, where he pled for the appointment of the earl's brother Sir Thomas Mortimer as justiciar. Both the earls of Ormond and Desmond were also present at this meeting. For the record of this meeting see *A Calendar of Irish Chancery Letters c.1244–1509* [*CIRCLE*], ed. Peter Crooks, Patent Roll 5 Richard II, 39. Crooks has also drawn attention to this later episode: *Factionalism and Noble Power*, 156.

8 Ibid. Crooks also explores the continuing positive Ormond-Mortimer relationship for the following generation of earls during the 1390s: 223–32.

9 Cadell's and Hopton's instrument can be found in the National Library of Ireland where they are catalogued together under D. 1268. Cadell's instrument has survived in an excellent state of preservation and includes his notarial signum. It is written in one hand throughout on one large membrane measuring 74.4 cm by 41 cm. Curiously, Curtis, who would have seen Hopton's instrument, does not mention it in his calendar.

10 The text in both versions of Hopton's instrument reads *coram populo et familia domini nostri domini Edmundi comitis Marchie*. Curtis's transcription omits *domini nostri*. Like Curtis I have silently expanded the abbreviations. See Dublin, National Library of Ireland, D. 1268.

11 Crooks has noted previously the household element among the witnesses, see Crooks, *Factionalism and Noble Power*, 127, fn. 4.

12 I have modernised the spelling of Christian names while retaining the form of the surnames given by Hopton. There is a discrepancy in the spelling of some surnames between Hopton's instrument and in the verbatim copy provided by Cadell. I have preferred those given by Hopton.

13 The chaplains are described as rectors of the dioceses of Lincoln, Salisbury and Hereford.

14 Given space and format constraints, I have not provided a biographical outline of all the witnesses.

15 G.A. Holmes, *The Estates of the Higher Nobility in Fourteenth-Century England* (Cambridge 1957; 2nd edition, 2009), 59.

16 Apart from the brief comments of G.A. Holmes almost 70 years ago, the most sustained work on the topic has been completed by Paul Dryburgh in his thesis on the first earl of March, which looks at the Mortimer affinity in the early fourteenth century: Paul Dryburgh, *The career of Roger Mortimer, first earl of March (c.1287–1330)* (University of Bristol, unpublished PhD thesis, 2002), 153–205. Since then brief discussions of the Mortimer affinity in the late fourteenth century have featured in: Ian Mortimer, 'The Mortimers in the Time of Richard II', *Journal of the Mortimer History Society: Volume 1*, (2017), 97–8; Brendan Smith, 'Transnational Lordship and the Plantagenet Empire: the Mortimer Lords of Wigmore, 1247–1425', *Welsh History Review/ Cylchgrawn Hanes Cymru*, 29/1 (2018), 27–50, 43–4; and David Simpkin, 'The Mortimer Retinue for War, 1277–1421', *Journal of the Mortimer History Society: Volume III* (2019), 49–58. Though valuable, these articles have not drawn upon the extensive corpus of surviving Mortimer estate and financial accounts from this period.

17 R.R. Davies, *The First English Empire* (Oxford, 2000), esp. chapter seven.

18 Robin Frame, *The Political Development of the British Isles* (Oxford, 1990), 179–87.

19 Peter Crooks, David Green, and W. Mark Ormrod, 'The Plantagenets and Empire in the Later Middle Ages', in iidem (eds), *The Plantagenet Empire, 1259–1453: Proceedings of the 2014 Harlaxton Symposium* (Donington, 2016), 33.

20 TNA, C 76/57, m. 10, from the AHRC-funded 'The Soldier in Later Medieval England Online Database' [*SLME*] www.medievalsoldier.org. Hopton's letters of protection for the expedition were issued in September 1374.

21 BL, Egerton Charter 7244.

22 BL, Egerton Roll 8727.

23 BL, Egerton Roll 8728. An edition of this account has been published in C.M. Woolgar, *Household Accounts from Medieval England: Part 1* (Midsomer Norton, 1992), 245–58.

24 Mortimer's will is preserved in Lambeth Palace Library [hereafter LPL], Register Courtenay, ff. 188r–189v. Kepeston's bequest can be found on f. 189r, his appointment as one of the earl's executors on f. 189v. An eighteenth-century transcription of the will can be found in J. Nichols, *A Collection of All the Wills, Now Known to be Extant of the Kings and Queens of England, Princes and Princesses of Wales, and Every Branch of the Blood Royal, From the Reign of William the Conqueror to that of Henry the Seventh Exclusive.* (London, 1780), 104–16. I have preferred throughout to refer to the transcription found in the register of Archbishop Courtenay.

25 *CIRCLE*, Close Roll 5 Richard II, 63.

26 Three letters from Kepeston and his fellow executors have survived sewn into a collection of accounts relating to the lordship of Radnor and its components. Two of them date from 26 June 1382, which indicates that Kepeston had returned from Ireland by then: TNA, SC 6/1209/15.

27 Three of his accounts for these later years have survived and are now kept in the British Library. They date from 5 January–23 April 1393, 24 April 1393–23 April 1394 and 24 April–2 June 1394. The first account can be found in Egerton Roll 8740 and the latter two (along with a short diet account) in Egerton Roll 8739.

28 LPL, Register Courtenay, f. 189v.

29 BL, Egerton Roll 8728.

30 BL, Egerton Roll 8727.

31 A discussion of the cartularies can be found in Barbara Wright, *Why Make Back-Up Copies? The Mortimer Cartulary and the Technological Revolution* (Otley, 2010). The suggestion that Stutvile composed at least one of the cartularies is my own.

32 Simon Walker, 'Lovell [Lovel], John, fifth Baron Lovell (*c.*1342–1408), courtier and royal councillor', *ODNB* (https://doi.org/10.1093/ref:odnb/53092).

33 Nigel Saul, *Richard II* (London, 1997), 247–8. See also 'Lovell, John', *ODNB*.

34 Ibid.

35 Ibid.

36 BL, Harley MS 1240, ff. 63r–v; Lord Frederick Campbell Charters, XVIII, 5.

37 *CCR 1374–7*, 96.

38 BL, Harley MS 1240, ff. 46v–47r.

39 Chelmsford, Essex Record Office, D/DHu M1, printed in K.C. Newton, *Thaxted in the Fourteenth Century: An Account of the Manor and Borough, with Translated Texts* (Chelmsford, 1960), 98. This expense has been struck out with no explanation from the auditor.

40 'Lovell, John', *ODNB*.

41 *CIPM: Volume XV: 1–7 Richard II*, 219.

42 *CPR 1381–5*, 452.

43 'Lovell, John', *ODNB*.

44 *CPR 1396–9*, 145. Robert was escaping legal problems in the lordship of Pembroke, *Handbook and Select Calendar of Sources for Medieval Ireland in the National Archives of the United Kingdom* [hereafter *HSCMI*], ed. Paul Dryburgh and Brendan Smith (Dublin, 2005), 161.

45 BL, Harley 782, f.74v; *SLME*.

46 *CPR 1377–81*, 485.

47 Simon Walker, *The Lancastrian Affinity* (Oxford, 1990; 2nd edn, 1996), 44–5. Wythfeld was also a Lancastrian retainer, retained by the duke, John of Gaunt, in 1372, though as Walker notes he 'served seven different commanders in the next ten years but never once with Gaunt'.

48 LPL, Register Whittlesey, f. 100r.

49 The inquisition post mortem of the earl of Hereford undertaken in 1373 records that Bromwich and his step-son Gilbert Talbot held two knight's fees in Gloucestershire: *CIPM*, XIII, 167. Bromwich's wife Elizabeth had died before April 1373 when her son Gilbert granted to Bromwich for life certain lands in Tynedale which had been held by Elizabeth for life: *CPR 1370–4*, 279.

50 These included the town of Bannow along with lands and lordships in Edermine and Jerpoint in the south-east of Ireland: *CPR 1370–4*, 87.

51 For an account of the campaign see James Sherborne, *War, Politics and Culture in Fourteenth-Century England*, ed. Anthony Tuck (London, 1994), 77–97.

52 *CCR 1374–7*, 96.

53 LPL, Register Courtenay, f. 190r. An eighteenth-century transcription of her will was published in Nichols, *Collection of All the Will*, 98–103.

54 *CPR 1377–81*, 391.

55 TNA, E 101/246/13.

56 *Documents on the Affairs of Ireland before the King's Council*, ed. G.O. Sayles (Dublin, 1979), 248–9.

57 'Private Indentures for Life Service in Peace and War 1278–1476', ed. Michael Jones and Simon Walker, *Camden Miscellany XXXII* (London, 1994), 96–7.

58 *CIRCLE*, Close Roll 3 Richard II, 47.

59 London, College of Arms, Lynch/2/88/55/1, accessed from Virtual Record Treasury of Ireland [VRTI], www.virtualtreasury.ie.

60 College of Arms, Lynch/2/87/36/2, accessed from *VRTI*.

61 A summary of his career can be found in Brendan Smith, *Crisis and Survival in Late Medieval Ireland: The English of Louth and Their Neighbours, 1330–1450* (Oxford, 2013), 71.

62 *CPR 1361–4*, 441.

63 *Ormond Deeds II*, 92–3.

64 *The Register of Milo Sweteman, Archbishop of Armagh, 1361–1380*, ed. Brendan Smith (Dublin, 1996), 39.

65 *CIRCLE*, Close Roll 43 Edward III, 44.

66 *CIRCLE*, Close Roll 4 Richard II, 47.

67 *CPR 1377–81*, 171.

68 The familial relationship between John and Walter can be seen in a quitclaim of Walter's son Thomas in *CCR 1419–22*, 195.

69 *Private Indentures for Life Service*, 87–9.

70 *CCR 1369–74*, 418.

71 *CPR 1377–81*, 345–6.

72 TNA, C 76/57, m. 10; *SLME*. In a list of the third earl's creditors Walter is noted as being owed 73s. from the account of the earl's treasurer, John Blake, in the 49th year (1375/6). This probably relates to the Breton expedition in 1375 but could conceivably include arrears from the previous campaigns. His arrears were paid in the account of John Vautort, the receiver-general, during the 50th year (1376/7): BL, Egerton Roll 8751.

73 *CPR 1381–5*, 116.

74 Ibid., 343–4. On the same day another writ was sent out from Chancery to the keeper of the same manor to ensure that Walter Bromwich received payment of his annuity of 20 marks and the arrears. One can only imagine Walter did not find this duty too difficult. See ibid., 176–7.

75 TNA, E101/40/33, m. 10; *SLME*.

76 BL, Egerton Charter 7228.

77 BL, Egerton Roll 8745.

78 A biographical sketch of Coneweye can be found in J.E Messham, 'Henry Conewey, Knight, Constable of the Castle of Rhuddlan, 1390–1407', *Flintshire Historical Society Journal* 35 (1999), 11–55. Messham's work is brief regarding Coneweye's service with the Mortimers and his earlier military career in Ireland. He (15) repeats the suggestion of George Holmes that Henry Coneweye may be identified with Henry Cornewayle (or Cornwaill as Messham spells his surname) who witnessed the making of Earl's Edmund will in May 1380; however, this is incorrect. Both Coneweye and Cornewayle were among Hopton's witnesses as can be seen in Table 1. I would like to thank Dr Adam Chapman for making me aware of this article. Chapman, in his doctoral thesis, provided a brief biography of Coneweye's career which fleshes out his military service in Ireland during the 1360s and 1370s. However, following Messham, he also incorrectly identifies Coneweye with Cornewayle: Adam Chapman, 'The Welsh Soldier: 1283–1422' (University of Southampton, PhD thesis, 2009), 234–5.

79 *HSCMI*, 313.

80 TNA, E101/31/25, m. 2; *SLME*.

81 *CIRCLE*, 44 Edward III Close Roll, 55.

82 *CPR 1370–4*, 90, 195.

83 *Private Indentures for Life Service*, 100–1.

84 Rotherwas, Herefordshire Archive and Records Centre, G33/1.

85 He was issued with letters of protection to go to Ireland in February 1380: *CPR 1377–81*, 409.

86 *Private Indentures for Life Service*, 100–1.

87 *CIRCLE*, Close Roll 5 Richard II, 17.

88 Ibid., Patent Roll 5 Richard II, 35; Close Roll 5 Richard II, 17. These writs tally with an entry in the *Annals of Ulster* that Edmund captured the castle of Athlone in 1381: *Annala Uladh: Annals of Ulster, otherwise Annala Senate, Annals of Senat; a chronicle of Irish affairs from A.D. 431 to A.D. 1540 [i.e. A.D. 431–1131; 1155–1588]*, 4 vols., ed. W.M. Hennessy and B. MacCarthy (Dublin, 1887–1901), sub anno 1381.

89 *CIRCLE*, Close Roll 5 Richard II, 16. In October Ralph Beltesford, clerk of the wages, was granted an allowance for the expenses of 'various hobelars and foot' who came from different parts of Ireland 'for the recovery of the castle of Athlone': ibid., 23.

90 *CPR 1381–5*, 119.

91 Ibid., 576.

92 *CPR 1385–9*, 9.

93 Ibid., 125.

94 Hawarden, North East Wales Archives, D/GW/1512.

95 *CPR 1381–5*, 576.

96 *CPR 1405–8*, 285.

97 As Haclyt is generally spelled Hakeluyt in most surviving life-records relating to him, I have preferred that form of the surname throughout the rest of this essay.

98 Dryburgh, 'The career of Roger Mortimer', 158. A summary of Hakeluyt's life can be found in *The House of Commons 1386–1421: Volume II Members A–D*, eds J.S. Roskell, Linda Clark and Carole Rawcliffe, 265–7.

99 *CPR 1354–8*, 321.

100 Dryburgh, 'The career of Roger Mortimer', 158.

101 TNA, C 76/56, m. 20; *SLME*.

102 TNA, C 76/57, m. 8; *SLME*.

103 *CPR 1381–5*, 119.

104 *CIRCLE*, Patent Roll 5 Richard II, 39.

105 *CPR 1381–5*, 88.

106 *CIRCLE*, Patent Roll 5 Richard II, 90.

107 Ibid., 100.

108 Shrewsbury, Shropshire Archives, 6000/2799.

109 BL, Egerton Roll 8730.

110 Dudley, Dudley Archives, DOH/V/1/2.

111 For his estates see *House of Commons II*, 265.

112 *CCR 1385–9*, 119, 495; *CCR 1392–6*, 278.

113 *CCR 1402–5*, 521; *CCR 1405–9*, 282.

114 An account of the events of these months can be found in Saul, *Richard II*, chapter nine.

115 Professor Given-Wilson called him the 'sixth Appellant': Chris Given-Wilson, *Henry IV* (New Haven and London, 2017), 45 n. 41.

116 *CPR 1391–6*, 481.

117 *CPR 1396–9*, 457.

118 Ibid., 185–6.

119 Ibid., 349.

120 TNA, SC 6/1184/23.

121 BL, Egerton Roll 8751.

122 A summary of Cheyne's life can be found in *House of Commons II*, 545–7.

123 *CPR 1358–61*, 100; *CFR 1356–68*, 321.

124 TNA, C 61/82, m. 12; *SLME*.

125 TNA, C 76/56, m. 14; *SLME*.

126 London, Senate House Library, MS 814/38.

127 *CPR 1391–6*, 500.

128 TNA, C 143/395/16.

129 TNA, C 76/57, m. 11; *SLME*.

130 *Private Indentures for Life Service*, 90–1.

131 LPL, Register Courtenay, f. 189v.

132 *CPR 1374–7*, 471.

133 *CIRCLE*, Patent Roll 5 Richard II, 50; Close Roll 5 Richard II, 48.

134 Ibid., 105.

135 He seems to have later returned (perhaps briefly), for in October 1382 he was granted letters of protection for royal service in Ireland: *CPR 1381–5*, 166. He was still in England a month later when he acted as a mainpernor for John Bromwich when he was granted the keeping of the English possessions of the alien abbey of Caen, see *CFR 1377–83*, 331.

136 BL, Harley MS 1240, ff. 46v–47r.

137 TNA, SC 6/1209/15. The other executors named were John, bishop of Hereford, Sir Peter de la Mare, John Kepston and John Piers, clerks.

138 Aberystwyth, National Library of Wales, The Mortimer Roll.

139 *CCR 1385–9*, 495, 657.

140 Anthony Goodman, *The Loyal Conspiracy* (London, 1971), 43.

141 BL, Egerton Roll 8739.

142 *CPR 1391–6*, 481.

143 On the Shrewsbury parliament see Saul, *Richard II*, 380–1.

144 University of Chicago, MS 224, f. 59v.

145 BL, Egerton Charter 58674.

146 TNA, SC 6/1184/23.

147 A transcription of this indenture can be found in Holmes, *The Estates of the Higher Nobility*, 130.

148 Médiathèque de l'Agglomération Troyenne, MS 1316, f. 50r.

149 University of Chicago, MS 224, f. 59v.

150 *Annala Rioghachta Eireann: Annals of the kingdom of Ireland by the Four Masters, from the earliest period to the year 1616*, 7 vols., ed. John O'Donovan (Dublin, 1848–51), sub anno 1398.

151 *CFR 1391–9*, 271–2.

152 Senate House Library, MS 814/38.

153 *CPR 1399–1401*, 60.

154 *CPR 1401–5*, 229.

155 Ibid., 231, 237.

156 LPL, Register Courtenay, f. 189v.

157 On Percy's short-lived revolt see Given-Wilson, *Henry IV*, chapter fifteen.

158 *CPR 1401–5*, 414.
159 *House of Commons II*, 547.
160 Crooks, Green and Ormrod, 'The Plantagenets and Empire in the Later Middle Ages', 33.
161 For the value of adopting a regional approach in the late medieval British Isles see Brendan Smith, 'The British Isles in the Late Middle Ages: Shaping the Regions', in idem (ed.), *Ireland and the English World in the Late Middle Ages: Essays in Honour of Robin Frame* (Basingstoke, 2009), 7–19.

9. FAMILY SUPPORT: MINORITY AND THE MORTIMER INHERITANCE, 1380–1425
Professor Chris Given-Wilson

1 G. Holmes, *The Estates of the Higher Nobility in Fourteenth-Century England* (Cambridge, 1957), 10.
2 *PROME [Parliament Rolls of Medieval England 1275–1504*, ed. P. Brand, A. Curry, C. Given-Wilson, R. Horrox, G. Martin, M. Ormrod and S. Phillips (16 vols, Woodbridge 2005)], iv.241. At the same time, they asked for a remedy against 'people who alienate their lands at the moment of death, and cause themselves to be carried from their manors [i.e relinquished legal ownership of them] in order to deprive the chief lords of the wardship of the same by deception'.
3 The petition stated explicitly that this was for 'the protection of such heirs' and that the guardian(s) should pay the true value of the estates each year (*PROME,* v.340). C. Given-Wilson, *The English Nobility in the Late Middle Ages* (London, 1987), 149–53, for the background.
4 Before 1350, enfeoffments to use by great nobles were rarities, but of the nine inheritances of great magnates who died between 1360 and 1380, seven were at least partly enfeoffed to uses. However, 'there does not in fact seem to have been any attempt to treat the whole of an inheritance in this way' (Holmes, *Estates*, 49–50, 57).
5 *CPR 1358–61*, 266–7. He had managed to recover almost all the lands forfeited by his grandfather the first earl, and since his grandmother Joan had died in 1358, he also acquired the very substantial Geneville lands which she had held in dower (Holmes, *Estates*, 16–17, 45–6). The Black Prince was less willing to respect the immunity of the Welsh lands.
6 The enfeoffment is in *CPR 1374–77*, 33–4, with remainder to his executors and councillors.
7 *SAC [St Albans Chronicle*, ed J. Taylor, W. Childs and L. Watkiss (2 vols, Oxford, 2003, 2011)], vol. I, 620–25. According to the chronicler, by the 'custom of the realm', the king should have retained the lands in his own hands; in November 1382 they had been reserved for the expenses of the royal household: A. Tuck, *Richard II and the English Nobility* (London, 1973), 88–9; *CPR 1381–5, 184.*
8 The estates were granted to Roger (the heir), the three earls and John Lord Neville in December 1383, for a rent of £4,000 a year. The custody of Roger, aged nine, was initially entrusted to Arundel, an arrangement confirmed on 27 July 1384, but a month later, on 23 August 1384, the king transferred it to Thomas Holand, earl of Kent (*CPR 1381–5*, 345, 377, 441, 452, 536).
9 A. Dunn, *The Politics of Magnate Power* (Oxford, 2003), 67–70, 148, 169–70; *The Chronicle of Adam Usk 1377–1421*, ed. C. Given-Wilson (Oxford, 1997), 38–41. Dunn also argues that the king used his ubiquitous favourite, William Lescrope, to undermine Roger's authority in Ireland between 1395 and 1397; he dismissed Roger as lieutenant of Ireland on 20 July 1398, before hearing of his death.

10 *CPR 1396–9*, 403, 408, 429, 514, 547 (however, Countess Eleanor was assigned her widow's dower).

11 These are the families associated with them in the 'Wigmore annal 1355–1377' printed by J. Taylor, *English Historical Literature in the Fourteenth Century* (Oxford, 1987), 285–300. Roger's marriage to the daughter of William, first earl of Salisbury, initially created a strong bond with the Montagues as well, but the two families fell out after Denbigh was restored to the Mortimers in 1354.

12 Warwick's mother was Katherine Mortimer, daughter of Roger, first earl of March. In 1390, Richard earl of Arundel (d.1397) married Philippa, the sister of Roger (d.1398), as his second wife.

13 *CPR 1399–1401*, 227 (Sir Edmund was the other executor); Dunn, *Politics of Magnate Power*, 100; C. Given-Wilson, *Henry IV* (New Haven and London, 2016), 190–201.

14 See for example C. Given-Wilson, 'The bishop of Winchester, the abbot of Titchfield, and the "pretended chapel" of Hook 1375–1405', in *People, Power and Identity in the Late Middle Ages: Essays in Memory of Mark Ormrod,* ed. G. Dodd, H. Lacey and A. Musson (London, 2021), 137–56, at 143. Dunn, *Politics of Magnate Power,* 100, estimates that between them the Percys may have made a profit of about £2,000 a year from the wardship of the Mortimer estates in 1400–1403.

15 Quote from the Dieulacres Chronicle in *Chronicles of the Revolution, 1397–1400,* ed. C. Given-Wilson (Manchester 1993, 40, 192–3).

16 G. Harriss, 'Richard of Conisburgh' *ODNB online;* T. Pugh, *Henry V and the Southampton Plot of 1415* (Southampton, 1987), 88–99; M. Ormrod, 'False Paternity and the Royal Succession in Later Medieval England', *Nottingham Medieval Studies* 60 (2016), 187–226.

17 Given-Wilson, *Henry IV,* 264–5.

18 Anne herself, however, had died in 1411, barely 20 years old, shortly after giving birth to their son, the future duke of York.

19 Pugh, *Southampton Plot,* 93–6.

20 *Chronicles of the Revolution,* 211.

21 *Henry IV,* 450.

22 *Usk,* 52–4.

23 Edward Charlton seems to have had little trouble in accommodating himself to the Lancastrian regime, taking a leading part in suppressing the Welsh rebellion and becoming a Knight of the Garter in 1407; it was his men who captured John Oldcastle in 1417.

24 For a different view of Sir Thomas's status, see Ian Mortimer's 'The Medieval Mortimer Family: an Outline Lineage' on the Mortimer History Website, https://mortimerhistorysociety.org.uk/wp-content/uploads/Mortimers/Genealogies/OUTLINE-LINEAGE-7.11.pdf 20–22; see also Andy King on his military record in chapter 6 of this volume (101).

25 Dunn, *Politics of Magnate Power,* 56–7.

26 *Usk,* 30.

27 *Usk,* 158.

28 See Andy King's analysis of Sir Edmund's military career in chapter 6 of this volume (110); and David Stephenson's assessment of Bryn Glas in chapter 2 of this volume (36–8).

29 *Usk,* 160; *Continuatio Eulogii: The Continuation of the Eulogium Historiarum 1364–1413,* ed. C. Given-Wilson (Oxford, 2019), 118.

30 The next chapter by Ian Mortimer provides a detailed assessment of what is known about Sir John Mortimer.

31 *PROME*, x.203 (from the *Chronicles of London*).

32 E. Powell, 'The Strange Death of Sir John Mortimer', in *Rulers and Ruled in Late Medieval England,* ed. R. Archer and S. Walker (London, 1995), 83–97.

33 *CPR 1413–16,* 45 (uncertainty about Edmund's age).

34 By 1422, about 90% of it had been paid, and the rest was discounted against the wages of war owed to him (*PROME*, x.107; Pugh, *The Southampton Plot,* 81, 86–7).

35 Harriss called him 'vacillating and contemptible', while Pugh believed him to have been 'greatly to blame for the tragic consequences' of the Southampton Plot (Harriss, 'Richard of Conisburgh', *ODNB online*; Pugh, *Southampton Plot,* 82, 162, 173). Yet none of the condemned conspirators accused Edmund of *consenting* to the plot, only that he initially agreed to listen to them, and contemporary chroniclers did not accuse him of betraying them: *Usk*, 254; *SAC,* vol. 2, 660–2; *Gesta Henrici Quinti: The Deeds of Henry V,* F. Taylor and J. Roskell (Oxford 1975), 19.

10. WHO WAS SIR JOHN MORTIMER?
Dr Ian Mortimer

1 Edward Powell, 'The Strange death of Sir John Mortimer: Politics and the law of Treason in Lancastrian England', in Rowena Archer and Simon Walker (eds), *Rulers and Ruled in Late Medieval England: Essays presented to Gerald Harriss* (1995), 83–97.

2 These translations are from the Magna Carta project: https://magnacarta.cmp.uea.ac.uk/read/magna_carta_1215/ all downloaded 17 October 2022.

3 C.L. Kingsford (ed.), *Chronicles of London*, 342. The instructions appear to have come from Robert Scott, deputy lieutenant of the Tower, as discussed on 198–9.

4 Sarah Stockdale, 'Blood on the Crown: Treason in the Royal Kinship Structure of Fifteenth-Century England' (Unpublished PhD Thesis, University of Winchester, 2018), 42–5.

5 *CIPM*, xxiv, no. 161. This specifies that Sir John Mortimer died on 25 October 1415, the date of the battle of Agincourt.

6 TNA, E 101/40/33, m. 6; E 101/40/34, m. 18; E 101/41/5, m. 13d.

7 Powell, 'Strange Death', 85–6.

8 F. Devon (ed.), *Issues of the Exchequer: being a collection of payments made out of His Majesty's Revenue, from King Henry III to King Henry VI inclusive* (London, 1834), 314; *Forty-Fourth Annual Report of the Deputy Keeper of the Public Records* (1883), 547.

9 TNA, E 101/45/2, m. 4; E 101/45/19, m. 3.

10 TNA, E 101/47/1, m. 1; C 76/98, m. 17.

11 TNA, E 101/51/2, m. 41.

12 J.L. Kirby (ed.), *Calendar of Signet Letters of Henry IV and Henry V* (London, 1978), 85 (no. 344).

13 *CIPM*, xviii, 255, 373.

14 *CFR, 1413–22,* 162.

15 *CCR, 1419–22,* 47, 64.

16 *CIPM*, xix, no. 874.

17 *CIPM*, xviii, no. 927.

18 *CPR, 1399–1401,* 47, 116, 393, 479.

19 TNA, SC 8/190/9475; *CPR, 1401–5,* 370.

20 *CCR, 1403–9*, 387.

21 *CCR, 1403–9*, 279. The deed was witnessed by John Dorewarde, John Wynter, Dru Barentyn (the goldsmith of London), Thomas Geney and Walter Stratton.

22 *Complete Peerage*, iv, 30, quoting a deed copied in BL MS Harleian 245, f. 47v.

23 TNA, CP 25/1/291/63, no. 48.

24 *CCR, 1413–19*, 356. The witnesses were: William Fulthorp and Ralph Yver, knights, and John de Aske esquire; Richard Fayrefax, and Robert Martyn of Yorkshire; Adam Persale and Richard Lakyn knights; and David Holbache and William Poynour esquires of Shropshire.

25 TNA, E 101/47/1, m. 1; C 76/98, mm 17, 19; E 101/45/2, mm 3, 4.

26 Anne Curry, *Agincourt: a New History* (Stroud, 2006), 137, 316.

27 *CIPM*, xxiv, no. 161.

28 Ibid., xxiv, no. 750.

29 *Forty-Fourth Annual Report of the Deputy Keeper of the Public Records* (1883), 624–5.

30 *CPR, 1416–22*, 84–5.

31 *CCR, 1413–19*, 456–7.

32 Powell, 'Strange Death', 86.

33 *CCR, 1413–19*, 483.

34 TNA, C 138/43/76, mm 1–2; *CIPM*, xxi no. 352.

35 *CCR, 1419–22*, 63.

36 N.H. Nicolas (ed.), *Proceedings and Ordinances of the Privy Council, 1386–[1542]*, 7 vols (London, 1834–7), ii, 296, 307–8, 311.

37 *CCR, 1419–22*, 196.

38 TNA, SC 8/125/6236; *Rot. Parl.*, iv, 160; *PROME*, ix, 310.

39 TNA, SC 8/24/1171.

40 *Proceedings and Ordinances of the Privy Council*, ii, 311-12.

41 *CPR, 1416–22*, 413.

42 *Issue Rolls*, 373.

43 Powell, 'Strange Death', 87, quoting J.G. Nicholas, *Chronicle of the Greyfriars of London* (1852), 15; *CPR, 1422–9*, 389.

44 Powell, 'Strange Death', 87–8.

45 *Proceedings and Ordinances*, ii, 332–3.

46 *Issue Rolls*, 384.

47 *Chronicles of London*, 342. For the cost of his journey, see *Issue Rolls*, 389.

48 *PROME*, x, 86.

49 *Chronicles of London*, 282–3.

50 *Chronicles of London*, 283.

51 *Rot. Parl.*, x, 87.

52 *Chronicle of the Greyfriars*, 15.

53 C.L. Kingsford, 'Register of the Grey Friars of London: Titulus de Monumentis', in *The Grey Friars of London* (Aberdeen, 1915), 70–133. *British History Online* http://www.british-history. ac.uk/brit-franciscan-soc/ vol6/ 70–133 [accessed 1 November 2021].

54 *Complete Peerage*, iv, 30–1. She died on 28 December 1432.

55 *CIPM*, xxii, no. 255.

56 *VCH Hertfordshire*, vol 3, parish of Hatfield, downloaded from https://www.british-history. ac.uk/vch/herts/vol3/pp91-111#h3-0006, 2 November 2021.

57 History of Parliament – https://www.historyofparliamentonline.org/volume/1386-1421/ member/harry-john-ap-1420 [downloaded 16 November 2021].

58 *PROME*, x, 68.

59 *Foedera*, x, 319.

60 See for example Augustine Vincent's statement in his *Discoverie of Errours in the First Edition of the Catalogue of Nobility Published by Raphe Brooke, Yorke Herald, 1619* (1622), 327, where he makes Sir John the younger brother of the fourth earl of March (1374–1398) and Sir Edmund Mortimer (1376–1409).

61 *Monasticon Anglicanum*, vi, 355.

62 *CPR, 1401–5*, 406.

63 J.L. Kirby (ed.), *Calendar of Signet Letters of Henry IV and Henry V (1399–1422)* (London, 1978), 25–6 (no. 25), 64–5 (no. 234).

64 John Anstis, *Observations Introductory to an Historical Essay upon the Knighthood of the Bath* (1752), appendix xxxviii (25).

65 C. Given-Wilson (ed.), *The Chronicle of Adam Usk, 1377–1421* (Oxford, 1997), 160–1.

66 *CIPM*, xxi, no. 351.

67 For his appearance in his brother's will, see Nichols (ed.), *Collection of all the Wills*, p. 115. For his brother's grants to him, see *CIPM*, xv, no. 552 (222); *CCR 1381–5*, 276; *CPR 1396–9*, 153.

68 The *Fundatorum Historia* states that he was killed in a tournament at Shrewsbury in 1328: *Monasticon Anglicanum*, vi, 352. The date might not be correct as in 1335 his mother made a settlement of her extensive Irish estates with remainder to her son, John. However, two years later she made a new settlement of her Irish lands, this time with reversion to her sole surviving son, Geoffrey: *CPR, 1334–8*, 152, 351.

69 *A Descriptive Catalogue of Ancient Deeds in the Public Record Office*, 6 vols (London, 1890–1915), i, no. B593; TNA, E 326/593.

70 *CCR, 1409–13*, 327.

71 *Catalogue of Ancient Deeds*, i, no. B1441; TNA E 326/1441. These amounted to 'lands and tenements, woods, &c., in Essenden and Bishops Hatfield, with the advowson of the chantry of St Anne in the church of Bishop's Hatfield, which the vendors had of the feoffment of Stephen Wolfe and Thomas Stoughton'.

72 *CIPM*, series 2, vol. 1 (London, 1898), no. 100.

73 *Dictionary of British Armoury* (1992), 105.

74 TNA, CP 25/1/90/95/661.

75 *CIM, 1377–88*, 196.

76 *CPR, 1348–50*, 248.

77 *CCR, 1409–13*, 418, 422.

78 *CCR, 1419–22*, 196.

79 *CPR, 1361–4*, 382.

80 *CPR, 1334–8*, 566.

81 *CPR, 1340–3*, 78.

82 *CCR, 1341–3*, 341–2; *CCR, 1343–6*, 304–5.

83 *CPR, 1391–6*, 481.

84 TNA, E 101/51/2, m. 7.

85 *CPR, 1399–1401*, 444. He was killed shortly before 27 May 1399. See *Calendar of Documents Relating to Scotland preserved in the Public Record Office and British Library*, 5 vols, ed. J. Bain (I–IV) and G.C. Simpson and J.D. Galbraith (V) (Edinburgh, 1881–1986), iv, 111.

86 Michael P. Warner, *The Agincourt Campaign of 1415: the retinues of the Dukes of Clarence and Gloucester* (Woodbridge, 2021), 184.

87 Anne Curry (ed.), *Agincourt 1415: Henry V, Sir Thomas Erpingham and the Triumph of the English Archers* (Stroud, 2000), 9.

11. Anne Mortimer's legacy to the House of York
Dr J.L. Laynesmith

1   University of Chicago MS, Codex 224, f. 59 digitised at https://www.lib.uchicago.edu/e/scrc/findingaids/view.php?eadid=ICU.SPCL.MS224;

2   *CPR 1405–08*, 173. Although no petition survives, the wording of the grant appears to be quoting a petition.

3   *CPR 1405–08*, 392

4   *CPL 1404–1415*, VI:132.

5   T. B. Pugh, *Henry V and the Southampton Plot of 1415* (Southampton, 1988), 100; see also the assessment of the significance of the marriage and the actions of Richard of Conisburgh by Chris Given-Wilson in chapter 9 of this volume (177–80).

6   T.B. Pugh, 'The Estates, Finances and Regal Aspirations of Richard Plantagenet (1411–1460) Duke of York,' in M. A. Hicks ed., *Revolution and Consumption in Late Medieval* England, (Woodbridge, 2001), 71.

7   https://inquisitionspostmortem.ac.uk/view/inquisition/22-467/471 [consulted 5/8/22].

8   Rosemary Horrox, 'Edward IV', *Oxford DNB*, https://doi.org/10.1093/ref:odnb/8520 [consulted 5/8/22].

9   Anthony Goodman and David Morgan, 'The Yorkist Claim to the Throne of Castile', *Journal of Medieval History* 11 (1985): 61–9.

10 Goodman and Morgan, 'Yorkist claim to the throne of Castile', 64.

11 Livia Visser-Fuchs, '"Honour is the Reward of Virtue": The Claudian Translation made for Richard, Duke of York, in 1445', The Ricardian 18 (2008): 66–82, 74.

12 College of Arms MS Num/Sch 3/16.

13 J.L. Laynesmith, '"To please … Dame Cecely that in Latyn hath litell intellect": Books and the Duchess of York', in Linda Clark (ed.), *Writing, Records and Rhetoric. The Fifteenth Century XV* (Woodbridge, 2017), 47–50.

14 Laynesmith, 'Books and the Duchess of York', 49–50; Sheila Delany, *Impolitic Bodies: Poetry, Saints and Society in Fifteenth-Century England* (Oxford, 1998), 15–24, 130–46.

15 Lesley Coote, *Prophecy and Public Affairs*, 119–201 and passim; Victoria Flood, 'Exile and Return: The Development of Political Prophecy on the Borders of England, c.1136–1450s', unpublished PhD thesis, University of York 2013, 229–42.

16 P.A. Johnson, *Duke Richard of York, 1411–1460* (Oxford, 1988), 78, 84.

17 Chris Given-Wilson et al eds. *PROME*, 'Introduction 1450' (Scholarly Digital Editions and TNA, Leicester, 2005).

18 D. Whitelock (ed.), *English Historical Documents c. 500–1042* (London, 1979), 837.

19 Ian Mortimer, *Medieval Intrigue: Decoding Royal Conspiracies* (London, 2004), 259–303.

20 It notably contradicted his own narrative for claiming the thrones of Castile and Leon.

21 *Rot Parl* v 373–8

22 A.S.G. Edwards, 'The Manuscripts and Texts of the Second Version of John *Hardyng's Chronicle*', in Daniel Williams ed., *England in the Fifteenth Century*, Proceedings of the 1986 Harlaxton Symposium (Woodbridge, 1987), 75–84.

23 BL Harley MS 116 42r. Raluca Radulescu, 'Yorkist Propaganda and The Chronicle of Rollo to Edward IV', *Studies in Philology* 100 (2003): 401–24.

24 Radulescu, 'Yorkist Propaganda', 418.

25 Radulescu, 'Yorkist Propaganda', 406.

26 Maree Shirota, 'Neither Roll nor Codex. Accordion Genealogies of the Kings of England from the Fifteenth Century' in Stefan Holz, Jorg Peltzer and Maree Shirota eds., *The Roll in England and France in the Late Middle Ages* (Berlin, 2019), 263–88.

27 Allan, 'Yorkist propaganda: Pedigree, prophecy and the "British History" in the Reign of Edward IV', in Charles Ross ed., *Patronage, Pedigree and Power in Later Medieval England* (Gloucester, 1979): 17–192, 172–3.

28 Kathleen L. Scott, *Later Gothic Manuscripts, 1390–1490, A Survey of Manuscripts Illuminated in the British Isles*, 6 vols. (London, 1996), 6:II:315–16.

29 For instance BL Lansdowne MS 456.

30 For instance Oxford Bodleian MS e. Musaeo 42 f. 30r.

31 Sonja Drimmer, 'A Political Poster in Late Medieval England: BL Harley MS 7353', in Julia Boffey ed., *Performance, Ceremony and Display in Late Medieval England*, Harlaxton Medieval Studies XXX (2020), 333–59.

32 Robert Bartlett, *Blood Royal: Dynastic Politics in Medieval Europe* (Cambridge, 2020), 151–3.

33 Henry Ellis ed., *Hardyng's Chronicle*, (London, 1812), 16. See also 337.

34 Ian Mortimer, *Medieval Intrigue*, 279–303.

35 Mary Giffin, 'Cadwalder, Arthur, and Brutus in the Wigmore Manuscript', *Speculum* 16 (1941): 109–120, 111.

36 University of Chicago MS, Codex 224, f. 51.

37 The line of kings descended from Brutus dies out with the first Christian British king, Lucius, after which Roman invasions and disorder follow until the reign of Constantine II. Although it is understood that Constantine is of royal British descent the line is not set out. Uther Pendragon is Constantine's third son and is the father of Arthur who is in turn succeeded by a Cornish kinsman also called Constantine. Even from here the line to Cadwaladr is more often of conquest than filial descent. See, for example, BL Lansdowne MS 456.

38 Cf e.g. John Morris ed., *Arthurian Sources: 5 Genealogies and Texts* (Phillimore, Chichester, 1995), 41–2, 58–63.

39 Mary Giffin, 'Cadwalader, Brutus and Arthur in the Wigmore Manuscript', *Speculum* 16 (1941): 109–20, 1179–18; Chris Given-Wilson, 'Chronicles of the Mortimer Family *c*.1250–1450', in Richard Eales and Shaun Tyas eds. *Family and Dynasty in Late Medieval England* (Donington, 2003), 70. The text is so littered with additions and small omissions that reaching an entirely firm date of composition is probably impossible.

40 Giffin, 'Cadwalader', 111.

41 For the likely history of composition of the chronicle, Chris Given-Wilson, 'Chronicles of the Mortimer Family', 67–86.

42 The pages were scraped clean of previous text and York's royal arms with a label for York are quartered with those of Mortimer and Ulster. Next to Cecily's shield is a list of her family members – their correct age order does not seem to have been recorded elsewhere so it is of interest for that alone. Anne was not yet duchess of Buckingham so it must have been written before 1444. Given-Wilson, 'Chronicles of the Mortimer Family', 76.

43 Mary Giffin, 'A Wigmore Manuscript at Chicago', *National Library of Wales Journal* 7 (1952): 316–25, 325 nn. 33–5.

44 Walter de Gray Birch, *Catalogue of Seals in the British Museum*, (London, 1887), 391.

45 Giffin identifies the birds as eagles but they lack the head tuft normal for eagles and York's own use of the falcon renders that bird far more likely. The sketch for Edward is too faint to be certain whether there is a crown on the lion's head.

46 James P. Carley, 'Arthur in English History', in W.R.J. Barron, *The Arthur of the English*, (Cardiff, 2001), 47–57.

47 Paul Dryburgh, 'The Career of Roger Mortimer, first Earl of March' (*c*.1287–1330), unpublished PhD thesis, University of Bristol (2002), 135–6.

48 Giffin, 'Cadwalader,' 113.

49 Juliet Vale, 'Arthur in English Society', in Barron ed. *The Arthur of the English*, 186.

50 Given-Wilson, 'Chronicles of the Mortimer Family', 73.

51 Dryburgh, 'Career of Roger Mortimer,' 134–8.

52 Carley, 'Arthur in English History, 50–51.

53 W. Mark Ormord, *Edward III* (London, 2011), 98–99.

54 Leo Carruthers, 'The Duke of Clarence and the Earls of March: Garter Knights and Sir Gawain and the Green Knight', *Medium Ævum* 70 (2001): 66–79.

55 BL Cotton MS Nero A X/2. The British Library online catalogue estimates the date of the manuscript's creation at 1375–1425.

56 Carruthers, 'Garter Knights and Sir Gawain', 75–6.

57 J. W. McKenna, 'Henry VI of England and the dual monarchy: aspects of royal political propaganda, 1422–32', *Journal of the Courtauld and Warburg Institutes*, 28 (1965), 145–62, 155.

58 *Hardyng's Chronicle*, 415.

59 BL Cotton Vespasian C vii ff. 69v – 72r. It uses Geoffrey of Monmouth's name for Cadwaladr's son, Ivor, rather than the name that appears in the Wigmore genealogies, Idwal.

60 BL Egerton 1076 f. 1v.

61 Sydney Anglo, 'The *British History* in Early Tudor Propaganda', *BJRL* 44 (1961): 17–48.

62 Scott, *Later Gothic Manuscripts*, 6:II:315-16; Shirota, 'Neither Roll nor Codex', *passim*.

63 Geoffrey of Monmouth, *The History of the Kings of Britain*, ed. Michael D. Reeve, trans. Neil Wright (Woodbridge, 2007), 278.

64 Geoffrey of Monmouth, *History*, 140–59; S. Anglo, 'British History', 34–6; Flood. 'Exile and Return', 25–6.

65 Hughes, Arthurian Myths and Alchemy. The Kingship of Edward IV (Stroud, 2002), 101, 136–7, 140; Anglo, 'British History', *passim*.

66 Judith Weiss, *Wace's Roman de Brut: A History of the British* (Exeter, 1999), 190–1.

67 F. Madden, *Layamon's Brut, or Chronicle of Britain* 3 vols. (London, 1847), III:290–1.

68 Madden, *Layamon's Brut*, III:297.

69 W.R.J. Barron, Françoise le Saux, Lesley Johnson, 'Dynastic Chronicles', in Barron ed., *The Arthur of the English*, 32.

70 Julia Marvin, ed. and tr. *The Oldest Anglo-Norman Prose Brut Chronicle* (Woodbridge, 2006), 142–5. It did acknowledge that the Britons believed Arthur would return, 178–9.

71 For example, F. W. de Brie, ed. *The Brut*, EETS 131, 136 (London, 1906), 58–9.

72 University of Chicago MS, Codex 224, f. 24v.

73 Robert A. Caldwell suggested that an early fifteenth-century Middle English 'Brut' story compiled out of Geoffrey of Monmouth and Wace, which includes the prophecies of Merlin (College of Arms Arundel MS 22), may have been assembled, like the Wigmore MS, to support the Mortimer claim to the throne. Unfortunately, his only basis for this is the manuscript's south-western provenance and the interest in earlier traditions of the British history. The manuscript is incomplete, breaking off before the angelic prophecy to Cadwaladr might have appeared. Robert A. Caldwell, 'The "History of the Kings of Britain" in College of Arms MS Arundel XXII', *PMLA* 69 (1954): 643–654, 654; Laura Gabiger 'The Middle English "History of the Kings of Britain" in College of Arms Manuscript Arundel 22', unpublished PhD thesis (University of North Carolina at Chapel Hill, 1993), 7.

74 Lister M. Matheson, *The Prose Brut: the Development of a Middle English Chronicle, Medieval and Renaissance Studies* 180 (Arizona, 1998), 3, 57–61, 92–7. The earliest instance was probably *Castleford's Chronicle,* but this work does not seem to have been used by other chroniclers so perhaps different motives were at play in different contexts.

75 Anne Lawrence-Mathers, *The True History of Merlin the Magician*, (New Haven, 2012), 70–94.

76 Flood, 'Exile and Return', 41.

77 Flood, 'Exile and Return', 57–69.

78 Flood, 'Exile and Return', 72–4; de Brie ed., *The Brut*, 72–6.

79 Flood, 'Exile and Return', 150–74.

80 Flood, 'Exile and Return', 211.

81 Flood, 'Exile and Return', 209.

82 Flood, 'Exile and Return', 226.

83 Hughes, *Arthurian Myths*, 156.

84 *Hardyng's Chronicle*, 179.

85 For instance de Brie ed., *The Brut*, 76. See Flood, 'Exile and Return', 38–41, 91–3.

86 Flood, 'Exile and Return', 166–96.

87 There are angels but one carries a trumpet and the other holds a sun, neither of which fit with the angelic prophecy, so they are perhaps simply connected with the broader theme of revelation.

88 H.T. Evans, *Wales and the Wars of the Roses* (Stroud, 1995, first published 1915), 6; Frederick Hepburn, 'The 1505 Portrait of Henry VII', *The Antiquaries Journal* 88 (2008): 222–57, 231 and n. 22.

89 The Percies are represented here but not as many of the second earl's children appear as in BL Add MS 18268A.

90 Scott, *Later Gothic Manuscripts,* 6:II:288–9.

91 libwww.freelibrary.org/digital/feature/medieval-edward-index [consulted 23/9/22].

92 https://blogs.bl.uk/digitisedmanuscripts/2019/06/toads-and-ermine.html [consulted 21/9/22] cf *Hardyng's Chronicle*, 31.

93 Scott, *Later Gothic Manuscripts*, 6:II:288

94 The website attributes the Holland arms to Edmund duke of York's second wife, but Anne Mortimer's mother is a far more likely connection.

95 Michael Powell Siddons, *Heraldic Badges of England and Wales*, 4 vols. (Woodbridge, 2009), 2:60.

96 Siddons, *Heraldic Badges*, 2:167–8. Howard de Walden and Evelyn Scott-Ellis, *Banners, Standards and Badges from a Tudor Manuscript in the College of Arms* (London, 1904), 32; Hughes, *Arthurian Myths*, 166–7.

97 J.L. Laynesmith, *Cecily duchess of York*, (London, 2017), 120.

98 Alison Allan, 'Political Propaganda Employed by the House of York in England in the Mid-Fifteenth Century', unpublished PhD dissertation, University of Swansea (1981), 392, citing Oxford, Bodley MS Digby 82, f. 16.

99 Ian Mortimer, *The Greatest Traitor* (London, 2003), 234.

100 W. de Gray Birch, *Catalogue of Seals in the Department of Manuscripts in the British Museum*, 6 vols. (1887) 3:391

101 Hepburn, 'The 1505 Portrait of Henry VII', 232.

BIBLIOGRAPHY

ARCHIVAL SOURCES

Bodleian Library, Oxford
MS Bodley 62, Prophesies (1465)
MS e. Musaeo 42, Accordion genealogy (*c.*1467)

British Library, London
Additional MS 6041, Mortimer cartulary
Cotton MS Nero A. iv, Llandaff Chronicle
Cotton MS Nero A X/2, Sir Gawain and the Green Knight (1375–1425)
Cotton MS Vespasian E vii, Pamphlet, emblazoned with the royal arms of England and Spain, the
    invented arms of Cadwaladr, and the Mortimer arms
Cotton MS Vespasian 18268A, Genealogical roll for Edward IV's accession
Egerton MS 1076, codex setting out Edward IV's right to the throne
Egerton Rolls 8723–8751, Mortimer and Badlesmere account rolls
Harley MS 116, *This brief tretys compiled for to bringe people oute of doute that haue not herd of the
    Cronicles of the lineall descenste vnto the Crowne of England and of Fraunce of Castell and of Legeons
    [Leon] and to the Duchie of Normandie sith that it was first conquest made*
Harley MS 1240, *Liber Niger de Wigmore* / Black Book of Wigmore
Harley MS 6033, a seventeenth-century notebook
Harley MS 7353, *Illustrated Life of Edward IV* or *The Edward IV Poster*

College of Arms, London
Lynch/2/88/55/1, Royal subsidy, 1380
Lynch/2/87/36/2, appointment of Sir Ralph Poley as steward of the liberty of Meath, 1380
Num/Sch 3/16, 'Dialogue … at the grave of Dame Joan of Acre'

Herefordshire Archives and Record Centre, Rotherwas
A 31/25, Account of James Leinthale, bailiff of the liberty of Wigmore, 1384/5
G 33/1, Receiver's account for the lordship of Clifford and Glasbury, 1377/8

Lambeth Palace Library, London
Register of William Whittlesey, archbishop of Canterbury (1368–1374)
Register of William Courtenay, archbishop of Canterbury (1381–1396)

Manchester, John Rylands Library
Latin MS 215, Mortimer family cartulary

The National Archives, Kew
C 76, Chancery, Treaty Rolls
C 81, Chancery Warrants, series I (Privy Seal)
C 133, Inquisitions Post Mortem, Edward I
C 135, Inquisitions Post Mortem, Edward III
C 136, Inquisitions Post Mortem. Richard II
C 145, Chancery, Miscellaneous Inquisitions
C 260, Chancery *Recorda*
CP 25/1, Court of Common Pleas, Feet of Fine
CP 40, Court of Common Pleas, Plea Rolls
E 31/2/1 Great Domesday Book
E 101, Exchequer Accounts (Various)
E 154, Exchequer, King's Remembrancer and Treasury of Receipt, Inventories of Goods and Chattels
E 159, Exchequer, King's Remembrancer, Memoranda Rolls
E 326, Exchequer, Court of Augmentations, Ancient Deeds series B
E 364, Exchequer, Foreign Account Rolls
E 372, Exchequer, Pipe Rolls
E 371, Exchequer, Originalia Rolls
E 403, Exchequer, Issue Rolls
JUST 1, Justices Itinerant, Assize & Eyre Rolls
KB 26, Court of King's Bench, Coram Rege Rolls
KB 27, Court of King's Bench, Plea Rolls
SC 1, Ancient Correspondence
SC 6, Ministers' and Receivers' Accounts
SC 8, Ancient Petitions
SC 11, Rentals and Surveys

National Library of Ireland, Dublin
D. 1268, Instrument of Philip Cadell and Henry de Hopton, 1381

University of Chicago
MS 224, *Fundatorum Historia* (Wigmore Abbey Chronicle)

PRINTED PRIMARY SOURCES

The Acts of Welsh Rulers, 1120–1283, ed. Huw Pryce (Cardiff: University of Wales Press, 2005)

Adae Murimuth Continuatio Chronicarum, ed. E.M. Thompson (London: Rolls Series, 1889)

Ancient Monuments Board for Wales Annual Report 38 (1991–2)

Annala Rioghachta Eireann: Annals of the kingdom of Ireland by the Four Masters, from the earliest period to the year 1616, 7 vols, ed. John O'Donovan (Dublin, 1848–51)

Annales Monastici, ed. H.R. Luard, 5 vols (London: Rolls Series 36, 1864–9)

The Annals of Clonmacnoise, ed. Denis Murphy (Dublin, 1896)

Annals of the Kingdom of Ireland, by the Four Masters, ed. John O'Donovan, 2nd edn, 7 vols (Dublin, 1856)

Annala Uladh: Annals of Ulster, otherwise Annala Senate, Annals of Senat; a chronicle of Irish affairs from A.D. 431 to A.D. 1540 [i.e. A.D. 431–1131; 1155–1588], 4 vols, ed. W.M. Hennessy and B. MacCarthy (Dublin, 1887–1901)

The Anonimalle Chronicle, 1307 to 1334: From Brotherton Collection MS 29, ed. W.R. Childs and J. Taylor (Leeds: Yorkshire Archaeological Society, 1991)

Arthurian Sources: 5 Genealogies and Texts, ed. John Morris (Chichester: Phillimore, 1995)

The Beauchamp Cartulary Charters 1100–1268, ed. Emma Mason, Pipe Roll Society, new series 43 (London, 1980)

Bracton, Henry de, *On the Laws and Customs of England*, ed. G.E. Woodbine and S.E. Thorne, 4 vols (Cambridge MA: Harvard University Press, 1968–77)

The Brut or The Chronicles of England, ed. F.W.D. Brie (London: Early English Text Society, Old Series 131, 1906)

Brut y Tywysogyon or the Chronicle of the Princes. Peniarth Ms. 20 version (Cardiff: University of Wales Press, 1952)

Calendar of Ancient Correspondence concerning Wales, ed. J. Goronwy Edwards (Cardiff: University of Wales Press, 1935)

Calendar of Ancient Petitions Relating to Wales from the thirteenth to the sixteenth century in the Public Record Office London (Cardiff, 1975)

Calendar of Chancery Warrants, 1: Privy Seals, 1244–1326 (London: HMSO, 1927)

Calendar of Close Rolls Preserved in the Public Record Office, Edward I–Edward IV, 42 vols (London: HMSO, 1900–49)

Calendar of Documents Preserved in France, ed. J.H. Round (London: HMSO, 1899)

Calendar of Documents Relating to Scotland preserved in the Public Record Office and British Library, 5 vols, ed. J. Bain (I–IV) and G.G. Simpson and J.D. Galbraith (V) (Edinburgh: H.M. Register House, 1881–1986)

Calendar of Fine Rolls Preserved in the Public Record Office, Edward I–Henry VII, 21 vols (London: HMSO, 1911–62)

Calendar of the Gormanston Register, eds James Mills and M.J. McEnery (Dublin: University Press, 1916)

Calendar of Inquisitions Miscellaneous (Chancery) Preserved in the Public Record Office, 8 vols (London, 1916–2003)

Calendar of Inquisitions Post Mortem and other Analagous Documents Preserved in the Public Record Office, Henry III–Henry VI, 26 vols (London: HMSO, 1904–2003)

Calendar of Ormond Deeds: Volume II, 1350–1413 A.D., ed. Edmund Curtis (Dublin: The Stationery Office, 1934)

Calendar of Papal Letters, Vol.2, 1305–1342, ed. W.H. Bliss (London: HMSO, 1895)

Calendar of Patent Rolls Preserved in the Public Record Office, Henry III–Richard III, 50 vols (London: HMSO, 1893–1916)

Calendar of Signet Letters of Henry IV and Henry V, ed. J.L. Kirby (London: HMSO, 1978)

Catalogue of Seals in the Department of Manuscripts in the British Museum, ed. Walter de Gray Birch, 6 vols (London, 1887)

Charters and Records of Hereford Cathedral, ed. W.W. Capes (Hereford: Cantilupe Society, 1908)

Chartes de l'Abbaye de Jumièges v. 825 à 1204, ed. J.-J. Vernier, 2 vols (Rouen, 1916)

Chartularies of St. Mary's Abbey, Dublin, ed. John T. Gilbert, 2 vols (London: Rolls Series, 1884)

Chronicles of the Reigns of Edward I and Edward II, ed. W. Stubbs, 2 vols (London: Rolls Series 79, 1882–3)

Chronicle of England by John Capgrave, ed. F.C. Hingeston (London: Rolls Series 1, 1858)

Chronicon Galfridi le Baker de Swynebroke, ed. E.M. Thompson (Oxford: Clarendon Press, 1889)

The Chronicle of Geoffrey le Baker of Swinbrook, ed. Richard Barber (Woodbridge: The Boydell Press, 2012)

Chronicle of the Grey Friars of London, ed. J.G. Nichols, Camden Society 53 (London, 1852)

Chronicon de Henrici Knighton vel Cnitthon Monachi Leycestrensis, ed. J.R. Lumby, 2 vols (London: Rolls Series 92, 1889–95)

Chronicon de Lanercost, 1201–1346, ed. J. Stevenson (Edinburgh: Maitland Club, 1839)

Chroniques de London, ed. G.J. Aungier, Camden Society, 28 (London, 1844)

Chronica Monasterii de Melsa, 1150–1506, ed. E.A. Bond, 3 vols (London: Rolls Series 43, 1866)

Cronica Adae Murimuth et Roberti de Avesbury, ed. E.M. Thompson (London: Rolls Series 93, 1889)

Chronica Adami Murimuthensis, 1303–1346, ed. T. Hog (London: Sumptibus Societatis, 1846)

Chronicles of the Revolution, 1397–1400, ed. C. Given-Wilson (Manchester: Manchester University Press, 1993)

Chronique de Ricard Lescot (1328–1344): Continuation (1344–1364), ed. J. Lemoine (Paris, 1896)

Chronica Monasterii S. Albani, ed. H.T. Riley, 7 vols (London: Rolls Series 28, 1863–76)

The St Albans Chronicle: The Chronica maiora *of Thomas Walsingham*, ed. John Taylor, Wendy R. Childs and Leslie Watkiss, 2 vols (Oxford: Oxford University Press, 2003–11)

'Chronicle of Saint Omer', in *The Battle of Crécy: A Casebook*, ed. Michael Livingston and Kelly DeVries (Liverpool: Liverpool University Press, 2015)

The Wigmore Chronicle 1066–1377. A Translation of John Ryland Manuscript 215, ff.1-8 and Trinity College, Dublin, MS.488, ff. 295-9, ed. Paul Martin Remfry (2013)

'Chronique de Normandie', in *Henrici Quinti, Angliæ regis, gesta, cum Chronicâ Neustriæ, gallicè*, ed. Benjamin Williams (London, 1850)

CIRCLE: A Calendar of Irish Chancery Letters, c.1244–1509: https://chancery.tcd.ie/content/welcome-circle

Continuatio Eulogii: The Continuation of the Eulogium Historiarum, 1364–1413, ed. Chris Given-Wilson (Oxford: Oxford University Press, 2019)

'De actibus tempore regis Henrici Sexti', *Incerti scriptoris Chronicon Angliæ de regnis trium regum Lancastrensium*, ed. J.A. Giles (London, 1848)

A Descriptive Catalogue of Ancient Deeds in the Public Record Office, 6 vols (London: HMSO, 1890–1915)

Dialogus de Scaccario, ed. C. Johnson (London: Thomas Nelson & Sons, 1950)

Dictionary of British Armoury (1992)

Discoverie of Errours in the First Edition of the Catalogue of Nobility Published by Raphe Brooke, Yorke Herald, 1619 (1622)

Documents on the Affairs of Ireland before the King's Council, ed. G.O. Sayles (Dublin: Irish Manuscripts Commission, 1979)

Early Yorkshire Charters, ed. C.T. Clay, W.T. Farrer and E.M. Clay, Yorkshire Archaeological Society Record Series, 10 vols (Edinburgh: Ballantyne, Hanson & Co., 1914–65)

English Historical Documents c.500–1042, ed. Dorothy Whitelock (London: Methuen, 1979)

Eulogium Historiarum, ed. F.S. Haydon, 3 vols (London: Rolls Series 9, 1858–63)

Excerpta è rotulis finium *in Turri londinensi asservatis, Henrico Tertio rege, A. D. 1216–1272*, ed. C. Roberts (London: Record Commission, 1835–6)

Flores Historiarum, III, ed. H.R. Luard (London: Rolls Series, 1890)

Foedera, conventiones, litterae et cuiucunque generis acta publica, ed. Thomas Rymer, 20 vols (London, 1704–35)

Foedera, conventiones, litterae et cujuscunque generis acta publica, 4 vols in 7 parts (London: Record Commission, 1816–69)

'French Rolls, Henry V', *Forty-Fourth Annual Report of the Deputy Keeper of the Public Records* (London: HMSO, 1883)

Gazetteer of Markets and Fairs in England and Wales to 1516, ed. Samantha Letters: https://archives.history.ac.uk/gazetteer/gazweb2.html

Geoffrey of Monmouth, *The History of the Kings of Britain*, ed. Michael D. Reeve, trans. Neil Wright (Woodbridge: Boydell, 2007)

Gesta Henrici Quinti: The Deeds of Henry V, ed. F. Taylor and J. Roskell (Oxford: Oxford University Press, 1975)

Gwaith iolo Goch, gol. Dafydd R. Johnston (Caerdydd: Gwasg Prifysgol Cymru, 1988)

Goch, Iolo, *Poems*, ed. and trans. Dafydd Johnston (Llandysul, 1993)

'William Gregory's Chronicle of London', in *The Historical Collections of a Citizen of London in the Fifteenth Century*, ed. James Gairdner, Camden Society, new series, 17 (1876)

Handbook and Select Calendar of Sources for Medieval Ireland in the National Archives of the United Kingdom, ed. Paul Dryburgh and Brendan Smith (Dublin: Four Courts Press, 2005)

Hardyng's Chronicle, ed. Henry Ellis (London, 1812)

Historia Vitae et Regni Ricardi Secundi, ed. G.B. Stow (Pennsylvania: University of Pennsylvania Press, 1977)

Inquisitions and Extents of Medieval Ireland, ed. Paul Dryburgh and Brendan Smith, List & Index Society 320 (Kew, 2007)

Issue Roll of Thomas de Brantingham, ed. Frederick Devon (London: J. Rodwell, 1835)

Istore et croniques de Flandres, ed. Kervyn de Lettenhove, 2 vols (Brussels, 1879–80)

Johannis de Trokelowe et Henrici de Blaneforde, Monachorum Sancti Albani, Necnon Quorundam Anonymorum, Chronica et Annales, ed. H.T. Riley (London: Rolls Series, 1866)

Layamon's Brut, or Chronicle of Britain, ed. F. Madden, 3 vols (London, 1847)

Livere de Reis de Brittanie e le Livere de Engleterre (Chroniques de Sempringham), ed. J. Glover (London: Rolls Series 42, 1865)

'Mac Carthaigh's Book', in *Miscellaneous Irish annals*, ed. Séamus Ó hInnse (Dublin, 1947)

Dugdale, William, *Monasticon Anglicanum*, ed. J. Caley, H. Ellis and B. Bandinel, 6 vols in 8 parts (London: Longman, 1817–30)

Monumenta Franciscana, Vol. 2, ed. R. Howlett (London: Rolls Series 4, 1882)

Munimenta Gildhallae Londoniensis: Liber Albus, Liber Custumarum, et Liber Horn, Vol. II, Part I, ed. H.T. Riley (London: Rolls Series, 1860)

Nicolai Triveti Annalium continuatio, ed. Anthony Hall (Oxford, 1722)

The Oldest Anglo-Norman Prose Brut Chronicle, ed. and trans. Julia Marvin (Woodbridge: Boydell, 2006)

The Oxford Dictionary of National Biography, eds H.C.G. Matthew and B.H. Harrison, 60 vols (Oxford, 2004–), online edition: https:///www.oxforddnb.com

Parliament Rolls of Medieval England, 1275–1504, eds P. Brand, A. Curry, C. Given-Wilson, R. Horrox, G.H. Martin, W.M. Ormrod and J.R.S. Phillips, 16 vols (Woodbridge: Boydell & Brewer, 2005)

Placita de Quo Warranto temporibus Ed. I, II and III in curia receptae scaccarij Westm. Asservata, ed. W. Illingworth (London: Record Commission, 1818)

Polychronicon Ranulphi Higden, Monachi Cestrensis: together with the English translations of John Trevisa and an unknown Writer in the Fifteenth Century, ed. C. Babington and J.R. Lumby, 9 vols (London: Rolls Series 41, 1865–86)

'Private Indentures for Life Service in Peace and War 1278–1476', eds Michael Jones and Simon Walker, *Camden Miscellany XXXII* (London, 1994)

Proceedings and Ordinances of the Privy Council of England, 1386–[1542], ed. N.H. Nicolas, 7 vols (London: Record Commission, 1834–7)

Proceedings before the Justices of the Peace, Edward III to Richard III, ed. B.H. Putnam (London: Spottiswoode, Ballantyne, 1938)

Radulfi de Diceto decani Lundoniensis opera historica. The Historical Works of Master Ralph de Diceto, Dean of London. 2 vols (London: Rolls Series 68, 1876)

Reading Abbey Cartularies, ed. B.R. Kemp, 2 vols, Camden Society 4th series 33 (London: Royal Historical Society, 1986–7)

Register of Edward the Black Prince, Vol. 4 (England), 1351–1365 (London: HMSO, 1933)

The Register of Milo Sweteman, Archbishop of Armagh, 1361–1380, ed. Brendan Smith (Dublin: Irish Manuscripts Commission, 1996)

A Roll of the Proceedings of the King's Council in Ireland 1392–93, ed. James Graves (London: Rolls Series, 1877)

Rotuli Hundredorum temp. Hen. III & Edw. I in turr' Lond' et in curia receptae scaccarij Westm. asservati, 2 volumes (London: Record Commission, 1812–18)

Rotuli Litterarum Clausarum in Turri Londoniensi Asservati, ed. T.D. Hardy, 2 vols (London: Record Commission, 1833–44)

Rotuli Parliamentorum, ed. J. Strachey et al., 6 vols (London, 1767)

Rotuli Scotiae in turri Londinensi et in domo capitulari Westmonasteriensi asservati, ed. D. Macpherson, J. Caley and W. Illingworth, 2 vols (London: Record Commission, 1814–19)

Sir Christopher Hatton's Book of Seals, eds L.C. Loyd and D.M. Stenton (Oxford: Clarendon Press, 1950)

Sir Thomas Gray: Scalacronica (1272–1363), ed. Andy King, Surtees Society 209 (2005)

Statutes of the Realm (London: Record Commission, 1810)

The Chronicle of Adam Usk 1377–1421, ed. C. Given-Wilson (Oxford: Oxford University Press, 1997)

Three Anglo-Norman Chronicles, ed. P.T. Ricketts, Anglo-Norman Text Society (Manchester, 2011)

'Translation of a French Metrical History of the Deposition of King Richard the Second', trans. John Webb, *Archaeologia* 20 (1824)

Vita Edwardi Secundi Monachi Cuiusdam Malmesberiensis, ed. and trans. N. Denholm-Young (London: Nelson's Medieval Texts, 1957)

Vita Edwardi Secundi: The Life of Edward II, ed. W.R. Childs (Oxford, 2005)

Thomae Walsingham, quondam monachi S. Albani, Historia Anglicana, ed. H.T. Riley, 2 vols (London, Rolls Series, 1863–4)

The Welsh Assize Roll, 1277–1284: Assize Roll no. 1147 (Public Record Office), ed. J.C. Davies (Cardiff: University Press Board, 1940)

Year Books 20–21 Edward I, ed. Alfred J. Horwood (London: Rolls Series 31, 1866)

SECONDARY WORKS

Allan, Alison, 'Yorkist propaganda: Pedigree, prophecy and the "British History" in the Reign of Edward IV', in Charles Ross (ed.), *Patronage, Pedigree and Power in Later Medieval England* (Gloucester, 1979): 171–92

—, 'Political Propaganda Employed by the House of York in England in the Mid-Fifteenth Century', unpublished PhD thesis, University of Swansea (1981)

Ambühl, Remy, *Prisoners of War in the Hundred Years War: Ransom Culture in the Late Middle Ages* (Cambridge: Cambridge University Press, 2013)

Anglo, Sydney, 'The *British History* in Early Tudor Propaganda', *Bulletin of the John Rylands Library* 44 (1961), 17–48

Anstis, J., *Observations Introductory to an Historical Essay upon the Knighthood of the Bath* (London: J. Woodman, 1752)

Ashbee, Jeremy, 'The Tower of London as a Royal Residence, 1066–1400', unpublished PhD thesis, Courtauld Institute of Art (2006)

—, 'The Structure and Function of the White Tower, 1150–1486', in *The White Tower*, ed. E. Impey (London: Yale University Press, 2008)

Ayton, Andrew, *Knights and Warhorses: Military Service and the English Aristocracy under Edward III* (Woodbridge: Boydell & Brewer, 1994)

'Military Service and the Dynamics of Recruitment in Fourteenth-Century England', in *The Soldier Experience in the Fourteenth Century*, eds Adrian R. Bell, A.C. King and D. Simpkin (Woodbridge: The Boydell Press, 2011), 9–61

Bailey, Mark, *After the Black Death: Economy, Society and the Law in Fourteenth-Century England. The Ford Lectures for 2019* (Oxford: Oxford University Press, 2020)

Barber, R., *Edward III and the Triumph of England* (London: Allen Lane, 2013)

Barron, C.M., *London in the Later Middle Ages: Government and People, 1200–1500* (Oxford: Oxford University Press, 2004)

Barron, W.R.J., 'The Penalties for Treason in Medieval Life and Literature', *Journal of Medieval History* 7 (1981), 187–202

Bartlett, Robert, *Blood Royal: Dynastic Politics in Medieval Europe* (Cambridge: Cambridge University Press, 2020)

Beattie, Cordelia and Stevens, Matthew (eds), *Married Women and the Law in Premodern Northwest Europe* (Woodbridge: The Boydell Press, 2013)

Bell, A.R., Brooks, C. and Dryburgh, P.R., *The English Medieval Wool Market, c.1230–1327* (Cambridge: Cambridge University Press, 2007)

Bell, Adrian R., Curry, Anne, King, Andy and Simpkin, David, *The Soldier in Later Medieval England* (Oxford: Oxford University Press, 2013)

Bellamy, J.G., *The Law of Treason in England in the Later Middle Ages.* (Cambridge: Cambridge University Press, 1970)

Binski, P., *Medieval Death: Ritual and Representation.* (London: British Museum Press, 1996)

Blackley, F.D., 'Isabella and the Bishop of Exeter', in Sandquist, T.A. and Powicke, M.R. (eds.), *Essays in Medieval History Presented to Bertie Wilkinson* (Toronto: University of Toronto Press, 1968), 220–35

Boase, T.S.R., *Death in the Middle Ages* (London: Thames and Hudson, 1972)

Borg, A.C.N., 'The State Prison', in *The Tower of London: its Buildings and Institutions*, ed. J. Charlton (London: HMSO, 1978)

Borman, T., *The Story of the Tower of London* (London: Merrell, 2015)

Brett, M., *The English Church under Henry I.* (Oxford: Oxford University Press, 1975)

Brooks, A. and Pevsner, N., *Herefordshire (The buildings of England)* (London: Yale University Press, 2012)

Brown, A.E., 'The castle, borough and park of Cefnllys', *Transactions of the Radnorshire Society* 42 (1972), 11–22

Brown, D.M. and Pearson A., *Cefnllys Castle, Radnorshire.* Aberystwyth: RCAHMW (2006): https://coflein.gov.uk/en/archive/6180112/

Brown, R.A, Colvin, H.M. and Taylor, A.J., *The History of the King's Works*, 6 vols (London: HMSO, 1963–82)

Bullock-Davies, Constance, *Menestrellorum multitudo: Minstrels at a Royal Feast* (Cardiff: University of Wales Press, 1978)

Butler L., 'Dolforwyn Castle, Montgomery, Powys. First report: the excavations 1981–1986', *Archaeologia Cambrensis* 138 (1989), 78–98

—, 'Dolforwyn Castle, Montgomery, Powys. Second report: the excavations 1987–1994', *Archaeologia Cambrensis* 144 (1995), 133–203

—, 'Dolforwyn Castle: prospect and retrospect', in Kenyon, J.R. and O'Conor, K. (eds), *The medieval castle in Ireland and Wales: essays in honour of Jeremy Knight* (Dublin: Four Courts Press, 2003), 149–62

Butler, L. and Knight, J.K., *Dolforwyn Castle, Montgomery Castle* (Cardiff: Cadw, 2004)

Butler, L.A.S., *Denbigh Castle, Denbigh town walls, Lord Leicester's Church, St Hilary's Chapel, Denbigh Friary*, revised edition (Cardiff: Cadw, 2007)

Caldwell, Robert A., 'The "History of the Kings of Britain" in College of Arms MS Arundel XXII', *PMLA* 69 (1954), 643–54

Carley, James P., 'Arthur in English History', in Barron, W.R.J., *The Arthur of the English* (Cardiff: University of Wales Press, 2001), 47–57

Carpenter, David A., 'A noble in politics: Roger Mortimer in the period of baronial reform and rebellion, 1258–1265', in Anne J. Duggan (ed.), *Nobles and Nobility in Medieval Europe* (Woodbridge: Boydell, 2000), 183–203

Carruthers, Leo, 'The Duke of Clarence and the Earls of March: Garter Knights and Sir Gawain and the Green Knight', *Medium Ævum* 70 (2001), 66–79

Cavell, Emma, 'Aristocratic Widows and the Medieval Welsh Frontier: The Shropshire Evidence. The Rees Davies Essay Prize', *Transactions of the Royal Historical Society*, sixth series 17 (2007), 57–82

—, 'Periphery to core: Mortimer women and the negotiation of the king's justice in the thirteenth-century March of Wales', *Journal of the Mortimer History Society* vol. 2 (2018), 1–20

Chapman, Adam, 'The Welsh Soldier: 1283–1422', unpublished PhD thesis, University of Southampton (2009)

Clarke, M.V., 'William of Windsor in Ireland, 1369–1376', *Proceedings of the Royal Irish Academy*, 41 (1932–4), 55–130

Cockayne, G.E.C., et al., *The Complete Peerage*, rev. & ed. Vicary Gibbs (13 vols, London, 1910–59)

Cook R., *Pendover Tower & Tudor lodgings, Ludlow Castle, Shropshire* (Lampeter: ArchaeoDomus Archaeological & Heritage Services, 2021)

Coote, Lesley, *Prophecy and Public Affairs* (York: York Medieval Press, 2000)

Crooks, Peter, 'Factionalism and Noble Power in English Ireland, *c.*1361–1423', unpublished PhD thesis, University of Dublin (2007)

—, with David Green and W. Mark Ormrod (eds), 'The Plantagenets and Empire in the Later Middle Ages', in iidem (eds), *The Plantagenet Empire, 1259–1453: Proceedings of the 2014 Harlaxton Symposium* (Donington: Shaun Tyas, 2016)

Crouch, David, 'The Complaint of King John against William de Briouze', in Janet S. Loengard (ed.), *Magna Carta and the England of King John* (Woodbridge: The Boydell Press, 2010)

Crump, J.J., 'The Mortimer family and the Making of the March,' in Prestwich, M.C., Frame, R.F. and Britnell, R.H. (eds.), *Thirteenth Century England* VI (Woodbridge, 1997), 117–26

—, 'Mortimer, Roger (III) (1231–82)', *ODNB*

Curry, Anne (ed.), *Agincourt 1415: Henry V, Sir Thomas Erpingham and the Triumph of the English Archers* (Stroud, 2000)

—, *Agincourt: a New History* (Stroud: Tempus, 2006)

—, 'After Agincourt, What Next? Henry V and the Campaign of 1416', in *The Fifteenth Century VII*, ed. Linda Clark (Woodbridge: Boydell, 2007)

Curtis, Edmund, *Richard II in Ireland, 1394–5* (Oxford: Clarendon Press, 1927)

Dalton, P. *Feudal Politics in Yorkshire 1066–1154*, unpublished PhD thesis, University of Sheffield (1990)

Daniell, C., *Death and Burial in Medieval England, 1066–1550* (London: Psychology Press, 1997)

Davey, R., *The Tower of London* (London: E.P. Dutton & Co., 1910)

Davies, J. Conway, 'The Despenser War in Glamorgan', *Transactions of the Royal Historical Society*, 3rd series 9 (1915), 21–64

—, *The Baronial Opposition to Edward II, its Character and Policy* (Cambridge: Cambridge University Press, 1918)

Davies, John Reuben, Davies, 'The execution of William Wallace: Saint Bartholomew's Eve, Monday 23 August 1305', Breaking of Britain: Cross-Border Society and Scottish Independence 1216–1314: http://eprints.gla.ac.uk/87808/7/87808.pdf

Davies, R.R., 'Colonial Wales', *Past & Present* 65 (1974), 3–23

—, 'Race Relations in Post-Conquest Wales: Confrontation and Compromise', *Transactions of the Honourable Society of Cymmrodorion* (1974–5), 32–56

—, *Lordship and Society in the March of Wales 1282–1400*, (Oxford: Clarendon Press, 1978)

—, 'Kings, lords and liberties in the March of Wales, 1066–1272', *Transactions of the Royal Historical Society*, 5th scr., 29 (1979), 41–61

—, *The Age of Conquest: Wales 1063–1415* (Oxford: Oxford University Press, 1991; reprinted 2000)

—, *The revolt of Owain Glyn Dŵr* (Oxford: Oxford University Press, 1995)

—, 'Frontier Arrangements in Fragmented Societies: Ireland and Wales', in *Medieval Frontier Societies*, ed. R. Bartlett and A. Mackay (Oxford: Clarendon Press, 1996), 77–101

—, *The First English Empire* (Oxford: Oxford University Press, 2000)

—, 'Mortimer, Roger, first earl of March (1287–1330), regent, solider, and magnate', *ODNB* (2008)

—, 'Mortimer, Roger (VI), second earl of March (1328–1360), magnate', *ODNB* (2008)

Davis, R.H.C., *The Early History of Coventry*, Dugdale Society Occasional Paper, 24 (Stratford-upon-Avon, 1976)

Delany, Sheila, *Impolitic Bodies: Poetry, Saints and Society in Fifteenth-Century England* (Oxford: Oxford University Press, 1998)

Devon, Frederick (ed.), *Issues of the Exchequer: being a collection of payments made out of His Majesty's Revenue, from King Henry III to King Henry VI inclusive* (London: John Murray, 1837)

Dibben, A.A., *Coventry City Charters*. Coventry Papers (Coventry, 1969)

Dickinson, J.C. and Ricketts, P.T., 'The Anglo-Norman Chronicle of Wigmore Abbey', *Transactions of the Woolhope Society* 39 (Hereford, 1969)

Dixon, W. Hepworth, *Her Majesty's Tower*, 5th edn (London, 1869)

Dobson, A.J., *The Origins of Ancrene Wisse* (New York: Oxford University Press, 1976)

Drimmer, Sonja, 'A Political Poster in Late Medieval England: BL Harley MS 7353', in Julia Boffey (ed.), *Performance, Ceremony and Display in Late Medieval England*, Harlaxton Medieval Studies XXX (2020), 333–59

Dryburgh, Paul, 'The Career of Roger Mortimer, first earl of March (c.1287–1330), unpublished PhD thesis, University of Bristol (2002)

—, 'Roger Mortimer and the Governance of Ireland, 1317–1320', in *Ireland and the English World in the Late Middle Ages*, ed. Brendan Smith (Basingstoke: Palgrave Macmillan, 2009), 89–102

—, '"The Mortimer has taken great pains to save and keep the peace": crown, city and community during the Bruce invasion and its aftermath', *Medieval Dublin XVII*, ed. Seán Duffy (Dublin, 2019), 224–38

—, 'For Queen and Country: The Interim Administration of Queen Isabella and Edward of Windsor, October–December 1326', in *English Medieval Government and Administration. Essays in Honour of J.R. Maddicott*, ed. Nigel Saul and Nicholas Vincent, Pipe Roll Society NS 65 (Woodbridge, 2023), chapter 17

Duffy, Seán, *Robert the Bruce's Irish Wars: the Invasions of Ireland, 1306–29* (Stroud: Tempus, 2002)

—, 'Irish and Welsh responses to the Plantagenet empire in the reign of Edward I', in Crooks, P., Green, D. and Ormrod, W.M. (eds), *The Plantagenet Empire, 1259–1453* (Donington: Shaun Tyas, 2016), 150–68

Dunn, Alistair, 'Richard II and the Mortimer Inheritance', in *Fourteenth Century England II*, ed. Chris Given-Wilson (Woodbridge: Boydell, 2002), 159–70

—, *The Politics of Magnate Power* (Oxford: Oxford University Press, 2003)

Edward II: His Last Months and Monument, ed. J. Barlow, R. Bryant, C. Heighway, C. Jeens and D. Smith, The Bristol and Gloucestershire Archaeological Society (Bristol, 2015)

Edwards, A.S.G., 'The Manuscripts and Texts of the Second Version of John *Hardyng's Chronicle*', in Daniel Williams ed., *England in the Fifteenth Century*, Proceedings of the 1986 Harlaxton Symposium (Woodbridge: Boydell & Brewer, 1987)

Egan, Simon, 'Richard II and the Wider Gaelic World: A Reassessment', *Journal of British Studies* 57 (2018), 221–52

—, 'A Task too great for One Dynasty? The Mortimer Earls of March, the de Burgh Inheritance and the Gaelic Nobility *c*.1370–*c*.1425', *Journal of the Mortimer History Society* 4 (2020), 1–20

Evans, B. Penry, 'The Family of Mortimer', unpublished PhD thesis, University of Wales (1934)

Evans, H.T., *Wales and the Wars of the Roses* (Stroud: Sutton, 1995, first published 1915)

Eyton, R.W., *Antiquities of Shropshire*, 12 vols (London: J.R. Smith, 1854–60)

Faraday, M.A., *Ludlow, 1085–1660: a social, economic and political history* (Chichester: Phillimore, 1991)

Finucane, R.C., *Miracles and Pilgrims: Popular Beliefs in Medieval England.* (London: Dent, 1977)

—, 'Sacred Corpse, Profane Carrion: Social Ideals and Death Rituals in the Later Middle Ages', in *Mirrors of Mortality*, ed. J. Whaley (London: Routledge, 1981)

Flood, Victoria, 'Exile and Return: The Development of Political Prophecy on the Borders of England, *c*.1136–1450s', unpublished PhD thesis, University of York (2013)

Frame, Robin, 'Power and Society in the Lordship of Ireland 1272–1377', *Past & Present* 76 (1977), 3–33

—, *English Lordship in Ireland, 1318–1361* (Oxford: Clarendon Press, 1982)

—, *The Political Development of the British Isles, 1100–1400* (Oxford: Clarendon Press, 1990)

—, 'The "Failure" of the First English Conquest of Ireland", in idem, *Ireland and Britain, 1170–1450* (London: Hambleton, 1998), 1–14

—, 'King Henry III and Ireland: the Shaping of a Peripheral Lordship', *Ireland and Britain*, 31–57

—, 'Ireland and the Barons War', *Ireland and Britain*, 59–69

—, 'Aristocracies and the Political Configuration of the British Isles', in *Ireland and Britain*, 151–70

—, *Colonial Ireland, 1169–1369* (2nd edn, Dublin: Four Courts Press, 2012)

Fryde, E.B., Greenway, D.E. and others, *Handbook of British Chronology*, 3rd edn (London: Royal Historical Society, 1986)

Fryde, N.M., *The Tyranny and Fall of Edward II, 1322–1326* (Cambridge: Cambridge University Press, 1979)

Gabiger, Laura, 'The Middle English "History of the Kings of Britain" in College of Arms Manuscript Arundel 22', unpublished PhD thesis, University of North Carolina at Chapel Hill (1993)

Gaydon, A.J. (ed.), *Victoria County History: Shropshire, Vol. 2* (London: Institute of Historical Research and Clarendon Press, 1973)

Giffin, M.E., 'Cadwalder, Arthur, and Brutus in the Wigmore Manuscript', *Speculum* 16 (1941), 109–20

—, 'A Wigmore Manuscript at the University of Chicago', *National Library of Wales Journal* 7 (1952), 316–25

Gillespie, James L., 'Thomas Mortimer and Thomas Molineux: Radcot Bridge and the Appeal of 1397', *Albion* 7 (1975), 161–73

Given-Wilson, C., *The English Nobility in the Late Middle Ages* (London: Routledge & Kegan Paul, 1987)

—, 'Richard II, Edward II, and the Lancastrian Inheritance', *EHR* 109 (1994), 553–71

—, 'Chronicles of the Mortimer Family *c*.1250–1450', in Richard Eales and Shaun Tyas (eds), *Family and Dynasty in Late Medieval England* (Donington: Shaun Tyas, 2003), 67–86

—, *Henry IV* (New Haven CT and London: Yale University Press, 2016)

—, 'The bishop of Winchester, the abbot of Titchfield, and the "pretended chapel" of Hook 1375–1405', in *People, Power and Identity in the Late Middle Ages: Essays in Memory of Mark Ormrod*, ed. G. Dodd, H. Lacey and A. Musson (London, 2021), 137–56

Goodall, J.A.A., 'The baronial castles of the Welsh conquest', in Williams, D.M. and Kenyon, J.R. (eds), *The impact of the Edwardian castles in Wales* (Oxford: Oxbow Books, 2010)

—, *The English castle, 1066–1650* (London: Yale University Press, 2011)

—, 'The early development of Alnwick Castle, *c*. 1100–1400', in Ashbee, J. and Luxford, J. (eds), *Newcastle and Northumberland: Roman and medieval architecture and art* (Leeds: Maney for the British Archaeological Association, 2013; Conference transactions; 36), 232–47

Gooder, A. and E.A., 'Coventry before 1355; Unity or Division? The Importance of the Earl's Half', *Midland History* 6 (1981), 1–38

Goodman, Anthony, *The Loyal Conspiracy* (London: Routledge & Kegan Paul, 1971)

—, and Morgan, David, 'The Yorkist Claim to the Throne of Castile', *Journal of Medieval History* 11 (1985), 61–69

Graham, B.J., 'Anglo-Norman Settlement in County Meath', *Proceedings of the Royal Irish Academy* C 75 (1975), 223–48

Gransden, A., *Historical Writing in England II: c. 1307 to the Early Sixteenth Century* (London: Routledge and Kegan Paul, 1982)

Griffiths, Ralph, 'Mortimer, Edmund, Fifth Earl of March and Seventh Earl of Ulster (1391–1425)', *ODNB*

Hamilton, J.S., 'Edward II: Favourites, Loyalty, and Kingship', in *Ruling Fourteenth-Century England: Essays in Honour of Christopher Given-Wilson*, ed. James Bothwell, Rémy Ambühl and Laura Tompkins (Woodbridge: The Boydell Press, 2019), 77–92

Harding, D.A., 'The regime of Isabella and Mortimer, 1326-1330', unpublished MPhil thesis, University of Durham (1985)

Harper, C.G., *The Tower of London: Fortress, Palace, and Prison* (London: Chapman and Hall, 1901)

Harrison, B.A., *The Tower of London Prisoner Book, 1100–1941* (Leeds: Royal Armouries, 2004)

Harriss, Gerald, *Shaping the Nation: England 1360–1461* (Oxford: Oxford University Press, 2005)

—, 'Richard of Conisburgh', *ODNB*

Hartland, Beth, 'Vaucouleurs, Ludlow and Trim: the role of Ireland in the career of Geoffrey de Geneville (c. 1226–1314), *Irish Historical Studies* 32, no. 128 (November 2001), 457–77

—, 'Reasons for leaving: the effect of conflict on English landholding in late thirteenth-century Leinster', *Journal of Medieval History* 32 (2006), 18–26

Hayden, A.R, *Trim Castle, Co. Meath: excavations 1995–8* (Dublin: Stationery Office, 2011)

Hemp, W.J., 'Denbigh Castle', *Y Cymmrodor* 36 (1926), 64–120

Hepburn, Frederick, 'The 1505 Portrait of Henry VII', *The Antiquaries Journal* 88 (2008), 222–57

Holden, Brock, *Lords of the Central Marches: English Aristocracy and Frontier Society, 1087–1265* (Oxford: Oxford University Press, 2008)

Holford, M.L., '"Notoriously unreliable": the valuations and extents [Fifteenth-century Inquisitions *Post Mortem*]', *The Fifteenth-Century Inquisitions Post Mortem*, ed. M.A. Hicks (Woodbridge, 2012), 117–44

Holmes, G.A., *The Estates of the Higher Nobility in Fourteenth-Century England* (Cambridge: Cambridge University Press, 1957)

—, *The Good Parliament* (Oxford: Clarendon Press, 1975)

—, 'Mortimer, Edmund, third earl of March and earl of Ulster (1352–1381)', *ODNB*

Horrox, Rosemary, 'Edward IV', *ODNB*

The House of Commons 1386–1421: Volume II Members A–D, eds J.S. Roskell, Linda Clark and Carole Rawcliffe (Stroud: Alan Sutton, 1992)

Hughes, Jonathan, *Arthurian Myths and Alchemy. The Kingship of Edward IV* (Stroud: Sutton, 2002)

Hume, P.R., 'The Mortimers and Radnorshire (part 1): the Conquest of Maelienydd', *Journal of the Mortimer History Society vol. 3* (2019), 17–36

—, 'The Mortimers and Radnorshire (part 2): Marriage and Inheritance – Radnor and Elfael', *Journal of the Mortimer History Society vol. 4* (2020), 63–70

—, *The Welsh Marcher Lordships Vol. 1: Central and North* (Eardisley: Logaston Press, 2021)

—, *On the trail of the Mortimers in the Welsh Marches*, new edition (Eardisley: Logaston Press, 2022)

Impey, E. and Parnell, G., *The Tower of London: The Official Illustrated History* (London: Merrell, 2000)

An inventory of the historical monuments in Herefordshire. 3. North-west (London: HMSO, 1934)

Ivamy, E.R.H., *Mozley & Whiteley's Law Dictionary*, 10th edn (London: Butterworths, 1988)

Johnson, P.A., *Duke Richard of York, 1411–1460* (Oxford: Oxford University Press, 1988)

Johnston, Dorothy, 'Richard II and the Submissions of Gaelic Ireland', *Irish Historical Studies* 20 (1980), 1–20

—, 'The Interim Years: Richard II and Ireland, 1395–9', in *England and Ireland in the Later Middle Ages: Essays in Honour of Jocelyn Otway-Ruthven*, ed. James Lydon (Dublin: Irish Academic Press, 1981), 175–95

—, 'Chief Governors and Treasurers of Ireland in the Reign of Richard II', in *Colony and Frontier in Medieval Ireland: Essays Presented to J.F. Lydon*, eds Terry Barry, Robin Frame and Katherine Simms (London: Bloomsbury, 1995), 217–28

Jones, N., *Tower: An Epic History of the Tower of London* (London: Hutchinson, 2011)

Kaeuper, R.W., *War, Justice and Public Order* (Oxford: Clarendon Press, 1988)

Keats-Rohan, Katherine, 'Aspects of Robert of Torigny's genealogies revisted', *Nottingham Medieval Studies*, 37 (1993), 21–7

Kenyon, J.R., *Castles, town defences and artillery fortifications in the United Kingdom and Ireland: a bibliography 1945–2006* (Donington: Shaun Tyas, 2008)

King, A., 'The Death of Edward II Revisited', *Fourteenth Century England IX*, ed. J.S. Bothwell and G. Dodd (Woodbridge: Boydell Press, 2016), 1–22

King, Mark, 'Richard II, the Mortimer Inheritance and the March of Wales, 1381–84', in *Fourteenth Century England VIII*, ed. J.S. Hamilton (Woodbridge: Boydell, 2014), 95–118

Kingsford, C.L., *The Grey Friars of London* (Aberdeen: Aberdeen University Press, 1915)

Knight, J.K., 'Excavations at Montgomery Castle. Part II. The finds: metalwork', *Archaeologia Cambrensis* 142 (1993), 182–242

—, 'Excavations at Montgomery Castle. Part III. The finds: other than metalwork', *Archaeologia Cambrensis* 143 (1994), 139–203

Knight, J.K. and Johnson, A. (eds), *Usk Castle, priory and town* (Almeley: Logaston Press, 2008)

Laborderie, O., Maddicott, J.R. and Carpenter, D.A., 'The Last Hours of Simon de Montfort: A New Account', *EHR* 115:461 (2000), 378–412

Larking, L.B., 'Inventory of the effects of Roger de Mortimer at Wigmore Castle and Abbey, Herefordshire', *Archaeological* Journal 15 (1858), 354–62

Lawrence-Mathers, Anne, *The True History of Merlin the Magician* (New Haven CT: Yale University Press, 2012)

Laynesmith, J.L., *Cecily duchess of York*, (London: Bloomsbury Academic, 2017)

—, '"To please ... Dame Cecely that in Latyn hath litell intellect": Books and the Duchess of York', in Linda Clark (ed.), *Writing, Records and Rhetoric. The Fifteenth Century XV* (Woodbridge: The Boydell Press, 2017), 37–56

Lewis, C.P., 'Mortimer, Roger de (fl. 1054–c.1080)', *ODNB*

—, 'Mortimer, Ralph de (c.1080–after 1115)', *ODNB*

Little, A.G., 'The Constitution of Provincial Chapters of the Minorite Order', in *Essays in Medieval History presented to T.F. Tout*, ed. A.G. Little and F.M. Powicke (Manchester: Manchester University Press, 1925), 249–67

—, *Franciscan Papers, Lists, and Documents.* (Manchester: Manchester University Press, 1943)

Lloyd, J.E., *Owen Glendower* (Oxford: Clarendon Press, 1931)

Ludlow, N., 'The castle and lordship of Narberth', *Journal of the Pembrokeshire Historical Society* 12 (2003), 5–43

Maddicott, J.R., *Thomas of Lancaster, 1307-1322. A Study in the Reign of Edward II* (London: Oxford University Press, 1970)

—, *Simon de Montfort* (Cambridge: Cambridge University Press, 1996)

Madox, T., *History of the Exchequer* (London: 1711)

Martin, A.R., *Franciscan Architecture in England* (Manchester: Manchester University Press, 1937)

Massey, Robert, 'The Lancastrian Land Settlement in Normandy and Northern France, 1417–1450', unpublished Ph.D. thesis, University of Liverpool (1987)

Matheson, Lister M., *The Prose Brut: the Development of a Middle English Chronicle, Medieval and Renaissance Studies* 180 (Arizona, 1998), 3, 57–61, 92–7

McAvoy, Liz Herbert, *Medieval Anchoritisms. Gender, Space and the Solitary Life* (Woodbridge: The Boydell Press, 2011)

McKenna, J.W., 'Henry VI of England and the dual monarchy: aspects of royal political propaganda, 1422–32', *Journal of the Courtauld and Warburg Institutes*, 28 (1965), 145–62

McNeill, T., *Castles in Ireland: feudal power in a Gaelic world*, 192 (London: Routledge, 1997)

Mears, K.J., *The Tower of London: 900 Years of English History* (Oxford: Phaidon, 1988)

Menache, S., 'Isabelle of France, Queen of England – A Reconsideration', *Journal of Medieval History* 10 (1984), 107–24

Messham, J.E., 'Henry Conewey, Knight, Constable of the Castle of Rhuddlan, 1390–1407', *Flintshire Historical Society Journal* 35 (1999), 11–55

Middleton, A.E., *Sir Gilbert de Middleton* (Newcastle: Mawson, Swan and Morgan Ltd, 1918)

Mileson, S.A., *Parks in Medieval England* (Oxford: Oxford University Press, 2009)

Minney, R.J., *The Tower of London* (New Jersey: Cassell & Co. Ltd, 1970)

Mitchell, Linda E., *Joan de Valence. The Life and Influence of a Thirteenth-Century Noblewoman* (Basingstoke: Palgrave Macmillan, 2016)

Moor, C. (ed.), *Knights of Edward I*, Harleian Society 80, 5 vols (London, 1929)

Moorman, J.R.H., *A History of the Church in England* (London: Adam and Charles Black, 1973)

Morris, R.K., 'Review article: Goodall, John, *The English castle*', *Transactions of the Ancient Monuments Society* 56 (2012), 129–36

Morris, W.A., *The Medieval English Sheriff to 1300.* (Manchester: Manchester University Press, 1968)

Mortimer, I., *The Greatest Traitor: The Life of Sir Roger Mortimer, 1st Earl of March, Ruler of England, 1327–1330* (London: Jonathan Cape, 2003)

—, *Medieval Intrigue. Decoding Royal Conspiracies* (London: Continuum, 2010)

—, 'The Chronology of the de Mortemer Family of Wigmore, c.1075–1185, and the Consolidation of a Marcher Lordship', *Historical Research* 89 (2016), 613–35

—, 'The Mortimers in the Time of Richard II', *Journal of the Mortimer History Society: Volume 1,* (2017), 91–110

Munden, A., *The Third Spire*, Coventry and Warwickshire Historical Association Pamphlets 17 (Coventry, 1991)

A New History of Ireland, II: Medieval Ireland, 1169–1534, ed. Art Cosgrove (Oxford: Clarendon Press, 1987)

Newton, K.C., *Thaxted in the Fourteenth Century: An Account of the Manor and Borough, with Translated Texts* (Chelmsford: Essex County Council, 1960)

Nichols, J., *A Collection of All the Wills, Now Known to be Extant of the Kings and Queens of England, Princes and Princesses of Wales, and Every Branch of the Blood Royal, From the Reign of William the Conqueror to that of Henry the Seventh Exclusive.* (London, 1780)

Nicolas, N.H., *Testamenta Vetusta*, 2 vols (London: Nicholas & Son, 1826)

O'Brien, K. and Fenlon, J., *Trim Castle, Co. Meath* (Dublin: Dúchas, the Heritage Service, 2002)

Ó Cléirigh, Cormac, 'The problems of defence: a regional case study', in Lydon, J.F. (ed.), *Law and Disorder in Thirteenth-Century Ireland: The Dublin Parliament of 1297* (Dublin: Four Courts Press, 1997), 25–56

Ormrod, W.M., 'Edward III and his family', *Journal of British Studies* 26 (1987), 398–422

—, *Edward III* (New Haven CT and London: Yale University Press, 2011)

—, 'False Paternity and the Royal Succession in Later Medieval England', *Nottingham Medieval Studies* 60 (2016), 187–226

Orpen, G.H., *Ireland under the Normans, 1169–1333*, 4 vols (Oxford: Oxford University Press, 1911–20)

Otway-Ruthven, A.J., 'The medieval county of Kildare', *Irish Historical Studies* 11, no. 43 (1958–9), 181–99

—, *A History of Medieval Ireland* (2nd edn, London: Barnes and Noble, 1980)

Owain Glyndŵr: A Casebook, ed. Michael Livingston and John K. Bollard (Liverpool: Liverpool University Press, 2013)

Owen, H. and Blakeway, R.B., *History of Shrewsbury* (London, 1825)

Parnell, G., *Book of The Tower of London* (London: B.T. Batsford, 1993)

Partington, Richard, 'The Nature of Noble Service to Edward III', in *Political Society in Later Medieval England*, ed. Benjamin Thompson and John Watts (Woodbridge: Boydell, 2015)

Perry, R., *Edward II: Suddenly, at Berkeley* (Wotton-under-Edge: Ivy House Books, 1988)

Phillips, J.R.S., *Edward II* (New Haven CT and London: Yale University Press, 2010)

—, 'Some Afterthoughts on Edward II', in *People, Power and Identity in the Late Middle Ages. Essays in Memory of W. Mark Ormrod*, ed. G. Dodd, H. Lacey and A. Musson (London: Routledge, 2021), 285–304

Plucknett, T.F.T, 'The Origins of Impeachment', *Transactions of the Royal Historical Society*, 4th series, 24 (1942), 47–71

Pollock, F. and Maitland, F.W., *The History of the English Law before the Time of Edward I*, 2 vols (2nd edn: Cambridge, 1898; reprinted 1968)

Potterton, Michael, *Medieval Trim: History and Archaeology* (Dublin: Four Courts Press, 2005)

Powell, E., 'The Strange Death of Sir John Mortimer', in *Rulers and Ruled in Late Medieval England: Essays Presented to Gerald Harriss,* ed. R. Archer and S. Walker (London: The Hambledon Press, 1995), 83–97

Power, D.J., *The Norman Frontier in the Twelfth and Early Thirteenth Centuries* (Cambridge: Cambridge University Press, 2004)

Prestwich, M.C., *Edward I* (New Haven CT and London: Yale University Press, 1997)

Priestley, S.C. and Turner, R.C., 'Three castles of the Clare family in Monmouthshire during the thirteenth and fourteenth centuries', *Archaeologia Cambrensis* 152 (2003), 9–52

Pugh, R.B., *Imprisonment in Medieval England* (Cambridge: Cambridge University Press, 1968)

—, 'The Knights Hospitallers as Undertakers', *Speculum* 56 (1981), 566–74

Pugh, T.B., *Henry V and the Southampton Plot of 1415*, Southampton Records Series 30 (1988)

—, 'The Estates, Finances and Regal Aspirations of Richard Plantagenet (1411–1460) Duke of York,' in M.A. Hicks (ed.), *Revolution and Consumption in Late Medieval England* (Woodbridge: Boydell & Brewer, 2001)

Radulescu, Raluca, 'Yorkist Propaganda and The Chronicle of Rollo to Edward IV', *Studies in Philology* 100 (2003), 401–24

Rátkai, S., *Wigmore Castle, north Herefordshire: excavations 1996 and 1998* (London: Society for Medieval Archaeology Monograph 34, 2015)

Raven, Matthew, 'The Loyal Mortimer: The Career of Roger Mortimer, 2nd Earl of March', *Journal of the Mortimer History Society* 2 (2018), 39–54

—, 'Parliament and the Trial of the 'Peers of the Land' in Henry of Lancaster's Revolt, 1328–29', Institute for Historical Research, Parliaments, People and Politics Seminar, 16 February 2021, available online: https://thehistoryofparliament.files.wordpress.com/2021/01/parliaments-politics-and-people-parliament-and-the-trial-of-the-peers-of-the-land-in-henry-of-lancasters-revolt-1328-29-2.pdf

Rees, William, *South Wales and the March, 1284-1415: a social and agrarian study* (Oxford: Oxford University Press, 1924)

Remfry, P.R., *The castles and history of Radnorshire*, revised edition [S.l.] (Castle Studies Research & Publishing, 2008)

Rogers, Clifford J., *War Cruel and Sharp: English Strategy under Edward III, 1327–60* (Woodbridge: Boydell, 2000)

St John Hope, W., 'The castle of Ludlow', *Archaeologia* 61 (1908), 257–328

Saul, Nigel, *Richard II* (New Haven CT and London: Yale University Press, 1997)

Scott, Kathleen L., *Later Gothic Manuscripts, 1390–1490, A Survey of Manuscripts Illuminated in the British Isles,* 6 vols (London: Harvey Miller, 1996)

Shepherd, E.B., 'The Church of the Friars Minor in London', *Archaeological Journal* 59 (1902), 238–87

Sherborne, James, 'Indentured Retinues and English Expeditions to France, 1369–80', *EHR* 79 (1964), 718–46

—, *War, Politics and Culture in Fourteenth-Century England*, ed. Anthony Tuck (London: Hambledon Press, 1994)

Shirota, Maree, 'Neither Roll nor Codex. Accordion Genealogies of the Kings of England from the Fifteenth Century' in Stefan Holz, Jörg Peltzer and Maree Shirota (eds), *The Roll in England and France in the Late Middle Ages* (Berlin: De Gruyter, 2019)

Shoesmith, R. *Castles & moated sites of Herefordshire*, revised edition (Almeley: Logaston Press, 2010)

Shoesmith, R. and Johnson, A. (eds), *Ludlow Castle: its history & buildings*, extended edition (Almeley: Logaston Press, 2006; first published 2000)

Siddons, Michael Powell, *Heraldic Badges of England and Wales*, 4 vols. (Woodbridge: Boydell, 2009)

Silvester, R., 'New Radnor: the topography of a medieval planned town in mid-Wales, in N. Edwards (ed.), *Landscape and settlement in medieval Wales* (Oxford: Oxbow Books, 1997)

—, 'Castell Blaenllynfi, Brecknock: a Marcher castle and its landscape', *Archaeologia Cambrensis* 153 (2004), 75–103

Simpkin, 'The Mortimer Retinue for War, 1277–1421', *Journal of the Mortimer History Society* 3 (2019), 37–58

Smith, Brendan, 'The British Isles in the Late Middle Ages: Shaping the Regions', in idem (ed.), *Ireland and the English World in the Late Middle Ages: Essays in Honour of Robin Frame* (Basingstoke: Palgrave Macmillan, 2009), 7–19

—, *Crisis and Survival in Late Medieval Ireland: The English of Louth and Their Neighbours, 1330–1450* (Oxford: Oxford University Press, 2013)

—, 'Dressing the Part in the Plantagenet Empire: The Death of Roger Mortimer, Earl of March and Ulster, in 1398', in *The Plantagenet Empire*, ed. Peter Crooks, David Green and W. Mark Ormrod (Donington: Shaun Tyas, 2016)

—, 'Transnational lordship and the Plantagenet empire: the Mortimer lords of Wigmore, 1247–1425', *Welsh History Review* 29 (2018), 27–50

Smith, J. Beverley, 'The Middle March in the Thirteenth Century', *Bulletin Board of Celtic Studies* 24 (1970), 77–94

Smith, Llinos Beverley, 'The Arundel charters to the lordship of Chirk in the fourteenth century, *Bulletin Board of Celtic Studies* 23 (1969), 153–66

Speight, Charles and Hopkinson, Martin, *The Mortimers, Lords of the March* (Almeley: Logaston Press, 2002)

Stephenson, David, 'Rhyd yr Onen Castle: politics and possession in western Arwystli in the later twelfth century', *Montgomeryshire Collections* 94 (2006), 15–22

—, 'The chronicler at Cwmhir abbey, 1257–63: the construction of a Welsh chronicle', in Griffiths, R.A. and Schofield, P.R. (eds.), *Wales and the Welsh in the Middle Ages* (Cardiff: University of Wales Press, 2011)

—, *Medieval Wales, c.1050–1332: Centuries of Ambiguity* (Cardiff: University of Wales Press, 2019)

—, *Patronage and Power in the Medieval Welsh March: One Family's Story* (Cardiff: University of Wales Press, 2021)

—, '"The Malice and Rebellion of Certain Welshmen": The Welsh Risings of 1294–1295', in Jobson, A.L., Kersey, H. and McKelvie, G. (eds), *Rebellion in Medieval Europe* (Woodbridge: Boydell, forthcoming)

Stockdale, Sarah, 'Blood on the Crown: Treason in the Royal Kinship Structure of Fifteenth-Century England', unpublished PhD Thesis, University of Winchester (2018)

Stones, E.L.G., 'The Date of Roger Mortimer's Escape from the Tower of London', *EHR*, 66 (1951), 97–8

Stretton, Tim and Kesselring, Krista J. (eds), *Married Women and the Law. Coverture in England and the Common Law World* (Montreal: McGill-Queen's University Press, 2013)

Strickland, M., 'Treason, Feud and the Growth of State Violence: Edward I and the "War of the Earl of Carrick", 1306–7', in *War, Government and Aristocracy in the British Isles, c.1150–1500. Essays in Honour of Michael Prestwich*, ed. C. Given-Wilson, A. Kettle and L. Scales (Woodbridge: Boydell Press, 2008), 84–113

—, '"All brought to nought and thy state undone": treason, disinvestiture and disgracing of arms under Edward II', in *Soldiers, Nobles and Gentlemen: Essays in Honour of Maurice Keen*, ed. P. Coss and C. Tyerman (Woodbridge: Boydell Press, 2009), 279–304

Suggett, R., *Houses & history in the March of Wales: Radnorshire 1400–1800* (Aberystwyth: RCAHMW, 2005)

Sumption, Jonathan, *The Hundred Years War III: Houses Divided* (London: Faber, 2009)

—, *The Hundred Years War IV: Cursed Kings* (London: Faber, 2015)

Tanquerey, F.J., *Recueil de lettres Anglo-Françaises, 1265–1399* (Paris, 1916)

Taylor, A., *The Welsh castles of Edward I* (London: Hambledon Press, 1986)

Taylor, J., *English Historical Literature in the Fourteenth Century* (Oxford: Oxford University Press, 1987)

Thurley, S., 'Royal Lodgings at the Tower of London 1216–1327', *Architectural History* 38 (1995), 37–46

Tuck, Anthony, 'Anglo-Irish Relations, 1382–1393', *Proceedings of the Royal Irish Academy*, 69 (1970), 15–31

—, *Richard II and the English Nobility* (London: Edward Arnold, 1973)

—, *Crown and Nobility, 1272–1461* (Oxford: Fontana, 1986)

—, 'Vere, John de, seventh earl of Oxford (1312–1360)', *ODNB*

Turner, R. and Jones-Jenkins, C., 'The history and digital reconstruction of Holt Castle, Denbighshire', *Archaeologia Cambrensis* 165 (2016), 241–82

Vale, Juliet, 'Arthur in English Society', in Barron, W.R.J., *The Arthur of the English* (Cardiff: University of Wales Press, 2001), 185–96

Visitations by the Heralds in Wales, ed. M.P. Siddons, Harleian Society New Series 14 (London, 1996)

Visser-Fuchs, Livia, '"Honour is the Reward of Virtue": The Claudian Translation made for Richard, Duke of York, in 1445', *The Ricardian* 18 (2008), 66–82

Walden, Howard de and Scott-Ellis, Evelyn, *Banners, Standards and Badges from a Tudor Manuscript in the College of Arms* (London: De Walden Library, 1904)

Walker, R.F., 'Bwlchyddinas Castle, Breconshire, and the survey of 1337', *Brycheiniog* 31 (1998–9), 19–30

Walker, Simon K., 'Profit and Loss in the Hundred Years War: The Subcontracts of Sir John Strother, 1374', *Bulletin of the Institute of Historical Research* 58 (1985), 100–6

—, *The Lancastrian Affinity* (Oxford: Oxford University Press, 1990; 2nd edn, 1996),

—, 'Lovell [Lovel], John, fifth Baron Lovell (c. 1342–1408), courtier and royal councillor', *ODNB*

Walker, Sue Sheridan, 'Proof of Age of Feudal Heirs in Medieval England', *Mediaeval Studies* 35 (1973), 306–23

Ward, B., *Miracles and the Medieval Mind: Theory, Record and Event, 1000–1215.* (London: Scolar Press, 1982)

Warner, Kathryn, 'The Adherents of Edmund of Woodstock, Earl of Kent, in March 1330', *EHR* 126 (2011)

—, *Isabella of France: The Rebel Queen* (Stroud, 2016)

Warner, Michael P., *The Agincourt Campaign of 1415: the retinues of the Dukes of Clarence and Gloucester* (Woodbridge: The Boydell Press, 2021)

Warren, Ann K., *Anchorites and their Patrons in Medieval England* (Berkeley: University of California Press, 1985)

Watson, F.J., *Under the Hammer. Edward I and Scotland, 1286–1307* (East Linton: Tuckwell Press, 1998)

Watson, G.W., 'Geoffrey de Mortemer and his Descendants', *The Genealogist*, new series 22 (1906), xiii, 1–16

Watson, Sethina, 'A mother's past and her children's futures: female inheritance, family and dynastic hospitals in the thirteenth-century', *Motherhood, Religion, and Society in Medieval Europe, 400–1400: Essays presented to Henrietta Leyser*, ed. Conrad Leyser and Lesley Smith (Farnham: Ashgate, 2011), 213–49

Watt, E.H., '"On Account of the Frequent Attacks and Invasions of the Welsh": The Effect of the Glyn Dŵr Rebellion on Tax Collection in England', in *The Reign of Henry IV: Rebellion and Survival, 1403–1413*, ed. Dodd, G. & Biggs, D. (York: York Medieval Press, 2008), 48–81

Waugh, S.L., *The Lordship of England: Royal Wardships and Marriages in English Society and Politics, 1217–1327* (Princeton: Princeton University Press, 1988)

Weiss, Judith, *Wace's Roman de Brut: A History of the British* (Exeter: University of Exeter Press, 1999)

Westerhof, Danielle, 'Deconstructing Identities on the Scaffold: The Execution of Hugh Despenser the Younger, 1326', *Journal of Medieval History* 33 (2007), 87–106

Wilkinson, L.J., *Women in Thirteenth-Century Lincolnshire* (Woodbridge: Boydell & Brewer, 2007)

—, *Eleanor de Montfort. A Rebel Countess in Medieval England* (London and New York: Continuum International, 2012)

Williams, G.A., *Medieval London: From Commune to Capital* (London: Athlone Press, 1963)

Williams, Gruffydd Aled, 'More than "skimble-skamble stuff": the medieval Welsh poetry associated with Owain Glyndŵr', *Proceedings of the British Academy* 181 (2012), 1–33

Williams, R., 'Early documents relating to Dolforwyn Castle, Newtown, etc.' *Montgomeryshire Collections* 28 (1894), 145–64

Wood, Herbert, 'The Muniments of Edmund de Mortimer, Third Earl of March, Concerning His Liberty of Trim', *Proceedings of the Royal Irish Academy* C 40 (1931/2), 312–55

Woolgar, C.M., *Household Accounts from Medieval England: Part 1* (Midsomer Norton, 1992)

Wright, Barbara, *Why Make Back-Up Copies? The Mortimer Cartulary and the Technological Revolution* (Otley: Flower Press, 2010)

Wright, T., *The History and Antiquities of Ludlow.* (Ludlow, 1826; reprinted, Manchester, 1972)

Wrottesley, George (ed.), *Crecy and Calais* (London: Harrison and Sons, 1898)

Dr Emma Cavell is a Senior Lecturer in Medieval History at Swansea University. She specialises in aristocratic women of the Welsh borderlands, law and litigation in England and Wales, and Jewish women in medieval England. Her recent publications include 'Widows, Native Law and the Long Shadow of England in Thirteenth-Century Wales' (*English Historical Review*) and 'The Measure of her Actions: A Quantitative Assessment of Anglo-Jewish Women's Litigation at the Exchequer of the Jews, 1219–81' (*Law and History Review*).

Dr David Stephenson has M.A. and D.Phil from Oxford; a former Bowra Senior Research Fellow of Wadham College, Oxford, he is now an Honorary Research Fellow at Bangor University. He has published and lectured widely, mainly in the field of medieval Welsh history. His *Medieval Powys: Kingdom, Principality and Lordships 1132–1293* (Boydell Press, 2016) won the inaugural Francis Jones Prize for Welsh history, administered by Jesus College, Oxford.

Dr John R. Kenyon is a leading authority on castles, and has been studying them, and later fortifications, since the later 1970s. He is the author of several books, and editor/ contributor to others, as well as numerous papers in a variety of journals. He has also written guidebooks for Cadw and English Heritage. He read History and Archaeology at the University of Southampton, and held posts in academic libraries, retiring in 2013 as the head librarian of the National Museum of Wales in Cardiff. He is a Fellow of the Society of Antiquaries of London and the Royal Historical Society. He was an Honorary Research Fellow at the National Museum of Wales and an Honorary Associate of SHARE, University of Cardiff. He was awarded his doctorate by the University of Cardiff based on his published work.

OPPOSITE: Wigmore Castle (© Laura Shepherds Lens Photography: www.laurashepherdslensphotography.com)

Dr Laura Tompkins is Research Lead at Historic Royal Palaces, the current custodians of the Tower of London, prior to which she worked as a Medieval Records Specialist at The National Archives, Kew. She completed her PhD on the subject of Alice Perrers, the mistress of Edward III, at the University of St Andrews in 2013 and has subsequently published a number of articles on Alice and the politics of 1360's and 1370's England. More widely, her research includes the study of royal favourites across the late medieval period, queens and queenship, kingship, the royal household and parliament. Laura is currently an Associate Fellow of the Institute of Historical Research.

Barbara Wright is a researcher and palaeographer of almost 40 years standing, and has been studying and transcribing texts relating to the thirteenth- and fourteenth-century Mortimer families for the last three decades. Early collaborations included with English Heritage for their in-house survey of Wigmore Castle when they acquired guardianship of it (2002), and with the BBC (*House Detectives at Large: Wigmore Abbey*, 2002). Her own papers and discoveries have provided factual contributions to many other people's publications. She is currently engaged in developing an enhanced version of *The Black Book of Wigmore*, the damaged and deficient Mortimer cartulary held in the British Library.

Dr Andy King is a Lecturer in History at the University of Southampton. His interests include Anglo-Scottish relations in the late Middle Ages; chivalry and the conduct of late medieval warfare; concepts of treason and rebellion; chronicles and historical writing; and castles. Amongst other work, he co-authored a monograph with Anne Curry, Adrian Bell and David Simpkin: *The Soldier in Later Medieval England* (OUP, 2013); and has co-edited collections of essays with David Simpkin: *England and Scotland at War, c.1296–c.1513* (Brill, 2012); and, with Andrew Spencer, *Edward I: New Interpretations* (York Medieval Press, 2020).

Dr Paul Dryburgh is President and a founder member of the Mortimer History Society. He also edits the Society's journal. Professionally, he works as a medieval records specialist at The National Archives (UK). His research interests are government, politics, warfare and economy in these islands in the thirteenth and fourteenth centuries. His doctoral thesis was on Roger Mortimer (d.1330). Paul is currently Co-Investigator of the Medieval Exchequer 'Gold Seam' on the Beyond 2022: Ireland's Virtual Record Treasury project, funded by the Irish Government. He is also Chair of the British Association for Local History.

PATRICK MCDONAGH is a PhD student in Trinity College Dublin researching the transnational lordship of the Mortimer earls of March and Ulster in the late fourteenth century across Britain and Ireland.

PROFESSOR CHRIS GIVEN-WILSON is Emeritus Professor of Medieval History at the University of St Andrews. He is the author or editor of a dozen books on late medieval English history including *Henry IV* (Yale, 2017), *The English Nobility in the Late Middle Ages* (Routledge, 2002), and *Chronicles: The Writing of History in Medieval England* (Hambledon, 2007). He is also general editor of *The Parliament Rolls of Medieval England* (Woodbridge, 2005).

DR IAN MORTIMER is a founder member of the Mortimer History Society and the author of 13 history books and numerous articles on the history of England between the tenth and twentieth centuries. He has been described by *The Times* as 'the most remarkable medieval historian of our time'. His first book, *The Greatest Traitor* (Vintage, 2010), was a biography of Roger Mortimer, 1st earl of March. He is best known, however, as the author of the four *Time Traveller's Guides – to Medieval England, Elizabethan England, Restoration Britain* and *Regency Britain* (Vintage, various dates). He is a Fellow of both the Society of Antiquaries and the Royal Historical Society.

DR J.L. LAYNESMITH is a Visiting Research Fellow at the University of Reading and Fellow of the Royal Historical Society. She has written and published extensively on elite women in medieval England, including prizewinning monographs *The Last Medieval Queens* (OUP, 2004) and *Cecily Duchess of York* (Bloomsbury, 2017).

INDEX

Katherine de Valois, queen of England
(m. Henry V) (d.1437) 176
Kells, Co. Meath, Ireland, battle of (1315) *see battles*
Kellistown, Co. Carlow, Ireland 110
Kenilworth Castle, Warks 196, *196*, 227
Kent, earls of *see Edmund [of Woodstock]; Holland*
Kepeston, John 150–2
Kildare, Co., Ireland 15, 126, 128, 133, 159
Kilkenny, Co., Ireland 126, *127*, 155–6
Castle *155*
King, William 185, 189, 198, 201, 203–4
Kingsland Castle and church, Herefs 13, *13*, *40*, 46
Kirkham, Yorks. ER 67
Knavesmire, York 90
Knighton, Radnors. *40*, 125–6, 141
Knighton, Henry, chronicler 67
Knucklas Castle, Radnors. 29–31, *40*, 50, 52, *52*
Kyre Wyard, Worcs 195

Lacon, Sir Richard 202–3
Lacy family of Ludlow xvi, 44, 92, 102, 128, 134, 142
Maud de (m. Geoffrey Geneville) 45
Lacy family, earls of Lincoln 132
Henry de, earl of Lincoln 47
John de, 2nd earl of Lincoln (d.1240) 15
Lambyn, Edmund 71
Lancaster, duke of *see John of Gaunt*
earls of *see Henry of; Thomas of*
Laois, county of, Ireland 14, 127–8, 142
Latimer, William, of Danby 137
Laȝamon 233
Leake, Treaty of (1318) 60
Lechlade, Glos 5–7
hospital of St John the Baptist 5–6
Leinster, Ireland 110, 126–8
Leinthale, James, bailiff of the honor of Wigmore 119
Leinthall (Starkes), Herefs 123
Leintwardine, village and Hundred of, Salop 123, 139, 143–4
Leon *217*, 220, 237–8
Lessorte, Thomas 71
Lestrange, John 12, *210*
Lewys Glyn Cothi, poet 51

'Liber Niger de Wigmore' *see Wigmore, chronicles of*
Linby, Notts 194, 201
Lingen, Herefs *40*
Lingeyn, John de 31
Lincoln, earl of 4
Lionel of Antwerp, duke of Clarence (m. Elizabeth de Burgh) (d.1368) x, xix, xxi, xxiv, 55, 116–7, 135, 137–8, 153–7, 169, 176, 205, *212*, 214–5, 220–2, 227, 230, 236, 240–1
Little Walsingham, Norf. *123*, 137
Llanddewi, Wales 31
Llangurig, Montg. 41
Llywelyn ab Iorwerth/ Llywelyn the Great, prince of Gwynedd (m. Joan, daughter of King John) x, xiv, xxiv, 8, 22–3, 39, 51, 185, 223–4
Llywelyn ap Gruffudd/ Llywelyn the Last, Prince of Wales (d.1282) xiv, xv, 10–13, *12*, 16, 19, 22, 25, 27, 35, 39, 49, 51, 54, 86, 90, 125–6, *142*, 227
Lockleys, Welwyn, Herts 207
London 24, 32, 58, 64, 71, 80, 85–6, 88, 91–2, 97, 99, 107, 152–3, 189, 197–9, 203–4
Bridge 86, 88, 199
constable of *see Segrave*
Greyfriars Church, Newgate *see Greyfriars*
mayors *see Bethune; Chigwell; Gisors*
St John's hospital, Clerkenwell 200, *200*
St Paul's Cathedral 65
Tower of xvii, xviii, xxv, 43, 46, 59–80, *74*, *78*, 103, 184, 189, *191*, 196
Long Crendon, Bucks *123*, 126
Louth, Ireland 130, 133
Lovell family 153–4
John, Sir 137, 150, 152–4, 167–8, 211
Robert 153
Thomas 153
Lower Lye, Herefs 123, 140
Lucy, Anthony de 94
Ludlow, Salop xi, xxiv, 90, 93, 128, 134–5, 140–1, 162–7
Castle *viii*, xvi–xvii, *xvii*, 4, *40*, 41, 43–6, *44*, *45*, *46*, 55–6, 58, 60, 70, *70*, *91*, 167, 215, 218, 223
St Laurence's Church *xi*, *66*, *151*
Ludwick
John de 207, 209
manor (Herts) 196, 201, 209
William de, Sir 209

319

Mortimer family of Wigmore
  Agnes (daughter of Roger d.1330, m. Laurence de Hastings) 169
  Anne, countess of Cambridge (daughter of Roger d.1398, m. Richard of Conisburgh) (d.1411) x, xxiii–xxiv, 44, 145, 169, 176–7, 180, 208
    legacy to the House of York [ch.11] xxiii–xxiv, **212**, 213–241
  Annora (m. Hugh d.1227) *see Braose*
  at arms [ch.6] xix, 101–19
  Beatrice (daughter of Roger d.1330, m. Thomas Beauchamp) 169
  Blanche (daughter of Roger d.1330, m. Piers de Grandison) 169
  castle builders [ch.3] xvi–xvii, 41–59
  Catherine, countess of Warwick (daughter of Roger d.1330, m. Thomas Beauchamp) x, 99, 169
  Edmund (son of Roger d.1330, m. Elizabeth de Badlesmere) (d.1331/2) x, xxii, 87, 90, 93–4, 133–4, 169, 208
  Edmund (son of Roger d.1282, m. Margaret de Fiennes) (d.1304) x, 13, 17, 29–32, 35, 59, 125, 128, 141, 144, 208
  Edmund, 3rd earl of March (son of Roger d.1360, m. Philippa of Clarence) (d.1381) x, xix, xxi–xxii, 96, 106–7, 114–6, 121–2, 135–8, 145, 147–69, **151**, 171, 173, 176, 208, 214, 240
    personal networks of [ch.8] 147–69
  Edmund, 5th earl of March (son of Roger d.1398, m. Anne Stafford) (d.1425) x, xxii, 37, 55, 111–6, 121, 138, 169, 174–82, 186, 188, 201, 205–8, 214
  Edmund, Sir (son of Edmund d.1381, m. Catrin Glyn Dŵr) (d.1409) x, 37, 110–2, 114, 116, 118, 169, 176, 182–5, 205, 208
  Eleanor (sister of Anne d.1411) (d.c.1414) 180, 214
  Eleanor (m. Roger d.1398) *see Holland*
  Elizabeth (daughter of Edmund d.1381, m. Henry 'Hotspur' Percy, Sir Thomas Camoys) x, 167, 169, 174, 201
  estates and economies of 119–47
  Geoffrey, Sir (son of Roger d.1330) x, 90, 169, 207–8
  Gwladus Ddu (m. Ralph d.1246) *see Gwladus Ddu*

Mortimer family of Wigmore cont.
  Hawise (daughter of Ralph d.1115–27) 2–3
  Hugh (son of Ralph d.1115–27, m. Maud le Meschin) (d.1181–5) x, xv, 3–4, 51
  Hugh (son of Roger d.1214, m. Annora de Braose) (d.1227) x, 6–8, 19, 141
  Isabel (daughter of Roger d.1282, m. John Fitzalan d.1272) (d.1292) 9–10, **10**, 12–20, **16**
  Isabel (m. Roger d.1214) (d.1252) *see Ferrers*
  Joan (daughter of Roger d.1214, m. Walter de Beauchamp) (d.1225) 6
  Joan (daughter of Roger d.1330, m. James Audley) 169
  Joan (m. Roger d.1330) *see Geneville*
  Mabel (m. Ralph d.1115–27) *see Mabel*
  Margaret (m. Edmund d.1304) *see Fiennes*
  Maud (m. Roger d.1282) (d.1301) *see Braose*
  Maud (m. Philip de Belmeis, Hugh Mortimer d.1181–5) *see Meschin*
  Melisende (m. Ralph Mortimer d.1115–27) *see Melisende*
  Philip (son of Roger d.1214) (fl.1215–44) 6
  Philippa (m. Edmund d.1381) *see Philippa of Clarence*
  Philippa (m. Roger d.1360) *see Montagu*
  Philippa (daughter of Edmund d.1381, m. John Hastings, Richard (III) Fitzalan) 169
  Ralph (son of Roger d.1214, m. Gwladus Ddu) (d.1246) x, 6–8, 51–2, 54, 185, 208, 223, 237–8
  Ralph (m. Melisende, Mabel) (d.1115–27) x, 1–3, 51, 123–4, 139, 143
  relationships with the Welsh [ch.2] xv–xvi, 21–41, 184
  Roger (fl.1054–78) 2
  Roger (elder brother of Hugh d.1181–5) (fl.1139) 3
  Roger (son of Hugh d.1181–5, m. Isabel de Ferrers) (d.1214) x, xv, 4–6, 23, 41, 51
  Roger (son of Roger d.1214) 6
  Roger (son of Ralph d.1246, m. Maud de Braose) (d.1282) x, xiv–xv, 7–11, 13–6, 25–9, 48–9, 51–5, 125–8, 141–2, 170, 208, 227
  Roger, 1st earl of March (son of Edmund d.1304, m. Joan de Geneville) (d.1330) x, xii–xiii, xvi, 9, 24–5, 34, 36, 43, 45–6, 52, 54–5, 58–89, **66**, **70**, **83**, 95–6, 99, 102–3, 112, 115, 117–8, 128–34, 141–2, 169–70, 206, 208, 218, 223, 227
    escape from the Tower of London xxv, 61–81